WORTHY OPPONENTS

GENERAL WILLIAM T. SHERMAN, U.S.A.
GENERAL JOSEPH E. JOHNSTON, C.S.A.

Edward G. Longacre

Rutledge Hill Press©
Nashville, Tennessee
A Division of Thomas Nelson Publishers
www.ThomasNelson.com

In memory of my cousin, Ellen Ewing Sherman

Published by Rutledge Hill Press, a division of Thomas Nelson, Inc., P.O. Box 141000, Nashville, Tennessee 37214.

Rutledge Hill Press books may be purchased in bulk for educational, business, fund-raising, or sales promotional use. For information, please e-mail SpecialMarkets@ThomasNelson.com.

Library of Congress Cataloging-in-Publication Data

Longacre, Edward G., 1946–
    Worthy opponents : William T. Sherman and Joseph E. Johnston : antagonists in war—friends in peace / Edward G. Longacre.
        p. cm.
    Includes bibliographical references and index.
    ISBN-13: 973-1-4016-0091-4 (harcover)
    ISBN-10: 1-4016-0091-3 (hardcover)
    1. Sherman, William T. (William Tecumseh), 1820–1891. 2. Johnston, Joseph E. (Joseph Eggleston), 1807–1891. 3. Generals—United States—Biography. 4. United States. Army—Biography. 5. Generals—Confederate States of America—Biography. 6. Confederate States of America. Army—Biography. 7. United States—History—Civil War, 1861–1865—Campaigns. I. Title.
E467 .L22 2006
973.7'30922—dc22
[B]   2006021518

Printed in the United States of America

06 07 08 09 10—5 4 3 2 1

TABLE OF CONTENTS

PREFACE

This book chronicles in parallel form the lives of two American soldiers, bitter rivals in wartime, who became fast friends once the guns ceased firing. For four years beginning in April 1861, Joseph Eggleston Johnston, C.S.A., and William Tecumseh Sherman, U.S.A., waged war against each other's army and nation, although not always in the same theater of operations. At intervals from May 1863 to July 1864 and again from February through April 1865—a period that encompassed some of the most celebrated engagements in the history of warfare—they directly confronted each other on the field of battle. During that time, while striving by every resource and stratagem to outwit, outmaneuver, and defeat each other, each developed a genuine respect for the intelligence and determination of his opponent.

Their mutual admiration increased after they came face to face to negotiate the surrender of Johnston's Army of Tennessee near Durham Station, North Carolina, at the close of the war in the West. In after years, although they led very different lives, their paths crossed with such frequency that they came to know each other in an entirely new context. They grew especially close in the 1880s, when both resided in Washington, Sherman as the commanding general of the United States Army and Johnston as a congressman from Virginia and then as United States commissioner of railroads, a position Sherman helped him gain and hold onto. They and their families dined, entertained, and traveled together, and whenever alone the two old soldiers good-naturedly refought the campaigns that had made their reputations. Johnston readily acknowledged that he spent more time with his former enemy than he did with the veterans of his own army. One of Sherman's subordinates, Maj. Gen. Oliver Otis Howard, observed that for the last twenty years or so of their lives, the old antagonists "behaved always toward each other as brothers."

On the surface, the two men were a study in contrasts. The compact, dignified, gentlemanly Johnston was thirteen years older than the gangly, garrulous, nervous Ohioan. Their regional influences, political views, and military experiences differed markedly. Yet they shared a number of personal and professional traits. As the sons of judges, from youth they evinced a deep interest in, and an abiding reverence for, the laws of the land, especially the United States Constitution, although differing in their interpretation of key provisions of that seminal document. Both espoused a conservative outlook on socio-economic issues, including slavery, an institution that each deplored but tolerated due to deep-seated doubts that a race long held in bondage could meet the full requisites of citizenship. Each had a high regard for personal honor and reacted strongly to perceived attacks on his name and reputation.

Their conservatism colored their military tactics. Both appreciated the inherent advantages of an entrenched army fighting on the defensive. When committed to the offensive, each preferred the indirect approach, relying heavily on feints, flanking maneuvers, and threats to lines of communication and supply as a means of drawing the opponent out of his field works and into the open, where he would be isolated and vulnerable. Each was concerned with husbanding and concentrating his strength so as to bring maximum power to bear against critical sectors of the enemy's position. Each took pains to avoid exposing his army's flanks and rear so as not to create an opening the other might exploit. During most of their confrontations, circumstances required Sherman to take the offensive, Johnston to maintain the defensive. Throughout, however, each maneuvered carefully, cautiously, aware that a false move might bring disaster. Occasionally, both felt compelled to take risks as Sherman did at Kennesaw Mountain during the Atlanta campaign and Johnston resorted to at Bentonville during the campaign of the Carolinas. Such instances, however, were rare, mainly because they proved costly. For the most part, each was too wary of the exploitative powers of his adversary to tempt fate or act precipitately.

Sherman went on record with the observation that Johnston was the shrewdest, cleverest opponent he ever faced. Thus he described Johnston's relief from command in mid-July 1864 as the greatest gift the Confederacy could have given him. For his part, Johnston admitted that Sherman was too savvy and vigilant to be drawn into a confrontation on terms even slightly advantageous to the Army of Tennessee. His greatest regret was Sherman's refusal during the 1864 campaign in Georgia to behave as his friend and superior, Ulysses S. Grant, did toward Grant's opponent in Virginia, Robert E. Lee. Had Sherman attacked him directly and repeatedly, Johnston argued, the Army of Tennessee would have emerged victorious from this, perhaps the most fateful epoch of the war. Yet Sherman's unwillingness to act as Johnston wished him to only increased the latter's admiration of the former.

It seems fitting that Sherman's and Johnston's mutual respect evolved into true friendship, for that progression mirrored the course of reunion and reconciliation during the latter years of the nineteenth century. Divided in war, united in peace, their relationship was, on an intensely personal level, the story of their battered and bloodied but durable and resilient nation.

In the course of preparing this book, several institutions provided research assistance; to them I am deeply indebted. Those most deserving of mention include the reference and special collections staffs of the Ohio Historical Society, the University of Notre Dame Libraries, Duke University's William R. Perkins Library, the Wilson Library at the University of North Carolina at Chapel Hill, and the William L. Clements Library of the University of Michigan.

Individuals who warrant special notice include Lia Apodaca of the Manuscript Division, Library of Congress; Art Bergeron at the U.S. Army Military History Institute; Susan M. Catlett of Old Dominion University's Patricia W. and J. Douglas Perry Library; Ruth Ann Coskie of the Museum of the Confederacy; Suzanne Christoff and Debbie McKeon-Pogue of the United States Military Academy Library and Archives; Mary Molineux and Susan Riggs of the Earl Gregg Swem Library, College of William and Mary; Cheryl Nabati at Langley Air Force Base's Herbert Bateman Library; Gregg Stoner of the Virginia Historical Society; and Sandra M. Trenholm and Ana Ramirez-Luhrs of the Gilder Lehrman Collection, now a tenant of the New-York Historical Society.

As always, my wife, Ann, accompanied me on my research trips, portable copier at the ready. Paul Dangel drew the maps, and Bill Godfrey reproduced the illustrations used in the book. My editor at Rutledge Hill Press, Geoff Stone, provided assistance throughout the project, as did Larry Stone, publisher emeritus. I also thank Rod Gragg, whose early support of the book made possible its publication.

ONE

THE SCHOOL
OF THE SOLDIER

Joseph Eggleston Johnston came from a large family—nine boys and one girl—whose American progenitor had emigrated from Scotland to the colony of Virginia in 1726. Joseph was the eighth son of Peter Johnston, who quit his college studies upon the first drumbeat of the American Revolution to serve in the patriot army of Nathanael Greene. By war's end, Peter, then all of seventeen, was a hard-bitten lieutenant in the mounted brigade of "Light Horse Harry" Lee, future father of Robert E. Lee. Returning to his family's home near Farmville, in Prince George County, the young veteran met, courted, and wed Mary Valentine Wood, a niece of the orator and statesman Patrick Henry. Through his bride, Peter acquired relatives who hailed from "many of the most prominent and influential families in the South, particularly in the Appalachian Mountains region."[1]

Peter's prospects for success in life were further strengthened when he returned to his books and took up the study of law. In quick succession he was admitted to the local bar, developed a thriving legal practice, and was elected a judge of the general court. Dissatisfied with the central Virginia circuit assigned to him, he swapped

Joseph E. Johnston

1

duties with a colleague and moved his rapidly expanding family to the equally bur-
geoning village of Abingdon, in the mountains of southwestern Virginia. There,
eight miles above the Tennessee border and less than sixty miles from Kentucky,
Peter established a small estate centered around a two-story log house that he christened "Panecillo." Although the countryside was thinly settled and the way of life
primitive, even for the era, Panecillo became a gathering spot for local barristers,
magistrates, and other public officials. At the time the house went up, Joseph
Johnston, who had been born at the family's former residence in Prince George
County, was in his fourth year.

Relatively little is known of Joseph's youth and adolescence. His most recent
biographer notes that he and his siblings "grew up amidst the contradictory influences of the Appalachian frontier and Abingdon society. Like other Abingdon
boys, they learned to ride, to shoot, and to cope with the rough and tumble life of
the frontier where courage and boldness were particularly admired." An earlier
chronicler, Joseph Johnston's nephew Robert Morton Hughes, asserts that from
boyhood Joseph was imbued with martial ambitions. This inclination had been
nurtured by the pride his father took in his military service, which was reflected in
the boy's name: Joseph Eggleston had been the elder Johnston's unit commander
during the War for Independence.[2]

Peter Johnston's pride was shared by other veterans who lived in the area, several of whom had fought under Gen. William Campbell at King's Mountain.
Indeed, the Abingdon country abounded in reminders of that celebrated engagement, for which one of the hills the town occupied had been named. The old soldiers never seemed to tire of reliving their war experiences, and they were
especially loquacious when an impressionable youth was within earshot. As
Hughes observes "the effect of such narrations on a boy naturally addicted to military matters, especially when reenforced by [the] not less daring exploits of his
father, may well be imagined. Young Johnston soon had the boys of the neighborhood, hardly less zealous than himself, organized into an 'army,' as he termed it;
and he was chosen as their 'general,' with one of his brothers as 'colonel.'" Hughes
adds that "the combined strength of the general and colonel was sufficient to
insure and enforce that obedience which is the foundation of discipline."[3]

Obedience and discipline were cardinal virtues of young Joseph, who gave the
impression of wisdom and maturity beyond his years. Although never grave or
melancholy, even as a youth he assumed an aura of dignity and decorum that may
have reflected his father's position in the community. Joseph honed his fund of
self-control whenever he and his brothers accompanied their father on the hunt,

one of Judge Johnston's favorite pastimes. The quest for the abundant deer and the occasional bear might consume days at a time; often it carried the hunters many miles from home, across the mountains into Tennessee or deeper into the wilderness of their own state. Joseph never grew too fatigued or bored to give his fullest attention to his role in the proceedings; if the game eluded the hunters, it was through no fault of his.

According to Hughes, Joseph and his brothers took an active part in the hunt "even before they were large enough to handle the long rifle which was the favorite arm of the pioneer." Under their father's tutelage, they learned to load, shoot, and respect firearms, with which they quickly became comfortable as well as conversant. Because he preferred to be a "driver"—flushing the game rather than waiting for it to be flushed—Joseph also became a proficient horseman. Although he grew up slight of build and somewhat below medium height, his affinity for the rugged life gave Joseph a deceptively powerful physique. In later life, his constitution would help him not only withstand the hardships of military service but survive several wounds received in action.[4]

Being an active youth, he experienced his share of childhood bumps and bruises—a fall from a cherry tree when quite young left him with permanent facial scars—but at age ten he suffered an injury that could have crippled him for life. Accompanying his father and brothers on a hunt several miles west of Abingdon, the boy undertook to demonstrate to a family slave named Robert his understanding of how a cavalry charge was conducted. He led Robert some distance from the rest of the party, then bade him dismount and, rifle in hand, take position as if to defend himself against a mounted attack. Hughes relates the upshot: "Joseph thereupon withdrew the horse to a sufficient distance to obtain the necessary impetus, and thundered down upon the stationary square. The horse, however, not being equally interested in the experiment, sheered off just before reaching the infantry, and did it so suddenly that his rider was thrown forward. . . . In the fall his leg was broken, the ends of the bone coming through the flesh."[5]

The boy lay quietly and without complaint while Robert went for Joseph's father and brothers. Neither then nor during the several-mile journey back to town, during which his brothers took turns carrying him upon their backs, did the victim give voice to his suffering. Upon obtaining medical aid, however, he found that his ordeal had only begun. The first doctor to treat him set the broken bone improperly, forcing a second, more competent, physician to reset it. Hughes observes that "the manner in which a boy of ten, in a time when anesthetics were not known, endured the operation[s] without a tear or groan, and his patience

under the three months of suffering which followed, showed his fortitude."
Already the judge's son had learned well the importance of upholding one's honor
and that of his family. One of the most effective ways was to accept misfortune
without flinching, bemoaning one's fate, or betraying weakness. Joseph Johnston
would be confronted by adversity time and again through the course of his life.
While his critics would not always agree, in every instance he would strive to repli-
cate the equanimity he had shown as a child, lying on a makeshift operating table
with his thighbone protruding through the skin of his mangled limb.[6]

Joseph's father was determined that his offspring develop intellectually as well as
physically. He and his wife tutored the children until they were old enough to
attend the local academy, of whose board of trustees the judge was a prominent
member. It was observed that from the first day he set foot in a classroom Joseph
did well in his studies. The classical education he received at the Abingdon
Academy influenced him through the rest of his life. Along with military texts,
his personal library would include works of classical literature, which he perused
whenever time permitted, even in the midst of active campaigning.

By the time he was ready for higher education, it had become a fixed fact in
his family that Joseph should matriculate at West Point. His father's prominence in legal and political circles, and the numerous professional connections
he had made during his years on the bench, facilitated the obtaining of an
Academy appointment for his son. It came through in the spring of 1825
through the agency of U.S. Sen. James Barbour of Virginia and Secretary of
War John C. Calhoun of South Carolina. On March 3, 1825, only hours before
Calhoun resigned his cabinet post to take the oath as vice president of the
United States, the celebrated statesman signed the appointment and forwarded
it to the judge's son.[7]

Joseph spent the next three months boning up on his studies in order to pass
the qualifying examination that would admit him as a member of the next cadet
class. By late June he was ready to start the tortuous journey to New York's Hudson
River Valley, site of the nation's finest engineering school, then commencing its
twenty-fourth year of instruction. Although eager to embark on the career he had
long ago chosen for himself, Joseph left home under tragic circumstances. Mary
Wood Johnston, who had long been in fragile health, lay dying; she would succumb to an unidentified disease within days of Joseph's departure, causing him to

4

wonder "how is it possible for me to bear the loss of such a mother, the best, the tenderest, and the most virtuous, with other than the greatest anguish?"[8]

By stage, train, and steamboat the heavy-hearted youth crossed his state, then traveled up the Atlantic seaboard via Washington, Baltimore, Philadelphia, and New York City. At any of these dazzling places Joseph, like other incoming cadets from small towns and isolated villages who had never ventured far from home, may have spent some days sightseeing. But as soon as he arrived at West Point, his pleasure seeking ended. He was thrown into the jarring routine of summer encampment, which preceded every academic year; he found it hectic and arduous, composed of hours on the drill plain and demanding physical exercises. When summer ended and the cadets moved into barracks, life became somewhat more predictable and less strenuous. It was occasionally made almost intolerable, however, by the hazing heaped upon the plebes by their elders, some of whom took fiendish delight in making their classmates' lives miserable. Still, as he had when breaking his leg on the hunt, Joseph endured the experience with a stoicism and self-restraint that impressed his fellows just as his dignified bearing and vigorous physical application impressed his instructors on the drill plain.

His study skills and classroom performances were a bit less formidable. During his first year he and the other plebes were subjected to only two courses, mathematics and French, the twin underpinnings of the Academy's engineering curriculum. Johnston distinguished himself in neither subject, although he improved his standing in French as the year progressed. In fact, by diligent application he rose from twenty-seventh place among the 105 cadets who entered the Academy in July 1825 to thirteenth in the forty-six-man class. During that period he was introduced to chemistry, mineralogy, rhetoric, military drawing, and the general science course known as natural philosophy. He performed ably in the pure engineering courses that predominated during his junior and senior years, especially drawing, where he displayed an aptitude for mapmaking that would influence his active-duty career.[9]

He also stood high in the tactics courses to which the cadets were exposed in their final year of study. His academic performance is all the more remarkable considering that the time he could devote to his studies was limited to the daylight hours. A lifelong tendency to night blindness—a relatively common affliction in the nineteenth century, when the prevailing diet, especially that of Southerners, was deficient in Vitamins A and B—prevented him from poring over his textbooks after the sun went down.[10]

One reason for his continued rise was his ability to avoid demerits which, by affecting a student's standing on the role of general merit, influenced his overall ranking. Penalties were doled out—arbitrarily, it often seemed—for a wide assortment of offenses, some quite trivial and without evident application to military service. This draconian code of conduct was the handiwork of the Academy's venerable superintendent, Brevet Lieutenant Colonel Sylvanus Thayer, for whom discipline was the glue that held the army together. Overall, his system achieved desired results although it took a toll of many cadets who, otherwise well suited to military life and capable of meeting most of the Academy's exacting requirements, received unrealistically low class rankings or washed out due to these black marks, two hundred of which, accumulated during any academic year, provided grounds for instant dismissal.

Joe Johnston never came close to the fatal total. During his first year at the Academy, he was gigged seven times for a total of sixteen demerits. His infractions ran the gamut of the mundane: inattention at drill, failing to police his quarters, wearing his hair too long to suit an inspecting officer. His deportment improved over his third-class year, during which he was cited only three times for punishable offenses. He collected nine and fifteen demerits, respectively, during his junior and senior years—an extraordinary performance. His few transgressions were mainly for visiting classmates after lights-out, indicating that despite the dignified air and the ramrod-straight posture that prompted fellow cadets to dub him "Colonel Johnston," he was sociable and approachable. Many of the associations he formed here lasted a lifetime; some paid career dividends—like him, several classmates would rise to high rank and prominence.[11]

Of these, the majority were of Northern birth, including future Union generals James Barnes, Ormsby McKnight Mitchel, and Catharinus P. Buckingham. Lesser-ranking Northerners also destined for distinction were Sidney Burbank, who attained an unblemished forty-one-year career in the regular infantry, and the military and frontier artist Seth Eastman. Southerners of future note with whom Johnston forged close ties included North Carolina-born Theophilus Holmes from his own class and upperclassmen Albert Sidney Johnston of Kentucky (no relation to him), who was destined for high command in the military forces of three nations including the Republic of Texas; and Leonidas Polk, another North Carolinian who would become an Episcopal bishop as well as a lieutenant general of Confederate troops.[12]

The Southerner with whom Johnston was most often thrown into contact was a fellow Virginian, Robert E. Lee, son of Peter Johnston's Revolutionary War commander. Although they were the only natives of the Old Dominion to graduate with their class, Johnston and Lee were never bosom friends. They were, however, unfailingly cordial and mutually supportive of each other's careers. Lee consistently attained a higher class standing than his classmate—he would graduate eleven places above Johnston on the roll of general merit. He also gained higher rank in the cadet corps, winning the coveted post of class adjutant. For his part, Johnston was promoted cadet sergeant during his second class year and the following summer briefly held the rank of lieutenant, only to lose the promotion for reasons that remain obscure. Perhaps because they were rivals for rank and position, Johnston's attitude toward his fellow Virginian was a combination of admiration and jealousy. That attitude would never change completely, but over time it would moderate. Years after Lee's death, Johnston would offer a more generous assessment of his colleague than any he could have rendered while both men lived:

> We had the same intimate associates, who thought, as I did, that no other youth or man so united the qualities that win warm friendship and command high respect. For he was full of sympathy and kindness, genial and fond of gay conversation, and even of fun, that made him the most agreeable of companions, while his correctness of demeanor and language and attention to all duties, personal and official, and a dignity as much a part of himself as the elegance of his person, gave him a superiority that everyone acknowledged in his heart. . . .[13]

One cadet with whom Johnston occasionally associated, not always to his pleasure, was Kentucky-born and Mississippi-bred Jefferson Davis of the class of 1828. Intellectually acute but lacking in self-discipline, Davis took part in numerous escapades during his Academy career and barely avoided dismissal on more than one occasion. The risks he took included frequent trips to Benny Havens's Tavern in nearby Highland Falls, an establishment strictly off limits to cadets and thus of great allure to the more adventurous among them.

Davis was at least peripherally involved in a bacchanal destined for an enduring place in West Point lore. On Christmas Eve of 1826 thirsty cadets, defiant of the regulations, celebrated the holiday by gathering in Room 5 in the Academy's North Barracks to enjoy prohibited amusements including eggnog laced with alcohol. When members of the Academy staff learned of the goings-on there as well as in a room one floor above and attempted to break them up, inebriated cadets ejected them bodily. Other officers who intervened were assaulted with chairs and pieces of kindling and even threatened with loaded muskets and bayonets. The proceedings nearly erupted into a full-fledged riot before order was restored and the most flagrant malefactors were placed in arrest.[14]

The offenders were turned over to the Academy's disciplinary officer, Maj. William J. Worth. Following a two-week court of inquiry under his direction, Worth recommended the permanent or temporary dismissal of seventeen cadets, not including Davis, who barely avoided disciplinary action. Worth's findings were approved by President John Quincy Adams. Although called as witnesses at the inquiry, Joe Johnston and Robert E. Lee had nothing to hide, having declined invitations to the "Egg Nog Riot." It is possible, however, that when the proceedings ended, Johnston and Davis argued over some aspect of the riot or its aftermath—if so, details remain lacking. Rumor had it that at another point in their Academy lives the two engaged in a physical altercation over their competing affections toward a certain young lady who was a regular visitor to the school. Something about the alleged incident rings false. Even so, when Davis graduated with his class in July 1828, he and Johnston appear to have parted on less than amicable terms.[15]

Upon his own graduation in 1829, Johnston had the satisfaction of knowing that he had made a favorable impression on the majority of his classmates and instructors while forging a record of scholastic achievement of which he might be proud. Nevertheless, his thirteenth-place finish failed to qualify him for a commission in the only branch of the service that Academy officials paid homage to, the Corps of Engineers. Robert E. Lee was tendered a berth in this elite unit, but Johnston had to settle for a second lieutenancy in the Fourth United States Artillery. He was, however, consoled to think that he was entering an arm of the service built on technological know-how as well as military proficiency. In such a position he believed he could do credit to his education, make his family proud, and achieve professional fulfillment.

Upon leaving the Hudson highlands, he returned to Abingdon for a brief reunion with the family he had visited only once since entering the Academy, during the three months' leave granted each cadet at the end of his third class year. By now most of his siblings had left home to make their way in the civilian world. Their departure would have made for a lonely life for Judge Johnston had he not recently remarried. Barely had the visitor in the new blue uniform begun to acquaint himself with his stepmother, the former Ann Bernard, than he had yet again to return to New York State, this time to embark on his career as an artilleryman.[16]

The long and tedious journey ended at Governors Island in the Hudson River off Manhattan, where Fort Columbus guarded the entrance to New York Harbor. In that already antiquated citadel of brick and masonry Johnston and his new unit, Company C of the Fourth Artillery, spent the next two years protecting America's largest city against an invasion force that would never materialize. During that generally uninspiring tour, Johnston learned the basics of leadership while making new friends among the officer corps and, whenever possible, availing himself of the attractions and entertainments the metropolis offered. In many respects, it was not an easy life. His junior status ensured him of a duty schedule heavier than that borne by many of the other officers. The instruction he received there—more often applicable to an officer of infantry than a leader of coastal artillerymen—was rudimentary and monotonous. Moreover, the living conditions at Fort Columbus bordered on the squalid. The fort's casemates, where the garrison was quartered, were dank, drafty, cramped, and vermin ridden—altogether a most unhealthy place in which to be confined for hours on end. The army diet was plain and tasteless, and on-post recreations were few and primitive.

Johnston was vastly relieved when, in the autumn of 1831, his unit boarded transports, sailed down the coast to Chesapeake Bay, and alighted at the tip of the Virginia Peninsula. There Company C became a part of the garrison of Fort Monroe, the largest and arguably the most historic military installation in the country. It shared with the rock pile on Governors Island undesirable characteristics including cramped quarters, but the local climate was more salubrious, and the transfer not only returned Johnston to his native state but also to a civilian community whose customs he understood and whose values he shared.[17]

His identity as a southerner, always a defining influence in his life, was undergoing strengthening and deepening thanks to major events with national repercussions. By 1831 increasingly stiff tariffs on imported goods were prompting southern farmers to challenge the authority of the federal government to impose such crippling legislation on their region. Some of the complainants' political spokesmen were talking openly about secession. The rising clamor would be dampened, if not quelled, by threats of reprisals from President Andrew Jackson, a strong nationalist despite his Tennessee roots. Even so, the crisis spawned a grievance against the central government that would long fester below the Mason-Dixon Line.[18]

Southerners had other concerns besides repressive enactments. In August

1831 a slave uprising in southern Virginia had stoked the darkest fears of slave-holders throughout the South. Late that month an African-American preacher, Nat Turner, the property of Mr. Joseph Travis of Southampton County, just across Hampton Roads from Fort Monroe, organized chattels from neighboring planta-tions into a small army that he led against slave-owning families. The rampage took the lives of at least fifty-five whites including women and children. The revolt had prompted the transfer of hundreds of troops, including Company C, Fourth Artillery, from northern posts to the threatened area.

By the time Johnston and his comrades reached Hampton Roads, the uprising had been put down bloodily, although violent reprisals were yet to come. Several of Turner's followers had been slain by militia and gun-toting citizens. Others, including the preacher himself, had been captured; they would die on the gallows in the weeks to come. The terror the slave army had unleashed, however, would linger for years in the minds of white southerners.[19]

Nat Turner's Rebellion may have made Lieutenant Johnston scrutinize his own attitudes toward the "peculiar institution." As the scion of a family that owned and managed slaves, he had accepted without question the efficacy, if not the morality, of forced servitude. It would appear that his relationships with the members of his family's black work force had been cordial; some, in fact, may have verged on real friendship.[20]

His relatively liberal attitude toward African-Americans would not have pro-tected him against the disapprobation of those who deplored slavery as a moral evil. During his two-year stint on the edge of Manhattan, he would have come in contact with many who openly disapproved of the institution and, therefore, of him, although such feelings would have been expressed by civilians, not by his colleagues in the ranks, most of whom displayed apolitical tendencies. How Johnston might have reacted to such criticism is unknown, although it can be supposed that it made him defensive about his identity as a white southerner. But while he might have been adverse to some of the more objectionable aspects of the institution, such as the callous dismemberment of slave families, he would not have been moved by the strident criticisms of abolitionists, more than a few of whom he undoubtedly encountered in New York society. He would have viewed members of this movement not as moralists or reformers but as political agitators of the most dangerous stripe, whose pernicious influence on the already widening sectional divide was deplorable.

Johnston appears to have had no personal involvement in the institution of slavery once he left home for West Point. At no time did he own slaves, and, according to his nephew, George Beverly Johnston, he had no inclination to acquire any: "I have heard him express himself more than once quite firmly against the institution of slavery." He never thought to defend it on any ground except economic necessity, and even that, he realized, was a shaky argument. Even so, he would have regarded an attack on slavery as a thinly veiled assault on the southern people, their value system, and their code of honor. This he would not have borne without resentment. The economic system that flourished in his homeland might have its unfortunate side, but the people behind it were morally superior to the corrupt officials, the money-mad industrialists, and the downtrodden laborers who populated the big cities of the North.[21]

Johnston's transfer to Fort Monroe paid social and professional dividends. It returned him to the company of West Point classmates including Lieutenant Lee of the Engineers, who was helping improve the defenses of the still-unfinished installation. It also gave him, a son of the Virginia upcountry, entrée to tidewater society. Along with fellow officers, he was a frequent guest in the homes of the best families of the area, whose daughters he happily squired about. A born romantic, Johnston was susceptible to the charms of many of these well-bred damsels, but he refused to admit to those he confided in—even to his favorite brother, Beverly—that he was ever smitten. As he put it, he regularly found himself in the company of so many attractive women that they effectively cancelled out each other in his mind and heart.[22]

For a time, his service at Fort Monroe was enlivened by study at the first branch-specific school in the army, the Artillery School of Practice. Once the novelty of the institution wore off, however, Johnston was oppressed by its stultifying routine, its physical demands, and its increasing emphasis on infantry-style training. Thus, when field duty in a far-off clime beckoned, he was anxious to respond. In the summer of 1832, his company became part of a punitive expedition, 850 strong, that Brig. Gen. Winfield Scott, a Virginia native and a hero of the War of 1812, organized for service against Indians rampaging through parts of the Northwest. Under Chief Black Hawk, members of the Sauk and Fox tribes had fled reservations in the Iowa Territory, to which they had been confined twelve years earlier, and had crossed the Mississippi to their old hunting grounds in northern Illinois.

Johnston, although probably aware that Black Hawk had violated a resettlement

Gen. Winfield Scott, USA

treaty that had been forced down his throat, resolved to do his duty as an officer of the United States Army. The assignment began late in June, shortly after his return to Hampton Roads from Abingdon, where he had attended the funeral of his father (who would soon be followed in death by two of Joseph's older brothers, one felled by disease, the other the victim of an accident). An excursion to Illinois would provide a respite from family tragedies and perhaps offer both adventure and career advancement. Yet, instead of howling savages in war paint, his unit spent most of the campaign battling diseases, the most virulent being cholera, which broke out aboard the expedition's transports as they crossed Lake Erie en route to the theater of operations. By the time the ships reached Fort Dearborn, outside the infant city of Chicago, almost six hundred of Scott's troops had been stricken with the insidious bacterial disease, and about one-fourth of the command succumbed to it. Most of the victims were enlisted men, although several officers, including the commander of Johnston's company, also contracted it. Johnston himself, although his health remained good, made it only as far as Dearborn, where Company C was held in quarantine.

For all its travail, the expedition never reached its destination. Before in position to confront Black Hawk and his followers, local militia ran them to earth, engaged them along Bad Axe River in the Michigan Territory, and forced their surrender. Chagrined to have missed the decisive action, General Scott had to make do with overseeing the negotiations that returned the Sauk and Fox west of the great river and resettled them on even less desirable land than granted them under the earlier treaty. Johnston was a witness to the proceedings, which were conducted at a fort on an island in the Mississippi, and as such affixed his signature to the new treaty. Thus ended his first, abortive involvement in war.[23]

TWO
THE BRIGHTEST
OF THE LOT

William Tecumseh Sherman came from a large family—six boys and five girls—whose American progenitor had emigrated from England to the colony of Massachusetts Bay in 1634. Tecumseh, as he was originally named ("Cumpy" or "Cump" to his parents, siblings, and friends) was the fifth child

William T. Sherman

and third son of Charles Robert Sherman, a proud descendant of Roger Sherman, signer of the Declaration of Independence and framer of the United States Constitution. In 1810, at the age of twenty-two, Charles left Connecticut, to which the family had removed one generation earlier, and migrated to south-central Ohio, eventually settling in Lancaster, Fairfield County.

In Connecticut, Charles had received a good education, had studied law and been admitted to the bar, and had married Mary Elizabeth Hoyt, his childhood sweetheart. Mary was also well educated, having graduated from a celebrated finishing school at

Poughkeepsie, New York. When Charles immigrated to the Northwest, he felt constrained to leave his wife behind; as soon as he put down roots in Lancaster, he returned for her and their firstborn, whom they christened Charles to honor both his father and his mother's eldest brother. As John Sherman, the fifth son, noted late in life, the budding family made the long, arduous trip to Ohio entirely by horseback, Charles and Mary "alternately carrying their infant child upon a pillow before them." To John, the rigors of the journey emphasized "the self-reliant character of the man, and the brave, confiding trust of his wife."[1]

Charles' decision to immigrate to the first state to be carved out of the Northwest Territory started a family trend. Four years later, upon the death of his father, Judge Taylor Sherman, his mother, in company with another son and a daughter, also made the trek to Ohio, settling in Monroeville and Mansfield, one hundred and seventy-five miles, respectively, north of Lancaster. Charles's mother and siblings made a happy life in the Buckeye State, but he himself attained the greatest measure of prosperity, short-lived as it seemed in retrospect. Not long after arriving in the town whose "natural beauty . . . and the charms of its already established society" had overcome his initial inclination to settle in Zanesville, the law practice he established there blossomed, and he and his family gained acceptance, then prominence, in the community.[2]

It helped that Charles was "a kindly, social man . . . greatly loved by his associates of the bench and bar. . . . He had a clear head, a generous heart, and a ready wit." Such traits augured well for professional success, but, as William T. Sherman noted in his memoirs, his father's position "was no sinecure." Charles's growing clientele required him to ride a circuit of courthouses, some as distant as Cincinnati and Detroit. John Sherman recalled that his mother would leave young Charles in the care of relatives and join her husband on his journey, which they made "always on horseback."[3]

When not accompanying Charles Sherman on his rounds, Mary was presenting him with sons and daughters, whom she reared with patient care. John recalled her as a gentle, guiding influence in the lives of her large brood: "I never knew her to scold, much less to strike, her children." But if she rarely raised her voice, she made her preferences known, especially when it came to the naming of her sons.[4]

In 1812, upon the outbreak of war with England, Charles Sherman interrupted his law practice to enlist in one of the volunteer units formed subsequent to the capture of Detroit and other Great Lakes ports by British regulars. Assigned to the commissary department of the local military department, he saw mostly staff duty but avidly followed the course of the war against the Redcoats and their Native American allies. Charles was especially impressed by the dramatic invasion of Canada that Maj. Gen. William Henry Harrison launched from recaptured Detroit in 1813. Twenty-seven years later, this feat, along with his earlier victory over the Indians of the Northwest at Tippecanoe, made Harrison the first successful presidential candidate of the Whig Party, of which Charles Sherman was an avid supporter.

Charles admired not only "Old Tippecanoe" but also his adversary in that celebrated encounter, Tecumseh, the great chief of the Shawnee Nation. The young attorney desired to bestow the chief's name on one of his first two sons, but when his wife insisted that both be named for her brothers, he acquiesced. By the time their third son came into the world, as he himself later explained, "mother having no more brothers, my father succeeded in his original purpose." The short form, "Cump," derived from the child's inability to pronounce the mouthful of a name, a defect shared by his younger siblings.[5]

That distinctive appellation might have stood unaltered had not his father died suddenly in June 1829, five years after being named a justice of the Ohio supreme court. Despite his professional attainments, he left his widow and children in what was euphemistically termed "circumstances of dependence," the result of debts he had assumed while serving as a local collector of internal revenue. Charles's many friends, some of whom were quite as prominent as he and much better off, stepped in to relieve Mary of her crushing burden by adopting several of the children. Only the three youngest would remain with their mother until maturity. The eldest sons, Charles and James, were already settled in college and professional life, respectively. Over the next three years the oldest daughters, Elizabeth and Amelia, married; one took in their ten-year-old sister, Julia. Of the younger children, seven-year-old Lampson went to live with a family friend, a newspaper publisher in Cincinnati, while five-year-old John moved in with an uncle in Mount Vernon, Ohio.[6]

Sen. Thomas Ewing

Meanwhile, nine-year-old Tecumseh was resettled in the Lancaster home of Thomas Ewing and his wife, the former Maria Boyle. Thomas Ewing, a forty-year-old native of Virginia, had been a close associate of Charles Sherman's as well as one of his warmest friends. Currently the prosecuting attorney for Fairfield and Athens Counties, he was moving up the ladder of politics. His rise within the Whig Party would culminate in his appointment, two years hence, as U.S. senator from Ohio. Following his single term in the Senate, he would serve as President Harrison's secretary of the treasury and as first secretary of the Home Department (later the Department of the Interior) under Zachary Taylor. A man of both physical and intellectual power, he counted among his friends the great solons of the era including Daniel Webster and Henry Clay. Socially conservative, Ewing had no great aversion to slavery as long as the institution was confined to the South, but he could not tolerate the growing number of threats by southern officials, angry over one or another policy of the federal government, to haul their states out of the Union. For this reason, in 1831–32 he publicly supported the efforts of Democrat Andrew Jackson to quash the Nullification movement.[7]

In addition to being a political animal, Ewing was a man of culture and refinement. Professional success had enabled him to build a large house on a hill overlooking the much more modest Sherman home, one adorned with expensive furnishings including the largest private library in the town. The house also abounded with children, although not as many as his friend Charles had fathered. By 1829 Ewing had sired eight-year-old Philemon (named for his father's law tutor), five-year-old Ellen, three-year-old Hugh, and the infant Thomas Jr. Over the next eight years, he and Maria would rear another son, Charles, and a daughter, Teresa. Despite their expanding brood, the Ewings were prosperous enough to take another child into their home, whom they would strive to treat as a true member of the family. And yet, perhaps out of consideration for Mary Sherman's sensibilities, they would never legally adopt the child.

Ewing had a preference for the one he would take in. He told the grieving widow, "You must give me the brightest of the lot, and I will make a man of him." Tecumseh's mother replied, "Take Cump, the red-haired one, he's the smartest." From the time he was a toddler, the child's intelligence had been a subject of remark in the family, and his common-school performance had validated their faith in his intellectual powers. Thus, on a day the boy would never forget, the tall, somber neighbor took Charles Sherman's third son by the hand and led him up the hill to his new home.[8]

Attempts by the Ewings to make the boy feel an integral part of the family achieved mixed results. Two years after he went to live with them, he appeared to Senator Ewing "bashful and not quite at home." Cump was nevertheless grateful for his foster parents' care, which they continued to demonstrate—in the form of financial assistance—well after he left their home to make a life of his own. He grew close to his adoptive siblings, especially Phil and, over time, Hugh (who, along with his younger brothers, Charles and Thomas Jr., was fated to follow Sherman into the Union army and to rise to star rank). On the other hand, Cump regarded Ellen as an inconvenient little sister until, some fourteen years after he joined the Ewing fold, she became the object of his romantic interest.

Perhaps because his mother lived for some years in the house at the foot of the hill and he saw her on a daily basis, Cump never completely shifted his affection to his foster parents. Sherman's biographers seem to agree that the circumstances of his transfer to the Ewings made him feel unwanted and abandoned, impressions that troubled him, to some degree, for the rest of his life. Michael Fellman, perhaps the most incisive of Sherman's biographers despite his sometimes excessive reliance on psycho-historical techniques, claims that "fear or betrayal and abandonment, bouts of depression, and diffuse and frequently explosive rage characterized the adult Sherman."[9]

Sherman's youthful sense of insecurity was not eased by the spirit of acceptance he found in the Ewing home. Although reserved and a bit distant even toward his biological children, Thomas Ewing was a caring and concerned parent. He tried to show that side of his personality to his ward, but he failed to win Cump's unalloyed affection. When Cump left Lancaster for West Point and, later, the army, and he wrote to his foster father, Cump invariably addressed him as "Sir." As he matured, he came to admire Thomas Ewing's public achievements and envy his financial success, but he was unable to regard him as anything more than a father figure—a surrogate for the true father of whom he had only sparse and clouded memories.

Maria Boyle Ewing dispensed her affection more freely than her husband, but she could also be a stern disciplinarian. Cump appears to have warmed to her maternal care, which she extended to him despite his refusal to call her "Mother." Perhaps he perceived her more admirable traits in her older daughter, which would explain why he developed such deep feelings for Ellen. One trait that Cump did not appreciate was Maria's religious devotion, which she tried to share with the boy for the comfort and peace of mind it would bring him. Born into an Irish Catholic family, Maria insisted on raising each of her children in the Church—a determination that Thomas Ewing, a life-long agnostic, refused to oppose. Cump's mother had professed adherence to the Protestant faith; born an Episcopalian, she later became a Presbyterian. Regardless, Maria sought and received her permission (whether overt or tacit) to have Cump baptized a Catholic.

According to family lore, the ceremony was performed by a visiting Dominican priest—at that time, Lancaster had a small Catholic church but no pastor—who at first refused to administer the sacrament. Appalled to learn that the boy had been named for a godless savage (however popular his public image), the priest insisted that he be given a proper Christian name. The date being June 25, the feast day of St. William in the church calendar, that name was bestowed upon the boy, Tecumseh being relegated to a middle name. It made no difference to the Shermans or the Ewings. To them, as well as to the numerous friends and colleagues he acquired in later life, he remained "Cump."[10]

The boy had not acquiesced in his baptism. He had no animus against Roman Catholicism (although late in life he decried the hold it exerted on its communicants), but he had no intention of obeying its precepts or participating in its rituals. Apparently his foster parents did not force him to do so; nevertheless, he resented his outward conversion, primarily because it had not been his idea. After marrying Ellen, he accompanied her to Mass, developed cordial relations with Catholic prelates, and generously supported the church's charitable institutions. In his heart, however, he was no Catholic, and never wished to become one.[11]

In fact, he rejected organized religion in any form. Although he professed a belief in the existence of God, he never became a Christian in the accepted sense of the term. He did not believe in the divinity of Christ, and he certainly did not accept the Catholic doctrine of a Holy Trinity composed of Father, Son, and Holy Spirit. His outward expressions of religious beliefs—few and far between as they were—suggest that he was a deist in the tradition of Jefferson, Franklin, and other founders of the American Republic. He supported the notion of a civil religion in which man turned inward in his quest for perfection rather than seeking inspiration from a Supreme Being.

For Sherman, as for all deists, God was an absentee landlord. He created the world, started it spinning on its axis, then took his attention from it, permitting it to function according to an all-encompassing set of natural laws. Those who inhabited the earth were left to work out their own relationships with the material universe. Yet God's refusal to intervene in the lives of men left a void to be filled by another object of worship. As a son of the early Republic, Sherman found an alternative deity in the American system of government. As one religious historian points out, "American political theory in the late eighteenth and early nineteenth century embodied the notion that American civil law was a reasonable expression of Divine law. Devotion to the civil law became primary because the Founding Fathers . . . had by sound reason uncovered the universal laws of human government and allowed them to be set in motion in the United States. Obeying the 'law of the land' became as fundamental as obeying the other universal laws of God."[12]

In addition to helping explain man's relationship with his fellow humans and the world they inhabited, the American political model, as mapped and guided by the Constitution (which every right-thinking citizen considered the most masterful document of its kind ever written), imposed on the nation a degree of order and stability critical to progress and prosperity. As Sherman biographer John F. Marszalek notes, even in his youth Cump appreciated that "order was necessary to success in life. . . . He saw any personal or public disorder as anarchy. . . ."[13]

More to the point, he regarded an orderly system of government as a curb on the chaotic tendencies of a democratic people. Democracies, he believed, spawned an ignorant populace easily manipulated by demagogues, corruptors, and other opportunists. For this reason, looking back at his boyhood, he applauded his foster father's opposition to Nullification while condemning the efforts of southern politicians to circumvent federal law in furtherance of regional economic interests.

⟶•⟵

If he resented being dragooned into religious conversion, young Sherman similarly took offense at the manner in which his life's course was laid out for him in total disregard of his own preferences. He appreciated the Ewings' efforts to secure a good education for him, noting that the Lancaster Academy, to which they sent him, "was the best in the place; indeed, as good a school as any in Ohio." There, at the hands of "excellent teachers," he received a broad, if not an especially deep, classical education laden with courses in ancient history and the dead languages.[14]

In his memoirs Sherman reduces this seminal period in his life to a single, unenlightening comment: "Time passed with us as with boys generally." His limited coverage of this period includes a recollection that at fourteen there was a break in his regular schooling. In the fall of 1834 he was selected, along with three other classmates, to assist in surveys preliminary to digging a waterway that would intersect the Ohio River canal at Carroll, eight miles north of Lancaster.

The work, which lasted until the following spring, was menial at best, but it paid a half-dollar per day, "the first money any of us had ever earned."[15]

Sherman is hardly more expansive in recounting how Thomas Ewing arranged, without the consent of his ward, to secure for him an appointment to West Point. Yet the reader readily understands that the decision was not altogether to his liking. He admits to having had "little knowledge" of that august institution "except that it was very strict, and that the army was its natural consequence." His phrasing suggests that for him the military life was not necessarily a happy prospect. In fact, he was ambivalent about a career in arms. He considered soldiering in defense of the nation a respectable and even an honorable profession. On the other hand, unlike Joseph E. Johnston, he harbored no childhood fantasies of becoming a dashing dragoon. Nor did family history incline him toward soldiering. Whatever reservations he might have harbored, however, were swept aside by Ewing's determination that he should receive a military education as well as by the ease with which he secured the necessary application.[16]

Having been accepted as a provisional member of the corps of cadets in May 1836, sixteen-year-old W. Tecumseh Sherman made the long, roundabout trip to upstate New York via relays of stagecoaches to Frederick, Maryland, by two-horse taxi to Washington, D.C. (where he shared Senator Ewing's boardinghouse room during a week of sightseeing), then by railroad to Baltimore, by boat to Havre de Grace, again by rail across Delaware, by steamer to Philadelphia, and by boat and railroad across northern New Jersey to New York City, where he spent another week with two of his uncles, residents of the great metropolis and its environs. On June 12 he finally made it to West Point, where he and two other plebes, his traveling companions, registered in the office of Lt. Charles Ferguson Smith, the Academy's adjutant and later its commandant of cadets.

Upon arriving, he joined the 139 other cadets who hoped to graduate with the class of 1840. Almost one hundred, however, were destined to drop out due to academic deficiencies, health problems, or other reasons. The survivors would include future soldiers of high rank and renown—some of these Sherman would fight alongside; others he would oppose. The list of future allies included George Henry Thomas of Virginia, George Washington Getty of the District of Columbia, Stewart Van Vliet of New York, and the Tennessean William Hays; all would become, like him, general officers in the Union ranks. His class also sported future Confederate generals Richard Stoddert Ewell and Thomas Jordan of Virginia, Paul Octave Hébert of Louisiana, James Green Martin of North Carolina, and Bushrod Rust Johnson, who hailed from Sherman's own state.

Gen. George H. Thomas, USA

While he made close friends of classmates from all regions, he was especially close to Thomas, whom he came to consider his best friend in the corps of cadets, and Edward Otho Cresap Ord, a Maryland-born member of the class of 1839. In addition to firm friendships, he forged casual acquaintances that would have an impact on his later career. The least promising but most beneficial of these was his brief association with Ulysses S. Grant, a fellow Ohioan transplanted to Illinois, who entered the Academy during Sherman's last year there. Until the Civil War threw them together, he remembered the fourth classman as an undersized country boy, the son of an acquisitive tanner—a good enough fellow but distinctive neither in his appearance nor in his intellectual attainments.[17]

Although he was one of the youngest members of his class, from his first days on the Hudson, Sherman's solid early education and natural aptitude for the mathematics courses that buttressed West Point's engineering-oriented curriculum assured him of academic success. He also demonstrated a facility for English composition and a talent for military drawing. Too, he possessed a broad and deep knowledge of national and world affairs. Years later Oliver Otis Howard, himself a West Pointer of acknowledged erudition, marveled at his classmate's grasp of the nuances of international diplomacy: "I don't think that any of us [at the Academy] could have equaled Sherman in his thorough mastery of that study." Howard also noted a particularly useful trait that characterized Sherman not only at West Point but throughout his military career: "He never forgot what he once learned."[18]

These abilities were reflected in his class standing. At the close of his first year, he stood ninth among the seventy-six cadets who remained in his class; succeeding years ended with him ranking sixth out of fifty-eight cadets; sixth of forty-six; and, upon graduation, sixth of forty-two. He would have stood two places higher on the roll of general merit, which reflected both classroom achievement and soldierly conduct, had he not seemingly gone out of his way to accumulate those freely dispensed demerits. In his four years at West Point, he amassed almost four hundred black marks.[19]

One historian of the nineteenth-century Academy suggests that Sherman's behavior was in keeping with the lax discipline that held sway during the superintendence of Lt. Col. R. E. De Russy. Even if this is true, his record also reflected his conflicted attitude toward military education and the military profession in general. While he did not wish to fail at the Academy, thus disgracing the Ewings, his own family, and himself, he refused to honor what he saw as the school's nitpicking, archaic, and unevenly applied regulations. The free-spirited cadet was frequently late for class, for drill, for reveille, for dress parade. Parade-ground instructors gigged him for talking in the ranks; inspecting officers marked him down for dirt on his musket as well as on his pants and shoes and for leaving his barracks room in disarray. The heaviest penalties he incurred were dispensed for visiting after lights out ("it is almost a natural impossibility to confine ourselves to our rooms," he informed Ellen, adding that "we often feel disposed to break over our imposed limits, and 'go forth'"). Not surprisingly, he was cited more than once for "going forth" from chapel before the chaplain had finished preaching.[20]

Largely as a result of these transgressions, he never won rank at the Academy although classmates of lesser intellect became corporals, sergeants, and lieutenants. Sherman explained his being passed over forthrightly enough: "I was not considered a good soldier. . . . Then, as now, neatness in dress and form, with a strict conformity to the rules, were the qualifications required for office, and I suppose I was found not to excel in any of these."[21]

The one attainment that did matter—a commission in the United States Army—was bestowed upon him on the day he was graduated, June 30, 1840. His class standing was certainly respectable, but it was not high enough to gain him entry into the elite fraternity of the construction or topographical engineers. Instead, like Joe Johnston, he was assigned a berth in a heavy artillery unit—in his case, the Third United States Regiment of Artillery. Given his aptitude for the technical side of soldiering, he would seem to be a perfect fit for that technologically driven branch.

He was far better versed in military science than in military art—he was no devotee of tactics or strategy. Although he had been a voracious reader at the Academy, he had not delved into the tactical manuals that crowded the shelves of its library, not even the works of Baron Antoine Henri Jomini, the preeminent theoretician of the age, interpreter of the campaigns of Napoleon and Frederick the Great. This dearth of formal study did not bother him, then or later. After the Civil

War, when invited to speak at his alma mater, he repeated to his audience a question frequently asked of him: From which books had he learned the secret of leading armies? His standard answer was that "I was not aware that I had been influenced by any of them." In place of book learning he had substituted a practical knowledge of men, weapons, and terrain gained by personal experience. His eyes were sharp, his reasoning was acute, and his brain was an amazingly efficient storage and retrieval system. By careful observation, by accumulating examples and filing them away for future reference, he had learned to judge the capabilities of the men he led and to motivate them to accomplish the difficult, even the seemingly impossible—to weather long marches under a blistering sun without ample water; to go for days or weeks at a time without a regular issuance of rations, clothing, and equipment; to reach, attack, and carry apparently impregnable objectives. "With this knowledge fairly acquired in actual experience," he asked rhetorically, "was there any need for me to look back to Alexander the Great . . . for examples?"[22]

He spent his postgraduate furlough visiting his two families in Lancaster. From there he traveled to Mansfield, where Charles Sherman Jr. was a practicing attorney and John Sherman was studying law under his tutelage. John's aptitude for his chosen profession would gain him prominence in Whig and, later, Republican party circles.[23]

Much of Cump's time in Lancaster was passed in the company of Ellen Ewing, herself just returned from the East in company with her father; she had been attending a Catholic girls' school in the Washington, D.C., suburb of Georgetown. At sixteen, Cump's foster sister was hovering on the brink of young womanhood; he felt attracted to her now as never before. On this occasion the couple may well have begun to plan a life together. There were attitude adjustments to be made and obstacles of many kinds to be surmounted, but just now they were happy to be reunited in the Ewing fold.

To celebrate his graduation, Ellen organized a party at which Cump was the honored guest. Her fiancé-to-be was neither Adonis nor Beau Brummell. Although in the flush of young manhood he was plain featured, with a long neck and a big head covered by an unruly mop of red hair, his physique tall, spare, and angular; and even in a dress uniform he could look unkempt and at times seedy. On this occasion, however, he rose to the demands of his celebrity, looking stylish in his new, unwrinkled uniform adorned with the gilt-edged shoulder straps of a second lieutenant of artillery. Although never a regular attendee at the dances West Point had hosted, he made an impressive showing on the dance floor with Ellen as his partner. Equally impressive was the way he took charge when a bat crashed the festivities. Through his efforts the winged intruder was ushered out the front door without damage to the household. The guests agreed that "General Sherman's first battle" had ended in glorious victory.[24]

Regretful that he must leave such pleasant surroundings all too soon, by late September he was heading east. After several days on the road and the water, he reported at the recruiting rendezvous on Governors Island in New York harbor. He took charge of the first military unit to be assigned to him, a party of raw recruits bound for Florida to make a dubious contribution to the seemingly endless guerrilla war against the Seminoles. In October Cump and his charges boarded a transport that descended the coast as far as Savannah. There they hailed another vessel bound for St. Augustine. By way of Indian River Inlet, they eventually reached their destination, Fort Pierce, where Cump joined Company G of the Fourth Artillery, part of the small garrison of that wilderness outpost.

The season for active campaigning was some weeks away; in the interim, Lieutenant Sherman settled into the routine of inspecting and drilling the squad of artillerists that had been entrusted to him. The dull regimen was brightened by the arrival in November of Bvt. Maj. Thomas Childs and a cadre of junior officers that included Cump's West Point classmate Stewart Van Vliet. The new arrivals brought the Fourth Artillery's force at Fort Pierce to two companies, enough to support active operations.[25]

The next several months were spent hunting scattered bands of Seminoles. Sherman found that the understrength enemy was too smart to offer battle; instead, they sank out of sight in their swamp- and canebrake-infested enclaves. They appeared content to wait out the soldiers, who, they could sense, were growing weary of waging a conflict they were ill-equipped, materially and psychologically, to win. Thus idled, Sherman spent much of his stint at Fort Pierce exploring the local terrain, which he described in a letter to John as "cut up by innumerable rivers, streams, and rivulets, which . . . gives rise in time to a heavy growth of live oak, palmetto, and scrub of every kind. These are the dreaded hummocks, the stronghold of the Indians, where he builds his hut, and has pumpkin and corn fields." These natural sanctuaries "have enabled the Indians thus far to elude the pursuit of our army."[26]

During Sherman's term in Florida, the army failed to bring its quarry to bay; the closest it came to a confrontation was a series of false alarms of impending attack.

24

The standoff dashed Sherman's hope of securing high rank and military distinction through a successful campaign in the field. He faced the gloomy prospect of remaining a junior lieutenant for years to come, his senses dulled by boring routine, his only compensation being the twenty-five dollars he drew every month—not nearly enough to support a wife and a family. He was keenly aware that Ellen's father desired him to resign his commission at the first opportunity, return to Ohio, and accept a managerial position in the salt wells that brought the Ewing family much of its income. Yet he saw no sense in leaving the only profession he had been educated and trained for. "Were I to resign," he informed Ellen, "I would have to depend upon someone till I could establish myself in some other field. . . . It would be madness at this late date to commence something new." At bottom, he had no desire to "depend" further on a foster father to whom he was already deeply indebted.[27]

To be sure, his profession had its compensations as well as its drawbacks. At least in some circles, there was a certain prestige to holding a commission. It gave him "a place envied by thousands and for which hundreds of the best young men of their country toil every year." The pride he took in being an officer deepened when, between early 1842 and mid-1843, his company did garrison duty in several cities in the Deep South, including St. Augustine, Mobile, and Charleston. At each of these stations, especially at Fort Moultrie in Charleston Harbor, he was welcomed into the society of some of the oldest, wealthiest, and most prominent families in the nation. All received him cordially; a few went so far as to suggest that as an officer and gentleman he was their equal, or something close to it. Theirs was an attitude Sherman found conspicuously absent in the garrison towns of the North.

He reciprocated by forming a generally favorable impression of southern culture and society. His regard was not unalloyed, for he was contemptuous of the dissipated plantation youth and the snobbish, decadent aristocrats whose company he could not always avoid. But he expressed a decided admiration for those small planters who earned their living by the sweat of their brow and were not too proud to toil in the fields side by side with their chattels.

His view of southern society was not tainted by a moral squeamishness about slavery. He did not hold southerners responsible for the institution; they had inherited it from their forebears and had to make the best of it. Slavery had become too important to the economic survival of the region to be done away with except gradually and with some idea of a viable replacement. Nor did he believe that slaves would prosper once given their freedom. He did not see them as inherently industrious or capable of self-sufficiency. Looking around, he ascribed the decay of certain parts of the South not to slavery itself but to the incompetence of the work force: "Many plantations have been wasted and blighted under the care and tillage of lowly irresponsible negroes."

A society in which a privileged few prospered from the labor of a voiceless underclass offended Sherman's sensibilities, mainly because of its inherent instability. Yet he feared that those who called for slavery's demise were opening a Pandora's box of economic ruin and social chaos. Slavery, he believed, rested on a base so rotten that in time it would collapse of its own weight, but he was content to wait for that day to come. The trick was to manage and contain the institution, to limit its influence and curb its expansion, without so antagonizing its practitioners that one third of the population rose up in arms to defend it. That prospect had an infinitely greater impact on Sherman's peace of mind than the possibility that slavery might go on, unabated, forever. It would continue to influence his view of American society throughout his military career and, in fact, through the rest of his life.[28]

THREE

WAR AND LOVE

The duties proscribed under the Tariff of 1832 were even more repressive than those of the Tariff of '28 (known to southerners as the "Tariff of Abominations"), which had ignited the Nullification crisis. Again southerners railed against the unbridled power of a central government that pandered to the interests of northern and western voters—power that some day, they feared, might be turned against chattel slavery. When renewed threats of secession worked their way into the oratory of local officials, President Jackson ordered troops elsewhere in the country to reinforce the southern garrisons. On December 23, 1832, Lieutenant Johnston and the other members of Company C, Fourth Artillery, were sent to man the forts of Charleston, South Carolina. The tense atmosphere that greeted the unit's arrival raised the troubling prospect that the young officer might be asked to raise his hand against the people of his region. He was vastly relieved when the crisis was defused without bloodshed through a series of compromises worked out in Washington. In the spring of 1833, Company C quietly returned to Fort Monroe.[1]

Johnston's renewed service on the Virginia Peninsula lasted a few months before being interrupted by another round of Indian campaigning, interspersed with a brief stint in the nation's capital. The first interlude saw his unit transferred to Fort Mitchell, Alabama, where it spent the winter of 1833–34 attempting to maintain peace between the usually placid Creeks and white settlers who had laid claim to portions of their reservation. It was dangerous and thankless duty, although it had its compensations. In letters to friends and some of his siblings, the normally reticent Johnston rhapsodized about the "very pretty Indian girls" with whom he occasionally consorted.[2]

In January 1836, at the close of a rather prosaic tour as a topographical draftsman in Washington, he entered upon an extensive and demanding campaign in the wilds of southern Florida, a region that one of his colleagues described as "that Indian-infested prison house of the army." The Seminoles, led by Chief Osceola, had refused to conclude negotiations toward moving them off tribal lands coveted by whites and onto less valuable territory west of the Mississippi. The poor faith in which the government's representatives negotiated had prompted Osceola and his four thousand followers—including hundreds of armed blacks, many of them fugitive slaves who had made common cause with the equally oppressed Seminoles—to attack isolated settlements. These they razed and looted, killing their occupants; they also ambushed and annihilated a column of soldiers under Maj. Francis Dade. Once again, military might was shifted into an environment hostile to white civilization.[3]

En route to his new duty station, Johnston enjoyed a furlough in Columbia, South Carolina, where two of his brothers and one of his cousins had gone to live. By mid-February he was at Savannah, Georgia, waiting for a steamboat to take him down the St. John's River to Picolata, Florida, on the border of Seminole territory. The mission that awaited him promised to be more frustrating than his truncated service against the Sauk, Fox, and Creeks, but at least he would serve in the capacity of aide-de-camp to General Scott, an unexpected honor tendered him in late February.[4]

His involvement in what became known as the Second Seminole War (the first had raged from November

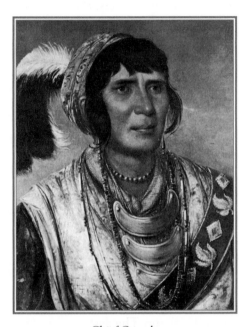

Chief Osceola

1817 through early 1819) began with outpost service at Fort Drane, a stockaded blockhouse in central Florida that served as the jumping-off point of Scott's campaign against the hostiles. The general's strategy was based on a three-pronged advance against Osceola's main enclave south of Fort Drane. The plan, however, was overly ambitious and unwieldy, and Scott proved himself unable to coordinate the movements it called for. Two of the columns were late in reaching their assigned rendezvous and failed to make contact as planned. In the end, having run short of provisions, both forces retreated to Fort Brooke, the principal military installation on Florida's Gulf Coast.[5]

Unaware of these developments, toward the close of March the third column, a mixed force of regulars and volunteers commanded by Scott himself and accompanied by Johnston, encountered Osceola's main body along the south bank of the Withlacoochee River. Scott placed his main body in flatboats and ferried it across the stream against light resistance. When the soldiers started inland, Osceola's people fell back to more defensible positions deeper in the swamps. Two days later, March 31, Scott's column drew fire from hostiles on one of the islands in the Withlacoochee; his troops stood their ground and then, upon command, attacked. Held close to Scott's side, Lieutenant Johnston observed from the rear as the regulars and citizen-soldiers, shouting a facsimile of a war whoop, charged up the riverbank, driving bands of red and black men from one position to another at the point of the bayonet. After a failed attempt to make a stand, the hard-pressed enemy gave up the fight and swam or splashed across the river to safety. Thanks to the nonappearance of the cooperating columns, which were to have cut off Osceola's retreat, Scott and his staff watched impotently as the survivors of their assault, including their chieftain, disappeared into the wilderness.

After securing the area, tending to his wounded, and burying the dead, Scott turned north to Fort Brooke. There most of his command idled away the next three months, as their leader pondered his lost opportunities and plotted a new offensive. He never put it to the test. Late in May he was transferred to Alabama to put down an uprising by disgruntled Creeks.[6]

Joe Johnston, now a first lieutenant in the Fourth Artillery, stayed on in Florida but without any pressing responsibilities. Life became especially static once Osceola was handed over to the army by tribesmen seeking the announced price on his head; thereafter, large numbers of his followers gave themselves up. Then a feud broke out between Scott and his successor in Florida, Brig. Gen. Thomas S. Jesup. The dust-up placed Johnston, who continued to be regarded as a "Scott man," in an unenviable position. His status as an "unwelcome supernumerary," combined with his chagrin over his uninspiring duty, the low pay he commanded, and the slow pace of promotion (a situation especially prevalent in the artillery, whose small size limited opportunities for advancement) made him consider leaving the army for civilian life.[7]

On May 31, 1837, following months of deliberation, he resigned his commission. A few days later he wrote his brother Beverly from Washington (to which he had returned following a few desultory months at Jefferson Barracks, near St. Louis, Missouri), explaining his action, which he ascribed to unful-filled ambition. It troubled him that "many of my juniors who had the luck to be assigned to regiments in which promotion was less slow than in that to which I belonged" had gotten ahead of him on the army's seniority list. He believed he could parlay his mapmaking experience into a more remunerative position as a civilian employee of the Topographical Bureau, in which he had served during his posting to Washington. His supposition was correct, but he neither expected nor appreciated his subsequent return to Florida, where he soon found himself once again battling the Seminoles.[8]

In the fall of 1837, the Topographical Bureau assigned its new employee to an expedition that was to survey the Florida coast from St. Augustine to Key West. The party, commanded by naval Lt. L. M. Powell, consisted of more than one hundred servicemen, including several African-American sailors (the navy had a minority recruiting program, something the army would continue to lack for another quarter-century). By mid-January 1838 this group, which was being fol-lowed down the coast by a company of regulars under 1st Lt. John Bankhead Magruder, a friend of Johnston's from West Point, had penetrated by boat to a point near the mouth of Jupiter Inlet, on the coast more than two hundred miles south of St. Augustine. Here, on the upper edge of the Florida Everglades, Powell's and Magruder's people intended to explore neighboring lagoons and the narrow, winding tributaries of the St. Lucie River.

The only trouble was that they were in close proximity to hundreds of those Seminoles who continued to resist removal even after the loss of their chief. Many had surrendered to Jesup only to flee when peace negotiations broke down. In fact, the surveyors had been trading skirmish fire with these people for a week or more. On the morning of the fifteenth, Powell, whose group had forged well ahead of Magruder's, discovered a Seminole village only a few miles off. Having unsuccessfully hunted Osceola's tribesmen during an earlier stint in Florida, the still frustrated Powell laid aside his surveying tools and took up his cutlass. Intent on attacking the village, he started inland with about sixty sailors and foot artillerists, half as many others having been left behind to guard the boats. Powell was accompanied by Johnston, who although a civilian had more military expe-rience than any of his uniformed associates.[9]

Guided to his objective by a captured Seminole woman, Powell was almost there when the inhabitants, alerted to his advance, turned out and opened fire. Powell wished to take the offensive, but the many raw recruits in his party refused to advance. A standoff ensued during which the Indians made casualties of many sailors and artillerists, including a couple of officers. During the firefight a bullet struck Johnston on the top of his skull, carrying away clumps of hair but doing no serious damage. By some accounts, dozens of rounds penetrated his loose-fitting clothing, while "a red sash which he wore, and which attracted the Indian aim on account of its conspicuous color . . . was literally riddled."[10]

Undaunted by these narrow escapes, Johnston took charge of the rear guard when a disgusted Powell was forced to call retreat. The civilian engineer covered the movement with an effective delaying action and even helped carry off a seriously wounded officer. By exploiting the defensive potential of every woodlot, swamp, and bayou, Johnston held off the hostiles until Powell's men reached their boats and paddled up the coast to safety. By the time they reached Fort Pierce, Johnston had won a reputation for "coolness, courage, and judgement." Modesty prevented him from glorying in his newly won fame, but he must have been pleased to have met at last the test of combat.[11]

<hr />

As Robert Hughes notes, Johnston's conduct at Jupiter Inlet "was worth something more than mere applause. It gained for him an appointment as first lieutenant in the topographical engineers, thus restoring him to his former rank and preventing him from losing anything by his resignation." His return to the army, in a capacity he much preferred to his former situation, took effect on July 7, 1838. That day he not only escaped the Indian-infested swamps of Florida and a war destined to grind on for seven more years but gained entrée to an elite branch of the army that his West Point grades had failed to secure for him.[12]

His new posting returned him briefly to Washington, D.C., and then took him to various sites in the East and Northwest. Over the next eight years, he supervised navigational improvements on the Black River in upstate New York (1838–39) and on Lake Erie (1841); helped survey the boundary between the United States and the Republic of Texas (1841, five years after Texas had won its independence from Mexico); plotted the border between America and the British Provinces (1843–44); and took a leading part in the Atlantic Coast Survey of 1844–46. He even found the willingness to return to Florida for some field engineering duty that did not involve him in combat.[13]

During this especially busy period in his renewed career, he tried to find a way to settle down. By May 1842 he was writing to his nephew John Preston Johnstone (an alternate spelling of the family's name), the son of his deceased brother Charles, about his love life. He admitted that he had a sweetheart, whose name he refused to divulge at first. Over the next three years, via long-distance correspondence when unable to secure leave from his multiplicity of duties, he courted this well-born young woman, whom he had met while on duty in the Topographical Bureau. She was Lydia Mulligan Sims McLane, daughter of Louis McLane, former congressman and senator from Delaware, U.S. minister to the Court of St. James, secretary of the treasury and later secretary of state during the Jackson administration, and now president of the Baltimore & Ohio Railroad. Having been brought up in the genteel setting of Maryland's Eastern Shore, "Lid" McLane had become a leading light in Washington-area society.

Lydia Johnston

The couple met through the agency of Lydia's brother, Robert, who as a subaltern in the First United States Artillery had headed a company of regulars that augmented Lieutenant Powell's surveying expedition following its battle at Jupiter Inlet. Robert had heard of Johnston's heroics during that action and, when he later became one of the man's colleagues in the Topographical Bureau, got to know him well and to think highly of him. Robert had paved Johnston's entrée into his family by praising not only his military skills but also his refined manner and courtly ways. His teenaged sister had been impressed with Johnston even before meeting him, and her regard for him grew over the years as the celebrated officer became a regular visitor in the McLane home. The extended but ardent courtship that followed ended on July 10, 1855, when the couple was married at St. Paul's Episcopal Church in Baltimore. The bride was twenty-three, the bridegroom thirty-eight.[14]

Despite the difference in their ages—perhaps because of it—theirs proved to be a happy union. Lydia, although not a classic beauty, was bright eyed and effervescent, with a piquant sense of humor that lessened the effect of her husband's sometimes overly dignified demeanor. For his part, virtually from the day they met, Johnston was deeply in love with Lydia and remained so to the day of her death after forty-two years of marriage. One of his closest friends in the army, fellow Virginian Dabney Herndon Maury, remarked that "I have never known two people more devoted to each other than they were." The couple's single regret was Lydia's inability to bear children, perhaps the result of the chronic illnesses that began to afflict her not long after she wed. "Her health was not robust," Maury observed, "and he watched over her in her illness with the greatest tenderness, and at all times paid her the delicate attentions of a lover."[15]

To a large extent Johnston filled the void in his life by showering his affectionate guidance on his nephew. He proudly watched as "Pres" followed his own career path by attending West Point and upon graduation accepting a commission in the artillery. Although their relationship approached that of father and son, Johnston begged Pres "to regard me . . . as a brother, and to let your intercourse with me be free and unrestrained, as if we were of the same age."[16]

Johnston and his bride had been together for only seventeen months when another war called him from Washington to southern climes. For many years tensions had flared between the United States and Mexico, mainly as the result of a campaign pledge by Democratic presidential candidate James K. Polk to add Texas to the American union, as a majority of her relatively sparse population appeared to desire. The government in Mexico City vocally objected to the permanent loss of its breakaway province, which it hoped to reclaim through carrot-and-stick tactics.

On March 3, 1845, one day before he relinquished the White House, John Tyler stole President-elect Polk's thunder by sending Texas president Sam Houston an annexation offer, one eventually accepted. Mexican officials protested vociferously but withheld an armed response. Tensions escalated yet again when Polk took office and announced his intention not only to acquire Texas but also to purchase for a reasonable sum California and New Mexico. Mexico City regarded the offer as an insult to national pride, and war drew closer.[17]

For a time neither country appeared willing to fire the first shot, but then Polk sent a small army under Brig. Gen. Zachary Taylor into the disputed territory between the Nueces River and the Rio Grande. When, in April 1846, Mexican troops retaliated by wiping out one of Taylor's patrols, Polk had the casus belli his political opponents believed he had been seeking. By mid-May, Congress had approved the president's request for a declaration of war, and the belligerents mobilized for a major confrontation.

Being on the scene in force, Taylor's "Army of Observation" saw early action. In two battles fought on the chaparral-fringed plain above the Rio Grande—Palo

Alto (May 8) and Resaca de la Palma (the following day)—Taylor repulsed his larger but less-well-trained-and-equipped enemy. The following September he attacked the defenders of Monterrey, Mexico, and after stubborn street-to-street fighting gained an even more dramatic victory. A fourth triumph came his way the following February, when Taylor got the best of another sizable but poorly disciplined enemy force at Buena Vista. The latter was commanded in person by Mexican president Antonio Lopez de Santa Anna, who a decade earlier had invaded Texas, had orchestrated the notorious massacre at Goliad, and had wiped out the garrison of the Alamo, only to be decisively defeated by Houston at San Jacinto, the event that gained Texas its uneasy independence.[18]

The success of Taylor, an avowed Whig, was gratifying to the American public, but it created problems for Polk, who saw the general as a presidential contender. As much for political as for military reasons, he ordered a second front to be opened along Mexico's Gulf Coast. After much deliberation, he entrusted command in that sector to Winfield Scott, who, although also a Whig, seemed less likely to parlay military success into a run for office.

Scott's plan of campaign, approved by Polk and his secretary of war, William L. Marcy, took material shape in February 1847 as twelve thousand troops began to assemble at and near New Orleans. Early the next month this force boarded transports and descended the Gulf to a landing three miles south of the fortified port of Vera Cruz. The debarkation, which began on March 9, marked the culmination of the largest amphibious operation by any army up to this time. Within four days, Scott's troops would encircle Vera Cruz, penning inside some twenty thousand defenders.[19]

Along with colleagues including Robert E. Lee, now-Capt. Joseph Johnston made the trip from New Orleans to Vera Cruz in the capacity of Scott's chief topographical engineer. His recent promotion had been highly gratifying, and he was thrilled by his return to the commanding general's military family. Like many another ambitious officer, he longed for an opportunity to "smell powder," comport himself competently, and advance in his profession. There was always the chance, of course, that he might meet his maker before that opportunity arose. On March 7, as his transports neared their landing sites, Scott accompanied Comdr. David Conner, U.S.N., aboard a steamer, the *Petrita*, to make a personal reconnaissance of the fortified city. Also on board were Scott's three division commanders, David E. Twiggs, Robert Patterson, and William J. Worth (commandant of West Point cadets at the time of the Egg Nog Rebellion), as well as several junior officers fated to attain celebrity in a future war, including Johnston, Lee (now also a captain), and Lieutenants Pierre G. T. Beauregard of Louisiana and George Gordon Meade of Pennsylvania. An engineer colleague with whom Johnston was on especially close terms, 2nd Lt. George Brinton McClellan, the pride of the West Point Class of 1846, was missing from the reconnaissance party. Thus "Little Mac" would have survived the day had the little steamer been struck by any of the numerous shells the Vera Cruz garrison hurled at her, some of which fell "so near the ship that a catastrophe was narrowly avoided." Scott's principal biographer, Charles Winslow Elliott, notes that "had a lucky shot sunk the *Petrita*, the whole course of later military history would have been altered."[20]

Johnston faced lesser dangers during the balance of the campaign, which ended with Vera Cruz's surrender on March 29. Scott's victory had been achieved virtually by artillery alone; over those three weeks, Vera Cruz had felt the impact of a half million tons of iron projectiles. Scott's chief "topo" took careful note of this outcome: by overruling his subordinates' desire to take the city by direct assault, Scott had achieved his goal via a siege that robbed the offensive of its drama and glory but kept casualties to a minimum.

Having established himself on the coast, Scott on April 2 led his army into the Mexican interior with the intention of attacking, capturing, and occupying the nation's capital, fully 250 miles to the west. The ensuing invasion, which lasted for five months thanks to intermittent interruptions, was punctuated by engagements large and small at points such as Cerro Gordo (April 17–18), Amazoque (May 14), and National Bridge (June 11–12). During the first of these, Captain Johnston had his wish for combat service fulfilled, but at a price. From April 9 to 11, Scott studied Santa Anna's strongly entrenched position at the mouth of the mountain pass through which ran the road between Vera Cruz and Mexico City. The American commander's ability to monitor his opponent's movements and deduce his intentions was facilitated by a series of daring reconnaissances led by Johnston, Lee, McClellan, and Lt. Z. B. Tower. The intelligence gathered on these missions persuaded Scott that he could turn the enemy's left flank via an encircling movement along a lightly defended trail.[21]

The reconnaissance that had gained most of this information, conducted by Captain Lee, had been a hazardous undertaking, but a subsequent scout that Johnston performed was no less dangerous. While conducting it, his small party attracted an artillery barrage and he fell wounded by grapeshot. The injury was so severe that he spent two weeks in a field hospital at Plana del Rio before being transferred to a better equipped facility in the city of Jalapa. At both places he was visited on a daily basis by his engineer colleagues as well as by his beloved nephew. A graduate of the West Point Class of 1843, 2nd Lt. John Preston Johnstone commanded a section of guns in a "flying battery." His immediate superior was Joseph Johnston's Florida companion, Capt. John B. Magruder of the First United States Artillery. Pres's newest colleague was a gangly young Virginian, Lt. Thomas Jonathan Jackson.[22]

While Johnston healed—a process assisted by the knowledge that his conduct at Cerro Gordo had gained favorable notice in the reports of his superiors (it would also win him the brevets of major and colonel)—an envoy from the State Department dispatched by President Polk arrived in Mexico in hopes of brokering a peace with Santa Anna. While the talks dragged on, combat operations went into recess. Even so, the army kept moving, this time to Puebla, eighty miles from Mexico City, where the majority of Scott's soldiers went into fixed camp.

During the respite, large numbers of reinforcements, including many volunteer units, reached expeditionary headquarters. The general promptly reorganized his enlarged command, forming units commanded by staff as well as line officers. Eager to win higher rank and station, Johnston, now recovered from his wound, leapt at the opportunity to transfer to a volunteer outfit. He was given the temporary rank of lieutenant colonel and executive command of a regiment of voltigeurs (riflemen). As Robert Hughes points out, the new position "did not prevent him from rendering freely his services as topographical engineer whenever there was need of them."[23]

Early in August, the effort to negotiate a peace having come to naught, Scott resumed his advance, approaching Mexico City from the south via the hamlets of San Antonio and Churubusco and a lateral movement toward the more westerly defenses of San Geronimo and Contreras. In concert with other troops, Johnston's regiment advanced on the first two positions. On August 20 he and his voltigeurs attacked and carried the works at Churubusco, clearing the main road into Mexico City. Johnston exulted in his first victory in command of field troops, a feat that would translate into higher rank and increased authority.

Johnston emerged from the action unwounded but not unscathed. After the fight a tearful Captain Lee sought him out and informed him that Pres Johnstone had been mortally wounded at Contreras the previous evening by an enemy shell. Lee never forgot the effect of the news, recalling that his colleague's "frame was shrunk and shivered with agony." In that instant, Johnston experienced what he

The Battle of Churubusco

later called "the full bitterness of grief." He wrote his brother Beverly: "I loved him more than my own heart. His profession made him peculiarly mine. Nobody else could love him as I have done."[24]

To Pres's sister Eliza, who lived in Richmond with her maternal aunt and her husband, future Virginia governor John B. Floyd, he elaborated on his sense of loss: "I looked upon him as the future companion of my military life—& saw in his high talents & courage, the certainty of future distinction—& then hoped too that his bright smile & tender & gay spirit would help my own wife to cheer my old age. These broken hopes can never be forgotten." He assured Eliza that as soon as able, he would escort her brother's remains to Abingdon for burial in the family cemetery.[25]

Somehow he repressed his grief and returned his attention to his riflemen. On the twenty-first he led them in an assault that helped drive the enemy beyond Churubusco and into the outer defenses of Mexico City. At this point Scott, although poised to make a final push against the walled and gated city, declared an armistice while Polk's emissary again tried to negotiate Santa Anna's surrender. After the talks stalled—as Johnston expected they would—on September 8 the Americans stormed Molino del Rey, a well-defended outwork southwest of the capital, overcoming a furious defense that took a heavy toll of the attackers. Five days later Scott's troops finally moved up to assault the fortified castle of Chapultepec, the last barrier to the fabled Hall of the Montezumas.[26]

At Chapultepec Johnston won new honors, this time in command of the detached right wing of his regiment, which had been halved to broaden the effect of its firepower. Following his lead, his voltigeurs rushed a redoubt at the foot of the towering edifice, then up a steep plateau toward its well-defended parapets. Every step of the way they were showered with musketry, which eventually forced them to fall back to the outer wall of the castle; there they huddled against the continuing storm. By then dozens of voltigeurs had become casualties, including their second-in-command, who had taken three painful, though not serious, wounds. From behind what little cover they could find, survivors returned the fire, covering comrades who came up from the rear carrying scaling ladders.

After catching their breath in a position protected from enemy fire, the storming party went forward under a renewed barrage. At Johnston's command, his voltigeurs left their imperfect sanctuary and rushed the works, taking charge of some of the ladders. With speed borne of desperation, they clambered up the rungs, Johnston in the lead. Reaching the top of the wall, they scaled the castle's parapets and once inside began to gouge out the defenders at bayonet-point. Soon the flag of Johnston's outfit was waving from the blood-stained ramparts— the first American banner to fly over the contested works.

After further, no less desperate, combat, the garrison abandoned the castle and fled out the road to the capital. But they did not make a stand there; before the day was out, Santa Anna withdrew from the city, permitting the *americanos* to take full possession. Although it would take another five months for Scott to "conquer a peace" with the signing of a treaty that secured all of his nation's war aims, the capture and occupation of Mexico City effectively concluded America's first war of territorial conquest.[27]

His performances at Churubusco and Chapultepec marked the pinnacle of Johnston's career in the United States Army. It won him—as had his conduct at Cerro Gordo—glowing praise in published reports. Perhaps the most effusive of these remarks came from his division commander, Maj. Gen. Gideon Pillow, who lauded "the very gallant and accomplished Lieutenant Colonel Johnston," whose three wounds received in the fight "did not at all arrest his daring and onward movements." To the promotions already won, Johnson would add a third brevet. Paradoxically, it made him a lieutenant colonel, although already a colonel by brevet.[28]

Inevitably, Johnston's service in the wake of Santa Anna's overthrow smacked of anticlimax. The occupation of the capital produced a major diminution of operations and an army-wide return to routine duty. That summer, the voltigeur regiment was disbanded and Johnston returned to his engineering duties. Although he was identified in official correspondence as a colonel and received the pay that went with the rank, his permanent grade remained that of captain. He would rise no higher until 1855.

During those seven years, he shouldered a variety of duties in far-distant places, to most of which Lydia accompanied him. While still on occupation duty, he headed expeditions to the Mexican coast for the purpose of escorting reinforcements and supplies to Scott's headquarters. When finally returned to the States, he was selected by Col. J. J. Abert, who commanded the topographical branch of the Engineer Corps, to conduct river surveys and explore wagon routes to the widely spaced garrisons in Texas.

He also studied the best places in which to construct a railroad that would cross the state, a project then in the planning stages. In the autumn of 1849 he formed two parties to survey proposed routes in the El Paso area. In the winter of 1851–52 his interest in plotting rights-of-way involved him in a private survey of a railroad route across west Texas. As Johnston's latest biographer, Craig L. Symonds, observes, although the venture had a certain military utility, "the distinction between private enterprise and public service was blurred. There is some evidence that Johnston might have expected to serve as president of the new company" that was to be formed as a result of the survey, but the project met a premature end due to a lack of funding.[29]

Beginning in 1853, Johnston transitioned from the deserts of the Southwest to the waterways of the Northwest. Over the next two years he supervised improvement projects on the Mississippi, Ohio, and Arkansas Rivers. The work was laborious and protracted, and it exposed him to health hazards that eventually laid him low with fever. Upon recuperating, he determined to leave the engineers for a commission in a line regiment. His desire was gratified when, upon the formation in 1855 of the army's first two regiments of cavalry (as distinct from the dragoon and mounted rifle units that had served the nation since 1833), he was appointed lieutenant colonel of the First Cavalry Regiment, second-in-command to Col. Edwin Vose Sumner. His new duties called him to the Kansas Territory, a move that reunited him with his friend George McClellan, now a captain in the same regiment.

From regimental headquarters at Fort Leavenworth, Johnston monitored the movements of potentially warlike Indians and surveyed the southern boundary of the territory, a prerequisite to Kansas's application for statehood. On the wind-swept plains he also observed some of the early skirmishes of the border wars between free-soil settlers and proslaveryites. The peacekeeping mission was fraught with danger, for at any time the First Cavalry might be caught in the crossfire of sectional conflict.[30]

Joseph E. Johnston as a lieutenant colonel

His months on the Kansas fron-tier, coupled with a brief interlude in neighboring Missouri, exposed Johnston to some of the severest weather he had ever experienced, but the storm that he feared the most was still gathering—the one seeded by sectional discord. Long before he was called east in September 1858 to serve on a board to regulate cavalry and artillery equipment, Johnston had come to believe that at some point in the not-distant future he would find himself embroiled in the fourth war of his military career, one that would make his service against the forces of Black Hawk, Osceola, and Santa Anna pale in terms of bloodshed, destruction, and suffering. When it came, he knew on which side of the dispute he would stand. But he could not say how long the storm would wreak havoc, what effect it would have on his personal and professional fortunes, and—when it finally abated—whether his ill-prepared nation would still be standing.

FOUR

DEAD COCK
IN A PIT

While at Fort Moultrie, Sherman frequently spent time on detached service. Temporary duty assignments took him to North Carolina, Georgia, Florida, and Louisiana. On one such excursion, early in 1844, he helped investigate claims against the government by Georgia and Alabama troops who had suffered matériel losses—horses, weapons, equipment—while fighting the Seminoles. Most of the work was conducted in Marietta, Georgia, just north of a nascent community that some years hence would be christened Atlanta. In off-duty hours he scouted the area, taking notes on the lay of the land, especially in the shadow of Kennesaw Mountain. At the time he did not know why he felt impelled to do so, but two decades later his findings would, as he wrote, prove of "infinite use to me, and consequently to the Government."[1]

In the summer of 1843 he detached himself from Charleston, taking an extended hiatus in the North for the first time since graduating from West Point. He returned to Lancaster, where he spent most of the three months granted him with his mother and his foster family. Although it cannot be determined how it came about, during this trip he appears to have retired his long-held conviction that the army was "a first rate place for a single man but no place at all for one that married." Whether by design or impulse, he proposed to Ellen, and she accepted. Not for another several months, however, did he seek her father's consent to the engagement. Perhaps he used the time to consider his decision, pronounce it correct, and reconfirm his commitment to Ellen. After some slight hesitation, the senator gave his approval.[2]

Considering that Ellen had been his sister, or something close to it, for the past fourteen years, their betrothal might have appeared strange in the eyes of some observers, but, as far as can be determined, no one in the Ewing or

Sherman families questioned its propriety. For their part, the couple reasoned that their relationship had evolved naturally, without either willing it into existence. Cump loved this woman, but he also saw decided advantages in their union. It would bind him to the powerful and influential family that had helped rear him—legal ties would take the place of the blood ties he could never forge. As John F. Marszalek points out, the marriage would not only resolve his "ambivalent feelings about his familial status" but would also mean that "he need no longer be the usurper of his dead father's place."[3]

The marriage would not take place for seven years, thanks in part to the intervention of political, diplomatic, and military events of far-reaching importance. By March 1845, with Cump back again in Lancaster on leave, this time to recuperate from injuries received in a riding accident near Fort Moultrie, Congress was passing its joint resolution to annex Texas and Zachary Taylor was preparing to lead his Army of Observation to the Rio Grande. A few months after a fully recuperated Sherman returned to South Carolina, Company E of his regiment, commanded by a colleague and close friend, Capt. Braxton Bragg, was ordered to join Taylor at Corpus Christi, Texas. Cump envied Bragg's chance to see action and win honors and promotion; he feared he himself would gain no such opportunity even by transferring to an infantry outfit, a proposition he briefly considered.[4]

His estimate of his prospects was accurate. When he left Fort Moultrie it was not for the theater of imminent operations; instead, he was placed on recruiting service in the North. The assignment disappointed and depressed him, but he determined to make the best of it. Early in 1846 he was in Pittsburgh, Pennsylvania, where, assisted by the increasing likelihood of war with Mexico, he quickly enlisted twenty-five would-be artillerymen. But when, returning to Pittsburgh after establishing a sub-recruitment depot at Zanesville, Ohio, he learned that shots had been fired at Palo Alto and Resaca de la Palma, he resorted to drastic measures to accelerate his career. First, he applied to the adjutant general to be transferred to "any active service." When a reply was not forthcoming, he handed over his recruits to a colleague, then hastened to Newport Barracks, Kentucky, across the Ohio River from Cincinnati—reportedly a staging area for Taylor's army.

His zeal to fight might have impressed some superiors but not the local commander, who "cursed and swore at me for leaving my post without orders, and told me to go back to Pittsburgh." His ardor doused, Sherman obeyed, only to find, upon his return, orders transferring him to Company F of his regiment, which was then awaiting transportation to California. The news thrilled and galvanized him. He wrote breathlessly to Ellen: "Is not this enough to rouse the most placid?

42

Indeed it is so great an event that I cannot realize it in its full force." Within days he was on board the twenty-gun sloop *Lexington* bound for Alta, California, via New York, Madeira, Rio de Janeiro, Cape Horn, and Valparaiso, Chile.[5]

He could hardly wait to see action in what he supposed to be a major theater of the conflict. But wait, he would—the sea voyage around the Horn, prolonged by extended stopovers at exotic ports, consumed more than six months. He made the journey jammed into a tiny stateroom that he shared with his Academy comrade Edward Ord. The close, fetid atmosphere aggravated the asthmatic condition he had endured since early youth. Consequently, he spent most of the voyage on deck or in the wardroom, where he wrote countless letters to family and friends, a majority of them to his fiancée. He stoically endured not only the cramped accommodations but also the tasteless meals served aboard ship (breakfast and dinner only), the lack of onboard exercise, and the rough seas that regularly pounded the *Lexington*. His main consolations were the friendships he made and renewed on the ship and the shore leave granted to the passengers when in port. He particularly enjoyed exploring the ancient ruins of Rio de Janeiro in company with another West Pointer, Lt. Henry Wager Halleck of the Corps of Engineers.[6]

The long voyage ensured that by the time he reached California, the fighting that had broken out there upon the formal declaration of war was a distant memory. The province was so vast and so distant from her parent country that, as the local Mexican commander realized, any effort to hold it would prove unsuccessful. In June 1846 a small but determined mob of farmers, army veterans, and mountain men had risen up to form the short-lived Republic of California. After overawing some Mexican outposts, the *americanos* allied themselves with a roving military force under Bvt. Capt. John Charles Frémont, the celebrated "Pathfinder of the West," as well as with a large naval presence under Comdr. John D. Sloat. Frémont and Sloat joined in claiming the Republic for the United States.

In late January 1847, when the *Lexington* entered Monterey Bay after 198 days at sea, the only combat being waged locally was a bitter and unseemly dispute between now-Lieutenant Colonel Frémont and Brig. Gen. Stephen Watts Kearny, recently arrived from New Mexico at the head of a small column of dragoons. Both officers cited authority from Washington to direct the military and civil affairs of the seized territory. By vote of the local settlers, Frémont had been elected governor, but Kearney, as Frémont's senior, disputed his claim to the position and ordered him to relinquish it. Frémont, backed by his own little army, refused. The standoff would continue until August 1847 when Kearny had his rival arrested. Subsequently Frémont was court-martialed and found guilty of

Monterey, Calif., in the 1840s

inciting mutiny. His sentence was remitted by presidential order, but soon afterward he resigned his commission in protest.[7]

Almost from his first day in Monterey, Lieutenant Sherman found himself serving as adjutant general to Col. Richard B. Mason of the First United States Dragoons, who headed the Tenth Military District, as California was now known to the army. Mason's primary responsibility was to serve as the territory's military governor. When he assumed these duties, he delegated much authority to Sherman, who saw to the implementation of military orders, while Lieutenant Halleck, whom Mason had named territorial secretary of state, oversaw matters of civil law.[8]

Sherman's job in Monterey was laden with power but awash in paperwork, which he did not relish. He came to appreciate the attractions of upper California, especially its beautiful vistas and striking landforms, but he disliked its mercurial climate, and he was not impressed with its mixed population of Hispanics, Americans, and Indians. He considered the majority of the inhabitants, especially the native Mexicans, dirty, lazy, and antagonistic toward their conquerors. ("They do not love us, they do not like our ways, our institutions, our restlessness. Our internal taxes, our labors are all too complicated from their brains, and lazy hands.")[9]

He also hated California's isolation, its remoteness from "the States" (the settled areas of the country farther east), and especially the irregularity of long-distance communication that prevented him from keeping in touch with Ellen and his family. He missed his fiancée terribly, and his loneliness was not assuaged by the few letters he received from her. In fact, many of them depressed rather than uplifted him, especially when she, as the daughter of a prominent anti-administration politician, attacked the ongoing war as an evil ploy to secure territory for the expansion of slavery. At other times—many other times—she upset him by sharp reminders that he had been baptized a Catholic and pleas that he profess devotion to the Church. She also distressed him by reciting a litany of health concerns, which she feared would turn her into an invalid some day. Sherman strove by return letter to calm her fears, but her near-constant complaints were a continual source of unease and concern.

What upset him most during his service in California was that he remained far from the scene of combat below the Rio Grande. To this campaign the army had committed a

John C. Frémont

preponderance of its strength, including every company of the Third Artillery except the one he was assigned to. From sketchy and belated accounts, he discerned that Scott's forces were riding an irresistible tide of victory on the road to Mexico City. Honors lay in store for those following him, but in his present position he was "banished from fame."[10]

During the spring of 1848, a year and a half after reaching California, his life changed suddenly and dramatically. In May gold was discovered at Sutter's Fort, near Sacramento. Within months of the word getting out, tens of thousands of fortune seekers were descending on the new El Dorado. Many hacked the precious metal out of mines, but most adopted the less strenuous process of panning for placer—deposits of gold found in surface soil and gravel. "The aged have called for their crutches," Sherman observed sarcastically, "and children have caught the common infection." Everywhere he looked he found freshly established diggings, causing him to marvel that "the lazy Californians are actually working!" The gold fever even lured two of his foster brothers to the boomtowns of the coast.[11]

Enough gold found its way into the local economy that the price of almost everything skyrocketed. Wages commanded by everyone including unskilled laborers soon dwarfed the meager and static pay of army personnel. Desertions became a major problem throughout the Tenth Military District, especially after February 1848, when Mexico's acceptance of the Treaty of Guadalupe Hidalgo formally ended the fighting, thereby removing the death penalty that deserters were subject to in wartime. On several occasions Sherman organized and commanded armed parties that ran down soldiers who had gone AWOL but had yet to disappear into the faceless population of the gold fields.[12]

By March 1849, having lost to gold fever numerous enlisted men, a couple of fellow officers, some civilian clerks, and a prized body servant, Sherman considered leaving the army, something both Ellen and her father were urging him to do. The following June he followed through with a letter of resignation, only to have it tabled by Brig. Gen. Persifor F. Smith, commander of the newly formed Division of the Pacific, who urged him to withdraw the request. He promised to give Sherman a choice position on his staff, to allow him to work for civilian wages in his off-duty hours, and at year's end to travel to army headquarters in New York, there to personally deliver dispatches to General Scott.

After wrestling with his options, Sherman agreed to stay on. His decision proved to be a profitable one. By hiring himself out as a surveyor to local developers, he made more money than he had ever seen in his life. He added to his purse by going into partnership with two other officers in a store that supplied rations, clothing, and tools to gold miners. The profit he made on the store almost matched his annual pay.

He finished out the year in a comfortable frame of mind, and when he sailed from San Francisco on New Year's Day 1850 he was financially able to support a wife. He intended to take one without further delay.[13]

The voyage east, this time by commercial steamer, consumed barely a month, a dramatic contrast to his endless passage aboard the *Lexington*. Reaching New York, he called on Winfield Scott, reported on his experiences in California, and received a coveted invitation to dine with the conqueror of Mexico. Afterward, Scott authorized his visitor to relay the dispatches he carried to the War Department. This tallied perfectly with Sherman's desires, for he was anxious to join Ellen and her family, who were living in Washington during Thomas Ewing's tenure as Zachary Taylor's secretary of the interior.

Sherman's visit to the capital was even more enjoyable than his excursion to Manhattan, for here he was treated as something of a celebrity—mainly, it would

Zachary Taylor

appear, because of his foster father's position. Sherman reported in person to Secretary of War George W. Crawford, presented his papers, and secured what General Smith had promised would be his for the asking: a six-month leave of absence. Thomas Ewing even arranged for him an interview at the White House, during which the president pumped Sherman about affairs, military and political, on the Coast. Though he had served under Taylor's remote command in Florida during 1840–41, the two had never met; Sherman came away impressed by his host's "blunt, honest, and stern character, that endeared him to the masses of the people, and made him President."[14]

The most rewarding event of his stay was his reunion with Ellen, whose family was residing in the Blair House on Pennsylvania Avenue. In the time they could snatch from the round of official functions the Ewing family was obliged to attend, the couple made final plans for their nuptials. The happy occasion took place on the evening of Wednesday, May 1, 1850, following Sherman's return to Washington from a visit to his mother and siblings in Ohio. It was a gala affair—a Catholic wedding at Blair House performed by the president of Georgetown College and attended by a small army of guests that included President Taylor; every member of his cabinet; senators Daniel Webster, Henry Clay, and Thomas Hart Benton; several justices of the Supreme Court; Britain's special envoy to Washington; a bevy of army and naval officers; and what Sherman called "300 Gentlemen & ladies of historical fame." Two of his closest friends in the army, Edward Ord and 1st Lt. James A. Hardie (USMA 1843), both of whom had been raised Catholic, were his groomsmen.[15]

After the ceremony, as Sherman noted in a letter to General Smith, Ellen and he made a honeymoon trip "through the Northern cities [including the obligatory visit to Niagara Falls] and West to Ohio, where we remained till July when we again came East, to remain here, till the time should come for me to go on duty." On July 4 they returned to Washington and ominous news. That afternoon the president had officiated at an hours' long patriotic celebration under a hot sun that left him fatigued and feverish. In the evening, after consuming a quantity of fruit and milk, he fell violently ill. Refusing outside medical attention, he grew rapidly weaker, dying on the ninth and plunging the capital, and the country, into mourning. At the direction of the adjutant general's office, Sherman served as an attendant at Taylor's funeral.[16]

The new president, Millard Fillmore, instituted a personnel shakeup as a result of which Thomas Ewing left the cabinet to return to the Senate by appointment of the governor of Ohio, and General Scott temporarily replaced George Crawford (the new treasury secretary) as acting secretary of war. The change in Ewing's fortunes forced his family to give up Blair House and return to Ohio. Taking his leave of the capital, Sherman escorted the family back home, where he would spend the balance of his leave. By now he had enjoyed the privilege of hearing Webster's last speech before leaving the Senate to become Fillmore's secretary of state. Cump had also sat in on the debates over the various pieces of legislation (including the soon-to-be-notorious Fugitive Slave Law) that would combine to form the Compromise of 1850.[17]

In early September, after more than a month in Lancaster, during which he resisted repeated appeals to resign his commission and become manager of the family's salt works in neighboring Chauncey, Sherman returned to active service, this time as an officer of the line, a member of Braxton Bragg's Company C, Third Artillery. When he reported to his unit's duty station, Jefferson Barracks, he traveled alone; Ellen, who was pregnant with their first child, remained with her parents. To her husband, she seemed only too willing to be apart from him. Over time, he would come to suspect that his wife was more emotionally dependent on her family than she was on him and more secure in its sheltering embrace. Ellen would find it difficult to leave the Ewing fold and accompany her husband on his assigned postings, even for brief periods. Only when he demanded her presence did she consent to join him along with the newborn daughter they had named for Maria Boyle Ewing but whom they came to call Minnie.[18]

Soon after reaching Jefferson Barracks, Cump received notice of his elevation to captain and his assignment to a coveted position in the army's recently expanded commissary department. His quick return to staff duty took him from the St. Louis suburbs into the city, headquarters of the local military department. He and his little family were settled in their new home only a few months when, in the summer of 1852, Ellen returned to Ohio for an extended visit. In the absence of wife and child, Sherman experienced bouts of loneliness and depression and was also troubled by a flare-up of his asthmatic condition. In the midst of his sufferings, he struggled with the conviction that the Ewing family was coming between him and his wife. The resentment he experienced made him feel like an ingrate, considering the financial and career assistance he had received from the foster father who was now also his father-in-law. His unsettling dilemma would continue until—and, in many ways, beyond—Thomas Ewing's death in 1871.

When, in October 1852, Sherman was transferred to New Orleans, Ellen was back in Lancaster preparing to deliver their second daughter, Lizzie (Mary Elizabeth Sherman, named for Cump's recently deceased mother). Not till after Christmas did Ellen, Minnie, and Lizzie reach Louisiana, accompanied by Cump's sister Frances. Perhaps because he was beset by financial difficulties (he had found New Orleans a terribly expensive place to live) and family pressures (Ellen had resumed prodding him to resign his commission and go to work for her father), Sherman, who in time would become a caring father, appeared at first to take little interest in his daughters. One biographer theorizes that he was unwilling to commit himself to them emotionally for fear they would soon be gone—back to Ohio with their homesick mother.[19]

Though he continued to reject the idea of managing a salt works, while in New Orleans Cump was sorely tempted to try life in the civilian world. An old friend from St. Louis, former captain Henry S. Turner of the First Dragoons, now a prosperous businessman, visited Sherman en route to bustling, gold-inundated San Francisco. There he was to open a branch of a St. Louis banking firm, Lucas & Symonds, at the behest of its co-founder, James H. Lucas, with whom Turner had gone into partnership. Turner floored his host by proposing that Sherman manage the new branch, insisting that his long service in, and knowledge of, California made him a natural for the position. The idea had immediate appeal to the financially strapped officer, especially after Mr. Lucas came down from St. Louis and personally made him an offer that included "a very tempting income, with an interest that would accumulate and grow."[20]

After some little hesitation, Sherman agreed to a trial period with the new branch. He applied for and was granted another six months' leave, this to test his ability to survive in the civilian economy. From that point on, events moved in rapid succession. As he remarked in his memoirs, "I dispatched my family up to Ohio . . . disposed of my house and furniture, turned over to Major [John F.] Reynolds the funds, property, and records of the office; and took passage in a small steamer for Nicaragua, en route for California."[21]

His return to the Pacific Coast was notable for a couple of events that he came to regard as bad omens. On the leg from Nicaragua to Acapulco he gallantly gave up his private stateroom to two well-dressed females who had been assigned accommodations below deck they considered unendurable. The price of generosity was his being forced to share a lower berth with five other passengers. Throughout the voyage "Captain Sherman and ladies" took their meals together at the best table in the dining room. His companions, whom he considered among "the most modest and best behaved" of anyone on board, explained that they were en route to San Francisco to join their husbands. Only upon reaching his destination did he learn that one of "his" ladies was a prostitute. His comment on the incident was succinct: "Society in California was then decidedly mixed."[22]

This incident had the power to embarrass; the second could have killed him. At four o'clock on the morning that his ship expected to berth at San Francisco, it struck a reef in Monterey Bay about a mile from shore. Although the vessel could not sink—she had hit bottom—the razor-sharp coral beneath her and the "white and seething water" pounding her hull threatened to tear the ship apart. Eventually lifeboats were lowered, and Sherman, after patiently waiting his turn, was rowed across the fog-shrouded bay. Landing north of San Francisco at Bolinas Creek, he hopped a schooner bound for the city with a load of lumber, only to be dumped into the water when the boat heeled over in high winds. Drenched but unhurt, he finally reached the city aboard a passing vessel; by then he had decided that "two shipwrecks in one day [was] not a good beginning for a new, peaceful career."[23]

The portents had a certain validity. His life during the next four years was plagued by an abundance of problems that, in the end, killed his hopes of becoming a successful banker. Early on, he discovered that his firm—Lucas, Turner & Company, housed in a building on Montgomery Street leased from a competitor that had moved into a more spacious facility across the street—was undercapitalized. Then there was the economic climate, a source of lingering concern. In contrast to its flimsy, impermanent appearance during and shortly after the Mexican War, San Francisco had acquired the look of a bustling, energetic city in the full flush of boom times. Even so, its economy was too dependent on transactions in precious metals— only gold was accepted as legal tender; paper money was banned—and it was highly susceptible to fluctuations in markets nationwide. The situation was worsened by state banking regulations. Those on the books were complex, confusing, and failed to meet the needs of the banking community. Other needed laws were nonexistent. There were no bank examiners, and no limits on usury—the prevailing interest rate exceeded 40 percent. Everyone seemed to be clamoring for a bank loan, but good collateral was scarce. As one of Sherman's more recent biographers, Lee Kennett, points out, "in a business community that had sprung up almost overnight there were no old established firms with a history of unimpeachable credit. . . . almost every borrower was something of an unknown quantity."[24]

Undaunted by these red flags, Sherman threw himself into his new career. He studied the banking business from top to bottom, scrutinized his competition (nineteen other banks served the city at the time of his arrival, although many soon went under), and cultivated local officials, business and civic leaders, and potential customers. He became so well known and so highly regarded in the community that in time he was offered the command of a locally based division of the state militia, with the rank of major general. He accepted the position only to resign it one month later when vigilante riots threatened to tear the city apart and he found himself powerless to suppress them. At about the same time, he was offered the backing of the local Democratic Party for the post of city treasurer. The pay, four thousand dollars, would have been "acceptable, and the office would have chimed in well with my present business," which he could have continued to manage. But a lifelong aversion to excessively partisan politics, which he considered one of the worst products of American-style democracy, impelled him to decline.[25]

By June, three months after opening the bank, Sherman felt sufficiently well established to have Ellen and the children join him. He took passage to New York by way of Nicaragua, then hurried to St. Louis via Lancaster. In St. Louis he met with Mr. Lucas, came to an agreement on the terms of his permanent employment, and secured from his boss a pledge to invest fifty thousand dollars into the construction of a new facility. He then returned to Lancaster to pry Ellen loose from a family who dreaded her leave-taking. Unable to tolerate the thought of a house devoid of children, the Ewings pleaded with Ellen and her husband to allow eighteen-month-old Minnie to remain with them. Once again Cump found his in-laws meddling in his personal life, but when he perceived that Ellen, who appreciated how lonely her parents would be in her absence, was willing to grant their request, he gave his consent.

Presently, Ellen, Lizzie, and he booked passage to San Francisco. One of his last acts upon leaving was to forward to the adjutant general's office his resignation, to take effect at the end of his leave, September 6, 1853. After almost a quarter-century of service to the army, he had committed himself to making a living "on the outside," as a civilian businessman.[26]

———◦◦◦———

The truncated family arrived in San Francisco late in October. Shortly after, Sherman gave up the small frame house he had rented on Stockton Street for a larger brick dwelling on nearby Green Street, and here the Shermans lived for the next year and a half. He thought he had provided well for Ellen, but she expressed dissatisfaction with everything about the local community, which she sarcastically called "the promised land." Referring to a hovel inhabited by a relative in Lancaster, she added, "I would rather live in Granny Walters cabin than live here in any kind of style." Her frame of mind did not improve even after the birth of their third child, William Ewing Sherman ("Willy"), in June 1854. Her husband appeared no more elated at the arrival of his first son than at the birth of his daughters, but in time Willy became the apple of his eye, even as the boy's father developed a more affectionate attitude toward Lizzie and her absent sister.[27]

Ellen's discontent peaked in the spring of 1855, when she abruptly left her husband and children to visit Lancaster (en route enduring a shipwreck comparable to the one Cump had experienced, but escaping unscathed). Cherishing her escape from California, she remained with her parents and Minnie for seven months. When she returned—again without her firstborn—the family moved into an even larger and more expensive house, but her outlook failed to improve. When business reverses began to trouble Cump, his depression was only deepened by his wife's discontent. The stress of trying to hold together a losing venture affected his physical as well as his emotional health; the asthma attacks he periodically suffered, which he attributed at least in part to the coastal climate, grew appreciably worse, keeping him awake at night and, when he slept, provoking feverish dreams.[28]

For the first two years or so of Sherman's financial career his employer's promises of support and the high standing he had attained in the community made him believe that Lucas, Turner & Company could make a go of it in San Francisco. But although his employer increased the institution's assets, the influx of capital was insufficient to overcome the many other problems that beset the enterprise. Operating expenses ate up the premium the bank charged on bills of exchange, "rendering the exchange business in San Francisco . . . rather a losing business." He could not recoup his losses through additional loans—too many of the bank's creditors defaulted, and deposits fluctuated so wildly week to week that they could not be used for loans. Many would-be depositors were discouraged from doing business by the local newspapers, whose editors vied with each other in spreading rumors—both well-founded and unfounded—of coming panics, imminent runs on savings institutions, and other stories harmful to business interests, especially banking. Some papers went out of their way to criticize Sherman's lending policies. Resentful and angry, he came to consider journalists the lowest form of humanity he encountered in San Francisco. His deeply held belief that every editor was a menace to society and a threat to him personally would endure long after he departed California.[29]

Vigilante justice in San Francisco, California

The banking business was also harmed by the social climate of the city. Corruption was endemic in local government. Elected officials violated the public trust with impunity, to the extent of releasing criminals who had the wherewithal to buy their cooperation. In response, vigilante groups composed of the "better class of people" sprang up to render extrajudicial justice. Both the vigilantes and their targets had the power to terrorize those citizens who were caught between them. The situation reached crisis proportions in May 1856 when a local editor shot and mortally wounded a rival (a former banker, of all things) whom he accused of defaming him in print, then sought sanctuary with the sheriff, whom he believed could be bought off. Two days after the victim succumbed to his wounds, an armed contingent of the Vigilance Committee marched on the jail, broke into it, spirited away the murderer and another prisoner being held for a capital crime, and hanged both of them from the roof of the building that housed the committee's headquarters.[30]

Vigilante justice shocked and revolted Sherman, who saw in the mob's assumption of police powers the worst possible violation of the political order. He had hoped somehow to prevent the hangings, as did San Francisco's mayor and state officials. After the deed was done, Gov. J. Neely Johnson asked Sherman—whose military experience appeared to recommend him for the job—to organize a body of law-abiding citizens, lead it against the mob, and arrest its leaders. With Johnson's covert support, Sherman arranged with the local military commander, Brig. Gen. John Ellis Wool, to supply the countervigilantes with arms and ammunition from the federal arsenal at Benicia Barracks. Wool even joined Sherman in inspecting the arsenal's holdings.

Understandably, Sherman believed he had secured the general's full cooperation. Thus he felt betrayed when Wool backed out of the agreement just as Sherman and his army of volunteers prepared to march on the committee's headquarters. Doubtful that the movement would succeed absent outside support and fearful that his well-known opposition to the vigilantes—who enjoyed the support of much of the business community—would harm Lucas, Turner & Company, Sherman withdrew from the effort he had helped organize, which quickly collapsed. Later, he expressed a measure of regret at his self-serving attack of discretion, which he feared had cost him the good opinion of the governor. As he admitted, Johnson "had a right to have some little feeling against me for deserting him at a critical moment."[31]

Even without Sherman's intervention, vigilante law in San Francisco eventually ran its course and the committee disbanded. By the time it did, its leaders were well on their way to winning control of city government via the ballot rather than the hangman's noose. Their electoral success confirmed Sherman in his belief that, rather than a grassroots organization of concerned citizens, the committee constituted a political party in opposition to the Democratic regime that had long ruled the city and that it desperately wished to unseat.[32]

Sherman's initially promising career as a man of business came to a quiet end on May 1, 1857, when the parent firm in St. Louis closed its San Francisco branch. Sherman was not surprised by the outcome: "We had an expensive bank, with expensive clerks, and all the machinery for taking care of other people's money for their benefit, without corresponding profit."[33]

He was not immediately out of work; James Lucas arranged that he should manage a new branch of his lending institution to be established in New York City. Sherman traveled there alone (Ellen happily went with the children to live with her parents), and on July 21, 1857, he inaugurated the enterprise, situated at 12 Wall Street. The business climate in Manhattan appeared a great improvement over that of boom-or-bust San Francisco and for a month or so the bank did well, but then a nationwide financial panic struck the city with full force. Two months later, Sherman's bank, along with hundreds of others in the city and around the country, closed its doors, never to reopen. The stigma of having presided over two business failures in the space of five months would long trouble him. When, two years later, he was offered a job with the English branch of an American banking house, he declined, explaining that "I was the Jonah that blew up San Francisco, and it only took two months residence in Wall Street to bust up New York, and I think my arrival in London will be the signal of the downfall of that mighty empire."[34]

Still in the employ of Mr. Lucas, in January 1858 Sherman returned yet again to San Francisco, where he attempted to recover monies owed to his old branch and to recoup investments he had made on behalf of several of his army friends. Although he resorted to "making sacrifices and compromises" with the firm's debtors, he secured little recompense—one evaded payment by feigning insanity. In July he returned dejectedly to Lancaster. Refusing to default on his own obligations, he covered his friends' losses from his pocketbook, an act of integrity that left him almost penniless.[35]

Having temporarily severed ties with James Lucas, he had to answer a daunting question: "What was I to do to support my family, consisting of a wife and four children [Thomas Ewing Sherman had been born in October 1856], all accustomed to more than the average comforts of life?" There was always the job at the salt works, but with the last measure of resistance he rejected his father-in-law's offer yet again. Eventually he was reduced to inquiring of friends still in the service if they knew of a way he might return to the army list; he was willing to take any position, but nothing was available. He remained unemployed or underemployed for a full year after departing San Francisco.[36]

Cump Sherman had hit bottom, and he was not hesitant to admit it, at least to former comrades. Shortly after his failure in San Francisco, he had encountered on the streets of St. Louis a West Point acquaintance who, like him, had left the army only to experience hard times and be pressured to go into a family business he dearly wished to avoid. To this man Sherman admitted that his life was in a shambles (he had become, as he later put it, "a dead cock in a pit"). Nor was he optimistic that he would be rescued by some dramatic reversal of fortune. He added that he regretted having tempted fate by leaving his secure existence in the army for the uncertainties of civil life.

Looking back on this incident, it seemed to him that his listener, Ulysses Grant, shared his regrets.[37]

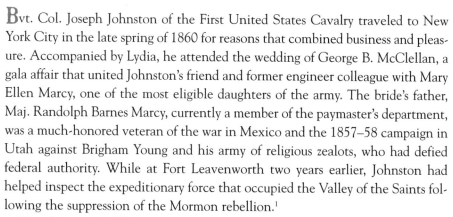

FIVE

TWO RESIGNATIONS

Bvt. Col. Joseph Johnston of the First United States Cavalry traveled to New York City in the late spring of 1860 for reasons that combined business and pleasure. Accompanied by Lydia, he attended the wedding of George B. McClellan, a gala affair that united Johnston's friend and former engineer colleague with Mary Ellen Marcy, one of the most eligible daughters of the army. The bride's father, Maj. Randolph Barnes Marcy, currently a member of the paymaster's department, was a much-honored veteran of the war in Mexico and the 1857–58 campaign in Utah against Brigham Young and his army of religious zealots, who had defied federal authority. While at Fort Leavenworth two years earlier, Johnston had helped inspect the expeditionary force that occupied the Valley of the Saints following the suppression of the Mormon rebellion.[1]

The Marcy-McClellan nuptials, which took place on May 22 at Calvary Episcopal Church in downtown Manhattan, was a happy occasion not only for the bridal couple but also for at least two of the well-wishers. Colonel and Mrs. Johnston were looking forward to spending time together in the civilized East—not only in New York but in Washington, Maryland, and Virginia. Only weeks before, the colonel had returned from his most recent (and most distant) posting, the New Mexico Territory, where he had served as inspector general of the local military department while also reassuming his duties as a topographical engineer. In addition to socializing, in Washington Johnston planned to conduct some regimental business in the office of the adjutant general. He also planned a courtesy call on Secretary of War John B. Floyd, a native of Abingdon and Johnston's brother-in-law. The former Virginia governor, who was foster father to Lizzie Johnston, daughter of Joseph's deceased brother Charles, had been appointed to his cabinet post in 1857, the first year of President James Buchanan's administration.

57

Soon Johnston had an additional reason to call on his relative. On or about June 10, by which time he and Lydia were back in Washington, they learned of the death of the army's quartermaster general, Thomas B. Jesup. Johnston leapt at the opportunity to succeed the deceased Virginian and thereby win promotion to star rank. He believed he had the requisite staff experience to make a success of the job, and his varied and lengthy field service had given him a good idea of the army's matériel needs in garrison, in the field, and in different climates.

At bottom, he wanted the position for the rank and prestige it commanded. Since his earliest days in the service Johnston had been as eager as anyone to advance in his profession. His great and constant ambition, and the continual thwarting of it by the army's fossilized seniority system, had been the primary cause of his May 1837 resignation from the artillery. Now he had a chance to move farther up the ladder than he could ever have imagined. Therefore— although no evidence exists that he lobbied for his preference—given his nature, it is likely that he at least notified Floyd of his interest in filling the vacancy.

Yet it was the prerogative of Winfield Scott, not his civilian superior, to choose Jesup's successor. Within days of the latter's demise, the commanding general made his selection—rather, his selections. Claiming that he could not choose from among four equally qualified candidates, he asked Floyd to do it for him. The names he submitted were those of Johnston; Robert E. Lee, now also a brevet colonel, the executive officer of the Second Cavalry; fifty-three-year-old Lt. Col. Charles F. Smith, a distinguished veteran of the Mexican War and the Mormon Expedition who had been commandant of cadets during William Sherman's years at West Point; and Col. Albert Sidney Johnston, the fifty-seven-year-old commander of Lee's regiment, who had been the ranking officer during the Utah campaign and, before that, secretary of war of the Texas Republic.[2]

It was, by any measure, a star-studded list; each candidate was capable of filling the vacancy honorably and effectively. In fact, despite a pristine record and wide experience in both staff and field positions, Johnston may have been the dark horse of the group. Smith was celebrated as a molder of future generals, while both A. S. Johnston and Lee had enjoyed more celebrated careers—certainly they were better known to the public. Then, too, both had the support of notable political figures—in Sidney Johnston's case, that of Jefferson Davis, now a powerful and influential senator from Mississippi.

For his part, of course, Johnston had John B. Floyd, and, in this case at least, a cabinet member trumped a senator. Within days of receiving Scott's list, Floyd selected his brother-in-law for the coveted position. His decision surprised many observers, shocked at least as many others, and outraged more than a few. Inevitably, charges of nepotism were hurled at him and his relative. The loudest protests came from inside the quartermaster's department, whose senior officers believed themselves entitled to the promotion.[3]

Floyd's action was highly gratifying to Johnston, who thereby became the first West Point graduate to fill a general officer's billet in the regular army. Two days after his promotion, he shared his elation with his niece. In gaining the position, he told Lizzie, he had surmounted the well-publicized opposition of Jesup's former subordinates, who had been "wishing to keep their generalcy for themselves." More than the promotion itself, he appreciated Floyd's endorsement of his qualifications, which gave proof of his "friendship & favorable opinion" (later he would characterize the war secretary as "the best friend my manhood has known"). That opinion, he told Lizzie, was "worth more to me than all the military rank in the Army."

Given the depth of his ambition, this last remark was an overstatement, but Johnston may have believed it at the time. He filled the rest of his letter to his niece with a summary of social affairs in the capital, where the Johnstons would be living for the foreseeable future. And he closed with an observation that in time would ring with irony: he and Mrs. Johnston enjoyed "as good a prospect as can [be had] in time of peace."[4]

Over the next ten months, Johnston served as the army's chief procurement, supply, and transportation official. He administered an annual budget in excess of seven million dollars, most of which went to cover the cost of subsistence and travel. He gave the fullest of his energy and ingenuity to the demanding position, but as his most recent biographer, Craig L. Symonds, observes, "as Quartermaster General Johnston was not an unqualified success. The characteristics that made him an effective troop commander in the field did not serve him well in his carpeted office in the War Department. A personable and compassionate commander, whose great strengths were the ability to win and keep the loyalty of subordinates and a willingness to put himself in the front of the battle, Johnston found the daily routine of continuous paperwork unfulfilling."[5]

As the summer of 1860 merged into autumn and the presidential canvass neared, Johnston found himself increasingly distracted by the worsening political situation. The sections had been on a collision course at least since the Nullification Crisis, but the process had speeded up following the raid of the fanatical abolitionist John

Brown on the federal arsenal and armory at Harpers Ferry, Virginia, the previous October. To many observers across the country, that aborted but violent attempt to foment a slave uprising—which for southerners rekindled horrific memories of Nat Turner's Rebellion—served notice that the uneasy compromise of sectional interests that Congress had enacted in 1850 was a dead letter.

It became increasingly clear that slavery, which had become the central issue in the national debate, could not be settled short of war. Its power to impassion, antagonize, and divide troubled many a moderate observer such as Johnston, but his attempts to inject rationality into the debate over slavery and secession proved unavailing. Years later he recalled that while in Washington "I heard the question of slavery much discussed by Southern M.C.s [members of Congress], especially the younger [ones], and never sensibly or rather, always foolishly. I tried often, to convince them that the division of the country would give the slaves of the border South[er]n States so near and safe a refuge that those states would soon cease to have slaves and be compelled by difference of interests to abandon the Confederacy and return to the Union." He realized, however, that logic had only so much power to persuade: "There has never been a question so hard to deal with as that of Negro slavery."[6]

The battle lines began to be drawn during the presidential campaign, which Johnston monitored as closely as any Washington insider could. When the Democratic Party split along sectional lines and nominated two candidates—former vice president John C. Breckinridge of Kentucky and Sen. Stephen A. Douglas of Illinois—and the new Constitutional Union Party, composed of moderate Democrats and former Whigs, chose John Bell as their candidate, the field became too crowded to ensure a victory for any one of these men. In November the candidate of the Northern-based Republican Party, former congressman Abraham Lincoln, also of Illinois, won a clear majority of electoral votes but less than 40 percent of the popular vote.

With a "Black Republican" bound for the White House, the lower South began to turn decades of fiery rhetoric into action. On December 20, two and a half months before Lincoln took office, South Carolina formally announced its departure from the Union, an action it claimed it had a right to take under the Constitution. Undoubtedly Quartermaster General Johnston would have agreed with this line of reasoning, but as a conservative in thought and deed he deprecated South Carolina's provocative act. His fear that one state's foolishness would trigger a chain reaction throughout the South began to be realized soon after the New Year came in. During the three weeks following January 9, 1861, six other

Deep South states left the Union. Then there was a pause, as if the country was attempting to come to grips with the enormity of what had been done so precipitately, so carelessly.

Southern officials, however, believed they knew what they were doing. Early in February delegates from the seceded states met in Montgomery, Alabama, to frame the governmental apparatus of a new nation, the Confederate States of America. On the ninth the members of the constitutional convention elected Jefferson Davis provisional president of the Confederacy and, as his vice president, Alexander H. Stephens, a former Whig from Georgia.[7]

Johnston's reaction to the choice of leadership is not known, but for personal reasons he could not have been pleased by Davis's selection. When in the U.S. Senate, Davis had opposed his promotion to quartermaster general. Furthermore, in 1855, when he was secretary of war in Franklin Pierce's cabinet, Davis had denied Johnston's appeal to be listed in the army's register of commissioned officers as a brevet colonel, rank conferred on him for gallantry at Cerro Gordo. To Johnston's profound indignation, Davis ruled that because Johnston's previous brevet had been that of major, his second brevet of the Mexican War should have been that of lieutenant colonel, the same grade he held in the First United States Cavalry. Davis's ruling had a major impact on Johnston's career because it robbed him, as the latter saw it, of the seniority to which his battlefield heroics entitled him. Given his acute sensitivity on matters of rank, he neither forgot nor forgave Davis's decision, which rankled him as much in 1861 as when it was rendered.[8]

Although Johnston needed no reminder of Davis's past opposition to him, Lydia, who as the daughter of a congressman and cabinet member felt comfortable making political pronouncements, warned her husband that the new president "hates you, he has power & he will ruin you" should Johnston accept a position that put him within the president's reach. Still, Johnston resolved to stand

Gen. Robert Anderson, USA

61

by Virginia should she leave the Union, whether or not she became a part of the Confederacy. If her actions brought him under Davis's influence, he would continue to do his utmost to defend his state, personal considerations aside.[9]

The breathing spell that followed the secession of the Cotton States was decisively broken on April 12, when South Carolina forces under Johnston's former engineer colleague Pierre Beauregard began to bombard the U.S. Army garrison inside Fort Sumter, Charleston Harbor. At the behest of Gov. Francis Pickens, Beauregard had demanded that the fort's commander, Kentucky-born Maj. Robert Anderson, evacuate Sumter and turn it over to state authorities. Although aware that he could not hold out indefinitely against such heavy opposition but believing he must make a show of resistance, Anderson refused. On April 13 he finally acquiesced to Beauregard's demand but only after enduring thirty-four hours of near-constant shelling that had reduced portions of his fort to rubble.

Reacting swiftly to this dramatic provocation, Lincoln, who had been in office for little more than a month, called for 75,000 troops for ninety days' service to put down an insurrection "too powerful to be suppressed" by lesser means. The appeal, which went not only to Northern governors but also to those in the upper South whose states had yet to secede, prompted the exodus of four of them. They included Virginia, where a secession convention had been sitting in Richmond since well before the crisis in Charleston came to a head.[10]

Until Lincoln's call, the convention delegates had appeared closely divided on the subject at question, a reflection of Virginia's historic ties to the Whig Party (in November the state had given her electoral votes to the conditional Unionist Bell, not the Deep South candidate Breckinridge). One of the delegates was Johnston's oldest living brother, Peter Johnston, a moderate on the secession issue. Initially Peter had expressed the conviction that his colleagues would not cave in to public pressure and vote to secede; he hoped they would produce some eleventh-hour compromise to preserve both the Union and state pride. "Mobs are gathered and paraded along the streets," he wrote his brother, "in one of which . . . the proposition was made to turn the Convention neck & heels out of doors, but I have no fear that our conservative majority will be, or can be, moved—the country has seen no body of men so calm and firm." When Lincoln's call for troops undercut the moderates' position, however, calmness and firmness went the way of all unrealistic hopes. On April 17 the convention passed a secession ordinance but also made provision for ratification via public referendum, to be held on May 23.[11]

Although a loyal son of the Old Dominion, Joseph Johnston had been unwilling to cut his ties with the military establishment of the United States until he had no alternative. Once the action of the state convention became known, he saw that the time had come. He had made it clear to his superiors—which now included Secretary of War Simon Cameron, John Floyd having resigned his post shortly after Christmas 1860—that he must conform his actions to those of his state. But he had not acted precipitately. Early in March, Jefferson Davis's secretary of war, Leroy Pope Walker, had written him offering a brigadier general's appointment in the Provisional Army of the Confederate States. Johnston had not replied to the offer; he had not even acknowledged it.[12]

Rumors of Walker's action made General Scott fear the loss of numerous accomplished officers of Southern birth or persuasion including the two Johnstons—Joseph and Sidney—as well as Robert E. Lee, the commanding general's favorite subordinate. Some time during the week that followed Fort Sumter's capitulation, the aged Scott appears to have made a personal appeal to his quartermaster general (as he did also to Colonel Lee) to remain with the army. Although Johnston's response is not known, it can be assumed that he dashed his superior's hopes even as he expressed regret at having to leave an army he had served faithfully for almost thirty-five years.

Mrs. Johnston's reply to a similar entreaty, which Scott made to her at a Washington gathering shortly afterward, was—according to the preeminent commentator on the Confederate social scene—direct to the point of bluntness. As Mrs. Mary Boykin Chesnut told the story, Scott asked Lydia Johnston to persuade her husband to stay with the Union, adding that "we will never disturb him in any way"—an implied pledge not to place him in a combat situation. Lydia was quick to answer that "my husband cannot stay in an army which is about to invade his native country." Scott countered: "Then let him leave our army—but do not let him join theirs." But Lydia was unmoved by his plea nor, she was certain, would her husband have been.[13]

She knew whereof she spoke. On April 22, one month before the voters of his state ratified the decision of the Richmond convention, Joseph E. Johnston, for the second time in twenty-three years, submitted his resignation from the United States Army. This time, the action was irrevocable.[14]

By June 1859, William Tecumseh Sherman was desperately seeking gainful employment. He would have accepted anything short of working in the salt wells of Chauncey, Ohio, a proposition his father-in-law continued to press upon him, and his wife continued to urge him to accept. It was to escape "that part of Ohio [to which] I had no fancy," Sherman wrote, that he had agreed, the previous September, to the Ewing family's counterproposition that he relocate to Leavenworth, Kansas, to manage a substantial amount of land that Senator Ewing had purchased and to turn one of the parcels into a farm that a relative intended to purchase. It was further arranged that he should go into partnership with his brothers-in-law, Hugh and Thomas Jr., who had established a legal practice in that frontier community. The "Boys," as they were known in the family, had tired of toiling in the gold fields and had come east to restart their lives in a semicivilized environment not so much different from the one they had left.[15]

Despite nagging misgivings that he was not cut out for lawyering, Sherman made the journey, alone, to Leavenworth. Seven years earlier he had viewed that town as an annex to the military community surrounding Fort Leavenworth; now, however, it had become a "handsome and thriving city, growing rapidly in rivalry with Kansas City and St. Joseph, Missouri." Although he missed his family, he settled fairly comfortably into the local society. Managing his father-in-law's property took less of his time than he expected, and so he threw himself into the affairs of the law firm of Sherman & Ewing. He received an attorney's license on "grounds of general intelligence," thus enabling him to forgo the normal period of study and/or apprenticeship. From the start, however, clients were few. In a way, this was good news for Cump, who dreaded having to argue a defense before a jury, something he was compelled to do on at least a couple of occasions when his brothers-in-law were late to court (both ended in a finding against his client).[16]

It soon became clear that Sherman & Ewing did not do enough business to support three partners. Cump picked up additional money as a notary public, and for a brief time he had a side business auctioning off surplus army horses and mules. The only truly remunerative enterprise to come his way was a gift from his West Point friend Stewart Van Vliet, now an assistant quartermaster on the staff of the local military department. Van Vliet offered him a contract to supervise repairs to the military road leading to Fort Riley, almost 140 miles west of Leavenworth. Sherman took the job out of economic necessity—he would have to provide not only for himself but also for Ellen and the children, who would join him that fall (all but Minnie, she being too attached to her grandparents to leave them at this time). The proffer was a godsend. His performance on the road was so satisfactory that the army contracted with him to fix some of the bridges the road crossed and to dig drainage ditches alongside it.[17]

After Ellen and the children arrived in November, the family wintered "very comfortably" as guests in the house Tom Jr. had erected in Leavenworth. Somehow, the firm grew; in January 1859 it took on a fourth partner, Daniel McCook Jr., a native Ohioan destined to achieve high rank in the Union Army and serve under Sherman. Even so, prosperity was elusive and Cump began to seek an occupation that would support his family in a style more in keeping with Ellen's upbringing. It was at this time that he began to repent having resigned his commission. He begged friends still in the service, including Van Vliet and Bvt. Maj. Don Carlos Buell of the adjutant general's office (West Point class of 1841) to help him return to the army. Though at first desirous of a position in the paymaster's department, which allowed the direct hire of civilians, over time he resigned himself to accepting anything that came along. For one thing, his family was growing again—Ellen was pregnant with their fifth child, Eleanor Mary ("Elly") Sherman. But the peacetime army remained extremely small—fewer than seventeen thousand officers and men, all told—and there were no vacancies.[18]

Major Buell, however, knew of an opening in the civilian world for someone with a military background. The state of Louisiana was seeking a "superintendent," i.e., president, for a military institute and college going up at Alexandria, almost 150 miles northwest of New Orleans. Buell sent his friend a copy of the job description and offered to recommend him for the position. Sherman penned a letter of application, sent it in without fanfare, and—probably to his amazement—got the job. It turned out that the vice president of the academy's board of supervisors, Gen. George Mason Graham, a "high-toned gentleman" who owned a plantation near Baton Rouge, was not only a former superior of Buell's but a half brother of General Mason, Sherman's commander in California. Furthermore, Graham's sister had taught at the Catholic girls' school in Georgetown that Ellen Ewing had attended, and she had fond memories of the girl who was now Sherman's wife. These connections helped Cump beat out eighty other applicants for the position.[19]

He entered upon his duties with characteristic dispatch. He escorted his family back to Ohio, inspected a military academy in Kentucky that might lend some insight into his new profession, and then, in October, headed south. He was immediately impressed with the facilities, especially the classroom building of the Louisiana State Seminary of Learning and Military Academy, which he found "very large and handsome," three stories tall, and situated on a four hundred-acre tract carved out of a pine woods on the edge of Alexandria. Conferring with Graham and the other supervisors, he learned that he would oversee the work of four instructors (one of whom would serve in the dual capacity of commandant of cadets) while, theoretically at least though not in actuality, taking on the additional duty of professor of engineering, architecture, and drawing. The pay was far from munificent—at thirty-five hundred dollars per annum, it was 70 percent of the salary he had commanded as a San Francisco banker—but the job represented steady work, had the support of state officials, and offered fringe benefits. The most attractive of these was that Sherman and his family would occupy, rent-free, a cottage to be erected on the campus.[20]

William T. Sherman as college president

Through the fall of 1859, Sherman, working closely with board members and the academic staff, developed a curriculum heavily based on the system in place at the well-regarded Virginia Military Institute (which, in turn, was based on the West Point model). He procured all manner of supplies, prepared advertising material, and helped thrash out a set of bylaws for governing the institution. On the second day of 1860 the school opened its doors to a first-year student body of sixty. Over the next twelve months the Ohio Yankee played the role of educator of southern youth. He deemed it the most prestigious position he ever held—and one for which he seemed to have the requisite aptitude. He got along well with General Graham and the other supervisors, with the members of the faculty (one of whom, David F. Boyd, professor of English and ancient languages, became his close friend), and with most of the families who had entrusted him with their sons' education. Two cadets were the children of the soon-to-be-famous Pierre Beauregard—a former artilleryman, now a brevet major of engineers, who had been two years ahead of Sherman at West Point. His physical presence, as well as his intellectual attainments and administrative abilities, attracted wide notice. A typical observer described him as "tall, angular, with figure slightly bent, bright hazel eyes and auburn hair, with a tuft of it behind that would, when he was a little excited, stick straight out."[21]

During Sherman's superintendency the institution prospered, and its student body expanded to more than 160. The teaching staff was held in high regard by supervisors and students alike, and under Sherman's watchful eye discipline was maintained despite his lack of statutory authority to administer it. Few untoward incidents caused that tuft of hair to protrude. The most dramatic and troubling was an abortive knife fight between two hot-tempered sons of the local aristocracy. Sherman managed to end the confrontation before injury occurred, and when he determined to expel both of the antagonists the board sustained him at the risk of antagonizing a couple of prominent families. Sherman even lobbied effectively for additional funds and resources, which the state authorities, impressed by the school's early success, agreed to provide—just as they raised his salary when informed that he was considering vacating his position to accept that banking job in London. As one historian has written, "Here in the deep South, Sherman had at last found a place of contentment."[22]

But it would not—it could not—last. Able to monitor national events from a state that was a cockpit of secessionist fervor, he watched helplessly and sick at heart as the country drew ever closer to the abyss. He saw in the students and their families a class of people to whom personal honor and regional pride counted for more than peace, harmony, and prosperity. Two months before the school opened, he had observed in a letter to Ellen that "Southern men . . . are as big fools as the abolitionists." When issues of race were discussed, "feeling runs so high . . . that, like religious questions, common sense is disregarded."[23]

The disputatiousness of those around him took on a more ominous form as 1860 wore on. Well before South Carolina declared for secession, a lead that Louisiana followed on January 26, 1861, Sherman realized that at some point in the not-too-distant future he must give up his position and leave the South, a region whose vistas and climate he had come to enjoy, whose attitudes and values he could appreciate if not wholly embrace, whose problematical institutions (such as slavery) failed to trouble him, but whose politics he could not abide.

As sectional antagonisms intensified, he tried to persuade his hosts, many of whom seemed to relish a shooting war to settle differences, that they were underestimating the opposition. As he told David Boyd, "You people speak so lightly of war. . . . You mistake too the people of the north. . . . You are rushing into war with one of the most powerful, ingeniously mechanical, determined people on earth—right at your doors. You are bound to fail. Only in your spirit and determination are you prepared for war. In all else you are totally unprepared, with a bad cause to start with. . . . If your people would but stop and think, they must see that in the end you will surely fail. . . ."[24]

Following the fall elections, the rush toward secession and conflict became unstoppable. Neither Sherman nor the people who had hired him believed the crisis would come so swiftly. If they had, the state would not have welcomed into its midst a soldier duty bound to side with his nation against enemies from within and without. From the outset, Sherman made no secret of where his allegiance lay; he was forthright in declaring that should any action of the state of Louisiana force him to choose sides, he would go north without qualm or hesitation. He had said as much before a bevy of state officials at a dinner party in the home of Gov. Thomas O. Moore, and they had applauded his candor and forthrightness even as they decried his views. Louisianans' expressions of high regard were all the more remarkable in light of the notoriety Sherman's brother had gained in southern circles. By 1860 John Sherman was not only well into his third term as a Republican congressman but was also considered a leading candidate for Speaker of the House. Although Cump denied that his brother was regarded back home in Ohio, as he was in the Deep South, as a "black abolitionist," he was aware that John had publicly endorsed Hinton Rowan Helper's *The Impending Crisis*, a novel that, by advocating emancipation, had been banned in Louisiana even while it became a best seller in the North. Such publicity embarrassed the southern educator, who more than once asked John to tone down his sometimes-radical rhetoric but not at the cost of losing his place in the Republican hierarchy.[25]

Although hopeful to the last that he would not have to take the final, irrevocable step, Sherman did so in late February 1861, tearfully bidding farewell to the faculty and shaking the hand of every remaining student. He had lingered in Alexandria for a full month after Louisiana voted for secession in order to receive his final pay as well as to tie up loose ends in a way that would ensure a smooth transition (whoever his successor turned out to be). In this way ended a stressful and trying experience, one immeasurably worsened after Governor Moore forced the surrender of the federal arsenal at Baton Rouge and stored two thousand of the rifles seized there on the grounds of Sherman's school, including the anteroom of his office and the parlor of his cottage. Because of the uncertainty, then the volatility of the local situation, Ellen and the children had not come down from Lancaster to turn that little house into a home.[26]

When submitting his resignation to the board of supervisors and to state officials, Sherman emphasized his chagrin at being compelled to depart. In turn, his employers accepted his action in a spirit of "no ordinary regret." On February 14 the board adopted a resolution that recognized "the able and efficient manner" in which Sherman had "conducted the affairs of the seminary during the time the institution has been under his control—a period attended with unusual difficulties, requiring on the part of the superintendent to successfully overcome them a high order of administrative talent." On April 1, the academic board issued a resolution of its own, praising "the manliness of character which has always marked the character of Colonel [*sic*] Sherman," who, it added, "is personally endeared to many of them [the faculty members] as a friend."[27]

By the time the professors proclaimed their regard and regret, Sherman was beyond range of any well wishes. On February 25, 1861, having shed the last of his administrative burdens, he left Louisiana by steamboat for Ohio.

SIX

SLEEPING
ON A VOLCANO

On the morning of April 23, 1861, Joseph and Lydia Johnston left the house in Washington they had occupied for the past two and a half years and entrained for Richmond. They departed the capital with little more than the clothes on their backs and Joseph's most precious heirloom, the sword his father had carried throughout the Revolutionary War. Travel problems delayed their arrival until the twenty-fifth, one day after Robert E. Lee, who had also submitted his resignation from the United States Army, reached the city to accept from Gov. John Letcher the commission of major general of Virginia troops.

After seeing Lydia comfortably settled in leased quarters, Johnston visited his West Point classmate and Mexican War comrade in his office in the state capitol. Lee not only greeted him warmly but recommended that Letcher elevate Johnston to the same rank that he himself held. The appointment was made without delay. Johnston was content, at least for the time being, to accept a berth in the defense forces of his state; Secretary Walker's offer of a brigadier generalship in the Confederate ranks had not struck him so favorably, perhaps because the centralized government that Walker represented clashed with

Gen. Robert E. Lee, CSA

70

the primacy of loyalty to one's state. By a thin margin of seniority—perhaps only by virtue of having arrived in the capital twenty-four hours earlier than Johnston—Lee was ensconced in the state's highest military office, outranking even its adjutant general, and Johnston, who had been Lee's senior in the old army, would have to serve under him. Despite his sensitive pride and the emphasis he habitually placed on military rules and customs, he agreed to subordinate himself to Lee. He did so because he admired the man's gifts and attainments and because, in this time of crisis and imminent war, it seemed the right thing to do.[1]

During or soon after their first meeting, Lee gave Johnston his first assignment as an officer of Virginia forces: to assemble, organize, inspect, and train the raw recruits who had been arriving in Richmond from all parts of the state since Sumter's fall and Lincoln's coercive proclamation. Documentation is too sketchy to form a determination of how well Johnston performed in this capacity. The assignment threw him into close contact with a number of junior officers, assigned as his subordinates, who would make their mark in the coming conflict, including Thomas Jackson, then a major of state forces, who as a young subaltern had served with Pres Johnstone in Magruder's battery. Not long after joining Johnston's staff, however, Jackson was promoted to colonel and was ordered to assume command of the troops that had gathered at Harpers Ferry, a strategic outpost in the Shenandoah Valley.[2]

At about the time Jackson left him, Johnston was abruptly demoted to the rank of brigadier general. The Virginia Convention, still sitting in Richmond and now charged with putting the state on a war footing, had voted to rescind all major general appointments except Lee's. By now, however, Johnston had become convinced that Virginia's war effort would be managed not by Lee and Letcher but by the fledgling government operating in Montgomery. Early in May, a fortnight after he had begun to collect and drill the Richmond recruits, Johnston accepted a brigadier's appointment in the Confederate Army.

He believed he knew where he stood in the new military establishment. Already the provisional Confederate Congress had passed legislation governing the transition of officers from the U.S. Army to that of the Southern nation. The law stipulated that the rank and seniority of these officers would transfer with them; thus, Johnston, as the highest-ranking officer to leave the old army, would become the senior general officer in Confederate service—senior even to Lee, who, though outranking him in the Virginia line, would not transfer to the Confederate ranks until two months after Johnston. This distinction was important to Johnston—indeed, it was essential to his view of himself as the premier soldier of the Confederacy. In time, however, the seniority issue would become a source of friction between him and Jefferson Davis.[3]

At this point, at least, he was appreciative of Davis's efforts to grant him high rank. When Davis asked him to report to Montgomery to receive instructions from him directly, Johnston promptly started south, accompanied by Lydia. Throughout the war that lay ahead, often even in the midst of field campaigning, husband and wife would be together whenever conditions permitted.

Johnston's visit to the first capital of the Confederacy (the seat of government would move to Richmond

Jefferson Davis

soon after the state's voters ratified her ordinance of secession) was brief and to the point. He conferred with Davis, Walker, and other members of the president's newly formed cabinet, while making himself and Lydia known to public officials that included members of both houses of the Confederate Congress and of Alabama governor Andrew B. Moore. During his visit Johnston was pleased to learn through unofficial circles that the Congress was about to pass an amendment to the law organizing the army that elevated every Confederate brigadier to full general (in the parlance of later American armies, four-star general).[4]

Johnston was also gratified by the respect and consideration shown him by everyone he met in Montgomery including Davis, who made it a point to inquire which command, if any, his visitor preferred. Johnston replied that he wished to remain in Virginia although not necessarily in the Richmond area, where he would continue to work with—and perhaps under—Lee. Nor did he favor a command in the northern part of the state, where defenders were gathering to counter a Yankee buildup in and around Washington, D.C. Davis listened politely and assured Johnston that he would assign him an important command elsewhere.

Soon Joseph and Lydia were returning to Richmond, having made a success of their southern tour. Once in the city, the general set about forming a staff and conferring with Letcher, Lee, and other state officials as to his initial posting as a

Confederate officer—his appointment reached him soon after his return from Montgomery. By mid-month, having bade Lydia a sorrowful farewell (believing the war would end quickly and he would soon return to her), he was on yet another train, this one heading west toward the verdant pastures, rolling hills, and majestic peaks of the Shenandoah Valley.

Johnston had been assigned to relieve Colonel Jackson in command of the garrison at Harpers Ferry, a key position in defense of the fertile corridor that would become famous as the "Breadbasket of the Confederacy." Not only did the Shenandoah Valley subsist the Confederate forces east of the Blue Ridge, its strategic byways connected that theater with the mountainous region beyond the Alleghenies, a potential avenue of enemy invasion. Harpers Ferry, which sat at the bottom—that is, the northern reaches—of the Valley, also commanded a network of north-south roads, some of them macadamized and of turnpike width, that connected southwestern Virginia with the country above the Potomac River, another likely invasion route. These facts made Harpers Ferry a strategic location that must be held if Virginia were to remain whole. Little wonder John Brown had made it the first objective of his campaign to divide and conquer the South through the medium of a slave revolt.[5]

On the trip from Richmond, the hopes Johnston entertained of a successful defense of his state were buoyed by the crowds of civilians that turned out at every railroad station to bid Godspeed to the defenders of the Shenandoah. These people, it seemed to him, displayed "great enthusiasm for the war against subjugation." Their numbers made him believe the general population of Virginia was large enough to support an all-out defense effort. Then he stepped from the train at the depot in Harpers Ferry and his ebullience began to fade. Obviously, Jackson had not been in place long enough to make a soldierly impression on these hard-looking but clueless recruits. The few thousand who comprised the local garrison appeared wholly ignorant of military life, as they showed by their slouching posture, variegated equipment, and heterogeneous weaponry. They were his Richmond recruits all over again, only in greater numbers.[6]

His concern only increased when he reviewed their imperfectly formed ranks. Their unsoldierly appearance was appalling. Many had no uniforms; those who did wore the garb of prewar militia units, in whose ranks they had absorbed only a smattering of training. As in Richmond, the men sported antiquated and inappropriate firearms, and little in the way of camp equipage. The only thing they had in abundance was a shared conviction—more accurately, a collective arrogance—that they could outshoot, outfight, and outwit any armed

Yankee who made the mistake of venturing their way. Johnston did not buy it. To a suggestion from a member of the Second Virginia that his outfit was ready and willing to go to war, Johnston replied, "I would not give a company of regulars for the whole regiment."[7]

As he scrutinized these would-be warriors, they sized him up in turn. The new commander was a smallish man, six or seven inches under six feet, but he carried himself well and gave the impression of strength out of proportion to his compact frame, which carried no more than 150 pounds of flesh and bone. An average observer would have guessed correctly that he was in his fifties (he had turned fifty-four a month before), and from his stature and bearing they would have gathered that he was a professional soldier. He was more distinguished looking than handsome. His thin, sensitive face was framed by elegant side whiskers and adorned with a neatly maintained Vandyke. He was balding; only a thin swatch of gray covered his head. Mrs. Chesnut heard that he had lost most of his hair virtually overnight, the result of a rare illness.[8]

In addition to his soldierly qualities, he gave the impression of a man of learning and erudition. One who knew him described him as exuding "intellectual power and cultivation." His demeanor tended to stiffness, but in seconds his face could light up with "a flashing, sunny smile, which betrayed . . . a genial nature & a ready appreciation of humor."[9]

Other intimates described a different side to this man. One noted that even though capable of displays of great charm and courtesy, Johnston was also "critical, controversial and sometimes irritable by nature." Under provocation he displayed a white-hot temper. Maj. John Cheves Haskell, one of his early-war staff officers, agreed that Johnston's "rather stern, but handsome face . . . could light up as brilliantly and look as kindly as it seemed possible for a face to look, yet it could change as suddenly to as stern and menacing [an] expression as any face ever could. It was a true index to his character, which was as affectionate and warmhearted, but as quick and passionate, as any I ever met; yet his passion . . . was sometimes of unseemly violence. . . ."[10]

Another of Johnston's early subordinates, Col. E. Porter Alexander of the Confederate artillery, was a witness to this passion and violence. One day during active campaigning an ambulance driver, whose vehicle shared the same narrow trail as Johnston and Alexander, unintentionally crowded the general off the road, causing him to rein in so abruptly that he nearly flew over his horse's head. This was bad enough but when the ambulance became mired in a slough it pinned Johnston and his mount against a fence. Alexander was shocked by his superior's reaction: "I don't think I ever saw any one fly into such a fury in my life. I had never before heard the general use an oath, but now with his face as red as blood, 'God damn you!' he shouted." In his rage he turned to Alexander and ordered him to "give me a pistol & let me kill this infernal blanketty blank." Only because the colonel pretended to be unarmed was the ambulance driver—by then "scared almost into a jabbering idiot"—able to clear the obstruction and tear off down the road.[11]

Yet another dimension to Johnston's personality, at least in the eyes of some who claimed to know him well, was a near-crippling reluctance to take responsibility for initiating action unless success could be guaranteed. A close friend of the general's family maintained that "never in his life could he make up his mind that everything was exactly right, that the time to act had come. There was always something to fit that did not fit." This man told Mary Chesnut a story to illustrate the point. Shortly before the outbreak of the war, Johnston and he were invited to use a celebrated game preserve in company with its owner, Wade Hampton III of Charleston, South Carolina, one of the wealthiest planters in the South. To the surprise of his companions, Johnston proved himself "a dead failure" as a hunter: "He was a capital shot, better than Wade or I, and we are not so bad that you'll allow. But . . . the bird flew too high or too low—the dogs were too far or too near—things never did suit [him] exactly. He was too fussy, too hard to please, too cautious, too much afraid to miss and risk his fine reputation for a crack shot. Wade and I . . . shot right and left—happy-go-lucky. Joe Johnston did not shoot at all. The exactly right time and place never came."[12]

If the new man at Harpers Ferry was to make a success of this, his first major command of the war, he would have to get over his self-defeating quest for perfection. Fortunately, he would be assisted in his labors by a crop of talented subordinates versed in the different arms of the service. They included not only Jackson, who after leaving the U.S. Artillery had been a tactics instructor at the Virginia Military Institute; but also Col. Ambrose Powell Hill of the Thirteenth Virginia Infantry; Col. James Ewell Brown ("Jeb") Stuart of the First Virginia Cavalry; Col. William Nelson Pendleton, Johnston's chief of artillery; and such reliable staff officers as Col. Edmund Kirby Smith, Johnston's chief of staff, who had experience in both infantry and cavalry campaigning; and Johnston's chief engineer, Maj. William Henry Chase Whiting, who had served alongside Johnston on prewar river and harbor improvement projects.[13]

As soon as he was able to reconnoiter his surroundings, Johnston saw that he would need all the support these officers could provide. If Harpers Ferry commanded the northern entrance to the Shenandoah, it was in turn commanded by the mountain ranges that surrounded it—Maryland Heights on the northeast, Loudoun Heights on the south and east, and on the west by Bolivar Heights. An enemy who placed well-supported artillery atop any of these eminences could easily shell the garrison into submission. Furthermore, the terrain at the bottom of this gigantic bowl "was more favorable to an attacking than to a defending force," he claimed. Then, too, "the Potomac can be easily crossed at many points above and below [the garrison], so that it is easily turned."[14]

Johnston had no doubt that an enemy force would attempt a turning-movement or seek to gain a foothold on the mountain—most likely, he would try to do both. One such force was nearly within striking range already, its elements having assembled at several points in western Maryland as well as south-central Pennsylvania. These eighteen thousand troops—mostly volunteers and militiamen, with a smattering of regulars—were led by Maj. Gen. (of Pennsylvania volunteers) Robert Patterson, a sixty-nine-year-old veteran of the War of 1812 and the Mexican campaigns who was an old and trusted comrade of Winfield Scott. Thus, within two weeks of Johnston's arrival at Harpers Ferry, his nearest enemy had accumulated enough men, guns, and support resources to make his position appear precarious in the extreme.

By early June, Johnston, via telegraphic communication with Richmond, had a pretty fair notion of what the enemy was up to, not only in his bailiwick but farther east. His findings troubled him no end. He had no doubt that Patterson, as soon as sufficiently concentrated, would be heading his way. At the same time, an even larger command massing in and around Washington, D.C., under Brig. Gen. Irvin McDowell, was expected to confront the northern Virginia Confederates of General Beauregard. As an experienced strategist, Johnston must have suspected that the Union's reigning triumvirate—Lincoln, Scott, and Secretary of War Simon Cameron—would strive to coordinate the movements of these armies. Given the raw material at Patterson's and McDowell's disposal and the distance between their headquarters—at least seventy-five miles, as the crow flew—this would not be easy, but if even a measure of cooperation were achieved the defenders of the Old Dominion would find themselves hard-pressed and quite possibly overwhelmed.

The threat that McDowell posed to northern Virginia in general and Richmond in particular was a matter of unease to Johnston, but Patterson was his primary concern. Only two days after reaching his post, Johnston was telegraphing his superiors that he feared Harpers Ferry was "untenable by us at present against a strong enemy." He lacked the manpower to hold both the town and the surrounding heights; in fact, he doubted the wisdom of holding either one. Winchester, twenty-eight miles to the southwest and connected to Harpers Ferry by railroad, was a more strategic, as well as a more defensible, point from which to guard the door to the Valley. He began to importune his superiors for authority to shift his garrison in that direction. But neither Davis in Montgomery nor Lee in Richmond considered such a move to be in the best interests of the Confederacy, if only because it might connote weakness, a fear of engaging the nearby foe. As he revealed in a series of communiqués through the first week of June, the president was adamant that Johnston not give up his current post unless forced to do so.[15]

This was not what Johnston wanted to hear, and his subsequent response marked the opening round of an extended and sometimes bitter difference of opinion between the two men. Jefferson Davis could not bring himself to abandon territory to the enemy; to his mind, every square inch of Southern soil was sacred ground. Yet Joe Johnston, as his words and actions would make quite clear, never occupied a position that he did not consider retreating from.

In early April 1861, a little over a month after giving up his cherished position in Louisiana, Sherman was again gainfully employed, although forced to take a pay cut. At a salary of two hundred dollars per month, he was the president of the St. Louis Railroad Company, another job that Henry Turner had suggested for him. Turner's partner, James H. Lucas, had set Sherman up in business in San Francisco and New York; now he bankrolled him a third time. As majority stockholder in the company (in actuality a horse car line that serviced a single city street), Lucas had the right of executive appointment.

Sherman had returned to St. Louis via Lancaster, where he had gone upon leaving the South. When he arrived, he had his entire family with him, this time including ten-year-old Minnie, whom he had finally wrested from her doting grandparents. The Shermans settled comfortably into the life of the midsized city that was enjoying the last weeks of peace before the bombardment of Fort Sumter changed American life forever.

As he embarked on his new occupation, Sherman seemed curiously detached, preoccupied, inattentive to the rumors of war making the rounds of this bastion of divided loyalties. Although still a soldier in mind and heart, he did not relish the idea of returning to uniform to wage war against some of the same people who had befriended him in the South. He was a businessman again, with a stake in the commercial prosperity of a major community, and he wished to pursue his reacquired occupation for as long as possible, if only to recoup the self-respect that had been damaged by so many career failures and disappointments.

Despite his best intentions, it must have been a Herculean task to concentrate on his job, for he was surrounded by reminders of the trouble abroad in the land. A house along the route of his rail line provided a headquarters of the city's Rebel element, including the pro-secessionist group known as the "Minute Men"; from its front door hung the flag of the fledgling Confederate government. At the end of town sat the camp of the local division of the Missouri State Guard, commanded by Gen. Daniel M. Frost, whom Sherman described as "a Northern man, a graduate of West Point, in open sympathy with the Southern leaders" and who had been appointed to his position by the state's pro-Confederate governor, Claiborne Jackson. The United States Army in St. Louis was represented by sixty-one-year-old Brig. Gen. William S. Harney, commander of the Department of Missouri, a native southerner who had no heart for confronting either Frost or Jackson. The only truly staunch representative of the federal government was Capt. Nathaniel Lyon, the fiery-tempered Connecticut Yankee who commanded the few companies of regular troops on duty at the local arsenal.[16]

The sorry state of Union war preparations in St. Louis mirrored the situation Sherman had found in Ohio upon returning from the South. It contrasted sharply with affairs in Louisiana, whose people he described as "earnest, fierce and angry, and [who] were evidently organizing for action." No one he met in Ohio or in the Unionist enclaves of Missouri matched them for determined bellicosity. Thus, "it certainly looked to me as though the people of the North would tamely submit to a disruption of the Union."[17]

John Sherman

Sherman had found a similar state of unpreparedness in the nation's capital. In fact, the pronounced apathy he encountered there appeared to pervade the inner circles of the government. While in Lancaster early in March he had received a letter from his brother John urging him to come to Washington. The summons carried more than normal weight, for John Sherman had risen to a position of power within the party that would administer the war that might break out despite the North's complacency. Following three consecutive terms in the House of Representatives and reelection to a fourth, John had been sent to the Senate by Ohio's Republican-controlled legislature; he would fill the seat vacated by Salmon P. Chase, Lincoln's secretary of the treasury.

Although ignorant of what lay behind his summons, Cump dutifully hopped an eastbound train. Upon arriving in the capital, he learned that John had arranged an interview for him with the new president. John hoped the meeting would provide an opportunity for his brother to return to the army at a higher rank than before. He also believed that Cump, thanks to his extended residence in Louisiana, could lend Lincoln some insight into the mind of the Deep South.

Instead, the interview with Lincoln merely confirmed the elder Sherman's suspicion that the North would not lift a finger in defense of the Union. When Lincoln asked him, "How are they getting along down there?" Sherman replied that the entire South was "getting along swimmingly—they are preparing for war." The president's response was understated, slightly jocular, and tinged with an irony that was lost on his visitor: "Oh, well, I guess we'll manage to keep house."[18]

Sherman recalled that upon this rejoinder "I was silenced, said no more to him, and we soon left." Once on the street, however, he vented his anger, cursing northern politicians as self-absorbed bureaucrats. He expended most of his wrath on John's Republican colleagues, who "have got things in a hell of a fix, and you may get them out as best you can." The country, he added, was "sleeping on a volcano that might burst forth at any minute." Cump washed his hands of the entire mess, informing John that he was "going to St. Louis to take care of my family, and would have no more to do with it."[19]

Sherman's determination to take no part in any effort to defend the Union remained in force for barely a month after he left the East for St. Louis. The week before Fort Sumter was fired on he received a telegram from Lincoln's postmaster-general, Montgomery Blair, a member of an old St. Louis family with prominent Republican credentials. Perhaps at John Sherman's instigation, Blair offered Sherman the chief clerkship of the War Department with a proviso that when the Congress, then in adjournment, next convened, he would be named an assistant secretary of war. Sherman turned Blair down, pleading the demands of business life and the overriding need to provide for his family. He was also motivated by pique, believing that Blair had blocked John's attempt to gain for him a desirable position in government service, head of the United States Sub Treasury in St. Louis. Cump's parting words to Blair failed to disguise either his anger with the man or his disgust at the state of affairs in Washington: "I wish the Administration all success in its almost impossible task of governing this distracted and anarchical people." Later Cump learned that this remark "gave offense, and that some of Mr. Lincoln's cabinet concluded that I too would prove false to the country." The administration's reaction might have irritated him, but it did nothing to make him modify the course he had set for himself.[20]

To the last he did his best to "keep out of the current" of events, although keenly aware of the direction in which it was rushing. From the start he had regarded the siege that South Carolina clamped on Fort Sumter at year's start as an act of war; thus he was not shocked when on April 13 he learned that his former colleague, Pierre Beauregard, had begun to shell the garrison commanded by Robert Anderson, Sherman's immediate superior at Fort Moultrie from 1843 to 1846.

Even now, with war an inescapable fact, he withheld his services from the government. He rejected an offer, relayed by John, from Secretary of War Cameron: command of the contingent of volunteers and militiamen that Ohio intended to commit to the war. The position went, instead, to George McClellan. At about the same time, he spurned an offer from Montgomery Blair's congressman brother Frank, one of St. Louis' staunchest Unionists, to return to the army and replace the fence-straddling General Harney. Sherman gave Blair the same excuse he had tendered his sibling: "I had made business arrangements in St. Louis, which I could not throw off at pleasure. . . ."[21]

He even refused John's plea that he return to Ohio to help form a regiment or regiments under Lincoln's call for seventy-five thousand three-months' volunteers. As a veteran of the regular service, Sherman had no desire to command those ignorant amateurs all too eager to answer the first call to duty. As he told John, he might be making a mistake, but "I cannot and will not mix myself in this present call. . . . The first movements of the government will fail and the leaders will be cast aside. A second or third set will rise, and among them I may be, but at present I will not volunteer as a soldier or anything else."[22]

He followed up his refusal with a letter to Secretary Cameron, dated May 8, five days after Lincoln issued a second, more realistic call for forty-two thousand volunteers to serve for three years unless sooner discharged. In this letter Cump sounded the same theme as on earlier occasions but in a more restrained, almost apologetic voice and with a hint that he might yet participate. Perhaps this caveat stemmed from his regret over the bad impression his letter to Montgomery Blair had created in official circles. "I hold myself now, as always, prepared to serve my country in the capacity for which I was trained. I did not and will not volunteer for three months, because I cannot throw my family on the cold support of charity, but for the three years' call made by the President an officer could prepare his command and do good service. I will not volunteer, because, rightfully or wrongly, I feel myself unwilling to take a mere private's place."

The closing remark was a deliberate exaggeration, indicative of his belief that were he to enlist he could expect rank only marginally higher than the subaltern's position he had filled in what was already becoming known as the "old army." He deserved better, he told himself, and so did his family, which was about to grow larger, Ellen being pregnant once again.[23]

Two days after writing Cameron, he seemed to have a sudden change of heart. On Friday, the tenth, he happened to be in the city along with seven-year-old Willy, the child he had come to view as a miniature version of himself, stirring his paternal pride as never before. That afternoon, urged on by Frank Blair, who had taken the lead in raising loyalist militia outfits to help defend Federal assets in the city, Captain Lyon led a six thousand-man contingent of this force, along with a column of regulars from the arsenal, to break up "Camp Jackson," the rendezvous of the pro-Confederate State Guard and to arrest every member who refused to take an oath of loyalty to the Union.

Contrary to the fears of local residents, many of whom lined the tree-shaded streets as Lyon's men passed by on their way to the camp, the confrontation ended peacefully when General Frost surrendered without a fight. By the time the victorious Federals marched back to the arsenal with Frost and most of his troops in tow, Sherman and his son had been joined on the street by Charles Ewing, just back from Washington where he had been conducting unspecified business of a military nature. The three formed part of a crowd that had grown to massive size, apparently composed of equal numbers of Unionists and Southern sympathizers. Numerous members of the latter group were jeering and cursing the passing troops. A "secesh gentlemen" who appeared to be inebriated suddenly attempted to break up the formation. For his intervention he was jostled rudely to the ground by a soldier. When the man rose he drew a pistol and fired a round that wounded a home guardsman. An instant later, panicky soldiers were returning fire, shooting wildly into and over the crowd.

Amid shouts and screams, the spectators scrambled for cover. Sherman and his brother-in-law hit the pavement, shielding Willy with their bodies. From the ground

Cump "heard the balls cutting the leaves above our heads, and saw several men and women running in all directions, some of whom were wounded." By the time the firing ceased, at least twenty-five civilians and three soldiers lay dead or mortally wounded. Fearful that violence might break out anew, Cump snatched up his son and took refuge in a gully, where they huddled until certain the danger had passed.[24]

As nothing else could have, the "St. Louis Riots" awoke William T. Sherman to the realization that, despite his determined attempt to hide from the war, it had found him—and his family. The jarring blow to his peace of mind drove home at last the magnitude of the crisis overtaking the nation and the need to make a personal commitment to it. Four days after he and Willy ran for their lives, he received a wire from Charles Ewing, who had returned to the capital to accept a commission as captain in the recently authorized Thirteenth United States Infantry. Charlie happily announced that Cump had also been commissioned into the regiment—as its colonel. He was wanted in the capital immediately.[25]

Convinced that at last the government was gearing up for the war, Charlie's in-law decided that "I could no longer defer action." He conferred with Lucas and Turner, explained his situation to them, and resigned his streetcar company position. A few days later he parted with his family, who would remain in St. Louis till his expected return. He supposed he would be allowed to choose the recruiting rendezvous of his new outfit; he intended it to be Jefferson Barracks. Only later, when it became clear that he would not return to St. Louis for quite some time, did he advise Ellen to give up their rented house in the city and take the children to Ohio.

Everything attended to, he lugged a suitcase to the railroad station and started east to begin his second career in military service. What lay ahead he could not predict, but the uncertainty did not bother him. As he told Ellen upon their parting, he had made up his mind to "trust to the fate of war."[26]

SEVEN

THE SHOCK
OF BATTLE

Throughout May and well into June 1861, Johnston kept trying to persuade his superiors that Harpers Ferry was too vulnerable to serve as an effective guard post at the entrance to the Shenandoah Valley. His concern over his position increased markedly after May 26, when he learned that his old friend George McClellan had ordered three columns of volunteers from southern Ohio into western Virginia. Ostensibly, McClellan acted to shield the Baltimore & Ohio Railroad, a major artery of supply for the Northern forces, and to protect the largely pro-Unionist population in that quarter. Johnston, however, suspected that "Little Mac" was heading his way, perhaps to strike from the left and rear while his attention was riveted on the buildup of Patterson's forces on the Potomac. If he could not defend Harpers Ferry against frontal assault, he had no hope of holding it against simultaneous attacks from two sides.

Johnston's attempts to explain his perilous situation to Richmond (to which the Confederate government had moved as soon as Virginians ratified their state's secession ordinance) achieved mixed success. On May 31 General Lee, still commanding the

Gen. George B. McClellan, USA

forces of Virginia, informed Johnston that outposts had been established on the upper Potomac at Leesburg and Point of Rocks and on the Leesburg Turnpike at Dranesville to facilitate communication between Harpers Ferry and Fairfax Court House, an advanced post on the "Alexandria Line," the primary cordon of defense in northern Virginia. Couriers from these points would inform Johnston of any threats to the rear of his position. Lee added: "In the event of such a movement, should you deem it advisable, and should you be unable to hold your position, I would suggest a joint attack by you and General Bonham, commanding at Manassas, for the purpose of cutting them off."[1]

Gen. P. G. T. Beauregard, CSA

Lee was referring to Camp Pickens, twenty-some miles south of Washington, D.C. That troop rendezvous, which was fast filling up with Southern volunteers, sprawled north of a shallow, meandering stream called Bull Run. Its current commander was Brig. Gen. Milledge L. Bonham of South Carolina. Reflective of the fast-changing situation in all parts of Virginia, one day after Lee wrote to Johnston, Bonham was superseded by Pierre Beauregard, now also a brigadier by virtue of his triumph against Fort Sumter. Under Beauregard's engineer's eye, the main line of defense would be moved to the south bank of Bull Run, its left flank resting about four miles north of Manassas Junction, where the east-west-running Manassas Gap Railroad met the north-south line of the Orange & Alexandria.[2]

Although currently manned by about six thousand raw levies, within six weeks or so the Alexandria line would be defended by twenty thousand troops of all arms. Like the soldiers already positioned along Bull Run, the newcomers were untrained and poorly equipped. Moreover, they constituted less than three-quarters of the force available to Irvin McDowell in and south of the Federal capital. Beauregard's principal consolation was that in any clash of arms his troops would enjoy the advantage of fighting on the defensive. They would, that is, unless Beauregard, whose admiration for the tactics of Napoleon impelled him to plan often and plan boldly, managed to persuade Richmond that Johnston and his men should leave the Valley and reinforce him, permitting him to take the offensive before the Yankees could strike south from their capital.[3]

Had Johnston learned of Beauregard's grandiose planning, he would have considered it both premature and presumptuous. And yet the idea of linking with the troops at Bull Run soon acquired a role in Johnston's own strategy. If any such junction were to occur, however, he would see to it that he led the combined force, not an officer who had been his junior in the prewar service. Then more pressing matters reclaimed Johnston's attention. On June 3, a large detachment of McClellan's command attacked the Confederate outpost at Philippi and routed its garrison. Ten days later another Federal force, under Col. Lewis Wallace, raided as far as Romney, little more than twenty miles from the Shenandoah. And on June 10, Johnston's scouts brought word that Patterson was moving toward the Potomac from his field headquarters at Chambersburg.[4]

These several events, which suggested a multipronged offensive converging on Harpers Ferry, convinced Johnston that he must act before he found himself caught in a pincers. Fortunately, he now had official authorization to withdraw from his position, although it had been granted somewhat less than graciously. As recently as June 7, President Davis had conveyed through Robert E. Lee his desire that Harpers Ferry be held as long as possible; its loss, he believed, would disrupt Confederate communications with officially neutral but Southern-leaning Maryland. Even so, Lee, speaking for the president, acknowledged that Johnston, as on-scene commander, had discretion to retire from the town if unable to withstand an enemy advance. A subsequent communiqué from Adj. and Insp. Gen. Samuel Cooper, the senior military man in the Confederate War Department, confirmed that Johnston had the right to exercise his judgment in the matter— something Johnston should have known all along. This remark was enough to irritate its recipient, but Cooper also implied that Johnston, by importuning his superiors so stridently and so frequently, was attempting to shift to them the responsibility for evacuating such an important post.[5]

Predictably, Johnston bristled at the implied rebuke; he replied, somewhat disingenuously, that he had not been trying to avoid accountability. Still, he was glad to have his preferred course sanctioned by the high command. On the day he learned of the Romney incursion, he dispatched three regiments under A. P. Hill to block additional advances by McClellan and his subordinates. As soon as Hill departed, Johnston began the task of evacuating Harpers Ferry. The operation came off smoothly; it was completed on the fifteenth, by which time every bridge over the Potomac between Point of Rocks and Shepherdstown had been destroyed; long stretches of railroad track had been dismantled; and public property, including the contents of the famous arsenal, had been removed, destroyed, or rendered unserviceable to the enemy.[6]

Leaving burning warehouses in his wake, Johnston marched his command—swelled by recent reinforcements to eight thousand officers and men—out the turnpike to Winchester, his preferred point of concentration and defense. That night he bivouacked near Charles Town, scene of John Brown's execution. There Colonel Stuart's scouts brought him word that Patterson's army was fording the Potomac at Williamsport, twenty-two miles to the northwest. Johnston countered by moving troops in that same direction so as to interpose between Patterson and Harpers Ferry. Johnston expected that by shifting toward Martinsburg he would bring on a clash of arms, an act that would show Richmond he was not afraid to fight. But his opponent failed to respond, and on the eighteenth Johnston, tired of waiting, completed his withdrawal to the environs of Winchester.

While at Winchester he was surprised to learn that Patterson had suddenly withdrawn to the north side of the river. Although his opponent would not learn the reason for some time, the elderly Pennsylvanian had been ordered to fall back by Winfield Scott, who had recently withdrawn from Patterson's army its entire complement of regular troops in order to bolster McDowell. The detaching left Patterson with approximately twelve thousand troops of all arms. Scott believed Johnston had about the same number, meaning that Patterson lacked the advantage he needed to give battle. For his part, Johnston began to view his adversary as overly cautious if not weak-kneed, an observation that, in the long run, would prove valid.[7]

At Winchester Johnston received additional instructions from Richmond. General Cooper reminded him that he was "to act as circumstances may require" in resisting invasion while keeping in regular communication with the War Department. Such advice might seem unnecessary except that a pattern had begun to emerge in Johnston's relationship with his superiors: he rarely kept them as closely posted on his plans and intentions as they wished. Instead of sending Richmond timely reports, he concentrated on augmenting and reorganizing his command. In late June, still at Winchester, he added an infantry brigade commanded by a promising young West Pointer from South Carolina, Brig. Gen. Barnard Elliott Bee. Bee's coming gave Johnston a force of approximately ten thousand, more than enough to compete successfully with Patterson, especially if

86

he were permitted to maintain the defensive. Around this same time he revamped his army into four brigades under the newly promoted Brigadier General Jackson; Col. Francis Bartow, a former congressman from Georgia, the only civilian among Johnston's senior subordinates; General Bee; and Brig. Gen. Arnold Elzey, a Maryland-born West Pointer who had distinguished himself in the Mexican War. Later a fifth brigade would be formed and assigned to Edmund Kirby Smith, now also a brigadier general.[8]

Late in June, Patterson, who had also been reinforced, appeared on the verge of crossing the Potomac a second time. To counter such a move, Johnston dispatched Jackson's foot soldiers, supported by Stuart's horsemen, to Martinsburg. There, in response to a recent order from General Cooper's office, Jackson was to destroy the rolling stock of the Baltimore & Ohio Railroad that had been seized and collected in that vicinity. Johnston had learned that his enemy was deficient in transportation; he was determined to prevent Patterson from commandeering additional resources.

Jackson did a thorough job of it: on June 21 he oversaw the burning and wrecking of forty-two locomotives and almost four hundred flat and box cars, more than a half million dollars' worth of stock. The action may have deterred Patterson but it also prevented Johnston from using the same resources to alleviate his own supply problems. Furthermore, the wholesale destruction raised a howl of protest among pro-Southern Marylanders, including state officials who had owned stock in the B & O. The furor may have worked to the detriment of Confederate interests in that strategic border state. For these and other reasons, at least one historian has described the destruction as an "egregious blunder," especially so because Johnston appears to have misinterpreted his instructions. The intent of Cooper's edict had been to demolish bridges, tunnels, and tracks of use to the enemy, not whole trains.[9]

On July 2, Stuart's vedettes, advancing from Martinsburg, reported that Patterson's army was indeed crossing the river, this time at Falling Waters, downriver from Williamsport. In compliance with his instructions from Richmond, Johnston sent Jackson to block the Union advance. A sharp skirmish ensued near Falling Waters—the first clash between Johnston and his Valley opponents. From the start outnumbered and eventually outflanked, Jackson landed only a few blows before forced to retire toward Winchester. As he moved south, Johnston headed north. Again resolved to force a confrontation; he moved his main body to Darkesville, three miles above Winchester, where Major Whiting laid out a defensive perimeter. But again Patterson failed to accept the challenge; he maneuvered as if willing to engage Johnston but withheld an attack. After four days of anxious waiting, Johnston's command stood down and returned to Winchester.[10]

By now it had become clear that the Yankees were not going to take the offensive. Patterson's evident intention was not to fight but to distract Johnston, holding him in place, preventing him from moving to join Beauregard. The transparent nature of these tactics would work to Johnston's advantage and to the advantage of his nation and his cause.

Colonel Sherman looked forward to assembling, organizing, and familiarizing himself with the personnel of the Thirteenth United States Infantry. He had a warm, emotional regard for the regiment, which he considered not only the key organizational element of any army but also its heart and soul: "The regiment is the family. The colonel, as the father, should have a personal acquaintance with every officer and man, and should instill a feeling of pride and affection for himself, so that his officers and men would naturally look to him for personal advice and instruction."[11]

To his great disappointment, he never became a father to the Thirteenth. Even as the outfit was being recruited, he was transferred from line to staff duty as inspector of the volunteer units assembling at Washington. His new job took him on a tour of the camps that extended in a wide semicircle from Alexandria on the south to the northwestern suburb of Georgetown. The work was important enough and it kept him occupied, but it was not why he had come east. His dissatisfaction with his noncombat role was heightened when, in mid-June, he traveled to the advance position of Patterson's army at Hagerstown, Maryland, where his brother John was completing a stint as a volunteer aide-de-camp. Sherman arrived to find the troops about to march to Williamsport prior to their initial crossing of the Potomac. There he renewed acquaintances with his best friend at the Military Academy, now-Col. George Thomas, who had left the regular cavalry to assume command of one of Patterson's infantry brigades. He also chatted amiably with the members of Patterson's staff, "all of whom seemed encouraged to think that the war was to be short and decisive, and that, as soon as it was demonstrated that the General Government meant in earnest to defend its rights and property, some general compromise would result." Although their visitor did not contradict them, he did not share this view of the future. To Sherman's mind, both sides were already in earnest, deadly earnest. The battle lines had been drawn, and the result would be bloody, long, and—probably for a time, at least—indecisive.[12]

As Patterson's army moved off, the Sherman brothers returned to Washington, where a special session of Congress was to meet on Independence Day. The message the president addressed to that body was, as Cump judged, "strong and good," a happy contrast to the weak image Lincoln had projected during their meeting at the White House. Lincoln's words showed that he "recognized the fact that civil war was upon us, that compromise of any kind was at an end; and he asked for four hundred thousand men, and four hundred million dollars, wherewith to vindicate the national authority." Sherman, who attended the opening session, was likewise pleased to observe that "the tone and temper of Congress had changed since the Southern Senators and members had withdrawn, and that we, the military, could now go to work with some definite plans and ideas."[13]

Sherman, for one, could go to work, for he had been relieved of his inspection duties. Perhaps through General Scott's assistance, in the last days of June he had been assigned command of a five-regiment brigade of volunteer infantry in McDowell's Army of Northeastern Virginia. The command was a component of the division of Brig. Gen. Daniel Tyler, a sixty-two-year-old West Pointer from New England who had left the army to manage canal and railroad companies. Having gone to war at the head of a regiment from Connecticut, Tyler had risen to become the most senior of McDowell's subordinates. Sherman found him a kindly, considerate superior who, though elderly by the standards of the day, seemed to know his business and, even more notably, was a firm disciplinarian.

Tyler offered his newest subordinate his full support in whipping his brigade into field-campaign shape. Any help would be a godsend, for soon after reporting at brigade headquarters on the Virginia side of the Potomac near the Aqueduct Bridge, Sherman discovered that his rather motley command—the Thirteenth, Twenty-Ninth, Sixty-Ninth, and Seventy-Ninth New York and Second Wisconsin Volunteers, plus a unit from Sherman's old regiment, Battery E, Third United States Artillery, under Capt. Romeyn B. Ayres—needed a lot of work before it would be ready to take on the Rebels. The great majority of its thirty-four hundred officers and men knew nothing of soldiering beyond what they had acquired in the two and a half months since their enlistment. Only two of their leaders, Col. Isaac F. Quinby of the Thirteenth New York and Lt. Col. Harry Peck of the Wisconsin regiment, had attended West Point, and only Quinby had graduated. Col. Michael Corcoran of the Sixty-Ninth New York had soldiered in his native Ireland but since coming to the United States twelve years before had been more politician than warrior. His prominence in the Irish-American community had brought him command of his regiment, which had its origins in the New York militia system and was largely composed of fellow immigrants. The single military qualification of Col. James Cameron of the Seventy-Ninth New York was that his brother was Lincoln's secretary of war. And Peck's immediate superior, Col. S. P. Coon, as Sherman put it, "knew no more of the military art than a child." To remove this "good-hearted gentleman" from the field, Sherman was forced to attach him to the brigade staff.[14]

For their part, the men of Sherman's brigade considered their new commander an odd duck. For one thing, he seemed to care little for military display. When not on the review or drill field, he went about clad partly or mainly in civilian attire, which was often rumpled and dusty. Even in uniform he looked somewhat disheveled; soldiers enjoyed commenting on his "tall gaunt form clad in a thread bare blue coat, the sleeves so short as to reveal a long stretch of bony wrist, the trousers at least four inches less than the usual length." His unmilitary bent extended to his grooming, or the lack of it. A "bushy untrimmed beard" and bristly crop of auburn hair, often carelessly combed, emphasized his less-than-attractive facial features including "hollow" cheeks, "a great bulging forehead," and "sharp piercing eyes." Oftentimes he appeared more like a civilian visitor at the camp than its commander.[15]

William T. Sherman

Although Sherman would claim that he commanded "one of the best brigades in the whole army," given his well-known antipathy toward volunteers this comment was probably the product of postwar reflection, when battles and honors won colored a man's memory of men and events. In July 1861, in fact, Sherman may have despaired of making soldiers of this gaggle of unmilitary civilians that had been entrusted to his care. The only sure way of achieving this objective was rigorous and repetitive drill and painstaking instruction. The problem was, he lacked the time for either.

Barely two weeks after assuming command, he was leading the Third Brigade,

First Division, Army of Northeastern Virginia toward the advance outposts of the Alexandria Line. Thirty thousand other eager but inexperienced volunteers were also in motion, clogging the roads leading south from the Potomac lowlands. On this morning of July 16, General McDowell had given in to mounting political and editorial pressure to march "on to Richmond" via Fairfax Court House, Vienna, and Centreville, Virginia.[16]

Sherman feared the result of a premature commitment, but the army's leaders hoped for the best. "You are green, it is true," General Scott had told McDowell, adding that "they [the troops of Beauregard] are green also; you are all green alike." Such an equation suggested an open, even contest—as long as the Confederates in the Shenandoah Valley did not interfere. When, days before the advance from Washington, General Tyler had asked the commanding general what would happen if Johnston were to reinforce Beauregard before McDowell reached Bull Run, an agitated Scott had replied that Robert Patterson would "take care" of Johnston. The Valley Confederates would not be permitted to slip away and head east before battle was joined. Cump's superior further tried Scott's patience by musing aloud in his presence (as he probably did in Sherman's) that, even so, he would be much surprised if "we did not have to contend with Jo. Johnson's [sic] army in the approaching battle."[17]

The withdrawal from Darkesville to Winchester disappointed many of Johnston's men, but their commander appreciated the folly of giving battle, even against a timid opponent, when heavily outnumbered. He believed Patterson had two to three times as many effectives as he himself. This seems a fantastic supposition, although Johnston's calculations were influenced by the large number of Confederates incapacitated by illnesses including measles, mumps, and dysentery. Looking back on the campaign, Johnston readily admitted that he and his adversary "overrated each other's strength greatly, as was generally done by the opposing commanders during the war."[18]

Over the next two weeks, Johnston's concerns were somewhat assuaged by the receipt of a couple of regiments from Richmond, personally dispatched by Jefferson Davis. His relief, however, was short-lived, for by July 15 Stuart's vedettes reported Patterson's sudden advance to Bunker Hill, about midway between his former post at Martinsburg and Johnston's headquarters at Winchester. Johnston kept a close eye on his enemy, who remained at Bunker Hill for two days before shifting eastward to the village of Smithfield. Though at first confusing, Patterson's movements were interpreted as the first step in an effort to outflank Johnston and interpose between him and Beauregard. Yet it remained to be seen whether Patterson had overcome his aversion to a confrontation.[19]

While Johnston sought to fathom and counter Patterson's tactics, Pierre Beauregard was again trying to persuade his superiors to order Johnston to his side. On the thirteenth he dispatched staff officers to place before President Davis two variations of the same plan, which the Creole's best-known biographer, T. Harry Williams, describes as "truly Napoleonic." Under its terms, Johnston would leave a small force at Winchester to hold Patterson in place and transfer the bulk of his army to Manassas Junction, enabling Beauregard to defeat McDowell. That done, Johnston's men would return to the Valley along with ten thousand of Beauregard's troops to attack and overwhelm Patterson. Johnston would then send a column to clear western Virginia of McClellan's Yankees. Finally, he would attack Washington from the rear by moving through Maryland while Beauregard left Bull Run and struck the enemy's capital in front.[20]

Both Davis and Lee—the latter now serving as chief military advisor to the president—dismissed Beauregard's strategy as unworkable, mainly for want of transportation and manpower (inadvertently or deliberately, the Creole had greatly overestimated Johnston's strength). But the concept of combining forces on the Alexandria Line was a compelling one, and Davis ordered it put in operation late on July 17 when he received word from Beauregard that McDowell was advancing, driving in the pickets on the roads south of Washington.

At 1:00 A.M. on July 18, 1861, Johnston received at Winchester a succinct telegram from Samuel Cooper: "General Beauregard is attacked. To strike the enemy a decisive blow, a junction of all your effective force will be needed." Johnston was to send every man incapacitated by sickness as well as his baggage trains to the supply depot at Culpeper Court House (an order he disobeyed because of the time it would take to implement), then march his command through the Blue Ridge to Beauregard's headquarters, a distance of fifty-some miles. Thirty minutes later Johnston received a plea for help from Beauregard himself, which had been sent concurrently with his dispatch to the War Department but whose transmission had been unaccountably delayed.[21]

Johnston had no recourse but to obey the twin summons. Although the plan of concentration had not been his own, he approved of the strategy that underlay it. From his first days in the field, he had become convinced that the only way the Confederate forces could prevail was to husband and mass their limited manpower.

He had made provisions for carrying out this concentration, should it be required of him: his route east would be via the railroad between Piedmont Station and Manassas Junction. As soon as Stuart assured him that Patterson had not left Smithfield, Johnston was ready to march. Leaving behind a couple of brigades of militia, the least desirable component of his command but whose numbers he considered "quite sufficient" to hold Patterson in place, Johnston placed his main body on the road to Ashby's Gap in the Blue Ridge. He had no idea how long it would take his still-raw recruits to reach the railroad and from there the scene of imminent combat. He could only hope that time was on his side.[22]

McDowell's army marched to battle at a glacial pace, stopping to skirmish with pickets who seemed to occupy every house, barn, and outbuilding between Fairfax Court House and Centreville and who fought and fell back slowly and defiantly. A frustrated McDowell ordered a portion of Tyler's division, which led the march, to move cross-country in the direction of Germantown with the intention of cutting off the Rebels' retreat, but the move was halted when Tyler discovered a substantial body of infantry drawn up in line of battle on the outskirts of Centreville. Eventually the road was cleared, the enemy having fallen back to Bull Run, and McDowell established his headquarters in the now-quiet village.

Sherman's brigade—minus the Twenty-Ninth New York, which he had left behind to guard his camps and equipage—saw no action during the first two days of the advance. This was fortunate, for, as Sherman observed in his memoirs, "the march demonstrated little save the general laxity of discipline; for with all my personal efforts I could not prevent the men from straggling for water, blackberries, or any thing on the way they fancied." They finally got a taste of combat on the afternoon of the eighteenth as the army drew to within rifle-shot of Beauregard's main position. Without authority from McDowell, General Tyler ordered his Fourth Brigade, under Col. Israel B. Richardson, to cross Bull Run at Blackburn's Ford, along Beauregard's right flank. The movement, officially styled a reconnaissance-in-force, brought on the first sustained fighting of the campaign, involving not only foot soldiers but cannoneers; in the fracas, both sides sustained several casualties.[23]

At first held near Centreville, three miles from the scene of action, Sherman's command was eventually ordered up as reinforcements for Richardson. Ayres's battery moved first, followed at an interval by the bulk of the brigade. The men arrived at the ford just as Richardson's men were retiring helter-skelter to the upper banks. Sherman recalled that his command "stood for half an hour or so under a fire of artillery, which killed four or five of my men." At that point the fighting dwindled down to minor skirmishing, and Sherman was ordered to return to Centreville. He retired convinced that little had been accomplished this day other than to confirm the enemy's presence in strong force on the far side of the stream and to give his would-be soldiers a little seasoning.[24]

Over the next two days, while other units probed Beauregard's position, Sherman's troops remained in their rear-echelon bivouac. Suddenly, on the evening of the twentieth, the brigade got the word to move out. Everyone in McDowell's army appeared to have received the same order—as if an encounter with Beauregard's main body was imminent. The thought did not frighten Sherman, but it bothered him nonetheless: "We had good organization, good men, but no cohesion, no real discipline, no respect for authority, no real knowledge of war." With those exceptions, the Army of Northeastern Virginia was ready to fight.[25]

<hr />

A little past 9:00 A.M. on the eighteenth, barely eight hours after receiving General Cooper's urgent telegram, Johnston's men were streaming southward from Winchester, Jackson's First Brigade in the lead. Although unused to hard marching, the troops moved with a sprightly step in response to repeated announcements, authorized by Johnston, that they were bound for a junction with Beauregard. The march, which was relieved by several badly needed rest stops, led to Millwood, near the banks of the Shenandoah River. That night Jackson's men, followed by the troops of Bartow, Bee, Elzey, and Kirby Smith, forded the Shenandoah. Once on the other side they pushed on to the hamlet of Paris, adjacent to Ashby's Gap. At Paris, as Johnston recalled, news was received of the fighting of the eighteenth, which indicated "that the Federal army was in the immediate presence of that of General Beauregard, so that a battle on Friday [the nineteenth] was probable—its occurrence later than Saturday very unlikely." As the men had required ten hours to cover the thirteen miles from Winchester to the Shenandoah River, Johnston realized that "there was no hope of reaching the field [of battle] in time, but by the railroad."[26]

The intermediate destination of everyone in the column, Piedmont Station, was reached at dawn on the nineteenth. There the footsore troops found Johnston, who had ridden on ahead to complete arrangements for shipping them to Manassas Junction. By noon, the single engine available at the depot, its passenger and freight cars weighted down with Jackson's troops, began the forty-mile run to Manassas. It took eight hours for the old and overburdened locomotive to cover the distance, whereupon it unloaded its human cargo, turned around on the siding, and started back for a second haul. It did not reach Piedmont Station until close to sundown, at which time half of Bartow's brigade climbed aboard the cars. The train did not return to Manassas till early on the morning of the twentieth. Some time after sunrise on the twentieth the next contingent, Bee's brigade, boarded a second train that Johnston had commandeered. How long it would take the rear of the army, Elzey's and Smith's brigades, to get in motion Johnston could not say, but he had been assured by the railroad's president that the last units would reach Manassas early that same day. By then, Stuart's cavalry, having ensured the immobility of Patterson's troops near Smithfield, would have reached Bull Run via overland march.[27]

Johnston left Piedmont Station in company with General Bee and his staff at about 7:00 A.M. on the twentieth. His train moved more swiftly that it had earlier; even so, it did not chug into Manassas until almost noon. As of that hour, only 40 percent of the Army of the Shenandoah was on hand to support Beauregard's Army of the Potomac, but the key fact was that McDowell had yet to attack. When he finally got around to it, he would find himself facing thousands of defenders who had not been on hand twenty-four hours earlier.[28]

As soon as he stepped down from the train, Johnston, accompanied by his staff, rode to Beauregard's field headquarters near the depot. Following a round of handshakes and introductions, the generals began to plot strategy. As they talked, Beauregard gave his superior a tour of his lines. Johnston was immediately struck by the rugged, heavily timbered terrain occupied by the Potomac army. The extensive wooded tracts prevented a broad view of the imminent battlefield; as a result, Johnston resolved to rely on the Creole's knowledge of his own position, and—as much as possible—that of the enemy.

Beauregard's troops manned a line that stretched for three and a half miles from Union Mills Ford. It was guarded by an infantry brigade commanded by Johnston's West Point classmate, Richard S. Ewell, northwestward across wooded, gently rolling terrain as far as a bridge of stone that crossed Bull Run near the point at which Col. Nathan G. Evans's undersized brigade anchored Beauregard's left flank. Between these extremes, four brigades had taken position, each covering a crossing site on the run. Two other brigades, which constituted Beauregard's reserve, were held in rear of Union Mills Ford. Beauregard appeared to have sufficient infantry and artillery to hold this perimeter, but his mounted contingent was small and scattered; Johnston immediately ordered Stuart's Virginians to augment it.

When the tour ended, Johnston authorized Beauregard, whose penchant for strategizing was well known, to draw up a plan of battle. Beauregard worked on it throughout the night and completed it early on Sunday, the twenty-first. When Johnston scrutinized the result some time before dawn (which must have been difficult, given his night blindness), he was surprised and disappointed by the vague and open-ended nature of Beauregard's strategy. The plan called for the combined armies to take the offensive before the enemy did—a tactic Johnston approved of—by attacking the Union left across Bull Run with the troops of Ewell, Brig. Gens. Theophilus H. Holmes and David R. Jones, and Col. Jubal A. Early, supported by some of the units assigned to the center and left-center of the line, including those fresh from the Valley under Jackson, Bee, and Bartow. The overall strategy was understandable, but the sequence of advance was unclear. Ill-defined circumstances would guide the successive movements toward McDowell's main camp at Centreville. Such generalities concerned the orderly minded Johnston, but there was no help for it. Soon after he finished studying the plan, the thump of enemy artillery told him that the battle was already on.[29]

It is an axiom of twenty-first-century military theory that no plan of battle survives the first clash of arms. This was certainly the case on July 21, 1861, which began with McDowell attempting what Beauregard had intended to do, attack and break his enemy's left flank. Not only did McDowell anticipate his opponents' strategy, he struck before they could, the result of orders missent and never received by several of Beauregard's attack elements.

Soon after daylight, McDowell had his artillery shell Evans's position near the stone bridge while he advanced a portion of Tyler's division (but not Sherman's brigade) down the road to Mitchell's Ford, there to catch and hold the attention of the troops defending the Confederate right. More than two hours earlier, McDowell had started a column, two divisions strong, on a fourteen-mile cross-country march to the west and south of Centreville, aiming for Sudley Springs Ford on Bull Run, which lay beyond Beauregard's left. It was this movement that Tyler was to assist with his feint.[30]

McDowell's plan was imaginative and enterprising, but it suffered in the execution. The green troops assigned to the turning movement marched too slowly, costing their commander the crucial element of surprise. By the time they reached Sudley Springs Ford, they were no longer shrouded in the darkness of early morning. Capt. E. P. Alexander (who later as a colonel) would observe Joe Johnston unleash his temper on a petrified ambulance driver) manned a signal station providentially located near the ford. Alexander detected the Yankees' crossing and relayed word to Colonel Evans, who rushed west at the head of his demi-brigade.

When word of McDowell's advance reached Johnston, he directed Beauregard, to whom he had delegated tactical control of the battle, to send Bee and Bartow to the Stone Bridge via a crossing of Young's Branch, a Bull Run tributary. Beauregard obeyed, adding to the effort a legion (a regiment-size force of infantry, cavalry, and artillery) just arrived at Manassas under Johnston's erstwhile hunting companion, Wade Hampton. Later Jackson's brigade moved in the same direction to take up a key position in that sector.[31]

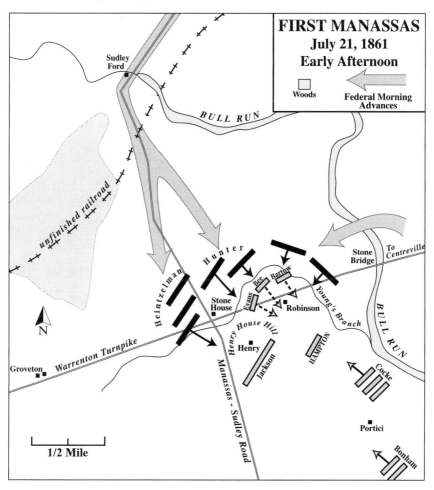

First Manassas, July 21, 1861, Early Afternoon

Joining Johnston on high ground known as Lookout Hill well in rear of the fighting, Beauregard—who still held to his initial impression that the attack on the left was a feint in favor of a heavier thrust farther east—received permission to implement a replacement for the original battle plan, which, quite clearly, had been overtaken by events. Instead of moving to attack Centreville, the combined armies would thrust themselves at the left flank of McDowell's turning column. But before the change of plan could be executed, the Yankees had forced their way across the ford and were pushing southward. Fighting heated up in competition with the rising sun as the fewer Confederates in that sector were shoved rearward until backed against an eminence known as Henry House Hill, a little more than a mile below Sudley Springs Ford. Upon reaching the crest of the hill, they were joined, a little past noon, by Johnston and Beauregard, who had galloped to the sound of the fighting.

The commanders had arrived to find a chaotic, near-desperate situation. The troops of Evans, Bee, and Bartow had been overwhelmed and most of them forced to retreat. Casualties had been heavy, especially in places where the defenders had been routed and scattered. Trying to rally some of them, Colonel Bartow had been killed. General Bee was soon to take a mortal wound, but not before giving Jackson's brigade, the only coherent force on this part of the field, an enduring appellation. "Yonder stands Jackson like a stone wall," he cried to the men of his Alabama, Mississippi, and North Carolina brigade, and urged them to "go to his assistance." Johnston added his efforts to this task, personally leading the Fourth Alabama of Bee's command—which had been broken and forced to retreat under irresistible pressure but had re-formed—into position on Jackson's right flank. Then Johnston left Beauregard and rode southeastward

Gen. Thomas J. "Stonewall" Jackson, CSA

to Portici, the manor house of a neighboring plantation, where he had established his headquarters. From there he ordered to Jackson's support regiments that had been engaged lightly or not at all on other parts of the field.[32]

The stand that Jackson's five regiments—the Second, Fourth, Fifth, Twenty-Seventh, and Thirty-Third Virginia—made on Henry House Hill would prove to be a turning point of the battle. Bolstered by continually arriving reinforcements from the center and right, the Virginians threw back a series of attacks. Then two well-placed artillery batteries got Jackson's range and began to pound his position. A regiment of New York "Fire Zouaves" in their colorful Algerian-style uniforms poised to sweep around his left flank. Seeing an opportunity to save the day, Stuart's cavalry charged the Zouaves, overrunning and trampling them and sending their survivors to the rear in panic and confusion. The New Yorkers' retreat uncovered the batteries; they were then charged by the Thirty-Third Virginia and supporting forces, who captured all but one of the eight cannons that had been lacing the crest of Henry House Hill. By now, 3:00 P.M. had come and gone. The antagonists had been grappling in the sweltering heat for more than six hours, but the outcome of the battle remained in doubt.[33]

Sherman's brigade had left its camp at Centreville at 2:30 that morning with the main body of Tyler's division, which McDowell had ordered to feint against the Confederates on the other side of Stone Bridge. The troops got into their assigned position some time after dawn and remained at the bridge until about 10:00 A.M., popping away at any target that showed itself on the south bank, thereby covering the movement of the flanking column farther east. Despite their best efforts, Sherman's riflemen could not prevent Rebels from double-quicking in the direction of Sudley Springs Ford. It seemed obvious that Tyler's diversion was falling short of maximum effect. Sherman tried to bolster the feint by having Captain Ayres shell selected targets across the water, but McDowell had ordered off the battery's two long-range rifled guns; the smoothbores that remained failed to reach the enemy's position. To avoid wasting ammunition, Sherman had Ayres cease firing. He unsuccessfully attempted to replace the lost rifles with a 30-pounder battery attached to the division.

Some time after noon, with the fighting between Sudley Springs Ford and Henry House Hill at full fury, Tyler was ordered to cross the run and join the free-for-all on the other side. Obediently, Sherman took his troops off to the left and marched them to the stream. Despite the steep bluffs that lined the water, the brigade experienced little difficulty crossing over near Sudley Springs Ford, the Irishmen of the Sixty-Ninth New York in the lead. As soon as his men reached the enemy's side, Sherman sheltered them behind an earthen bank that lined the road from the ford, giving the command time to close up. From this vantage point the scouts of the Sixty-Ninth spied a body of the enemy that appeared to be falling back toward Henry House Hill. Without orders, Lt. Col. James Haggerty spurred his horse toward the retreating troops as if determined to cut them off all by himself. For his rashness he fell from the saddle with a fatal wound.[34]

This was but the beginning of Sherman's travail. Ordered by General McDowell, whom he discovered on the ground personally directing the turning movement, to pursue what appeared to be a demoralized mass of Rebels, Sherman started forward with his regiments arrayed in line of battle, Quinby's Thirteenth New York now in advance. Topping a rise north of the hill and nearing the position where, minutes before, the Federal batteries had been overrun, Quinby's men suddenly encountered a severe fire of artillery and musketry that halted and staggered them. As they reeled backward, the rest of the brigade pressed ahead, passing them. Peck's Second Wisconsin, the next in line, made its way up the slope of Henry House Hill and advanced against the line that Jackson had staked out and his supports had strengthened. The Badger regiment pressed forward resolutely until it found itself caught in a deadly crossfire from the Confederates on the hill and the nearest Union troops to the west, the brigade of Brig. Gen. William B. Franklin. Like more than a few Northern outfits, the Second Wisconsin had gone to war in uniforms of gray cloth. Since gray was the predominant color shown by the enemy, Peck's soldiers were taken for Rebels by many of Franklin's men, whose misdirected fire claimed several casualties. Thrown into confusion, the Second Wisconsin fell back to the Sudley Springs Road, where it halted, rallied, and went forward once again, only to be forced back in disorder the moment it passed the brow of the hill.[35]

In this early morning of the war, Union and Confederate commanders had not learned the most effective way to commit multiple ranks of troops to battle. Sherman was clearly lacking in this skill. Instead of sending his brigade forward in strength sufficient to overwhelm the opposition, he continued to put in one regiment at a time. Now it was the turn of Cameron's Seventy-Ninth New York, whose officers were dressed in pants of tartan pattern and many of whose enlisted men wore kilts, the battle dress of generations of Scots, the predominant nationality of the outfit. The exotic attire may have stirred ethnic pride, but it provided no protection from the musketry and artillery fire to which the regiment was subjected. In his after-action report, Sherman cogently described the result of the Scotsmen's advance: "They rallied several times under fire, but finally broke and gained the cover of the hill." By then they had suffered dozens of casualties, including the mortal wounding of their colonel.[36]

Almost frantic at the losses his men were absorbing without commensurate gain, Sherman committed his last unit, Corcoran's Sixty-Ninth. The Irishmen went gamely up the slope of the hill but encountered a reinforced enemy line against which it could make no impression. Most of Franklin's men having withdrawn, Corcoran lacked the flank support his comrades had enjoyed. As Sherman observed, the regiment was exposed to "firing [that] was very severe. . . . It was manifest the enemy was here in great force, far superior to us at that point."[37]

Corcoran, evidently undaunted, led his men into the maelstrom, only to be beaten back and then attacked by a phalanx of screaming, shooting horsemen. Corcoran disappeared in the midst of these attacks, which applied the finishing touch to Sherman's repulse. Long after the Sixty-Ninth fell back in panic and disorder, it was ascertained that Corcoran had been taken captive. He would spend a year in Rebel prisons before he was exchanged, released, and permitted to rejoin his outfit.

When the last of his regiments withdrew, Sherman rallied them in a less exposed position in the rear. Aware that his men had been fought out—laid low not only by enemy bullets but also by fatigue, thirst, and heatstroke—he kept them well in hand but attempted no further assaults. Then, some time after 2:00 P.M., began what Sherman called "the scene of confusion and disorder that characterized the remainder of the day." McDowell's army, which only hours before seemed to have a complete and dramatic victory in hand, began to withdraw as a body—at first, slowly and in good order, but then, unaccountably, in panic and chaos. It was, Sherman thought, a fitting way to end a day filled with errors and missed opportunities, especially considering the much smaller numbers of the enemy (it would be days before McDowell confirmed that Johnston's men had joined Beauregard's before the battle had begun). For Sherman, however, the most disheartening aspect of the retreat was that he could not prevent his brigade from being swept up in it.[38]

From his vantage point at Portici, where he continued to locate and forward reinforcements to the front, Joe Johnston had a difficult time assessing the direction the battle was taking. The staccato report of rifle fire and the thump of artillery could tell him only so much—not enough to give him an accurate guide to his army's fortunes. Some time after 3:30 P.M., however, he began to fear that the fight was getting away from him, that the forces holding Henry House Hill were on the brink of being overwhelmed by the heavier numbers of the enemy. Then a staff officer galloped up from the rear with breathless word that Yankee infantry had captured Manassas Junction.

The first reaction of Johnston, who had long harbored the fear that Patterson would follow him from the Valley, was that all was lost. Caught between forces front and rear, his army—four regiments of which had yet to arrive from Piedmont Station—could not hope to survive. Within minutes, however, other couriers brought word that the new arrivals, some of whom wore blue uniforms, were members of the rear echelon of the Army of the Shenandoah, under General Kirby Smith. At once Johnston knew that victory was at hand.

By 3:30, Smith had reached Portici for an emotional reunion with his superior and friend. At his suggestion, Johnston personally directed Arnold Elzey's brigade to the battlefield; he placed it under Smith, whose own command was still en route from Piedmont Station. As the troops went into action on Jackson's left, driving the last Federals from Henry House Hill, Smith fell wounded, to be replaced by Elzey. At this moment, another fresh brigade, Jubal Early's, appeared on the scene. It went in shoulder-to-shoulder with Elzey's men, enabling the Confederate battle line to extend so far to the west that it curved around the right flank of the enemy.[39]

Within an hour of Elzey's and Early's advance, which Johnston described as "executed . . . gallantly and well," what remained of McDowell's battle line had been shattered and its shards thrust back across Bull Run in full retreat. "The enemy was driven from the long-contested hill," Johnston would recollect, "and the tide of battle at length turned" in favor of the defenders. No Union army was going to march on to Richmond this day, nor for many days to come.

Johnston rejoiced that "the victory was as complete as one gained in an open country by infantry and artillery can be." He rejoiced, too, in the knowledge that primary credit for a stellar passage of arms would go—as was right and proper—to the senior officer in the army of the Confederate States of America, Joseph Eggleston Johnston.[40]

EIGHT
SELF-INFLICTED WOUNDS

Battles fought by inexperienced troops have a way of disorganizing, and often disabling, the victor as well as the vanquished. Some time before 5:00 P.M. on July 21, with McDowell's army streaming north in two columns, Johnston ordered General Bonham, whose brigade covered Mitchell's Ford on the Confederate right, to pursue, with his own command and that of General Longstreet, the more easterly Union column, which was heading out the turnpike to Centreville. A small force of cavalry was also directed to follow this column and strike it in flank, while Stuart's horsemen, supported by a light battery, harassed the westerly body, retreating via the Sudley Springs Ford.

All efforts at overtaking the foe and preventing his escape proved unavailing. McDowell's men were furiously intent on returning to the safety of the Washington defenses, and most of them enjoyed too great a head start to be brought to heel. Then, too, the scattered forces that sought to dog their heels were slowed at almost every step by the road-clogging debris of retreat: the bodies of dead men, the carcasses of dead horses, abandoned wagons, shattered caissons and limbers, and piles of cast-off weapons and equipment. Hundreds of stragglers were rounded up, and the cavalry cut off a few small groups of demoralized troops, but no coherent body of the enemy was brought to bay. When an erroneous report warned that Federal infantry was approaching Bull Run by the Union Mills Road, those few troops that had been put in motion were recalled. Bonham's and Longstreet's troops had already returned to their original positions in response to similar rumors, also unfounded.[1]

How to mount a better organized pursuit became an issue of contention among Johnston, Beauregard, and Jefferson Davis, who joined his generals on the field of battle as the sun was going down. Failing to get accurate reports of the day's fighting at his office in Richmond and unable to stand the suspense, the president had fled the capital by train, leaving General Lee behind. Even when he arrived at Manassas Junction, Davis could not gauge from the sights that met his eyes whether the Southern arms had prevailed. Thus he was both elated and relieved when he reached Portici by horseback, escorted by Beauregard's chief of staff, Col. Thomas Jordan, and learned from Johnston himself that the day had been won.

Late that night, after Davis rode out to the firing lines where he was greeted with hearty cheers, he rejoined his generals at Beauregard's headquarters. After the trio exchanged words of praise and congratulations, Johnston and Beauregard presented a summary of the day's operations. At some point the issue of a pursuit came up. Johnston explained that he had attempted to organize one but that it had been unproductive. At the suggestion of Colonel Jordan, Davis dictated an order calling for a full-scale pursuit. But then conflicting reports of the enemy's demoralization made him change his mind; he directed, instead, that only a reconnaissance-in-force take place in the morning. That operation came to naught, mainly because a postbattle downpour had turned the roads toward Washington into gumbo, preventing a concerted advance.[2]

By all indications, a full-scale pursuit such as Davis originally called for was beyond the capability of Johnston's and Beauregard's troops; even with a battle under their belts, they could hardly be called soldiers. Nor did the army enjoy enough cavalry—that arm was in short supply on both sides of the field—to make a pursuit truly effective. Yet because no Union army would leave a later battlefield in such confusion and disorder, once the sensations of relief and euphoria began to fade, the victory at Manassas came to appear, in the eyes of many Southerners, incomplete. The prevailing belief was that an army susceptible of being destroyed had been permitted to escape.

In later weeks, Davis and his commanders would engage in a long, volatile, and unseemly squabble over who was to blame for the failure to chase the panicky foe all the way to Washington. Davis contended that he had ordered a full pursuit, but Johnston heatedly disagreed. The record would appear to sustain Johnston, but too often the general would defend himself with arguments that appeared spiteful, petty, even disingenuous. The principal reason why Johnston reacted so harshly to criticism on this point, it would appear, was his fear that it tarnished, if it did not rob him of, the first great triumph of his long and honorable military career.[3]

The fighting at Manassas had confirmed Sherman's suspicions about the matériel at his disposal. Yet instead of ascribing the outcome to the rawness of his troops and their insufficient instruction, he blamed himself for their lack of tenacity and staying power. On the morning after the battle, Brig. Gen. E. D. Keyes, one of Sherman's comrades in the Third Artillery, now a fellow brigade commander under McDowell, had returned to the Washington suburbs with his demoralized command (he had witnessed soldiers throwing down their rifles "with a gesture as violent as they would throw off a venomous reptile"). Keyes was resting in his tent after twenty-seven hours in the saddle when Colonel Sherman entered alone. "His countenance," Keyes recalled, "was that of a disappointed man. After resting in silence twenty minutes, he arose and departed. I am not certain whether Sherman had troops or company with him or not."[4]

In fact, during Sherman's army's retreat, many regimental and brigade commanders had become separated from their leader, some of whom, in their haste to get back to their camps along the Potomac, had raced ahead of him. Other men—the better part of the brigade—were straggling back in leaderless groups large and small. They did so under what Sherman called "a slow, mizzling rain" that fit the prevailing mood perfectly: "Probably a more gloomy day never presented itself."[5]

Unwilling to show his despondency to the men, he fought off the black mood that had enveloped him. Soon he lost himself in the process of restoring some semblance of order to his command. By the twenty-third he had drawn each of his regiments inside or close to a work he had christened Fort Corcoran. Within another two days he had assessed his casualties, taken steps to fill the gaps rent in the officer corps, composed and forwarded his report of the battle, and "had my brigade about as well governed as any in that army."[6]

He had to work hard to keep watch over the most demoralized soldiers, especially those who had signed ninety-day enlistment papers and considered their obligation to the government paid. Several such men, who were especially numerous in the ranks of the Sixty-Ninth New York, became so unruly that Sherman feared a mutiny. Believing he must take drastic action, he had Captain Ayres unlimber his battery in the midst of the regiment's camp with orders to fire on anyone attempting to leave without Sherman's permission. When a company officer announced that he was going to Washington to resign his commission and return to his law practice, Sherman vowed to shoot him down "like a dog," a threat that impressed not only the officer but onlooking enlisted men.[7]

In time, the crisis abated and most of the men agreed to abide by the ruling of the army's adjutant general as to when their obligation ended. Thereafter, to keep the brigade busy, Sherman drilled it almost incessantly, leaving officers and enlisted alike too tired to air their grievances in a group setting. His efforts to raise morale, or at least keep the men from brooding over their unhappy lot, were aided by a couple of events that occurred within days of the army's return from the battle. On the twenty-third, George B. McClellan, whose series of small but dramatic victories in western Virginia had won him nationwide publicity and the title "Young Napoleon," replaced McDowell in command of the forces around Washington, which he named the Army of the Potomac. The men quickly warmed to the soldierly image Little Mac presented, and they enjoyed the pomp and pageantry that accompanied his every outing. When he visited their camps astride his big black charger, trailed by his impressively large staff, the soldiers clustered about him and talked freely of their wants and needs, which he promised to attend to as expeditiously as possible.[8]

Wherever he went, McClellan seemed to exude energy, strength, and confidence, qualities the army had never discerned in his portly and dour predecessor. In Sherman's mind, McClellan's only failing was that his visits were too infrequent. "Instead of coming over the river, as we expected," the colonel observed, "he took a house in Washington, and only came over from time to time to have a review or inspection." He called on the commanders of his brigades and regiments even less frequently. On one of those few occasions, he informed Sherman that he intended to organize an army one hundred thousand strong, supported by one hundred batteries of artillery. This was heartening news, but "I still hoped he would come to our side of the Potomac, pitch his tent, and prepare for real hard work, but his headquarters still remained in a house in Washington City."[9]

If Little Mac would not come around regularly, his commander in chief did. A few days after the return from Bull Run, Sherman spied a carriage coming down the road from the ferry crossing to Georgetown. He thought he recognized one of the occupants. It turned out to be Mr. Lincoln, come to see and be seen by the army in company with his secretary of state, William H. Seward. When he spied Sherman by the side of the road, Lincoln remembered him from their White House meeting; he asked the colonel to join them. Sherman climbed in and gave the coachman directions to the camp of his brigade, which lay at the top of a steep hill. On the way there he inquired if the president intended to address the troops.

To Lincoln's affirmative reply, Sherman made bold to suggest that when doing so he should discourage "all cheering, noise, or any sort of confusion; that we had had enough of it before Bull Run to ruin any set of men, and that what we needed were cool, thoughtful, hard-fighting soldiers—no more hurrahing, no more humbug."[10]

Far from taking offense at this unsolicited advice, Lincoln acknowledged it with a solemn nod. When they reached the camp, Sherman had his command turned out and placed at parade rest. Lincoln stood up in his carriage so that all could see him and delivered what Sherman considered "one of the neatest, best, and most feeling addresses I ever listened to, referring to our late disaster at Bull Run, the high duties that still devolved on us, and the brighter days yet to come." When, at a few points, some of the soldiers began to cheer, the president restrained them, acknowledging that while he himself liked the sound of it, "Colonel Sherman here says it is not military; and I guess we had better defer to his opinion." This pleased Sherman, as did the praise Lincoln bestowed on him for the order and neatness of the brigade's camp.[11]

He was even more appreciative of the way the president upheld the authority of a commanding officer to discipline his men. When his address ended, Lincoln spoke informally with many officers and men, including the subaltern who had attempted to take unauthorized leave. When the man complained to Lincoln that Sherman had threatened to shoot him, the president looked at Sherman, then turned back to the aggrieved officer, and in a stage whisper audible to the entire regiment, replied: "Well, if I were you, and he threatened to shoot, I would not trust him, for I believe he would do it." Sherman recorded the upshot: "The officer turned about and disappeared, and the men laughed at him."[12]

Abraham Lincoln

Lincoln's visit was a memorable occasion, but it was not the high point of Sherman's summer. A few weeks later an emissary from Washington arrived at Fort Corcoran with a list of officers recently promoted to brigadier general of volunteers, one of whom was William Tecumseh Sherman. Acutely aware that everyone else on the list shared the blame for Bull Run, Sherman was openly incredulous. So was an elderly colleague who had made the list, Col. Samuel P. Heintzelman. The crusty regular exclaimed within earshot of Sherman and other apparent promotees: "By———,———, it's all a lie! Every mother's son of you will be cashiered!" But on August 24 a special order confirming the omnibus promotions was published by General Scott's office. Sherman's appointment was back-dated, for purposes of seniority, to May 17, only three days after the date of his commissioning as colonel of the Thirteenth Infantry.[13]

Yet another who received a star was George H. Thomas, who, despite the botch his superior had made of it, had performed creditably throughout the campaign to distract Joe Johnston and confine his army to the Shenandoah. Thomas's promotion was a real feat for, as a native Virginian, his loyalty had been a matter of doubt to Lincoln, Secretary of War Cameron, and other government officials. Sherman could take partial credit for the outcome, for at every opportunity he had praised his West Point classmate as a skillful soldier dedicated to the salvation of the Union.[14]

Before the close of August 1861, Sherman, stars proudly adorning his shoulders, said his good-byes to individual officers and the assembled enlisted men of his brigade. Handing over the command to another newly minted brigadier, Fitz John Porter, he promptly departed Virginia for Kentucky, where a new and even more challenging assignment awaited him. Two weeks earlier, Sherman had received a summons from his old commander at Fort Moultrie, Robert Anderson, himself a newly promoted brigadier general (in the regular service, not the volunteer army), to visit him at his room in Willard's Hotel in Washington. Sherman went at once; he found Anderson closeted with political officials from his native state. When able to break away, Anderson informed his visitor that Kentucky—which another of her native sons, Abraham Lincoln, had vowed to keep in the Union—was approaching a military and political crisis. State authorities including a majority of the legislature were poised to proclaim Kentucky's loyalty to the national government but only if the administration backed them with military resources. At present, two columns of Confederate troops based in Tennessee appeared ready to invade the Bluegrass State: one, under Sidney Johnston and Brig. Gen. Simon Bolivar Buckner, via Nashville; the other, led by Brig. Gens. George B. Crittenden and Felix Zollicoffer, by way of East Tennessee and Cumberland Gap.

To combat these threats, Lincoln had authorized the formation of the Department of the Cumberland, embracing Federal forces in all corners of Kentucky (except for the area bordering Cincinnati, Ohio) and Tennessee (except a section along the Mississippi River). The president had appointed Anderson to the command and had authorized him to select as his ranking subordinates any four of the newly appointed brigadiers. Anderson informed Sherman that he had asked for him as well as for Thomas; Sherman's benefactor in Kansas, Don Carlos Buell; and Ambrose E. Burnside of Indiana (West Point class of 1847).[15]

Sherman immediately accepted the proffered assignment ("I always wanted to go West, and was perfectly willing to go with Anderson, especially in a subordinate capacity"). Keenly aware of the tactical errors he had made at Bull Run and of his own relative inexperience above the small-unit level, Sherman did not consider himself worthy of independent field command. Until he learned the ropes, he preferred serving under an old regular he trusted and admired. He explained this preference to Lincoln when the latter came to Willard's to confirm Anderson's acceptance of the departmental command and to review his choice of lieutenants. When Lincoln learned of Sherman's "extreme desire" to serve in a secondary capacity, he seemed amused, explaining that "his chief trouble was to find places for the too many generals who wanted to be at the head of affairs. . . ."[16]

Days later Sherman and his superior were sharing a seat on a train bound for the Commonwealth of Kentucky, that "dark and bloody ground" of divided loyalties, strategic opportunities, and daunting challenges.

For a few days following the battle of the twenty-first, before the controversy over who ordered or countermanded a pursuit to the Potomac robbed the victory of its glow, all was quiet if malodorous at the headquarters of Johnston's army. Having assimilated Beauregard's command, it now called itself the Army of the Potomac. For the next three months, until it was officially changed, Johnston's command would share that title with George McClellan's army. While detachments moved gingerly in the direction of the picket posts the Yankees had established along the fifteen-mile-long corridor between Fairfax Court House and Washington, other soldiers, heavily assisted by slaves impressed for the task, tended to the unenviable chore of interring corpses in blue as well as in gray.

Johnston had expected that before he quit the battlefield McDowell would have interred most of his dead. The retreat, though, had been too sudden and precipitate, and the work had been left to the victors. They got around to it slowly. For days, bodies lay rotting under the July sun, producing an odor that wafted through the camps of Johnston's regiments and that contributed, in the minds of reporters who visited the scene, to unusually high sick rates in the Confederate ranks. Johnston denied allegations that the unburied dead produced "camp-fevers tenfold more fatal than the bullets of the enemy," but he agreed to move some of his camps to less malodorous climes. A brigade he had assigned to his former engineer officer, now-Brig. Gen. W. H. C. Whiting, was moved to Bristoe Station on the Orange & Alexandria Railroad although Johnston insisted the transfer was made "on account of complaints of bad water." At about the same time, Evans's brigade was removed to Leesburg, near which it would repulse a Union demonstration three months hence in a fight known as the battle of Ball's Bluff. The brigades of Longstreet, Jones, Brig. Gen. Philip St. George Cocke, and Col. John H. Forney were shifted to the vicinity of Centreville. By early August Jackson's brigade had moved to Centreville as well. Stuart's cavalry, supported by Elzey's infantry, was held well in advance of these camps, keeping tabs on enemy movements and intentions by capturing and interrogating Yankee solders and civilians leaving the capital.[17]

Perhaps because he had won a triumph in the field while his superiors in Richmond remained chained to their desks, within days of the great battle Johnston began to quarrel with those whom he believed had failed to support him or show him the proper respect. On July 24 he objected strongly to the continuing flow of directives from General Lee, who was serving as a sort of deputy secretary of war to Jefferson Davis. In Johnston's view, because Lee did not command troops or head a bureau or department, he had no authority to order anyone to do anything. Directives could come only from the president, Secretary of War Walker, or General Cooper. Johnston's resentment skyrocketed when Lee sent Capt. Dabney Maury to Manassas to fill the position of chief of staff that had been vacant since Kirby Smith's promotion. A fellow Virginian, Maury was an old friend of Johnston, who received him warmly while loudly rejecting his right to the appointment. As Johnston explained in a subsequent letter to Cooper, he had already selected a new chief of staff and thus had no room for Maury. Johnston went on to assert his claim to "ranking General of the Confederate Army," which precluded Lee or any other inferior officer from telling him what to do.[18]

Johnston's stiffly worded protest won him no admirers. When Jefferson Davis read it, he labeled it an act of insubordination. The dispute did not become a major issue, but an incident that occurred early in September not only spiraled into a furious controversy but forever poisoned the Davis-Johnston relationship. The root cause was a message Davis sent to Congress on August 31, formally identifying the five appointees to the rank of full general in the Confederate army. As expected, Johnston's name was on the list, but he was livid when he learned the order of seniority that Davis proposed: Cooper, Sidney Johnston, Lee, Joseph Johnston, and Beauregard.

Davis had calculated seniority on the basis of when each officer had been grad-uated from West Point and their standing within their class. To be sure, this was an arbitrary ruling and undoubtedly reflective of the president's preferences and prej-udices. He wanted Cooper at the top of the list because at sixty-three he was sen-ior in terms of years in service, and his administrative expertise (and thus his rank) was critical to the smooth functioning of War Department bureaucracy. The next in line, Sidney Johnston, was Davis's favorite field commander. He had champi-oned the man's advancement through the ranks of the United States Army, such as when supporting him for quartermaster general in 1860. Quite simply, he desired that Johnston enjoy unrivaled authority among the Confederacy's field leaders. After Johnston, Robert E. Lee was Davis's beau ideal as a soldier. The Virginian had established an excellent working relationship with Davis, and more than anyone else the president relied on him for counsel and advice.

By prioritizing according to class standing, Davis had an excuse to rank Joseph Johnston, whom he considered a less gifted and more difficult subordinate, behind Lee. Although Davis was already having a falling-out with the last man on the list and for that reason might have been tempted to leave his name off of it entirely, he felt constrained to include Beauregard, who had emerged in the mind of the public, Northern as well as Southern, as the victor of Manassas.[19]

Because the prerogatives of rank and seniority meant so much to Joseph Johnston, when he learned of Davis's ranking system, he bitterly protested the way it had been arrived at. The Confederate Congress had passed more than one act recognizing the equitable transfer of rank from the United States Army to the Confederate service. Johnston had been the only general officer to cast his lot with the defense forces of the South; legally, he had an ironclad claim to the title of senior Confederate officer. Davis later attempted to defend his low rank-ing by maintaining that since Johnston (like Lee) had joined the Virginia forces prior to entering Confederate service, he was not covered by Congress's action. Johnston angrily rejected this bit of sophistry, as he did Davis's subsequent expla-nation that Johnston's rank as quartermaster general, U.S.A., did not transfer to the Confederate service because the former position had been a staff, not a field, appointment. To refute Davis's logic, Johnston had only to point out that Cooper had also been a staff officer in the old army.

His temper at white heat, on September 10 Johnston composed an impassioned response to what he considered a spiteful and malicious act directed at him. He declared that Davis's ruling had been designed to penalize an officer with a long and unblemished record of service to two armies: "It seeks to tarnish my fair name as a soldier and a man, earned by more than thirty years of laborious and perilous service. I had but this, the scars of many wounds, all honestly taken in my front and in the front of battle, and my father's Revolutionary sword. It was delivered to me from his venerated hand, without a stain of dishonor. Its blade is still unblemished. . . ."[20]

Johnston did not at once forward to Richmond this rambling, emotionally laden missive, which revealed both the severity of his wounding and the depth of his rancor toward Davis. But upon rereading it two days later he decided that it perfectly expressed his state of mind, and he dated and sent it to the president's office.

Davis's response, although brief and couched in formal language, may have infuriated its recipient even more than the object of his ire: "I have just received and read your letter of the 12th instant. Its language is, as you say, unusual; its arguments and statements utterly one sided, and its insinuations as unfounded as they are unbecoming." In Johnston's mind, the president's refusal to address any of his allegations confirmed their validity.[21]

Never again would Johnston and his president enjoy cordial relations, a situation with ominous overtones for Confederate military fortunes. Their mutual enmity even spilled over into the drawing rooms of Richmond society, where Lydia Johnston and the first lady, Varina Howell Davis, carried on at a lower level the war between their husbands. As Craig Symonds points out, "previously close, they now formed rival salons where they indulged in catty remarks about one another, remarks that were soon passed on to members of the rival circle."[22]

The ever-widening breach gave birth to opposing camps within the Confederate Congress. Although capable of gentlemanly conduct and generous impulses, Jefferson Davis could also be haughty, condescending, and rude to those who did not agree with his policies, whom he considered not misguided but willfully wrong. At times he seemed to go out of his way to make enemies, whose opposition he took quite personally. In turn, the latter were willing to use every resource at their disposal to thwart the president and derail his agenda. In time, Johnston would join in this rivalry on the side of Davis's congressional opponents.

The president was not the only public official Johnston quarreled with in the months following his great victory. Beginning in October—by which time the newly christened Army of Northern Virginia had been divided into corps commanded by Beauregard and Maj. Gen. Gustavus Woodson Smith, a Kentucky-born West Pointer with whom Johnston had shared engineering duties in Mexico—the army leader engaged in a series of disputes with Davis's favorite cabinet member.

This was Judah P. Benjamin, a former New Orleans lawyer who recently had replaced the overmatched Leroy Walker as acting secretary of war. He had a brilliant legal mind and was talented in many areas, having served as Davis's attorney general; later he would become Confederate secretary of state. However, Benjamin lacked experience in military matters and was unfamiliar with, and had little respect for, many of the high-ranking officers whose operations he supervised. It seemed only a matter of time before he injured the sensitive pride of the victor of Manassas.[23]

The Benjamin-Johnston contretemps began with a misunderstanding over the construction of shelters the army was to inhabit when it went into winter quarters. The following month, Johnston and Benjamin clashed over a more serious incident, the latter's attempt to implement Davis's desire to reorganize the army along sectional lines, forming brigades of regiments from the same state as befit the political

Judah P. Benjamin

ideology of the Confederacy. Johnston considered the policy, while commendable in the abstract, too unwieldy to execute as quickly as Davis wished. He dragged it out for a year, much to the displeasure of the president and his war secretary.[24]

In November and December, the cabinet member and the general clashed over an intemperate letter sent to the War Department by General Whiting, Johnston's subordinate and friend. Whiting, who had been promoted for his staff services in the battle of Manassas, had been assigned to command an infantry brigade consisting of five recently organized regiments from Mississippi. In a letter to General Cooper forwarded by Johnston (and thus tacitly approved by him), the tart-tongued Whiting had asked, "What are they sending me unarmed and new regiments for? Don't want them. . . ." In subsequent correspondence with Richmond, he not only restated his disgruntlement but criticized Davis's handling of army affairs in general. Benjamin, writing to Johnston on behalf of the president, reacted angrily to this "very insubordinate letter." He demanded that Johnston return Whiting to his former rank of major and order him to report to

Stonewall Jackson for engineering duty. Benjamin also scolded Johnston for act-ing as a conduit for Whiting's dissatisfaction and directed that "you will hereafter decline to forward to him [Davis] communications of your subordinates having so obvious a tendency to excite a mutinous and disorganizing spirit in the Army." Johnston bristled at this expression of official disfavor, but both he and Whiting had to apologize before Davis rescinded his ruling.[25]

Another issue of dispute between Benjamin and Johnston was the secretary's attempt to impose on the army policies designed to persuade solders who had gone to war in one-year regiments to reenlist for the duration of the conflict. Mandated inducements included a liberal leave program and the right of enlisted men to elect or reelect their regimental officers. Johnston considered the incen-tives an unwarranted intrusion into his affairs, one detrimental to the army's strength, morale, and efficiency. This time, however, Benjamin had his way. Davis rejected Johnston's subsequent protest and sustained his cabinet member and close friend.[26]

The Benjamin-Johnston conflict with the greatest potential for harming the army occurred in January 1862 as the result of a dispute between General Jackson and one of his more peevish subordinates, Brig. Gen. William Wing Loring. Three months after Manassas, Davis—against Johnston's wishes and without his consent—returned Jackson and his command to the Shenandoah to supervise local defenses and operate against the Yankees in that region, now led by Brig. Gen. William S. Rosecrans. On January 10, Jackson occupied strategic Romney, which the enemy had evacuated, thereby threatening the line of communica-tions connecting Rosecrans's army to Union forces on the upper Potomac.[27]

When Jackson withdrew his main body from Romney, he left Loring's com-mand to hold the town through the balance of the winter. The mission did not sit well with the division leader and some of his subordinates, who believed they had been placed in a position vulnerable to recapture. The aggrieved officers addressed a formal complaint to Jackson, who disapproved it but forwarded it, as per regulations, to the War Office. After studying the document, Jefferson Davis directed Johnston—who remained Jackson's nominal commander—to investi-gate the basis of Loring's protest. Johnston failed to do so personally, however, and the report filed by the inspector general he sent to Romney in his stead failed to resolve the impasse.

At this point Benjamin, who saw validity in the complaint, stepped in. He peremptorily ordered Jackson to withdraw the division from its exposed position. Stonewall did so but followed with a letter complaining of bureaucratic interference in his command and requesting a transfer to a staff assignment. He added an ominous threat: "Should this application not be granted, I respectfully request that the President will accept my resignation from the army."[28]

Johnston was horrified by the turn the matter had taken. Only his strenuous pleading and the urging of Governor Letcher persuaded Stonewall to rescind his application and remain in the service. Not content to let the matter rest, Johnston complained bitterly to Davis of Benjamin's latest and most harmful intrusion into army operations. To prevent further disturbances within his command, Johnston asked that Jackson's force be withdrawn from the Department of the Potomac. Again, Davis sided with his war secretary, curtly reminding Johnston that he was subject to Benjamin's authority.[29]

Thus Johnston had drawn another rebuke for (as he saw it) an attempt to uphold his rights and prerogatives as commander of the Confederacy's principal fighting force. The quarrels that Benjamin had precipitated—primarily, it would appear, through ignorance rather than any conscious effort to violate military rules and customs—caused the continuing feud between his boss and Johnston to acquire ever greater heat and intensity. The seemingly endless clash of wills and temperaments constituted a war within a war, one that Johnston, by virtue of his statutory subordination to Davis's authority, could not hope to win.

And yet, he could fashion small, short-term victories. In late February 1862, Johnston was a guest at a dinner party in Richmond attended by public officials including congressmen inimical to Davis and his hand-chosen subordinates. Urged on by one of these, Johnston rashly voiced his conviction that the Confederacy could not hope to win its independence as long as it was saddled with meddlers and obstructionists such as Judah Benjamin. The secretary's enemies used this oft-quoted complaint as ammunition to help derail congressional action on Davis's nomination of Benjamin to the permanent position of secretary of war. The no-confidence vote that resulted compelled the president to withdraw the nomination and instead appoint George Wythe Randolph, a substitution that Joseph Johnston greatly favored. The general's success, however, was to prove both unsatisfying and fleeting.[30]

NINE

THREATS REAL AND IMAGINED

Anderson, Sherman, and Thomas reached Cincinnati on September 1, 1861. In that city, by prior arrangement, they met with a number of influential Kentuckians including state senator James Speed, a future attorney general under Lincoln. The meeting was for the purpose of determining the most effective and also the most discreet way to use military force to keep the Bluegrass State in the Union fold. The turbulent political situation back home had impelled the emissaries from Louisville to conduct their business out of state. In May, Kentucky's divided citizenry had forced its secessionist-leaning governor, Beriah Magoffin, to proclaim the state's neutrality. How long the fence straddling could prevail was anyone's guess. In Kentucky, as in Missouri, the State Guard (militia) was effectively controlled by Southern sympathizers. It answered to Magoffin, and its military commander was Simon Bolivar Buckner, soon to be appointed a brigadier in the Confederate service. Yet Unionists had recently won some victories that promised to strengthen the state's loyalty to the administration of its native son, Abraham Lincoln.

Upon the outbreak of war, a slim pro-Union majority prevailed in the legislature, but in August elections had greatly increased that margin. Then, too, as a condition for appropriating large sums for arming state forces including the Guard, the loyalist majority had transferred control of military affairs from Magoffin to a five-man commission, most of whose members were Unionists. And although threatened by Rebel invasion, the state had authorized the establishment of two recruiting camps for Federal volunteers, near Jeffersonville and Nicholasville.[1]

During the strategy session, Anderson pledged to do his utmost to prevent the Confederates from overrunning his state. He feared, however, that the recruiting camps had not produced enough defenders to turn back Sidney Johnston, Crittenden, and Zollicoffer. Thus it was decided that General Sherman should solicit additional manpower from the governors of Indiana and Ohio as well as from the man who had become the most powerful military officer (and, arguably, the most influential political figure) in Missouri, the once-disgraced army explorer John Charles Frémont. Sherman was off on his errand almost immediately, but it proved a futile effort. In Indianapolis he found Gov. Oliver P. Morton too busy forming regiments for the armies of McClellan and Frémont to divert any to a neighboring state, even one as critical as Kentucky. Sherman met the same response in Springfield, where an apologetic but unbowed Gov. Richard Yates begged off on Anderson's request.

A disappointed Sherman then sought out Frémont, who had established his presence in St. Louis in the manner of a Middle Eastern potentate—ensconced in luxurious quarters attended by a colorfully attired and fiercely loyal staff, including many of European descent, and protected by a small army of bodyguards. Although warned that the general would never give an interview to a mere brigadier who lacked an appointment, Sherman gained entrée to Frémont's headquarters and had an hour-long conversation with the man who gloried in his old army nickname of "Pathfinder of the West." The meeting was cordial enough, Frémont inquiring about the situation in Kentucky and explaining the state of military and political affairs in his own realm. The latter had been especially volatile since early the previous month, when a Union column under the recently promoted Brig. Gen. Nathaniel Lyon had been defeated and its leader killed by the Confederates of Sterling Price at Wilson's Creek, near Springfield. In the end, all Frémont did for his visitor was to assure him that, as soon as he drove Price from the state, he would "turn his attention down the Mississippi"— presumably to assist General Anderson.[2]

When the interview ended, Sherman, now fully discouraged, entrained for Louisville, where Anderson had established his headquarters. He found the city awash in rumors but picked up one hard fact: the legislature had unambiguously declared its intention to remain in the Union rather than cast its lot with secession. To some extent, the decision had been prompted by the recent occupation of Columbus, on the far western edge of the state, by Confederate forces under Maj. Gens. Leonidas Polk and Gideon Pillow (Joseph Johnston's West Point classmate and Mexican War superior, respectively). Sherman saw the long-threatened incursion as a "signal for action," one that Anderson must counter. The trouble was that Kentucky's Unionists were unprepared for a confrontation, while their enemy, as

Sherman believed, "were fully prepared." Reflective of this readiness was the September 18 seizure of Bowling Green, in the south-central portion of the state, by Buckner. The next day, General Zollicoffer established a Rebel foothold in the southeastern corner at Barboursville, adjacent to strategic Cumberland Gap.[3]

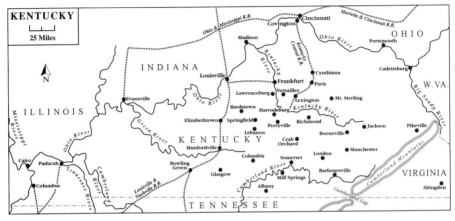

Kentucky

Dating from the receipt of this news, wrote Sherman, "the excitement ran high in Louisville." He began to believe the boasts of Rebel sympathizers that at any hour Buckner would march on Louisville or Frankfort. Sherman's anxiety deepened on the day he learned that General Anderson had been conferring with the president of the state's most important railroad, the Louisville & Nashville. The official reported that a strategic bridge on a fork of Salt Creek, thirty miles south of the city, had been burned ("whether to prevent Buckner coming into Louisville, or us from going out, was not clear"). Several nigh-irreplaceable trestles over Salt Creek were in danger of being destroyed as well. An even more ominous report had Buckner's troops heading for Louisville by train. If Buckner was indeed coming, Sherman thought, he would probably stop at the State Guard camp of instruction at Muldraugh's Hill, roughly midway between Bowling Green and Louisville. Thanks to a Unionist saboteur, Buckner's train hit a missing piece of track and derailed, giving Anderson additional time to prepare to meet him.[4]

Sherman's superior agreed with the L & N official that the imperiled trestles must be protected. He ordered Sherman to see to it at the head of a column composed of some of the volunteers and home guards who had congregated at the training camp at Jeffersonville. Sherman hurried there, collected upwards of one thousand men, and led them to the L & N depot, where he put them aboard the cars. Reaching their destination the next morning, the soldiers not only secured the trestles but took possession of the camp at Muldraugh's Hill. Sherman remained in the occupied training facility for two days, assimilating reinforcements from Louisville and overseeing repair work on the bridge that had been fired. While there he ascertained, to his immense relief, that the reports of Buckner's approach had been false. Buckner had yet to leave Bowling Green, whose defenses Johnston was still building up.

By now Sherman had at Muldraugh's Hill perhaps three thousand men. These were too few to defend an entire state, but in case they had to make the effort, the brigadier instituted a crash program aimed at turning eager, ignorant volunteers into something akin to soldiers. The prospect of leading these raw levies against confident invaders including well-disciplined militia—Kentucky had one of the most admired militia organizations of any state, North or South—gave him great concern. His problems, however, had just begun. On October 5, his superior recalled Sherman to Louisville where he was informed that the responsibilities Anderson had borne for the past month had become so onerous and stressful that to save his health he was relinquishing command of the department. The decision placed Sherman in a position he had tried mightily to avoid: overall command of a state in danger of enemy takeover. Alarmed and upset, he informed Washington that he did not want to succeed Anderson in "direct violation of Mr. Lincoln's promise to me." The best the War Department could do was to assure him that an old friend, Don Carlos Buell, would be sent to supersede him. But Buell was then in California, and Sherman knew how long it would take him to reach Louisville.[5]

Left on his own, he began to panic. The memory of his less-than-stellar performance at Bull Run haunted him, but his subordinate status had saved him from bearing the full weight of defeat. Now he would be held personally responsible for any error of commission or omission. He could not imagine leading into battle troops even less reliable than those who broke and ran on July 21, troops whose reputation for attacking chicken coops and smokehouses made them a greater terror to loyal farmers than to the Confederates. With this rabble he would have to take on three columns of Confederates led by some of the most brilliant military minds in the country.

In actuality, Sherman's outlook was not nearly so bleak as he imagined. His department consisted of some eighteen thousand troops of all arms, albeit scattered about the state, many of them in out-of-the way places. Moreover, he was not alone in having to contend with manpower, ordnance, and logistical problems—so were Johnston, Buckner, and Zollicoffer. Yet Sherman could see only his own difficulties and deficiencies, and he despaired for the future—Kentucky's, the Union's, and his own. To George Thomas, now commanding the training camp near Nicholasville, he confessed that he "could hardly sleep" at night for anxiety and worry. He feared being driven from the state by the "vast force" opposing him: "It is impossible to say how or where we shall winter," he wailed. "This will depend on our enemies. They will not allow us to choose." He saw himself as surrounded by a disloyal population committed to aiding and abetting the invaders. He came to believe that spies were everywhere, including, perhaps, inside his headquarters. He suspected that farm and dray wagons had been covertly collected for miles around to augment Johnston's supply facilities.[6]

He had been in command of the Department of the Cumberland barely a week when he had the opportunity to place his concerns before the secretary of war. Simon Cameron, late in returning to Washington from St. Louis where he had been investigating irregularities in Frémont's administration, happened to be in Louisville in company with Adj. Gen. Lorenzo Thomas. At Sherman's urging, Cameron, while awaiting rail connections to the east, agreed to meet with him in his room at the Galt House.

Sherman might have been expected to approach the secretary warily. After all, he had rejected Cameron's offer to command Ohio volunteers, and three months later the man's brother had been mortally wounded during those piecemeal attacks on Henry House Hill. Regardless of the consequences, however, he read his visitor a laundry list of administrative and operational concerns and called his situation "as bad as could be." The main problem, Sherman advised, was twofold: a lack of manpower and a dearth of serviceable weapons. Neither had been properly addressed by the government, which seemed intent on dispatching all available resources to McClellan in Virginia and Frémont in Missouri. In consequence, Kentucky was ripe for Rebel takeover. Its defense force was only large enough to be "tempting to such a General as we believed Sidney Johnston to be . . . if Johnston chose, he could march to Louisville any day."[7]

Cameron was shocked by this grim assessment. He had not been informed of any such problems, and, perhaps perceiving a degree of panic in his host's voice, he was not certain whether to believe him or not. After some thought, he asked Sherman how many troops he believed were needed to stabilize the situation. Sixty thousand, was the reply, although Sherman quickly added that these would be sufficient only for defensive purposes. If, as reports had it, the government expected him to take the offensive against Johnston and his subordinates, two hundred thousand men would be required. At this, Cameron bolted upright and exclaimed, "Great God! Where are they to come from?" When the secretary calmed down, the talk turned to peripheral matters such as recruiting, a problem with which, Cameron believed, Kentucky might yet receive outside assistance. When the meeting concluded, their parting was cordial enough, leading Sherman to believe he had opened the secretary's eyes to a problem that affected the nation as a whole and the commander at Louisville in particular.[8]

Only in later weeks did he appreciate the impact of the concerns, predictions, and estimates he had shared with Cameron. The cabinet member had been accompanied to Sherman's room not only by General Thomas but also by several unidentified civilians whom Sherman suspected were newsmen, a class he continued to regard with scorn and reproach. Cameron had assured him that he could speak freely and frankly in their presence, but two weeks after the meeting at the Galt House, a *New York Tribune* reporter who had attended it published an article based on a memorandum of Cameron's trip compiled by General Thomas. The memo related that Sherman had presented "a gloomy picture of affairs" in his department. It stressed his prediction that two hundred thousand additional troops were needed in Kentucky without explaining that Sherman had considered a much smaller force adequate for the state's defense. Other newspapers in the East and Northwest reprinted the article; Sherman probably read it in the *Cincinnati Daily Commercial*, the largest-circulation newspaper in his part of the country.[9]

At the time the piece appeared, its subject was feeling, even more keenly than before, the burden of departmental command. On November 1 he wrote Ellen of the virtual certainty that Johnston was about to strike Louisville: "Rumors and reports pour in on me of the overwhelming force collected . . . across Green River." The stress of waiting for the crisis to break was affecting him both physically and mentally. Even a newsman sympathetic to the general described him as "a bundle of nerves, all strung to the greatest tension. . . . he devotes but little time to sleep. . . . He was always at this office [the Louisville Press Agency] during the evening, often remaining until three o'clock in the morning, when the closing of the office would force him to retire to his rooms at the hotel. During these hours he would pace the floor of the room apparently absorbed in thought and heedless of all that was going on around him. . . ." Other reporters were not so charitable; some spread a rumor that Sherman had gone crazy. It was a dramatic claim, one that resonated with editors desperate for good copy about the war. Over time, the charge— strictly on the basis of its constant repetition—acquired a degree of verisimilitude that made it difficult for those who knew differently to refute it.[10]

Throughout his ordeal, Sherman kept pleading for Washington to relieve him.

He importuned McClellan, successor to Winfield Scott as general in chief, to hasten Buell to his relief or, failing that, to send Sherman's old comrade Henry Halleck instead. Buell, however, was still en route, and Halleck was on the verge of moving to St. Louis to replace Frémont, whose erratic generalship, lax bookkeeping, and penchant for politicking had cost him the support of the government.

In the second week in November, new and ominous reports of Confederate movements brought Cump to the end of his tether. Overwork, lack of sleep, and unrelieved stress caused him to sink into a morbid depression that threatened to disable him. An alarmed aide took drastic measures by sending to Lancaster for the general's wife and family, hoping their presence would be a tonic to him. Instead, when Ellen made the fourteen-hour journey to Louisville accompanied by her brother Phil, she found her husband on the brink of a nervous breakdown, if not something worse. The next day she wrote to John Sherman: "Having seen Cump on the verge of it [insanity] once in California, I assure you I was tortured by fears, which have been only in part relieved since I got here."[11]

At once she ministered to her husband, ensuring that for the first time in weeks he got regular meals and sufficient sleep. While he recuperated, McClellan agreed to relieve him from command, although unsure what to do with him afterward. On November 15 Buell finally arrived and took over departmental affairs. By now Cump had recovered his equilibrium to the point that Ellen felt she could return to Lancaster. He remained in Louisville for a week after her departure to help facilitate the transition of command.[12]

When he left Louisville it was to go to St. Louis, where General Halleck had taken over Frémont's headquarters as commander of the Department of Missouri. Halleck had heard reports of Sherman's erratic behavior in Louisville but was willing to overlook them. He gave his colleague a warm welcome and took him on as a subordinate. To ease Sherman back into the field, he sent him on an inspection tour of his fiefdom, with authority to assume command of any camp or outpost he believed threatened by the enemy.

Reaching Sedalia on November 23, Sherman was shocked to find the defense forces there as well as at Otterville, twenty miles to the east, loosely positioned, "with no concert between them." When rumors reached him that Sterling Price was somewhere in that part of Missouri, perhaps headed for Sedalia, the nerve-jangling situation that had almost incapacitated Sherman in Kentucky threatened to repeat itself. He sent a rather strident call to St. Louis, advising Halleck to send whole divisions to Sedalia to resist attack. When his superior was slow to respond, Sherman issued "preliminary orders looking to that end" in Halleck's name.[13]

Sherman believed he was being prudent and proactive, but "the newspapers kept harping on my insanity and paralyzed my efforts. In spite of myself, they tortured from me some words and acts of imprudence" that seemed to confirm the earlier diagnosis of mental instability. Perhaps his boss thought so, too; on the twenty-sixth, Halleck telegraphed him to "make no movement of troops without orders." Two days later Sherman was told to report at St. Louis; the message recalling him contained the ominous news that "Mrs. Sherman is here." Obviously, Ellen had come to take him back to Lancaster.[14]

Gen. Henry W. Halleck, USA

By the time he was reunited with his wife, Cump was ready to go home. He believed his usefulness to Halleck—perhaps to any other superior—had been destroyed by his own infirmities and the malicious slanders in the public press. In fact, the newspapers attributed his recall from Sedalia, as they had his relief from Louisville, to mental aberration, "though in fact I had done nothing, except to recommend what was done immediately thereafter on the advice of Colonel [James B.] McPherson, on a subsequent inspection."[15]

Looking back on this, the darkest hour of his military career, perhaps of his life, Sherman related the sad conclusion to three hellish months of service in Kentucky and Missouri: "Seeing and realizing that my efforts were useless, I concluded to ask for a twenty days' leave of absence, to . . . allow the storm to blow over somewhat. It also happened to be mid-winter, when nothing was doing; so Mrs. Sherman and I returned to Lancaster, where I was born, and where I supposed I was better known and appreciated."[16]

Despite their several acrimonious run-ins, Joseph Johnston and Jefferson Davis managed to lay aside their animosities, put their heads together, and thrash out a strategy for dealing with the enemy. Their willingness to confer, however, did not mean they saw eye-to-eye on every important issue. Moreover, whenever they failed to reach a consensus each tended to blame the other for the result and then act as he himself thought proper.

Their first face-to-face occurred on October 1, 1861, a few weeks before Johnston's military realm was formally designated the Department of Northern Virginia and Beauregard was given command of one of its three elements, the District of the Potomac. (Jackson in the Valley and T. H. Holmes at Fredericksburg headed the other components.) Davis came up from Richmond to Beauregard's command post near Fairfax Court House, and Johnston joined them there. The discussion that followed centered on the possibility of taking the offensive against the still largely quiescent McClellan. Johnston favored such a course, but he insisted that he lacked the manpower to pull it off. His newly defined department encompassed some forty-seven thousand troops of all arms, but a count taken in October revealed that only thirty-one thousand of these were in Johnston's immediate area of operations. He and his subordinates informed Davis that for offensive purposes they would require another twenty thousand to thirty thousand troops.

In response to the president's logical question—where would the additions come from?—Johnston, in keeping with his mania for massing limited resources, proposed taking them from the coastal defenses of the Carolinas. Those states, he argued, would remain safe if the army was successful in Virginia. Davis, who favored a cordon defense of Southern territory, dared not, for political reasons, strip any state of local defenders. He offered a counterproposal, that Johnston invade Maryland to cut off a large but exposed detachment of McClellan's army opposite Evansport, Virginia. Johnston rejected the idea for want of transportation, explaining that by the time enough supply vehicles were on hand, the critical element of surprise would be lost. The conference thus ended on a note of indecision that pleased none of the attendees. Immediately afterward Johnston recalled his forces from the Fairfax Court House vicinity—which he considered the most advantageous position from which to launch an attack but not a good place to keep an army committed to the defensive—and established his headquarters at Centreville, eight miles farther from Washington.

It took Johnston only two months to decide that he had not pulled back far enough. By then his troops had spent a rather dismal Christmas in the field, their first of the war. Throughout the army, morale appeared to be sagging. The euphoria of the triumph at Manassas had worn off. The army had yet to be materially strengthened. It had taken up residence in rude and ramshackle huts that provided

Confederate winter quarters near Centreville, Va.

little protection against the winds and snows of the season. Finally, the long-lethargic Yankees had begun to assert themselves in ways that both surprised and worried their opponents.

Some of the gloom that pervaded Johnston's camps dated to December 20, when a force of combined arms under now-Brig. Gen. J. E. B. Stuart encountered a sizable column of foragers near Dranesville, on the turnpike to Leesburg. After a several-hour engagement Stuart had been forced to retire, having suffered three times as many casualties as the Federals, who had been led by Sherman's old friend, Edward Ord. This, the first major setback of Confederate arms in northern Virginia, made Johnston fear that his lines remained too extended, too vulnerable to being taken by surprise by the suddenly active foe.[17]

His confidence in his ability to hold his position seemed to drop another notch after January 1862, when Beauregard, on whom he had come to rely for tactical advice as well as for ammunition to rebut Davis's more farfetched ideas, accepted an opportunity to go west. There he would be second-in-command of all Confederate forces beyond the Alleghenies as senior subordinate to Albert Sidney Johnston. The latter was still headquartered at Bowling Green, although within a month he would be falling back though Tennessee into Mississippi, the result of Union successes against all sectors of his defensive perimeter in southern Kentucky. Johnston's long-threatened plunge into the heart of the Bluegrass State, which had unstrung and unseated Sherman, had not materialized.[18]

Gen. Albert Sidney Johnston, CSA

As much as possible, Joseph Johnston made good the loss of his ranking subordinate. He halved the large corps Beauregard had commanded and assigned its divisions to Maj. Gens. James Longstreet and Daniel Harvey Hill. The much smaller corps G. W. Smith commanded was reduced to division size as well. Johnston's command now totaled a little over thirty-six thousand, but its slight strengthening over the winter had not eased his mind about its overextended position, which stretched for eight miles from Centreville to Manassas. The area in between was served by a single railroad line on which the army depended for all its supplies.[19]

By mid-February 1862 Johnston was seriously considering withdrawing to the Rappahannock River, about midway between Washington and Richmond. Rumors of his dissatisfaction with his current position reached Richmond, and on the nineteenth Jefferson Davis (one day after taking the oath of office as "permanent" president of the Confederacy) called him to the capital and invited him to attend a session of his new cabinet. The meeting began with a discussion of unhappy news from Tennessee, where strategic defenses on the Tennessee and Cumberland Rivers had been attacked and forced to surrender to the U.S. Navy and a land force under a general named Grant. Equally grim intelligence had been received from North Carolina, where the

Gen. James Longstreet, CSA

garrison on Roanoke Island had fallen to Brig. Gen. Ambrose Burnside, who now seemed poised to move against Norfolk and perhaps also Richmond.

Johnston, whom Davis asked for a candid assessment of his army's situation, outlined the withdrawal operation he had in mind, adding, however, that it should be deferred until spring, when dry roads would permit an orderly movement. Davis had mixed feelings about the idea, believing that northern Virginia should be held as long as possible. Yet he recognized that the defense of Richmond, the paramount object of Confederate strategy in the East, would be better accomplished by an army situated thirty-five miles closer to the city. The meeting ended with Johnston believing he had received authority to withdraw as soon as he wished and Davis supposing that the army would maintain its present position until forced to fall back. When or if a retreat was ordered, Davis expected to receive ample warning.[20]

The result of this misunderstanding was that Johnston implemented his decision far too soon to suit Davis and without letting the president know in advance. One reason for the precipitate movement, as Johnston later explained, was his concern that operational secrecy had been compromised. Within hours of his attendance at the cabinet meeting, word of the pending withdrawal was making the rounds of the capital. If Richmond was aware of what lay ahead, Washington would soon be as well. Better to make the move before McClellan could mass to stop it or at least interfere with it.[21]

Johnston's preference for acting sooner rather than later appeared validated on March 5, when General Whiting, whose command held an advance position, reported "unusual activity" in the enemy's camps a few miles to the north. By now Johnston's engineers had laid out a defensive position south of the Rappahannock, "strengthened by field-works, and provided with a depot of food." In that area, Johnston believed, "we should be better able to resist the Federal army advancing by Manassas, and near enough to Fredericksburg to meet the enemy there, should he take that route; as well as to unite with any Confederate forces that might be sent to oppose him should he move by the Lower Rappahannock or Fort Monroe." The last-named point, which sat on the southern tip of the Virginia Peninsula, off Hampton Roads, was one of only two U.S. Army installations on Southern soil that had not fallen into Confederate hands; it would soon figure prominently in McClellan's plans.[22]

The army's withdrawal, which Johnston considered carefully planned, began on the morning of the seventh with the fall-back of the most advanced forces, three brigades that had held the lower Occoquan River near Evansport (now

Quantico) and Dumfries. On the eighth and ninth the main body of the army—units posted between Centreville and Manassas—began their retrograde. By early on the eleventh, Johnston's infantry and artillery were crossing the Rappahannock, with Stuart's troopers covering the rear. Johnston placed a large portion of his army below the stream, on either side of the Orange & Alexandria trestle. Another portion he positioned at Culpeper Court House, ten miles farther south, with the rest at various points in between. Most of the cavalry was stationed above the river, at and near Warrenton Junction to provide timely word of the enemy's approach. Johnston established army headquarters near the railroad bridge, south of the stream.

Only on March 13 did Richmond receive official word of the movement, and then only the news that it had ended. A surprised Davis informed Johnston that "I was as much in the dark as to your purposes, conditions, and necessities, as at the time of our conversation on the subject about a month since." The president also complained of the "many and alarming reports" received in the capital that in withdrawing from Manassas and Centreville Johnston had not only burned many of the huts and cabins in which the army had wintered but had abandoned numerous batteries on the Occoquan and Potomac Rivers. Perhaps more troubling was a report that, before evacuating, Johnston's men had burned or otherwise destroyed massive quantities of rations, equipment, and supplies, including the contents of a meatpacking plant the Confederate commissary had established on the railroad northwest of Manassas. In later weeks Johnston was assailed by similar accusations from editors, politicians, and disgruntled soldiers who had lost personal baggage on the move or been forced to destroy provisions they would sorely miss.[23]

Characteristically, Johnston took exception to the wave of official and private complaints, which he countered with a lengthy recitation of the pains he had taken to avoid wasting precious resources. A general scarcity of transportation had prevented him from bringing off every item he would have preferred to remove. On this score, at least, he had given Richmond ample warning. As early as February 22 he reported the removal of private property at and near Manassas. Several times over the next three weeks he called Davis's attention to "the accumulation of subsistence stores at Manassas," which he had repeatedly urged the commissary department to cease sending. He had also warned of the problems posed by "the vast quantities of personal property in our camps . . . [that] must be sacrificed in the contemplated movement," even at the cost of "great suffering."[24]

Over Johnston's protests, Secretary Benjamin, at Davis's behest, opened an inquiry into the abandonment and destruction of war goods. Johnston and several of his subordinates were forced to defend themselves in official memoranda, a time-consuming chore that did nothing to lessen past animosities. In time, events of more far-reaching significance crowded the story of the lost supplies off the front pages of Southern newspapers. Able to complete his work beyond the public spotlight, Benjamin eventually concluded that no acts of criminal waste had been committed by anyone at any level.

By the standards of the period, the marriage of Ellen and William Sherman was an unconventional one. Having been reared in relative luxury, the pampered daughter of a powerful and influential public figure, Ellen had a strong sense of self that did not require validation by her husband's status or wealth. From an early day, Sherman understood that he could not impose his will on his wife, nor could he gain by demanding from her anything she did not care to give. For his part, Cump never bowed to her demand that he adopt her vision of domestic bliss, that he become subservient to her domineering father, and that he share her moral and religious values.[25]

Ellen and Tommy Sherman

As their wartime and postwar correspondence reveals, in many ways theirs was a stormy union, punctuated by outbursts of raw emotion, expressions of discontent and unhappiness, and caustic commentary on each other's flaws and failings. Perhaps the most divisive influence in their married life was their religious differences. Although in many respects a committed deist, Sherman sometimes gave Ellen the impression that he was an unbeliever, an atheist. She, on the other hand, was insistent that as a Catholic by baptism he must practice his faith. She never ceased praying for his acceptance of church teachings and his participation in its services. It was a fruitless endeavor, although after Ellen's death their children secured for her a victory of sorts by seeing to it that their father, as he lay unconscious on his deathbed, received the last rites of the Church.[26]

If their union was contentious and abrasive, it was also characterized by a mutual devotion to their children (who now numbered six, their daughter Rachel having been born in July 1861), to their extended families, and to each other. It was manifest to all who knew them that, for all their differences of temperament and outlook, they complemented each other in fundamental ways and that, more importantly, they needed each other. In his psychobiography of Sherman, Michael Fellman seeks to explain his subject's "wild and free" nature by describing him as an antelope, but "also a sheep or goat, a resentful but willing domestic animal. To him, the mystifying and insufferable Ellen was his hunter and his wife for life. To her, this peculiar, wild, cold, and injured vagabond, so unlike her rock-solid father, so disappointing to her, so alienated from her home, her town, and her Father in heaven, and of course from her, was also her kind and wounded husband for life."[27]

Ellen's solicitude for Cump was no better exhibited than during the most wounded period of his life, when he returned with her to Ohio after losing command positions in Kentucky and Missouri. He spent the pre-Christmas season 1861 in Lancaster, a joyless holiday during which he nevertheless recuperated in body, mind, and spirit—at least until he read a notice from the *New York Times* that had been picked up by a local paper. Reporting on conditions in the department he had just left, the writer noted that Brig. Gen. Franz Sigel had replaced Sherman, "whose disorders have removed him, perhaps permanently, from his command." A couple of days later the *Cincinnati Enquirer* ran new and more dramatic allegations of the general's insanity ("it appears that he was at times when commanding in Kentucky stark mad. . . . It seems providential that the country has not to mourn the loss of any army through the loss of the mind of a general into whose hands were committed vast responsibilities. . . ."). The St. Louis papers copied this story as well, while the *Enquirer's* rival, the *Cincinnati Gazette*, stated flatly that "the family and friends of Sherman desire to keep his insanity a secret."[28]

Because the target of this smear campaign appeared unable or unwilling to defend himself, Ellen and her family went into action in his behalf. She wrote John Sherman in Washington, encouraging him to assure the administration that her husband's mental health had not been impaired. She provided her brother-in-law with ammunition to prove that Washington had contributed to the distress that had brought him down: Why, she asked, were there reinforcements "now pouring into Kentucky to sustain General Buell, when Sherman's requests had gone unheeded?" She also castigated General McClellan, whose respect for his civilian leaders she knew John Sherman questioned, for abandoning her husband to an intolerable situation in Kentucky. The general-in-chief, she charged, had "ignored Cump, refused him any regular troops or men that had had any discipline and suffered him to be driven out of the position by his neglect without raising a finger."[29]

Her letter did a certain amount of good. Although not pleased that his brother had permitted himself to be driven out of Kentucky, Senator Sherman secured an audience with Lincoln during which he explained that most of Cump's well-publicized problems were not of his own making. He depicted the newspapers as having exaggerated his brother's difficulties in order to pump up readership. After the meeting, John reported to Ellen that the president had expressed his kind intentions toward her husband. He had cited Cump's energy, administrative expertise, and devotion to the cause and had given his assurance that he did not hold the general responsible for his public fall from grace.

Finally persuaded to join in his own defense, from Lancaster Sherman solicited expressions of support from his military superiors. Asked if he believed that Sherman had shown any "want of mind" on the job, General Halleck said no. He assured Cump that he had been relieved not for diminished mental capacity but for compromised physical health. Halleck even wrote on Sherman's behalf to the editors of some St. Louis papers, declaring that his subordinate had performed his duties creditably up to the day he went on leave. In a letter to Ellen, Halleck, who had suffered similar abuse at the hands of reporters, proposed "a Yankee trade with him—I will take all that is said against him, if he will take all that is said against me. I am certain to make 50 per cent profit by the exchange."[30]

Ellen wanted her husband to extend his leave through the winter, but on December 18 he left for St. Louis. He was not psychologically prepared to return; he was convinced that he had humiliated himself and disgraced his profession by his erratic, unmilitary behavior. The experience had cost him self-confidence; as he explained to Phil Ewing, "I am fully conscious now of grave errors, but I am not fit for a leader in such a war, and have from the first desired to keep in the background." He attributed his recent misfortunes to his long residence in Louisiana: "I have no doubt I have been much biased by my association with Southern people, and that in consequence I have overrated their power. I certainly have not their temper and purpose. . . ."[31]

Despite his lingering unease, he wished to get back into the field and make amends. Halleck, however, took one look at him and decided he was not ready for an operational command. To prolong his relief from major responsibilities, Halleck sent him to Benton Barracks, a major troop rendezvous on the north side of St. Louis. There Cump took on the arduous but manageable task of turning hundreds of raw recruits into soldiers. After he settled into the position, he began to hope he could remain there until the war in the West began to display signs of real progress. He would not feel comfortable taking on a heavier workload until he received some assurance that the Rebels were not on the verge of overrunning Missouri.

Aware that her husband remained troubled and at times despondent, Ellen decided to write personally to Lincoln. Believing (or at least hopeful) that the president thought well of Cump, she sought "some intervention in my husband's favor & in vindication of his slandered name." She considered his current subordinate status "an endorsement of the slander" that had been heaped on him by malicious editors and enemies of the administration. These "cruel attacks" had wounded her as well as Cump, and thus she appealed "for a speedy relief from the sorrow that has afflicted me in this trial to my husband."[32]

There is no evidence that Lincoln ever responded to the letter. Unwilling to consider her efforts in her husband's behalf stymied, in January 1862 Ellen and her father traveled to Washington, where they visited the White House and laid Sherman's case before the one person to whom Ellen believed she could "appeal with confidence." The visitors ended their conference with Lincoln in high spirits. The president had praised Ellen's mate as a skilled and dedicated officer in whom he retained confidence, an opinion that dated from his visit to Cump's brigade at Fort Corcoran. In a letter to her husband at Benton Barracks, Ellen stressed that Lincoln "seemed anxious for us to know, and said that he wanted you to know, that he had entertained the highest and most generous feelings towards you, and that he still entertained them . . . [that] recent reports were unfounded [and] your abilities would soon secure promotion. . . ."[33]

Only days after Cump received this upbeat prediction, it appeared to come true. Halleck, perceiving that Sherman had done a good job with his recruits and convinced that the man had regained his old confidence and at least a portion of his self-respect, recalled him to headquarters for a strategy session. When they met in his office Halleck hauled out a map of his department, and they studied the positions occupied by the Confederates in southern Kentucky, including Sidney Johnston's enclave at Bowling Green. That once-formidable perimeter now looked considerably shorter than it had been only a few months earlier. The previous November a Union column had attacked Johnston's far left flank by crossing the Mississippi River to Belmont, Missouri, and breaking up a Confederate encampment before being forced into hasty retreat. Two months later, a small army under George Thomas had defeated near Mill Springs and Logan's Cross Roads the force that had secured Johnston's right, in the process killing General Zollicoffer. Now, asked Halleck of Sherman, where should the Union forces strike next? Sherman did not hesitate: "Naturally, in the center."[34]

Halleck nodded as Sherman drew a line through the midpoint of what remained of Johnston's line, where the Tennessee River flowed south into the heart of the western Confederacy. That, said Halleck, would be the objective of the next Union advance in his realm, and Sherman would play a major role in it. Sherman's reply, if indeed he made one, would go unrecorded. Perhaps the magnitude of the revelation drove him to silent contemplation. A return to the field meant taking on responsibilities so demanding and worrisome he might find himself again reduced to a state of abject panic. And yet Halleck would not be offering him such a position unless convinced he could handle it. Now all Sherman had to do was convince himself of the same thing.

TEN

"MY GOD! WE ARE ATTACKED!"

Sherman always gave Halleck the credit for devising the strategy that culminated in the capture of Forts Henry and Donelson, "the first real success on our side" in the war. But he was not the sole claimant to the honor. At about the same time that Halleck predicted a thrust through the heart of Sidney Johnston's realm, Ulysses Grant, then an obscure brigadier commanding a district in Halleck's department with headquarters at Cairo, Illinois, was coming to see the efficacy of such a move.

Grant had recently invaded western Kentucky in remote cooperation with Thomas's drive on Mill Springs. His two columns of volunteers, under the redoubtable Charles F. Smith and politician-general John A. McClernand, a former Illinois congressman and a personal friend of Abraham Lincoln, had spent more than a week "splashing through the mud, snow and rain" fighting the foul weather more than they did the enemy.[1]

Grant had found the operation unsatisfying, but while conducting it he had envisioned a less weather-

Gen. John A. McClernand, USA

beaten offensive south and east of Columbus, along the half-frozen rivers of upper Tennessee, one he hoped to conduct with the cooperation of the navy. Soon after

134

returning to Cairo, he laid before Halleck a plan for an advance against Forts Henry and Heiman on the Tennessee River and Fort Donelson on the Cumberland. Each of these works was strategically important as a door to the Confederate heartland, but each was also lightly held. Grant considered all three vulnerable to capture, especially if a land assault by the army could be coordinated with a gunboat attack on the rivers. Curiously—perhaps because he believed he had thought of the idea first and did not wish to entrust its execution to just anyone—Halleck turned down his subordinate's proposal. However, a resubmitted plan, one endorsed by Flag Off. Andrew Hull Foote, who would provide the naval support, won Halleck's apparently grudging approval.[2]

Even though initially he reaped no credit for it, Grant's plan fulfilled every expectation of its author. Staging out of Paducah, Kentucky, northeast of Cairo, on February 2, 1862, his eight-thousand-man expeditionary force swept down on Fort Heiman on the west side of the Tennessee, found it abandoned, then crossed the river to the larger Fort Henry. His plan called for army and navy to converge on Henry on the sixth, but a late start and an errant march delayed Grant's contingent. Attacking on his own, Foote scored so many hits on the fort that the garrison evacuated and hustled over land to more heavily defended Fort Donelson, a dozen miles to the east. Feeling cheated of a sure triumph, Grant, once he overcame delays caused by logistical and manpower problems, followed up the escapees and lay siege to their refuge on the Cumberland. On the sixteenth, after Smith's troops repulsed a desperate attempt at a breakout, Grant accepted the surrender of perhaps fifteen thousand defenders under Simon Buckner (Buckner's superior, Maj. General John B. Floyd, Joe Johnston's brother-in-law, had fled the fort to avoid the consequences should he, as a former United States cabinet member, fall into Union hands). The victory made Grant the first true Union hero of the war. The demand he had made in response to Buckner's request for terms dovetailed nicely with his initials, and he quickly became known throughout the North as "Unconditional Surrender" Grant.[3]

During Grant's advance on Donelson, Sherman had returned to field duty after an absence of three months. Considering his rehabilitation complete, Halleck on February 13 ordered him to Paducah, to assume command of Grant's former district. Arriving in that river village at the northern terminus of the railroad to Union City, Tennessee, Sherman found instructions waiting for him. "Send General Grant," Halleck ordered, "every thing that you can spare from Paducah and [neighboring] Smithland." Halleck's dispatch informed Sherman that, as a result of Fort Henry's capture, General Johnston had evacuated Bowling

Green, ending the threat he had long posed to loyal Kentuckians as well as to William T. Sherman's state of mind.[4]

The news of Johnston's retreat, and especially Fort Donelson's fall, exhilarated Sherman even as it calmed old fears. Speaking for himself and other Union commanders in the Bluegrass State, he claimed that "probably at no time during the war did we all feel so heavy a weight raised from our breasts, or so thankful for a most fruitful series of victories." Although he continued to hail Halleck as the brains behind the victory, Sherman readily recognized the enterprise, determination, tenacity, and tactical acumen that Grant had displayed in gaining victories that many observers considered unattainable except at excessive cost. Using his head as well as his fists, Grant had prevailed at a cost of one-sixth the loss he had inflicted on his opponents. Sherman was vastly impressed with the fellow West Pointer who until recently had been to him a wisp of memory, an almost faceless nonentity.[5]

During the run-up to Donelson, Sherman had taken pains to make himself known to the squat, bearded, cigar-chewing Illinoisan. He had written from Paducah that he should like "to hear from" Grant, learning his needs, wants, and intentions. In a spirit that would have been foreign to someone such as Joseph Johnston and although senior to Grant, Sherman promised to "do everything in my power to hurry forward to you reinforcements and supplies, and if I could be of service myself would gladly come, without making any question of rank with you or General Smith." Again Sherman was making known his preference for subordinate command, as long as he could serve under someone he trusted and admired.[6]

Grant appreciated the logistical support he received from Sherman, and he responded gratefully to the older man's willingness to waive rank and serve under him. Sherman further ingratiated himself with Grant after the latter unaccountably fell from grace with Halleck only weeks after his momentous victories on the Tennessee and Cumberland. Thanks to a saboteur who had access to his communications, probably a civilian telegrapher, without knowing it Grant failed to keep in touch with Halleck at St. Louis. The department commander attributed the breakdown to indifference or laxity on Grant's part. He was afraid that Grant had succumbed to the head-turning praise bestowed on him as the captor of Henry and Donelson. Because the regular telegraph link was not functioning, he sent messages to Grant via Sherman at Paducah. When this expedient failed to resolve the problem, Halleck complained to Washington of Grant's apathy, charged him with insubordination, and even accused him of having taken to drink, a habit that had forced him to resign his captain's commission in 1854. In early March, when

Gen. Charles F. Smith, USA

at last able to get in touch with Grant, Halleck effectively shelved him, forcing him to turn over his recently enlarged command (soon to be known as the Army of the Tennessee) to General Smith. Grant's senior subordinate was thereby placed in charge of a campaign—the preliminaries of which were already underway—to confront Sidney Johnston in his new refuge, Corinth, Mississippi.

From Paducah, Sherman sympathized with Grant's plight, which he judged to be unmerited, but he maintained a charitable view of Halleck. As he noted in his memoirs, "Halleck was evidently working himself into a passion, but he was too far from the seat of war to make due allowance for the actual state of facts. General Grant had done so much, that General Halleck should have been more patient." Meanwhile, Sherman kept busy providing resources, not only men and supplies but also troopships, to Halleck, Grant, and General Buell, the latter having occupied Nashville, Johnston's headquarters after evacuating Bowling Green.[7]

While at Paducah Sherman had received a pledge from Halleck that, as soon as he collected sufficient troops to be of service to Grant or Smith, he would be permitted to lead them into the field. That day came on March 10, when four newly organized brigades under Sherman—infantry, cavalry, artillery, and support arms—started down the Tennessee River in nineteen transports. Sherman was glad to be returning to the field, but

Gen. Ulysses S. Grant, USA

he had no illusion about the material at his disposal. "My division was made up of regiments perfectly new," he wrote, "nearly all having received their muskets for the first time at Paducah. None of them had ever been under fire or beheld heavy columns of an enemy bearing down on them." They would have that experience sooner than any of them, their commander included, could have anticipated.[8]

When he reached Fort Henry at the head of his unlettered command, Sherman reported to Smith, who reluctantly had taken over the force formerly assigned to Grant. He would command it for only a few weeks before being laid up by a virulent infection, the result of a boating accident, that would take his life before the end of April. Smith's savvy tactics and rock-solid demeanor would be sorely missed, but the army, and the war, would go on without him.[9]

The flotilla that Sherman became a part of at Fort Henry comprised twenty-five thousand troops and sixty-some transports. Its ultimate objective was Johnston's point of concentration in northern Mississippi, but its first mission was to sever the latter's railroad lines east of Corinth. Primary targets included that stretch of the Mobile & Ohio west of Crump's Landing on the Tennessee River and, several miles to the south, the right-of-way of the Memphis & Charleston near Burnsville. The first expedition, conducted by Brig. Gen. Lewis Wallace (the Romney, Virginia, raider) inflicted light damage on its objective before its leader, concerned about reports of large enemy force in his area of operations, retreated to Crump's Landing. The second mission, which Smith entrusted to Sherman, was defeated by a sudden deluge that raised the Tennessee River above flood stage, leaving almost every landing in the vicinity of his objective under water. When his troops finally debarked east of Burnsville late on the fourteenth of March, they floundered over waterlogged roads and rain-swollen creeks so deep that Sherman was compelled to return them to their transports and continue upriver, looking for drier ground. He found it when the ships bumped to a halt against the almost one-hundred-foot-high bluffs that lined the river at Pittsburg Landing, twenty-three miles above Corinth. Once on land, he started southward to cut the railroad he had failed to reach two days earlier, but he quickly encountered a sizable body of Rebels. The firefight that broke out convinced him that an overland movement would not succeed, and he recalled his men to Pittsburg Landing.[10]

Now he concentrated on helping later-arriving divisions under Smith find suitable camping grounds in the same vicinity. He considered the ground west of the landing expansive enough to accommodate "a hundred thousand men" and the terrain capable of "easy defense by a small command." In a matter of days the countryside for miles around was dotted with campgrounds, drill fields, artillery and wagon parks, and cavalry cantonments.[11]

Although originally limited to the fifty-two thousand troops under Smith, the area would soon be occupied by a force of approximately equal size, Buell's Army of the Ohio. Until recently, its addition had been a matter of speculation. General Halleck had been attempting for months to secure Buell's cooperation in striking toward Corinth, but the army leader had used one excuse after another to delay participating. As of March 11, however, Halleck, by Lincoln's order, had become the commander of all Union forces west of the Alleghenies. He no longer reported to McClellan, whom the president had relieved of his general-in-chief's duties so that he could concentrate on leading the Army of the Potomac. Halleck's increased authority gave him the power to compel Buell's cooperation.

Suddenly, Buell was eager to comply. He proposed, however, to join Smith's forces on the Tennessee by way of an overland march from Nashville. The link-up was to take place at Savannah, a village on the east bank of the river six miles upstream from Pittsburg Landing. Although Halleck expected him to arrive much earlier, Buell's decision to cross more than one hundred miles of rugged country inundated by rains and lacking good roads would prevent him from reaching Savannah until near the end of the first week in April.[12]

While Buell prepared to move, the forces at and near Pittsburg Landing settled into their new camps and began the waiting game. On scene by the end of March were the divisions of Sherman, Hurlbut, McClernand, Smith (now commanded by Brig. Gen. W. H. L. Wallace), and Brig. Gen. Benjamin M. Prentiss. Lew Wallace's division remained at Crump's Landing, four miles upriver. Wherever situated, the army used the time to catch up on its training, something especially important to Sherman's troops. The men underwent company, battalion, and regimental drill while their equally inexperienced officers pored over tactics manuals.

Because they would take the offensive as soon as Buell arrived, none of Smith's subordinates seriously considered shoring up his camps with field works or entrenchments. Sherman was especially opposed to fortifying; he assured nervous subordinates that the nearest Rebels were miles off, probably huddling in fear of the assault being prepared for them. Thus his own position remained open and vulnerable on all sides, from its right flank on the banks of Owl Creek—the westernmost point on Smith's line—to its left. In between sat an abandoned woodland chapel known as Shiloh Meeting House.[13]

139

After Johnston's army fell back to the Rappahannock, the Yankees probed its new position but without evident intent of bringing on a battle. They also overran the winter camps the enemy had left behind, confiscating as many rations and as much equipment as had escaped the torch and trying to understand the need for such an abrupt and precipitate withdrawal. One clue was the trees that Johnston's men had felled, painted, propped up on firing platforms facing McClellan's camps, and covered with brush to make them appear, from a distance, like cannons. Evidently the Rebels believed themselves too few to hold their position without resorting to subterfuge.

During the first week after their retirement from the Manassas-Centreville line, the Confederates remained along their river of refuge. Then, on March 16, Johnston led all units except Ewell's division and Stuart's troopers farther south to even more defensible positions below the Rapidan River. Here the army also enjoyed easier access to the defenses of Richmond as well as to those troops on the Virginia Peninsula commanded by Johnston's prewar comrade John B. Magruder and at Norfolk under Maj. Gen. Benjamin Huger.[14]

Most of Johnston's officers and men, even those who had been opposed to the retreat, admitted that their new position was a formidable one. So too did President Davis and General Lee, who visited Johnston's headquarters at Fredericksburg soon after the troops reached the Rapidan. Lee came clothed in newly-won authority, having been assigned to duty "at the seat of government under the direction of the President with the conduct of military operations in the Army of the Confederacy." Theoretically, the new position, as fixed by congressional statute, placed Johnston as well as Magruder, Huger, Holmes (who commanded the troops around Fredericksburg), and Jackson (who remained in the Valley) under Lee's supervision. In actuality, Lee's authority was limited to what his most esteemed biographer, Douglas Southall Freeman, calls "the minor, vexatious matters of detail and the counseling of commanders in charge of the smaller armies." As before, the president would consult closely with his favorite aide on matters large and small, "but in no single instance was Lee given a free hand to initiate and direct to full completion any plan of magnitude."[15]

Only hours after Davis and Lee concluded their visit and returned to Richmond, scouts in Hampton Roads reported the arrival of an ominous-looking fleet of transports and warships, the first wave of an invasion force more than one hundred thousand strong. His original plan to advance overland on Richmond having been thwarted by Johnston's fall-back, McClellan had determined to take the Confederate capital from below by placing his entire army at Fort Monroe and advancing up the Peninsula toward the capital via Yorktown, on the York River. On the twenty-fifth a worried Davis inquired of Johnston how many troops he could send to the assistance of Magruder and Huger. The Richmond authorities had yet to fix the composition and origin of the armada, but the prevalent opinion was that it came from McClellan's department.[16]

Until the force could be specifically identified, Johnston, who habitually favored concentration of forces rather than their dispersion across multiple fronts, was reluctant to commit the main body of his command to the Peninsula. Moreover, he did not consider that venue the proper point at which to confront an invasion force; he strongly recommended, instead, the transfer of his army and all other available forces to Richmond. His advice was quickly rejected; Davis ordered him to send ten thousand troops to Magruder at and near Yorktown. By March 28, however, the president was considering having Johnston withdraw his entire army in the direction of the Peninsula.[17]

By the first days of April, 1862, it had become clear to Magruder, who continued to monitor the build-up at Fort Monroe, that McClellan was on the Peninsula in force. By the fifth, the Yankees were advancing up that narrow strip of sandy earth in two columns, one heading for Yorktown, the other for Warwick Court House, on the other side of the ten-mile-wide corridor. When the news reached Richmond, Davis ordered Johnston to fall back on the capital with all of his troops except a small force to deal with a Yankee force that had been observed north of the Rappahannock. Thought to be making a diversion for McClellan, this body nevertheless demanded to be watched until its intent could be determined.

Though Johnston would have preferred to remain at Richmond, Davis sent him, soon after he reached the city, to Yorktown. There he conferred with General Magruder and inspected the three lines of defense that had been erected across the peninsula. Johnston considered these works not only incomplete but also too weak to withstand attack; moreover, he considered Yorktown vulnerable to the fire of those U.S. Navy gunboats already stationed in the York to support McClellan's advance. And yet Johnston had to admit that Magruder was making maximum use of his resources, marching his troops from one end of his line to the other and back again, making enemy observers believe his 13,500-man command was at least twice that size. Magruder's theatrics had the desired effect. Convinced that he was facing an army equal in numbers to his if not larger, McClellan halted on the outskirts of Yorktown, which he decided to bombard into submission. He settled down to siege operations, sending up from Fort Monroe dozens of heavy guns and mortars, which he placed in battery south and east of the city.[18]

Union mortar batteries outside Yorktown, Va.

While McClellan went to ground, the advance of Johnston's army arrived to occupy Yorktown and the line of defense west of it. Upon returning to Richmond in company with Generals Smith and Longstreet for a conference with Davis and his advisors, Johnston had argued against committing more troops to the Peninsula, where they would be outnumbered and subject to heavy artillery and gunboat fire. Supported vocally by Smith but not by Longstreet, who remained strangely silent throughout the meeting, Johnston once again requested a concentration of forces around Richmond—his, Magruder's, and Huger's, augmented by troops from the Deep South. He pledged that once he reached the capital, he would not sit back and allow McClellan to take the initiative. He assured Davis that "the great army thus formed, surprising that of the United States by an attack when it was expecting to besiege Richmond, would be almost certain to win; and the enemy, defeated a hundred miles from Fort Monroe, their place of refuge, could scarcely escape destruction. Such a victory would decide not only the campaign, but the war. . . ."[19]

Davis's brain trust, General Lee and Secretary of War Randolph, rejected

Johnston's plan as too risky, militarily and politically. They would not counte-nance abandoning the strategic port of Yorktown or, across the water, Norfolk with its well-equipped naval yard. (It was there that the armored warship *Virginia* had been prepared for her devastating assault on Union shipping in Hampton Roads and, on March 11, her less successful but history-making clash with the ungainly Yankee ironclad *Monitor*).

The general and the war minister had another reason for dissuading Johnston from abandoning the Peninsula. They believed that an invader must be con-fronted as close as possible to his point of debarkation; he could not be allowed to advance on and lay siege to the southern capital. The loss of Richmond, either by attack or investment, would kill the Confederacy's hopes of gaining political and diplomatic recognition around the world, especially from those European powers who might lend it military support.

By the time the conference broke up in the wee hours of the fifteenth, Davis had accepted Lee and Randolph's view and rejected Johnston's. The army com-mander and his subordinates saluted, left Davis's office, and rejoined their troops as the last of them marched through Richmond en route from the Rappahannock. Disappointed by the high-level decision that had gone against him, Johnston nev-ertheless rode proudly at the head of his smartly stepping column as crowds of civilians cheered, clapped, and waved flags in honor of its passage.[20]

Reaching the Yorktown front on the seventeenth, Johnston assimilated Magruder's garrison, assumed command of the combined force (now more than fifty thousand strong), and moved his troops into the siege lines opposite the enemy. From there he continued to barrage Davis, Lee, and Randolph with pleas for mass-ing the army around Richmond and forcing a showdown with McClellan. His supe-riors continued to resist the idea, and they had new ammunition for their objections. On April 18 Irvin McDowell, who after Manassas had been relegated to corps com-mand under McClellan but had been withheld from the army that landed at Fort Monroe, had occupied Falmouth, Virginia, across from Fredericksburg. From Richmond, the presumption was that McDowell intended to join McClellan, adding another thirty thousand or more troops to Little Mac's nearly prohibitive advantage in strength. Johnston's presence at Yorktown, effectively interposing between the enemy forces, made the junction less likely. Thus they rejected every argument the army leader put forth in favor of abandoning his present position.[21]

Through the remainder of April 1862, as spring rains inundated roads and filled the watercourses of the Peninsula, discomfiting the troops on both sides and limiting their mobility, Johnston stared down his much weightier enemy. As he wrote after the war, "we had nothing to do but to finish the works begun, between Yorktown and the head of the inundations [of the Warwick River, which crossed the Peninsula], and observe the enemy's operations. They were limited to a little skirmishing at long range, and daily cannonading." Meanwhile, McClellan's engineers, supported by fatigue parties, continued work on the fifteen batteries whose heavy guns would soon be trained on the town. Johnston was acutely aware that his opponent would be able to blast Yorktown's fieldworks into splinters in a matter of hours.[22]

Throughout this period Johnston made no further mention to Richmond of his preferred strategy; in fact, he acted as if he had come to share his superiors' view of things. In actuality, he was biding his time until events proved his idea the only one worth pursuing: "I determined to remain in the position only so long as it could be done without exposing our troops to the powerful artillery which, I doubted not, would soon be bought to bear upon them." As early as the twenty-fourth he was hinting in dispatches to Davis and Lee that he would soon be forced to pull up stakes and move in their direction. That hour came on May 1, by which time the first operational batteries had begun to shell Yorktown, albeit sporadically. The next evening, shrouded in darkness, the evacuation got under way.[23]

Johnston led his army out two northwestward-leading roads that ran parallel for much of their length before joining two miles below Virginia's colonial capital, Williamsburg. Both roads were so spongy from the recent rains that in places they barely supported the passage of supply wagons, artillery batteries, horses, and foot soldiers. Guns became mired, some hopelessly so, in the porous earth, but at least one was hauled out of the mud by a fatigue party that included Johnston himself. The general had cheerfully dismounted to help manhandle the piece onto dry ground, oblivious of the muck that soon covered him from boot to cap but appreciative of the cheers of passing troops.[24]

Despite the occasional breakdowns and the inevitable confusion such an operation generates, the evacuation proceeded so smoothly that by the morning of the third the army's vanguard was passing through Williamsburg, sixty miles from Richmond. Progress was sufficient to please the architect of the operation. It is not farfetched to think that Johnston may have been buoyed up by the image of George Brinton McClellan preparing to rain fire upon his enemy's lines only to find them abandoned. The mingled look of rage and disappointment on Little Mac's face would have been worth seeing.

In a sense, Johnston, by his eleventh-hour evacuation, was playing a cruel joke on an old friend; but he could tell himself that it was McClellan's own fault. Little

Mac should have suspected that his opponent, having retreated from well-established positions at Harpers Ferry and Manassas, would have relinquished his foothold at Yorktown without a second thought or backward glance.

On March 17, 1862, Ulysses S. Grant arrived at Savannah to reclaim his army, superseding the bedridden General Smith. The difficulties that had imperiled Grant's relations with Halleck, and which Halleck's enmity had complicated and worsened, had been straightened out. Halleck's rise to command of the entire western theater had removed any motive for persecuting Grant. Then, too, Lincoln's recent demand that he prove the charges he had leveled against his subordinate had persuaded Halleck to restore the man to field command as well as to the good graces of the government.[25]

Upon arriving, Grant expressed pleasure to have Sherman by his side. He remained impressed by the latter's willingness to forgo seniority and serve under him—a moot point now, as Grant had been promoted to major general of volunteers for his recent victories. Sherman, he saw at once, had done a good job of establishing the army at Pittsburg Landing and preparing its campsites. Over the next three weeks the two men worked closely to refine strategy and inspect the army's position. When time permitted, they swapped reminiscences of West Point and their shared experiences as soldiers and civilians in the palmy days before Fort Sumter.

Grant endorsed Sherman's decision (one that General Smith had also approved) not to throw up works and dig rifle pits along the front of his division, most of which had been posted to cover the main road to Corinth and the Owl Creek crossing of the Purdy-Hamburg Road. "We did not fortify our camps," Sherman asserted in his memoirs, "because we had no orders to do so, and because such a course would have made our raw men timid. The position was naturally strong. . . . At a later period of the war, we could have rendered this position impregnable in one night, but at this time we did not do it, and it may be it is well we did not" (in his mind, fieldworks just as often invited as discouraged an attack). His explanations aside, it would appear that Grant and his subordinates did not fortify because they did not expect to be assaulted. They did not believe that General Johnston would leave his secure position at Corinth, march twenty miles through open territory susceptible of observation, and launch a surprise attack. Besides, Buell's troops were only days away from making contact with Grant's. No right-minded opponent would strike at such a juncture.[26]

During the first days of April, Grant should have realized that such thinking was badly flawed. On the third, Rebel troops who were not supposed to be any-where in the vicinity opened fire on some of the army's pickets. On the fourth, one of Sherman's outposts was surprised and captured by Confederate cavalry; a detachment attempting to recover the position ran up against a battle line manned by infantry and supported by field guns. The confrontation ended when the Federals withdrew, unaware that they had been attacked by an advance ele-ment of Johnston's army. When the detachment's commander reported the fight to Sherman and wondered aloud if it presaged a battle, the division leader is sup-posed to have muttered: "You militia officers get scared too easily." The following day Sherman reported to Grant that "the enemy is saucy, but got the worst of it yesterday, and will not press our pickets far. . . I do not apprehend anything like an attack on our position."[27]

He had to swallow his words the next morning, April 6, 1862, when, at about five o'clock, a Union patrol discovered a body of gray-clad infantry advancing through a cotton field in front of General Prentiss's position, east of Sherman's encampment. A fight broke out that lasted for several minutes before the patrol was forced to break contact and fall back. By then a fully manned Confederate battle line was striking Prentiss's camp, routing its sleeping occupants, and shooting them down or chasing them to the rear. Some time after seven o'clock, the onslaught turned in Sherman's direction. His division became the target of the Arkansas, Mississippi, and Tennessee brigade of Brig. Gen. Patrick Ronayne Cleburne, part of the corps of Maj. Gen. William J. Hardee, supported by several brigades from the corps of Maj. Gens. Leonidas Polk and Braxton Bragg, Sherman's colleague and friend from the Third U.S. Artillery.

Moments after hearing the first shots of the day, Sherman, telescope in hand and accompanied by his staff, had galloped out to the position of his advance guard, Col. Jesse Appler's Fifty-Third Ohio Infantry, on the east side of the road from Pittsburg Landing to Corinth. For a few minutes Sherman's spyglass, survey-ing the valley in front of his camp, hit upon nothing suspicious looking, but when an Ohio soldier shouted that he should look to his right, bullets began to fly in the general's direction. Dropping the telescope, he exclaimed: "My God! We are attacked!" An instant later his orderly, Tom Holliday, who had been standing next to Sherman, toppled dead. "The shot that killed him," Sherman later told Ellen, "was meant for me." As it was, he was hit in the hand by a piece of buck-shot. Over the next several hours he would also be struck by balls that tore his hat and strap, the latter causing a painful shoulder injury.[28]

Blood dripping from his sleeve, the general mounted, galloped back to his main body, and had the division's drummers call out any men who had not already awakened to the shooting. As soon as the troops turned out—half-dressed, sleep-befogged—Sherman whipped them into lines of battle. For the next hour they exchanged shots with Cleburne's attackers, both sides taking heavy casualties. As Sherman observed in his after-action report, "the valley afforded the enemy a partial cover, but our men were so posted as to have a good fire at him as he crossed the valley and ascended the rising ground on our side."[29]

Opening of the Battle of Shiloh

For about an hour Sherman's men, supported by a couple of batteries, had to worry only about the Rebels directly in front of them, but by eight o'clock Sherman spied "masses of infantry to our left front in the woods . . . and became satisfied for the first time that the enemy designed a determined attack on our whole camp." Even as the new arrivals moved across his line of vision toward the left, additional bodies of troops in gray and butternut advanced frontally. Try as he might, Sherman could not prevent the attackers from interposing between his position and those of McClernand and Prentiss. Soon the sound of hundreds of muskets blasting away to the east told him that Prentiss's camps were being overrun. When the racket diminished some time after nine, he suspected correctly that his colleague had been

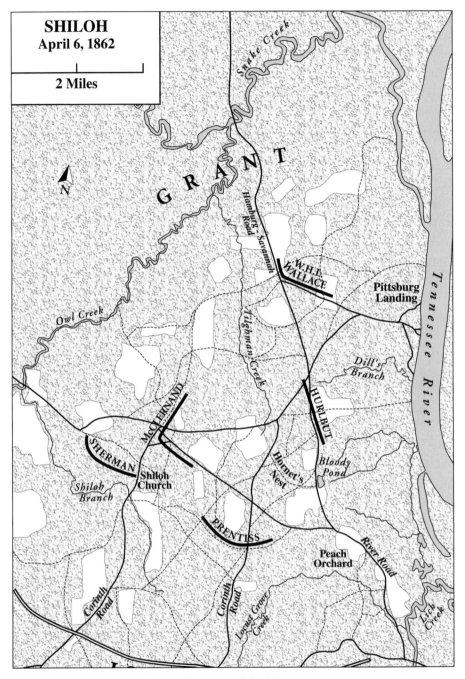

Shiloh, April 6, 1862

forced into retreat. Two hours or so later Prentiss would rally his survivors in a woods along a sunken road struck on all sides by so many spiteful missiles that it became known as the Hornet's Nest. The defenders would repulse no fewer than eight attacks before being hopelessly cornered and forced to surrender.[30]

Not long after the enemy outflanked him, Sherman saw that portions of his line were crumbling. Appler's regiment, part of Col. Jesse Hildebrand's brigade, had vacated its exposed position almost as a body and in great disorder, followed by equally hard-pressed comrades from the Fifty-Seventh Ohio. Their flight exposed the guns of Capt. Allen C. Waterhouse's Battery E, First Illinois Light Artillery. For what Sherman called "some time," the three regiments in immediate support of the battery, including the remnant of Hildebrand's command, resisted the onslaught but eventually all ran for the rear, whereupon the enemy seized three of Waterhouse's pieces. With more than a third of his division in retreat, Sherman's entire position was in danger of going under, but he considered the vicinity around Shiloh so vital that he ordered the commanders of his remaining brigades, Cols. John A. McDowell (younger brother of Irvin McDowell) and Ralph P. Buckland, to hold their ground to the last. Sherman's fourth brigade, under Col. David Stuart, had been detached to the far end of the army's line, two miles or more from the rest of the division; it too would be overwhelmed and scattered before the morning was over.[31]

By ten o'clock the Confederates had brought up artillery, which soon found the range of Sherman's left rear. When shells began landing there, imperiling his line of retreat, the general decided that it was time to shift position. At his command, McDowell and Buckland withdrew their men as far to the east as the Pudry-Hamburg Road. They fell back in tolerably good order, although a battery Sherman rounded up to assist them proved ineffectual when its captain was shot from his horse and his gunners fled, abandoning five more cannons to the Rebels.

Sherman's new position did not hold for long. At about ten-thirty, the Confederates came on with even greater force than before, forcing him to abandon the ground just occupied at the intersection of the Purdy-Hamburg Road and the road to Corinth. Under his personal direction and that of the division staff, his soldiers took up yet another position, this close upon General McClernand's right flank. The men were able not only to hold this line but to attack out of it. When the oncoming Rebels appeared to shift in McClernand's direction and the latter's line began to waver, Sherman threw McDowell's still-intact brigade at them, slowing their progress and giving McClernand time to regroup.

Granted a brief respite by the enemy's withdrawal, Sherman strengthened his new position, shoring up its flanks with what reserves he could find and telling his men to avail themselves "of every cover—trees, fallen timber, and a wooded valley to our right." He stalked back and forth along the front of the position, oblivious to flying missiles, his teeth clamped around a cigar, shouting instructions and advice. The men responded positively to the image of strength and solidity he projected in the midst of crisis—bravado that had already cost him three horses, shot from beneath him. An aide later remarked that Sherman's bearing instilled in all around him "a feeling that it was grand to be there with him." This day Sherman was his old, confident self. The crippling anxieties, the paralyzing insecurities that had plagued him when behind a desk in Louisville and on his inspection rounds at Sedalia were distant memories.[32]

Likewise impressed by Sherman's coolness and composure was Grant, who, along with his staff, visited his subordinate on the firing line some time after 10:00 A.M. The commanding general was hurting, the result of a fall from a horse that had put him on crutches, but he seemed heartened by what he observed on Sherman's front. He expressed satisfaction with the job the division commander was doing and confidence in his ability to hold his ground to the last. Grant only wished he felt as sanguine about the battle raging on the other end of the line, where the divisions of Hurlbut and W. H. L. Wallace were hard-pressed and in danger of being forced back to the banks of the Tennessee. At length, Grant and Sherman exchanged salutes and the army leader rode to a scene of greater concern.[33]

In fulfillment of his superior's expectations, despite mounting opposition Sherman held his position on McClernand's immediate right for upwards of four hours, "sometimes gaining and at other times losing ground," but determined to resist heading to the rear until he could no longer prevent it. That time came at about 4:00 P.M. By then, Hurlbut had been thrown back to the river, denying Sherman and McClernand support on that end of their line. Having been informed by Grant that Lew Wallace's division would soon arrive from Crump's Landing to shore up his right, Sherman consulted with McClernand and the two agreed to fall back, as slowly and carefully as possible, toward the Tennessee. The new position they selected, which ran roughly parallel to the Hamburg-Savannah Road, constituted the far right flank of their army's last defensive position of the day. Sherman was careful to cover the bridge over Snake Creek that Wallace would have to cross in coming down from Crump's Landing. The latter would not arrive, however, till after dark, the result of confused and time-consuming marching and countermarching over roads that led away from, rather than toward, the scene of the fighting.[34]

When falling back to the Hamburg-Savannah Road, Sherman gathered up troops who had been cut off from their commands. The prodigals helped him hold his new position, as did the timely appearance of a battery that poured a destructive fire into the flank of the Confederates assaulting not only his lines but also those of McClernand. Sherman was pleased to find that in his new location his men were protected by a cleared field two hundred yards or more wide, which discouraged the enemy from pressing forward. Thus relatively secure, "I . . . contented myself with keeping the enemy's infantry at that distance during the rest of the day."[35]

When afternoon began to merge into evening and the enemy's assault finally lost momentum, the Army of the Tennessee held onto its position along the Tennessee by its fingertips. Each of its divisions except Lew Wallace's had been battered and broken, and one of them, Prentiss's, had ceased to exist. Officers and men were exhausted and stressed from hours of exposure to musketry and shelling that in many cases had reduced regiments to battalion or even company size. Despite the gloomy situation, when the Rebels broke contact and pulled back under gathering darkness, Grant grew confident that the battle had not been lost and was going to be won. During the night, which was sodden with rain, he made the rounds of his senior subordinates. To Sherman, as to the others, he declared that come morning they would attack all along the line and recover the ground that had been relinquished. It is not known whether everyone he gave this pep talk to believed it, but Sherman did. Just as his actions this day had inspired confidence in many of those who beheld them, so too did Grant inspire Sherman. If Grant believed the army was on the verge of victory though hard-pressed all day and forced into successive retreats, Sherman believed so too.

In fact, Grant had a firm basis for his prediction. Not only had Lew Wallace found his way to the battlefield at last, so had the advance echelon of Buell's army, which had begun crossing the Tennessee in time to bolster Grant's left flank as the fighting neared its close. The better part of two divisions of the Army of the Ohio would be on Grant's side of the river before sunrise on the seventh. The newcomers would spearhead the counteroffensive Grant had in mind, accompanied by the more intact and less demoralized elements of his own army.

Grant was yet unaware of another event of incalculable value to his strategy for victory. At the height of the fighting just concluded, General Johnston, while in the saddle directing his army's assault on the Union left, had stopped with his leg a rifle ball—quite possibly, an errant round from one of his own units. Although the wound appeared so slight that its victim did not seek medical attention, an artery had been severed and Johnston bled to death on the field. His second in command, Pierre Beauregard, was not as confident of success as his late superior; it was he who, upon the approach of evening, had suspended the attack on Grant's compressed position at the river, believing that in the morning he could finish off his adversary before Buell arrived to reinforce him.[36]

Grant proved to be a much better judge of what was possible on the seventh. At about 7:00 A.M., with Buell's men in the advance and Lew Wallace's division bolstering their right, Grant's battle-scarred troops—rookies who had become veterans in a matter of a few hellish hours—attacked out of their lodgment along the river and headed back toward the camps they had abandoned twenty-four hours earlier. During the night the enemy had retired to the south side of the Purdy-Hamburg Road but had failed to secure his line with fieldworks. The armies of Grant and Buell met them on the open ground and began to drive them back. Crossing the deep and broad ravine known as Tilghman Branch, Sherman's, McClernand's, Hurlbut's, and Lew Wallace's divisions swept forward in a shared spirit of evening the score.

Progress was particularly evident on Sherman's front. Aided by the heavy, well-directed fire of a battery of 24-pounder cannons that the usually irreligious brigadier claimed to have found "by almost Providential decree" and closely supported by Brig. Gen. Lovell H. Rosseau's brigade of Buell's army, by 4:00 P.M., as Sherman proudly observed, "we stood upon the ground of our original front line and the enemy was in full retreat. I directed my several brigades to resume at once their original camps." Soon afterward, the Confederates on all portions of the field were in full withdrawal toward the Mississippi line.[37]

The fighting this day had validated some cherished beliefs and confounded others. Grant had been right to believe that if he refused to give up the fight he could seize the initiative and turn the battle around. Beauregard had been wrong to suppose that time remained to finish on Monday the job of destroying the Army of the Tennessee nearly complete by late on Sunday. For his part, Sherman had been both wrong and right—wrong in believing that no Rebel would dare surprise the mighty host at Pittsburgh Landing, and right to believe that if anyone could transform near-defeat into decisive victory, that man was Ulysses S. Grant.

ELEVEN
RECUPERATION AND REDEMPTION

Once he recovered from the shock of finding the Confederates gone from his front, McClellan started out after them, but only after deliberating for several hours. When it finally began, the pursuit from Yorktown was more lukewarm than hot. McClellan's cavalry, under Brig. Gen. George Stoneman, along with four artillery batteries, was sent ahead of the rest of the column assigned to the mission, which consisted of one division each from the Third and Fourth Corps. While these forces sought to overtake the fugitives by land, another body of foot soldiers would ride transports up the York and Pamunkey Rivers, disembarking at West Point and moving inland in hopes of cutting off the enemy's retreat.

Even had the weather cooperated, it is not likely that the Army of Northern Virginia would have reached its destination without taking a few knocks, at least from Stoneman's horsemen. The recent rains, however, had so mistreated the roads that the army had no hope of clearing the Peninsula before the enemy overtook it. Every step of the way to Williamsburg, the army bogged down in the deep and viscid mud. Johnston came to see that his rear guard would have to turn about and give battle if the main body was to make its escape. He assigned to the task not only Stuart's troopers but the infantry division of "Pete" Longstreet, a subordinate Johnston had come to think of as a strong right arm, much as his successor would some day.[1]

At about noon on May 4, 1862, Stoneman finally overhauled the Confederate column and sparred briskly with his primary adversary, Stuart. Despite being roughly handled, Jeb held back the Yankees until Longstreet could occupy defenses south of Williamsburg that General Magruder's engineers had laid out months before. The next day, the infantry in Stoneman's rear reached the scene, and Longstreet took them on. The result was an intense clash under a steady rain that generated so much noise that a worried Johnston, who had left Williamsburg with the main body, returned there with D. H. Hill's division, which he deployed on Longstreet's left. The additions helped stem a blue tide that had threatened to inundate Longstreet's position. Despite losing half of Jubal Early's brigade in an unsuccessful assault against a battery that had been shelling a key fortification on Longstreet's line, the defenders emerged victorious from this encounter, which, despite its occasional severity, Johnston labeled an "action" rather than a battle.[2]

Thanks to the stout fighting of the rear guard, Johnston's army continued on to Richmond, its progress slowed only by the mud, not by the enemy. Not even the flanking force that McClellan had sent by water brought it to bay. On the seventh, as the army passed Barhamsville, a Yankee column that had sailed up the York to its confluence with the Pamunkey moved inland from Eltham's Landing, intent on bringing the Rebels to heel. Short of its objective, it was intercepted, halted, and thrown back by two of General Smith's brigades, one commanded by Wade Hampton, the other by a young brigadier whom Johnston would come to regard as a loyal disciple and then as a Judas, John Bell Hood.[3]

Spared from further pursuit, the retreaters shuffled, trotted, and rumbled up the Peninsula in two columns, Smith's and Magruder's divisions by way of New Kent Court House, Longstreet's and Hill's via Long Bridge on the Chickahominy River, a brackish stream that flowed south by southeast across the Peninsula. While the army caught its breath near Baltimore Cross Roads, Johnston determined to move to the north bank, placing another significant barrier between him and his slow-moving enemy. The move would help relieve his concern for the safety of his flanks, a concern triggered by the recent news that both of the rivers that bordered the Peninsula were in McClellan's possession. By now, too, it was known that—as Davis and Lee had anticipated—Norfolk had fallen in the aftermath of Yorktown's evacuation. Before the city's defenders fled, they scuttled the once-mighty *Virginia* to prevent her from falling into the hands of the Union navy. Taking advantage of a lack of opposition, on May 15 the *Monitor* and several other gunboats ran up the James River and attacked the batteries at Drewry's Bluff, on the doorstep to the Confederate capital.

Although the attack was repulsed, that same day Johnston's army crossed the Chickahominy and hastened on to its safe haven, the intricate, well-designed fortifications that encircled Richmond. The troops took position in advance of the outer line of works, about three miles from the city proper. Johnston placed Hill's division in the center of this line, astride the road from Williamsburg, Longstreet on the right, covering the River Road, and Magruder on the left, along the Nine Mile Road. Smith's corps took up a position in rear of Hill's left flank and Magruder's right.

These dispositions complete, Johnston conferred with his superiors to determine how to confront McClellan when the latter finally arrived. The alternatives appeared equally grim: attack head-on with about half the manpower at his opponent's disposal or permit Little Mac to mount a siege that Richmond could not possibly survive. In the end, the first option was deemed preferable, although Davis and Lee steadfastly refused to consider (even to acknowledge) Johnston's repeated urging that all available forces be concentrated at Richmond and thrown against the enemy.[4]

By the last week in May, McClellan's army, having crawled to within five miles of the capital, appeared poised for the kill. The Union leader, already inundated with manpower, would soon have even more at his command. On the seventeenth of May McDowell's thirty-five-thousand-man corps at Falmouth had received the go-ahead to join the Army of the Potomac. Johnston believed, and his superiors agreed, that he had to strike before the junction took place. Fortunately, any attack would exploit McClellan's faulty logistics. The Army of the Potomac was straddling the high-banked Chickahominy, three of its five corps on the north side, the other two on the south, their positions connected by a couple of rickety-looking bridges.

Johnston's logical objective was the body on the north bank, with which McDowell planned to link via overland march. An attack in that sector was a risky proposition, especially for a commander who felt much more comfortable on the defensive, but at least Johnston would not have to take on McClellan's entire force. In fact, he would have to defeat even fewer troops than he imagined, for he believed that only the Fourth Corps, commanded by E. D. Keyes (upon whose cot a weary and heartsick William T. Sherman had thrown himself the day after the debacle at Bull Run), was on the south side. Until recently Samuel P. Heintzelman's Third Corps had been on the north bank; Johnston believed it still was.[5]

Almost at the eleventh hour, Johnston revamped his battle plan to accommodate a dramatically altered situation. In response to a plea for help from Richmond, Stonewall Jackson—whose Army of the Shenandoah remained a part of Johnston's department although it had long received its orders from General Lee—resumed the campaign of threat, bluff, diversion, attack, and withdrawal that he had been engaged in, at the expense of overmatched Union leaders in the Valley, since March. Now, at the head of a slightly enlarged force, Stonewall launched a powerful diversion in Johnston's behalf, routing the garrison at Front Royal, then advancing against occupied Winchester. On the twenty-fourth, he attacked that communications hub and after heavy fighting sent its defenders streaming across the Potomac in utter rout.

Jackson's masterful offensive generated so much publicity throughout the country and so much concern in Washington that on the twenty-eighth President Lincoln ordered McDowell to halt his movement to the Peninsula, turn right, enter the Valley, and force Stonewall to cease and desist. Early that day, as Johnston was fine-tuning his strike north of the Chickahominy, Stuart's scouts reported McDowell's changed course.[6]

Presumably with a sigh of relief, the army leader immediately shifted attention to the smaller enemy force south of the river, aware that if he could drive it away the emotionally delicate McClellan might overreact, panic, perhaps even retreat. Johnston continued to believe that things were looking up even after a May 30 reconnaissance by Hill revealed that Heintzelman's troops had joined Keyes's in the projected area of attack, which was defined by a prominent stand of trees, Seven Pines, and a depot on the nearby Richmond & York River Railroad, Fair Oaks Station. Johnston's hopes of a successful assault rose when a heavy rain, accompanied by lightning strikes fatal to soldiers in both armies, fell throughout that day, raising the river and diminishing the possibility that reinforcements would reach the forces Johnston planned to strike.[7]

In the predawn darkness of May 31, 1862, a dry but chilly and overcast day, Johnston began to put into motion one of only two full-scale assaults he would ever execute. It called for simultaneous advances by three widely spaced columns: from the northwest by Longstreet's division on the Nine Mile Road, from the west by D. H. Hill on the Williamsburg Road, and from the southwest via the Charles City Road by the division of Benjamin Huger, which had just reached Richmond from Norfolk and Petersburg. Chase Whiting's division would also occupy the Nine Mile Road at Old Tavern, ready to assist Longstreet or meet any Union counterattack. The divisions of Magruder and A. P. Hill shared the unenviable mission of making a diversionary attack on the Yankees on the north bank.[8]

Johnston's battle plan was well conceived and well crafted. But it called for a complex series of interconnected movements, each predicated on the successful completion of its predecessor. D. H. Hill was to attack first; only when his men opened the battle was Longstreet to move out. Hill, however, was to withhold his advance until he received word that Huger had got into his assigned position on the Charles City Road, which lay well to the south and east of Huger's pre-battle position. These were difficult movements under any circumstances but

Gen. Benjamin F. Huger, CSA

especially for an army most of whose men had never fought a battle. The tactics involved would also prove to be beyond the ability of Johnston's staff to coordinate. Johnston further complicated matters by failing to acquaint General Huger with important details of the plan. Later the South Carolinian would claim it had not been made clear to him that Johnston actually intended to attack Keyes and Heintzelman.[9]

The biggest impediment to success turned out to be James Longstreet, who failed to understand what Johnston expected of him. This may also have been Johnston's fault. Although he issued written orders to every other senior subordinate (including, presumably, Huger), he gave oral instructions to Longstreet. Either they were garbled or Longstreet simply failed to heed them, for when the attack began early on the thirty-first he precipitated a chain of errors that virtually doomed the operation.

Instead of advancing on the road assigned him, in morning darkness Longstreet countermarched his division south to the Williamsburg Road, in the process delaying Whiting's movement. Longstreet's mistake—the exact cause of which has never been determined—went unnoticed by Johnston for some hours, even though the army leader had established his field headquarters on the Nine Mile Road. When Johnston finally sent staff officers to locate the subordinate he trusted so implicitly, he could not be found.

Longstreet did not get in touch with his superior until 4:00 P.M. By then the division leader had not only thoroughly confused D. H. Hill, who could not guess why the attack had been delayed, but had blocked Huger's division as it tried to move into position on the Charles City Road. Huger reached that highway first, but when Longstreet caught up with him he insisted that his own division precede Huger's. Huger was forced to stand idly by until Longstreet's men filed onto the road and took the advance. Apparently Longstreet gained Huger's assent to this major alteration in the battle plan by falsely claiming seniority over him.

The upshot of Longstreet's misadventure was that the attack did not commence until some time after 1:00 P.M., when Hill, tired of waiting for the signal to go ahead, advanced independently of his fellow commanders. He struck Keyes's line at Seven Pines, the point where the Nine Mile Road connected with the Williamsburg Road. Smashing into the most exposed Union division, he slowly enveloped its position. The outpositioned Yankees resisted stubbornly, but after a two-hour struggle broke for the rear. In gaining this success, however, Hill suffered severely, one of his regiments losing 60 percent of its strength to casualties.[10]

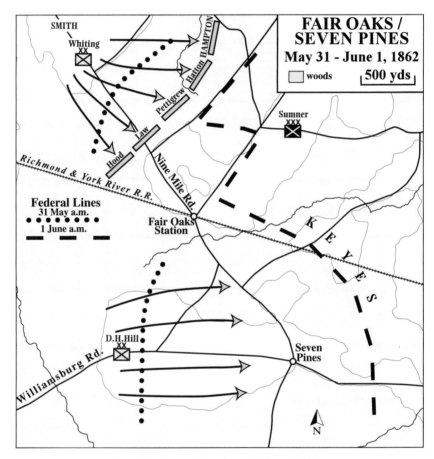

Fair Oaks/Seven Pines, May 31-June 1, 1862

The flight of Keyes's most exposed division placed his entire line in peril, but reinforcements from Heintzelman at least temporarily stabilized it. Heartened by the timely support, Keyes attempted to take the offensive but his attack was thrown back, and both sides withdrew to regroup. Then, shortly before 4:00 P.M., new troops from both armies reached the field. Whiting's division, ordered into action by Johnston, came down the Nine Mile Road to Fair Oaks Station, while McClellan's Second Corps, under Edwin V. Sumner, Joe Johnston's commander in the First United States Cavalry, began to cross the swaying bridges. It reached the field of battle just in time to prevent Whiting from overrunning Keyes's again-tenuous position. After some of the most desperate grappling of the war to this time, Whiting's men were driven away and the Fourth Corps' line was saved. When the principal fighting died out, a little after 6:00 P.M., Johnston's plans lay in ruins, thanks largely to Longstreet, whose failure to adhere to orders had kept seven of the thirteen brigades assigned to Johnston's offensive out of the fighting.[11]

Throughout the chaotic battle, Joseph Johnston had made little effort to influence execution of his battle plan. For most of the day he remained well to the rear, fretting that the fight was not progressing as he had intended but powerless to right things. He failed to contact Longstreet for hours after the latter began his errant advance, and when he did, he neglected to ensure that Old Pete rectified his mistakes. Strangely, he would never censure Longstreet for his sins of omission and commission, not even in his postwar memoirs. Moreover, he would let stand the absurd claim Longstreet made in his after-action report, that Huger was personally and solely to blame for the foul-up on the Williamsburg Road. That charge effectively ended the South Carolinian's career with the Army of Northern Virginia.

Johnston, after remaining too long and too far from the point where earlier in the day his leadership might have made a difference, made the mistake of riding through early evening darkness to the sector where Whiting's men has regrouped, having been repulsed by Sumner's late-arriving corps. Believing that the fighting would be renewed the next day and confident that ultimate success was achievable, Johnston was trying to smooth the serried ranks of Whiting's command when a rifle ball slammed into his right shoulder. Although the impact sent him reeling, he refused to go to the rear for medical attention until certain that his troops were in shape to renew the attack come morning. As he rode forward once again, shells came in over a stand of trees toward which he was riding. When a member of his staff was seen to flinch at the sound, the wounded general remarked heartily enough: "Colonel, there is no use of dodging; when you hear them they have passed."[12]

Johnston himself failed to hear the next round, which exploded in front of him, showering him and his staff with shell fragments. One penetrated his chest, fracturing ribs and knocking him unconscious to the ground. His alarmed aides rushed to his side, lifted him on their shoulders, and carried him a quarter of a mile to the rear, where a stretcher was hastily sent for. Before it arrived, the general regained consciousness and seemed to take in everything that had happened. His staff tried to keep him still and quiet, but Johnston was visibly agitated that his sword and sidearms had not made the move with him. Unconcerned about his own condition, he kept pleading for someone to fetch them. The sword, the one his father had carried throughout the Revolution, was more precious to him than his own life: "I would not lose it for ten thousand dollars. Will not some one please go back and get it . . . ?"[13]

Only after an enlisted man returned to the spot where the general had fallen, retrieved the cherished heirloom, and brought it to him, did Johnston consent to be carried from the field of battle.

Like the Confederates after Manassas and the Federals following the evacuation of Yorktown, Grant's army was unprepared to pursue when Beauregard broke off the battle and retreated. Not until the morning of April 8, 1862, did the victors of Shiloh set out to follow, if not to overtake, their enemy. Sherman took on the mission at the head of two brigades of "fatigued troops" and a small body of cavalry. The compact force trooped down the road to Corinth, passing field hospitals crammed with the dead, the dying, and the wounded Beauregard had been forced to leave behind. En route, Sherman was joined by Brig. Gen. Thomas J. Wood's infantry division of Buell's army. When the combined force reached a fork in the road, Sherman sent Wood down the left-hand road while he himself proceeded down the more westerly trail.

Sherman may have regretted splitting his force, for about a half-mile beyond the fork he passed through a woods and stumbled upon a still-occupied encampment. A phalanx of horsemen—part of Beauregard's rear guard under the already celebrated Col. Nathan Bedford Forrest—poured out of the camp and charged the new arrivals. The unexpected assault broke the formation of Sherman's advance regiment, the Seventy-Seventh Ohio, as well as that of the Fourth Illinois Cavalry, which had been supporting the Ohioans.

As foot soldiers and horsemen raced to the rear, Sherman blocked the road with the balance of his command. Upon hitting this barrier, Forrest's men recoiled and fell back in some confusion, having suffered several casualties including the severe wounding of their leader. At Sherman's order, his troopers charged in turn, hastening the suddenly demoralized Confederates down the road and into the distance.

Discovering the enemy gone and the roads leading south "very bad, and . . . strewed with abandoned wagons, ambulances, and limber-boxes," Sherman called off the pursuit. After tending to his wounded, burying the dead of both sides, collecting and interrogating his prisoners, and burning the captured camp, he started back to his old bailiwick along Owl Creek. His withdrawal effectively ended the Shiloh campaign.[14]

At first that campaign was considered, at least in Union circles, an unalloyed triumph, a feat of arms creditable to the officers and men who had fought it and the generals who had directed them. Within weeks, however, Northern newspapers began to carry the eyewitness accounts of soldiers and reporters who described the fight as a desperate, chaotic struggle from first to last. When it became known that Johnston's attack had taken the army by surprise, and especially after casualty figures began to be reported—more than thirteen thousand Union soldiers had been killed, wounded, or captured (early accounts had the count even higher)—the high command came in for some of the harshest criticism ever leveled at an American army by editors and politicians. Grant became a target of the most flagrant abuse. Rumors spread that the man who had lost his commission to drink had returned to old habits. It was said that he had been stupidly drunk before the battle (why he had fallen from his horse), drunk throughout the two days of fighting, and when the fight ended too drunk to mount a pursuit worthy of the name.

Sherman, who could not tolerate the attacks of journalists, was incensed that his superior and friend should be treated so viciously and unfairly. "The hue and cry against Grant about surprise," he informed his father-in-law in a letter home, "is wrong. . . . It is outrageous for the cowardly newsmongers thus to defame men whose lives are exposed." With his own participation fresh in mind, he added: "The real truth is, the private soldiers in battle leave their ranks, run away and then raise these false issues. The political leaders dare not lay the blame where it belongs."[15]

Sherman refused to confine his denunciations of Grant's critics to his personal correspondence. A few weeks after the battle he engaged in a heated war of words with Lt. Gov. Benjamin Stanton of Ohio, who, in reaction to the critical comments of soldiers from his state, had caused to be published what Sherman called "a most abusive article about General Grant and his subordinate generals." In actuality, Stanton criticized only two officers, Grant and Prentiss. However, although he himself escaped censure, Sherman felt impelled to defend his defamed superior and a colleague who had fought to the last ounce of resistance and was now in a Confederate prison camp. His caustic reply to Stanton's charges was published two months after Shiloh, ironically in the *Cincinnati Commercial*, one of the newspapers that loudly and often had labeled Sherman insane. Stanton responded in a letter printed in a subsequent issue of the paper, and Sherman, determined to get in the last word, returned fire yet again.[16]

Sherman's choice of weapons in his fight with Stanton—newspaper publicity—seems strange given his disdain of the Fourth Estate. He continued to regard journalists as "the most contemptible race of men that exist, cowardly, cringing, hanging around, gathering their material out of the most polluted sources." When he wrote Ellen to assure her that he had safely passed through the "big battle where they Shot real bullets," he boasted that reporters "keep shy of me as I have said the first one I catch I will hang as a Spy. I now have the lawful right to have a Court martial, and if I catch one of these Cincinnati Newspapers in my camp I will have a court and they will do just as I tell them."[17]

Sherman's attitude was not modified by the generally favorable commentary his performance at Shiloh received in the press. His coolheaded generalship under great and constant pressure won especial praise. Even those reporters who had called for his ouster in the wake of his misadventures in Kentucky and Missouri now considered him one of the few high-ranking heroes in the army. Perhaps typical was the account of Whitelaw Reid, the rising young star of the staff of the *Cincinnati Gazette*, who pictured Sherman "dashing along the line, encouraging them [his troops] everywhere by his presence, and exposing his own life with the same freedom with which he demanded their offer of theirs." When his division was outflanked and nearly surrounded, instead of giving way to the prevailing panic, Sherman showed himself "indefatigable in collecting and reorganizing his men. . . . Whatever may be his faults or neglects, none can accuse him of a lack of gallantry and energy when the attack was made on his raw division that memorable Sunday morning."[18]

Commentary such as this went far to erase the stigma of the insanity charge that had dogged Sherman for so long. As he remarked to Ellen with relief but also with a trace of bitterness, "So at last I Stand redeemed from the vile slanders" of his tormentors, one of the most prominent of whom had been Whitelaw Reid. John Sherman agreed, writing his brother from Washington that "all the absurd stories of the past were discredited by Shiloh."[19]

Sherman's military superiors echoed the verdict of the press. Grant thanked him warmly for the tenacity he had displayed in meeting the opening attack, which had kept the right wing from breaking at a time when it would have been disastrous to the army as a whole. On April 13 Halleck wrote Lincoln's new secretary of war, Edwin McMasters Stanton, that "it is the unanimous opinion here that Brig. Gen. W. T. Sherman saved the fortune of the day on the 6th instant, and contributed largely to the glorious victory on the 7th." Halleck joined Grant in recommending that Sherman be rewarded with a promotion to major general of volunteers. Stanton endorsed the recommendation and Abraham Lincoln gratified political interests, including Thomas Ewing, John Sherman, and other members of Ohio's congressional delegation, by making the appointment, which was dated May 1, 1862.[20]

Although quietly pleased by his newly won celebrity and pending elevation, Sherman, still encamped on the field of victory, turned to the mundane task of reorganizing his command, which remained in some disorder days after the battle. He consolidated his four brigades into three, only one of which (McDowell's) retained its former commander. The other two went to newcomers, one a prominent politician, the other a proven soldier: Brig. Gen. James W. Denver, a former governor of the Colorado Territory (his name adorned the territory's largest city) and Colonel Morgan L. Smith, who on April 7 had performed with high ability under Lew Wallace.[21]

Sherman expected that in a matter of days he would lead his leaner, battle-tested command to Corinth to finish the job of destroying the Army of Mississippi that had begun on the second day at Shiloh. He expected, too, that as senior general officer in West Tennessee Grant would supervise the effort at the head of Buell's army as well as his own. Sherman was disabused of this notion on April 11, when Halleck arrived at Pittsburg Landing by steamboat from St. Louis and announced that he was taking command of the forthcoming movement. He would personally direct not only Grant's and Buell's commands but also the smaller army of Maj. Gen. John Pope, which in March had sailed down the Mississippi from central Missouri to attack and capture Rebel defenses at New Madrid and Island No. 10. Called to Tennessee, Pope's command gave Halleck a force that exceeded one hundred thousand officers and men.

Halleck's coming appeared a vote of no confidence in Grant, whom the departmental commander had failed to defend against the recent public criticism of his actions at Shiloh. That impression was strengthened when Halleck issued orders dividing his rather unwieldy multitude into four segments. He assigned its left wing to Pope, its right wing to George Thomas (who had commanded a division in Buell's army not present at Shiloh), its center element to Buell, and its reserve to McClernand. Sherman might have reflected on the assignment of Thomas, and especially McClernand, with some resentment. Like Buell and Pope, both were major generals, and although recently appointed, they were senior to Sherman.

Thomas, however, had been Sherman's junior when both were brigadiers, and McClernand lacked a professional military background. Sherman did not begrudge the ascendancy of Thomas, who remained his close friend. But although he had fought alongside McClernand in the recent battle and believed the man had comported himself ably enough under the circumstances, Sherman turned a jaundiced eye on any political general, especially one who appeared to have received his stars through wire pulling and influence peddling.[22]

However he may have felt about his own status, Sherman was distressed to discover that as a result of the army's reshuffling, Grant appeared to have been shelved. Officially he was second in command to Halleck, but it was an anomalous position, without authority. Throughout Halleck's movement on Corinth, which began on May 2, he issued orders directly to the army's wings and reserve without going through Grant and, in many cases, without notifying him. After more than a week of such treatment, Grant, who believed he was being penalized for the unfavorable publicity Halleck's department had received after Shiloh, complained to his superior that "my position differs but little from that of one in arrest." He asked for quick restoration of his former authority, or to be relieved from duty. Halleck did not answer him directly but denied he was punishing Grant for anything he had done or failed to do.[23]

Grant's unhappiness mounted as the movement to Corinth continued at the feeble pace with which it had begun. Corinth was only twenty miles from Pittsburg Landing, but with the overly cautious Halleck at the helm it took the Federals three weeks to reach their destination, mainly because at almost every stopping point Halleck had them entrench as if Beauregard's people were lurking behind every tree. When the command finally drew within striking distance of Corinth, it found the place empty. Beauregard, fearfully outnumbered even after assimilating a small army out of Arkansas under Maj. Gen. Earl Van Dorn, had slipped away to regroup in the vicinity of Tupelo. An embarrassed Halleck staged a limited pursuit but called it off on June 11, permitting to escape a quarry he had not truly wished to bring to bay.[24]

By the time the army occupied Corinth and began to strengthen the local defenses in response to their commander's continuing insecurity, Grant had had enough. In letters to his wife, Julia, he stated that he would soon take leave of the army, the implication being that he would never return to it. He did not share his intentions with Sherman, but the latter learned of it through an unimpeachable source. By early June 1862 Sherman had been ordered, at the head of his own division and General Hurlbut's, to the rail depot of Chewalla, fourteen miles northwest of Corinth. The combined force was to salvage what remained of some rolling stock that Beauregard had ordered destroyed when beginning his march to Tupelo.

The arduous and prosaic mission was one of many moves that Halleck made in the aftermath of the Corinth campaign that displeased Sherman. As he wrote in his memoirs, "The army had no sooner settled down at Corinth before it was scattered: General Pope was called to the East [to command the so-called Army of Virginia, which was to cooperate with McClellan's command], and his army distributed among the others; General Thomas was relieved from command of the right wing, and reassigned to his division in the Army of the Ohio; and that whole army under General Buell was turned east along the Memphis & Charleston [Rail]road, to march for Chattanooga. McClernand's 'reserve' was turned west to Bolivar and Memphis. General Halleck took post himself at Corinth. . . ."[25]

For all his questionable dispositions, Halleck as a military mind retained a high place in Sherman's estimation. As he wrote his father-in-law, the departmental commander (whose nickname in the prewar army had been "Old Brains") was "as competent a theorist as we have—naturally of good strong mind—a head as strongly marked as [Daniel] Websters." Halleck also remained his friend; thus, a few days before leaving Corinth for Chewalla, Sherman stopped at army headquarters, where he found the general in an expansive mood. In the course of their chat Halleck mentioned that he had approved Grant's petition for a thirty days' leave. Sherman, who was aware of Grant's discontent, believed he knew what was behind the request.[26]

Upon leaving headquarters, Sherman rode to Grant's camp north of Corinth. He found his friend only hours away from leaving. Grant confirmed his visitor's suspicions, explaining that "I am in the way here. I have stood it as long as I can, and I can endure it no longer." He gave Sherman the impression that he was referring not only to the criticism of his leadership at Shiloh but to the scurrilous charge that he had been drunk throughout the fight.[27]

When Grant mentioned that he was going home to his family in Missouri, a decision that had a quality of permanence to it, Sherman begged him not to leave, "illustrating his case by my own." He related in some detail his trials and tribulations in Kentucky, explaining how his self-confidence had been worn away by the burden of command and his own overactive imagination, and how his reputation had been almost destroyed by accusations of mental instability. He might have quit the field at that point—indeed, he had nearly done so, convinced that he could be of no further use to the army. Instead, through the intervention of family, friends, and sympathetic superiors, he had stayed on with the result that he was now in "high feather" thanks to a single battle that "had given me new life." The same could happen to Grant: "I argued with him that, if he went away, events would go right along, and he would be left out; whereas, if he remained, some happy accident might restore him to favor and his true place."[28]

Sherman's host appreciated the advice and apparently saw merit in it. After some thought, Grant admitted that he might be acting too hastily, motivated by his own interests instead of those of the army. He agreed to remain, at least for a time, and he promised not to leave without speaking to Sherman first. Satisfied with the response, Sherman shook hands with his friend, saluted, and started on his mission to Chewalla. A few days later, he received a letter from Grant stating that he had reconsidered his course and would stay on with the army.

The episode cemented the Grant-Sherman relationship in a way that nothing either man did on the battlefield could have. In later years, when asked about the nature of that relationship, Sherman would reply, half in jest and half seriously: "He stood by me when I was crazy and I stood by him when he was drunk, and now, sir, we stand by each other always."[29]

When borne by ambulance to the rear at Seven Pines, Johnston, who remained conscious throughout the trip, encountered President Davis and General Lee, who had journeyed from the capital to monitor the progress of the battle. The president dismounted, offered Johnston his hand, and asked if there was anything he could do for him. The victim feebly shook his head and remarked that he did not know the extent of his injuries. In his memoirs Johnston admits that despite their mutual antipathy, Davis showed "great concern, as he continued to do until I was out of danger." Moved by the apparent seriousness of the general's condition, the president wrote his wife that "the poor fellow bore his suffering most heroically."[30]

Johnston was conveyed to a house in the capital that had been turned into a general hospital. There his wounds were treated and he slept through the night under the influence of opiates, his worried staff standing watch outside his room. The next day the patient was removed to a quiet neighborhood in the southeastern section of the capital. He was put to bed at the Crenshaw home on Church Hill, adjacent to Richmond's oldest house of worship, St. John's Episcopal. Lydia joined him there to serve as his principal nurse.[31]

His recuperation progressed slowly. The shoulder wound was not serious, but the shell fragment that had broken his ribs left him victimized by recurrent attacks of pleurisy. As he convalesced, he kept abreast of the war news. He learned to his dismay that the attack he had planned for June 1 and which he had entrusted to General Smith had gone awry and that Davis had removed Johnston's senior subordinate from command. Robert E. Lee was put in Smith's place, and under him the army returned glumly to its former positions outside the capital.

Johnston endorsed Lee's ascendancy, mainly because the man enjoyed Davis's unwavering confidence. "Now they have in my place one who does possess it," Johnston told a well-wisher who had expressed regret over the change in command, "and who could accomplish what I never could have—the concentration of our armies for the defence [sic] of the capital of the Confederacy." Even so, Johnston blamed Davis for waiting too long to order the succession: "If, on my being unhorsed May 31st, he had put Lee in command . . . the battle would have been continued with all the chances in our favor."[32]

To an extent, at least, Johnston's prediction that Lee would command a more concentrated force came true. The armies remained relatively quiescent for a month after the battle along the Chickahominy while Lee took hold of his new command and devised a way to drive McClellan from the gates of the capital. When fighting resumed late in June, Stonewall Jackson was on the verge of joining the Army of Northern Virginia, his spectacularly successful Valley campaign at a close. With his newly added strength, on the twenty-sixth Lee attacked the far right of McClellan's position, a Union corps isolated on the north side of the Chickahominy. Although this command withstood the blow, McClellan withdrew his entire army a considerable distance to the southeast before the fighting ended.

Psychologically bruised by Lee's aggressiveness and agility, the Union leader continued his retreat over the next six days despite gaining the tactical advantage in most of the five battles that followed. By the first day of July, his army was huddling along the James River near Harrison's Landing, almost twenty miles from the city it had confidently expected to take by storm or siege. There it would remain, posing no further threat to Richmond, until withdrawn to Alexandria by water in mid-August.[33]

Although gratified to learn of the success achieved by the army he continued to think of as his own, Johnston wondered if he would regain command once recovered from his injuries. The newspapers told him that Lee was attracting praise bordering on hero worship. Johnston's West Point classmate had been hailed as a godsend to the Confederate cause and the savior of his nation, encomiums that had never been bestowed on his predecessor. Under the circumstances, only the most confirmed stoic would have failed to succumb to resentment and jealousy. Joseph Johnston had not displayed such impassiveness since, at age ten, he lay silent and uncomplaining on a doctor's table, a bone protruding from his leg.

By mid-June, although still affected by his wounds, Johnston was able to sit up and receive visitors. One of the first to call was Confederate senator (and former United States senator) Louis Trezevant Wigfall, a South Carolina native and transplanted Texan who had served in a quasi-military capacity at Fort Sumter and, briefly, as a brigadier general in Johnston's army. Here in Johnston's sickroom the two renewed their acquaintance. Repeat visits strengthened the bond between them. Johnston not only appreciated his visitor's well wishes but admired his connections. Wigfall, who was serving as a volunteer aide on the staff of Johnston's favorite subordinate, Longstreet, was a valuable source of information not only on the progress of the war but also on political matters affecting the army. Johnston came to appreciate the insider's knowledge the man freely shared. More than anything else, the two were drawn together by a shared dislike of Jefferson Davis. Johnston's policy differences with the president were well known, and Wigfall was one of Davis's most outspoken congressional opponents.[34]

Before Johnston's convalescence was well along, the two men had become close friends—so close that they agreed that General and Mrs. Johnston should move into the Richmond home of Senator and Mrs. Wigfall. The arrangement proved mutually beneficial. Not only did general and congressman complement each other militarily and politically, but Charlotte Wigfall became one of Lydia Johnston's most cherished friends. Lydia also became extremely fond of Charlotte's two daughters, whom she came to regard as the children she never had.[35]

Louis T. Wigfall

Not long after the couples began living under the same roof, Wigfall, who until then had supported Davis occasionally and grudgingly, became his avowed enemy, the result of the president's veto of a bill on military administration that might have originated with

Johnston and which Wigfall had not only sponsored but also shepherded through both houses of Congress. Davis's action merely confirmed the senator's preconceived notion—one that a number of other congressmen shared—that Davis was too enamored of his prerogatives and especially of his power to govern the army. At bottom, the Wigfall bloc viewed Davis as too nationalistic to rule a nation founded on the principle of decentralized authority.

From the start Wigfall saw in Joseph Johnston a potential means of curbing Davis's influence over the military and perhaps over the Confederacy as a whole. He and like-minded colleagues could portray Johnston as a highly competent, morally upright soldier whose valid claim to seniority had been denied and whose strategic and tactical talents had been circumscribed and misused as the result of Davis's autocratic nature and especially his penchant for making appointments based on favoritism. For his part, Johnston saw Wigfall's power and influence as a means of advancing policies that promoted his own interests as well as the army's.[36]

As his friendship with the powerful and influential but volatile and erratic lawmaker flowered, at least occasionally Johnston must have looked past the mutually advantageousness of their association and seen himself for what he had become, a weapon in the hands of Davis's political antagonists. Yet he seemed increasingly comfortable with his new identity as his recuperation continued, the war went on, and his chances for regaining command of the Army of Northern Virginia grew smaller and smaller.

Sherman's prediction of a reversal of fortune for Ulysses Grant came true with amazing speed. On July 11, 1862, Henry Halleck realized his highest ambition when Lincoln, tiring of his role as de facto general in chief of the army, called him to Washington as commander of all United States military forces. Upon Halleck's departure from Corinth on the sixteenth, Grant, as senior subordinate, took his place although denied titular command of the Department of the Mississippi. Regardless, Grant's authority encompassed everything between the Tennessee and Mississippi Rivers as far north as Cairo. His forces included not only the Army of the Tennessee but also the Army of the Mississippi, now commanded by Maj. Gen. William S. Rosecrans, McClellan's ranking subordinate in western Virginia in 1861.[37]

In moving to Corinth, Grant relinquished his most recent assignment, command of the District of West Tennessee with headquarters at Memphis. He had filled that position for barely three weeks, but it had provided a good introduction to the task of administering civil as well as military affairs in the heart of an enemy's country. As of mid-July, that task and the headaches that went with it devolved upon Sherman in accordance with one of the last orders Halleck issued before heading east. At his new post and in his new role as a major general, Sherman would head his own division as well as Stephen Hurlbut's, the latter known officially as the Fourth Division, District of Memphis.

Sherman reached his station on the Mississippi on the twenty-first. He placed most of his own troops inside partially completed Fort Pickering, and Hurlbut's between the fort and river. Despite the intense heat of a West Tennessee summer, Sherman spent weeks drilling his troops, Hurlbut's included, to within an inch of their lives. At the same time, he tried to maintain security on his communication lines, with special reference to the Memphis & Charleston Railroad, a popular target of both uniformed Confederates and local guerrillas.[38]

Much of Sherman's time during the four months he spent in Memphis was taken up with civil affairs. Upon arriving, "I found the place dead; no business doing, the stores closed, churches, schools and every thing shut up. The people were all more or less in sympathy with our enemies, and there was a strong prospect that the whole civil population would become a dead weight on our hands." Because the river north of the city was in Union hands, Sherman felt secure issuing orders that reopened the stores, banks, and public institutions, thus restoring the flow of commerce almost to prewar levels. He even permitted the local Episcopal Church to hold services although its rector refused to alter the customary prayer for the president—President Davis. Sherman allowed the practice to continue, assuring the clergyman that "Jeff needs your prayers badly. It will take a great deal of praying to save him."[39]

Fully cognizant of his wide-ranging authority and the power behind it, Sherman intended to rule with as light a touch as possible. He tried to treat the populace not as enemies but as fellow countrymen. He did his utmost to restrain his soldiers from pillaging and vandalism. Such behavior violated the societal order which he believed must be maintained even in wartime. He issued receipts on the U.S. Treasury for goods his quartermaster and commissary officers commandeered from local sources. Consistent with his orders and his personal attitudes, he refrained from interfering with ownership of private property, including slaves. He informed the mayor that he had "the most unbounded respect for the civil law, Courts & authorities and Shall do all in my power to restore them to their proper use viz. the protection of life, liberty & property." He added philosophically: "Civil war prevails in the land and necessarily the Military for the time being must be superior to the Civil Authority but does not therefore destroy it."[40]

Despite his sympathetic intent toward the local community, Sherman quickly became convinced that it was unwilling to grant him the same consideration. Townspeople, including many of prominent standing, aided and abetted the guerrillas in attacking his outposts, breaking his railroad, and harassing Unionist citizens. Such covert support infuriated Sherman, mainly because he seemed powerless to stop it. He was particularly incensed that local partisans should hide along the banks of the river to snipe at passing gunboats, transports, and commercial vessels. In late October guerrillas grounded and burned a supply vessel south of the city at Ship Island. On other occasions, they killed and wounded Union seamen and their soldier passengers.

At first Sherman attempted to combat the insurgents by conventional means. Whenever guerrillas were observed in his district, infantry units converged on their supposed hideouts and cavalry swept the surrounding countryside. These efforts proved unavailing, as Sherman must have suspected they would. The faceless, nameless enemy not only moved too quickly to be overtaken but once his work of sabotage, destruction, or murder was done, he folded seamlessly into the civilian population. By late September Sherman was complaining to a subordinate of the futility of trying to "reach the actors, for they come from the interior and depart as soon as the mischief is done."[41]

Before long, Sherman was forced to switch tactics. Instead of pursuing the irregulars themselves he began to retaliate against the general populace. In response to continuing attacks on his troops and supply lines he threatened to exile several pro-Confederates and their families. When guerrillas ambushed a foraging party near Wolf River, killing a number of soldiers, he rounded up known Southern sympathizers and shipped them to a prison camp in Kentucky. He countered other attacks by burning the homes of leading secessionists, a tactic he vowed to repeat whenever depredations occurred.

His policy of reprisal culminated on September 24, when he sent two companies of foot soldiers on a dawn raid against the river village of Randolph, where partisans had fired on passing gunboats. Sherman instructed the commander of the raiding party: "You will destroy the place, leaving one house [standing] to mark the place." Afterward he reported that the party "has returned and Randolph is gone. It is no use tolerating such acts as firing on steamboats. Punishment must be speedy, sure and exemplary. . . . The town was of no importance, but the example should be followed up on all similar occasions."[42]

He left no doubt that he, for one, intended to follow up. The razing of Randolph halted attacks on the river, but only for a few weeks. When they resumed, Sherman had one of his most trusted subordinates march his regiment down the west bank of the Mississippi and destroy all homes and farms along the fifteen-mile stretch where sniper fire had been observed. The subordinate, although sparing a few houses and farms, torched the property of every civilian he suspected of complicity in the attacks.[43]

Sherman's retaliatory efforts appear to have been only partially successful. Guerrilla operations continued, but as his reprisals grew ever harsher, attacks on his posts and lines dwindled and in some areas stopped altogether, although they broke out again elsewhere in his realm. But by making examples of civilians suspected of supporting the insurgents, Sherman at least had the satisfaction of believing he was doing something to quell resistance to his regime.

Impelled to explain his actions, which some observers, North as well as South, might have considered excessive and even barbaric, on October 4 Sherman wrote to Grant that "we cannot change the hearts and minds of the South, but we can make war so terrible that they realize the fact that, however brave and gallant and devoted to their country, still they are mortal and should exhaust all peaceful remedies before they fly to war."[44]

In making such pronouncements, Sherman was, as Michael Fellman comments, "turning an emotional corner in his conception of the war against the South." Sherman's experiences with the shadow warriors who disrupted his operations and with the respectable citizens who supported them even as they professed a desire to live in peace with their occupiers had driven him to a conviction that the only way the war could be won was to make Southern society bear the consequences of its actions. This conviction would form the basis of a policy that some contemporary observers, and many latter-day historians, would erroneously label "total war." It was, more accurately, a form of hard war, less restrained and less civilized than that practiced heretofore but neither unlicensed nor unbounded. This distinction, however, would be lost on the people of Georgia and the Carolinas, upon whom Sherman would practice his philosophy on a larger and more destructive scale two years hence.[45]

TWELVE

RETAKING THE FIELD

From having to deal with the partisans who plagued him in Memphis, Sherman developed a strategy that he believed could be successfully applied wherever Union forces occupied southern territory. The vulnerability of outposts and extended lines of communication and supply made assigning sizable resources to protect them counterproductive. Instead of holding fixed points, the Federals should take the war to the enemy by forming large, highly mobile strike forces whose power to destroy and disrupt would not only limit the Confederacy's ability to oppose them but would erode its will to resist. If guerrillas could play the raiding game, so could well-organized, well-disciplined regular units, whether of company, regimental, or brigade size.

For Sherman, the resource that enabled an occupation force to raid effectively was not the railroad, but the river, especially the Mississippi. Even when the railroad was "in full operation," he told Grant in early October 1862, the enemy "can keep pace with us up and down." River-borne operations, on the other hand, would permit the army to land virtually anywhere it chose and inflict damage where it would do the enemy the most harm. Destruction should not be limited to military objectives but extended to the civilian populace when it could be proven that the citizens were assisting the enemies of the United States, whether in or out of uniform. Such a policy would cause disaffection by showing the southern people that their government could not protect them against the loss of personal property, including homes, crops, and slaves. By now Sherman had come around to the view espoused by Lincoln (who was on the verge of issuing his preliminary Emancipation Proclamation) as well as by many military commanders including Grant, that only by depriving the South of its servile work force could the Confederacy's ability to wage war be curtailed.[1]

From hard experience Sherman had learned, as he informed Grant, that no matter how humanely their occupiers treated them, Southerners could not "be made to love us, but may be made to fear us, and dread the passage of troops through their country. With the Mississippi safe, we could land troops at any point, and . . . could make ourselves so busy that our descent would be dreaded the whole length of the river, and by the loss of Negroes and other property [they] would in time discover that war is not the remedy for the political evils of which they complained."[2]

With the Mississippi safe. That was the key to making Sherman's strategy work. As of the fall of 1862, the Mississippi was safe to Union shipping only as far south as Vicksburg, Mississippi, where heavily fortified defenses atop virtually inaccessible river bluffs prevented military and civilian vessels from reaching Union-occupied New Orleans. A second, less formidable outpost 130 miles downriver at Port Hudson, Louisiana, likewise blocked Union navigation, although dependent for its continued existence on the security of Vicksburg.

The inability to access the full extent of the river had an economic dimension. It posed problems not only for the United States Army and Navy but also for the citizens of the Northwest, especially farmers and merchants who had to ship their goods to market via the more costly medium of the railroad. Growing discontent among these interests had resulted in the election to state and national office of men whose willingness to obstruct the war effort was a source of concern to the Lincoln government.[3]

From Memphis, Sherman hoped to persuade Grant to leave northern Mississippi behind and operate against "the Gibraltar of the Confederacy" by water. Grant appeared willing to consider such a proposal, having recently disposed of threats to his department from two of the four Rebel armies operating in the western theater, Maj. Gen. Earl Van Dorn's fourteen-thousand-man Army of West Tennessee and Sterling Price's corps-sized Army of the West. The other commands were the Army of Tennessee, a reincarnation, with some adjustments, of Beauregard's Army of the Mississippi, led by Braxton Bragg; and the Army of East Tennessee, under Edmund Kirby Smith, now a major general.

In September, while Bragg and Smith appeared ready to join forces for an invasion of Kentucky, Van Dorn and Price were also planning to link, then to attack Grant's lines in West Tennessee. Deciding to land the first blow, Grant sent two of his senior subordinates, Rosecrans and Sherman's friend Edward Ord, to attack Price at Iuka, Mississippi, east of Corinth. Errors spoiled Grant's plan and the contemplated one-two punch never materialized. Even so, on September

19 Rosecrans, after withstanding several attacks, drove Price from the village. By botching a pursuit, however, he allowed Price to make a wide circuit to the south and join Van Dorn. After the battle, Rosecrans took position at Corinth.[4]

Grant was not in the town when Price and Van Dorn attacked Rosecrans on October 3. Although the Rebels made inroads along some sectors of the recently strengthened Union defenses, their assault ended in repulse and retreat when cooperating forces under Ord, Hurlbut (dispatched from Memphis by Sherman), and Brig. Gen. James B. McPherson rushed to Rosecrans's assistance. Again Rosecrans mounted an ineffective pursuit, which infuriated Grant and made him consider firing his subordinate. He did not have to; on October 30, the War Department named Rosecrans head of the Army of the Ohio in place of Buell, whose performance in ousting Bragg's army from Kentucky had been lackluster at best (Kirby Smith had opted out of joining Bragg for the invasion that ended at Perryville).[5]

With the exception of sending Hurlbut to reinforce Corinth via Jackson, Tennessee, Sherman had been kept out of the recent fighting; therefore, by early November he was ready and eager to relinquish his occupation duties and return to the field. He himself was at least partially responsible for the strategic situation that made his desire reality. Having recently assumed command of the Department of Tennessee, which included north Mississippi, Grant had put on paper his thoughts on operating against Vicksburg. The proposal, which Grant eventually laid before Halleck, reflected his own long-held thoughts on the subject but quite obviously was influenced by Sherman's musings on the desirability of raiding through Rebeldom.

Like Sherman, Grant saw Vicksburg as the next major objective of the Union forces in this theater. Its capture would not only unblock the Mississippi, it would fracture the Confederacy by severing the communications link between its western and trans-Mississippi theaters. Then, too, as Sherman envisioned, it would open the enemy's interior to raids large and small. Unlike Sherman, however, Grant favored an advance on Vicksburg not by water from above but by an overland march from the east. He pictured a movement along the axis of the Mississippi Central Railroad through Oxford and Grenada, with a turn to the west near the state capital, Jackson, then on to a confrontation with the local commander, Lt. Gen. John C. Pemberton, and the thirty thousand Rebels available in northern Mississippi.[6]

Grant's plan won the approval of Halleck, who pledged to forward to his once-neglected subordinate as many additional troops as he needed. A large number of these would come from Wisconsin, Illinois, Iowa, Ohio, and elsewhere in the Northwest where recruiting was under way in response to Lincoln's most recent call for volunteers. Already, in fact, hundreds of recruits were en route to Memphis and other points on the Mississippi. They were not, however, earmarked for Grant's use, but for John McClernand's.

In August the politician general had persuaded Lincoln to give him command of as many volunteers as he could personally recruit for an advance on Vicksburg by river in cooperation with a naval fleet under Flag Off. David Dixon Porter. Lincoln, who believed he needed the support of his War Democrat friend to secure reelection in 1864, gave McClernand the impression not only that he would have an independent command but also that his wants would receive priority over anyone else's. At the last minute, however, Secretary of War Stanton, who was wary of McClernand's lack of military experience and his low standing among professionals such as Halleck, inserted a significant caveat in the secret orders he handed the general on October 20, 1862: McClernand would be permitted to command only those troops that Grant did not require for his own operations in the same theater. Seizing on this limitation, Halleck intended to ensure that Grant—whom he had mistrusted not so long ago, but never as much as he did McClernand—got the jump on the politician general. On November 11 he wrote Grant at his field headquarters at La Grange, Tennessee: "You have command of all troops sent to your department, and have permission to fight the enemy where you please."[7]

Adm. David D. Porter, USN

With Halleck's covert but solid backing, Grant determined to use for his own purposes the recruits being dispatched to Memphis. On the fifteenth he directed Sherman to meet him at Columbus, Kentucky, the army's main supply base, for a strategy session. Sherman went at once, tearing himself away from his family. Ellen and the children had arrived for an extended visit at departmental headquarters, which Sherman, who thought little of creature comforts, had finally transferred from a tent on the edge of the city to a large house adjacent to Fort Pickering.

During the meeting, Sherman learned that Grant had already begun to advance down the railroad at the head of two columns commanded by Maj. Gens. Charles S. Hamilton and James McPherson (the latter only recently promoted to two-star rank). In response to the movement, Pemberton, with a large detachment of his command, had assumed a defensive position behind the Tallahatchie River near Holly Springs, fifty miles southeast of Memphis. Grant intended to take Holly Springs, a station on the Mississippi Central, where he desired to establish a supply depot to support the balance of his campaign.

Grant did not intend to advance toward Vicksburg on his own. He desired Sherman to organize a second expeditionary force, one that would move parallel to, and west of, his own, until the two could unite for a drive against the river fortress. Sherman should leave enough troops at Memphis to form a "proper garrison" and lead the rest toward a junction with Grant, on the Tallahatchie, by "a certain date."[8]

That day never arrived. Immediately after the meeting ended Sherman returned to Memphis and made preparations to depart yet again. On November 24, having kissed Ellen and the children good-bye, he left the town in the hands of General Hurlbut and his "three small divisions" and embarked on what amounted to his first stint in corps command. Without opposition, he reached the town of Wyatt, Mississippi, on December 2, where he learned that Pemberton, having been threatened by an infantry-cavalry expedition out of Helena, Arkansas, had withdrawn from close contact with Grant and had fallen back to the Yalobusha River near Grenada.[9]

By the fifth, Sherman was only ten miles from Grant's field headquarters at Oxford. He hastened there only to learn that his superior had revamped his strategy for Vicksburg. With Pemberton ensconced below the Yalobusha after tearing up the railroad from Grenada south, Grant felt temporarily stymied. The roadblock had materialized just when time mattered most—McClernand would soon be at Memphis to claim his recruits and assert his right to an independent operation against Vicksburg.[10]

Grant now proposed an advance on Vicksburg by water as well as land. With his force on hand, augmented by troops from Corinth as well as by two of Sherman's divisions, he would keep Pemberton occupied while Sherman organized an amphibious operation on the Mississippi. With his remaining division Sherman was to return yet again to Memphis, gather up the recruits assembled there, load them aboard transports, then steam down to Helena and pick up the locally based division of Maj. Gen. Frederick Steele. The combined force would then pass into the Yazoo River, convoyed by Porter's ships, disembark on the bluffs north and west of Vicksburg, and attack the city's depleted garrison from that quarter. Should Pemberton fall back to the city in response to Sherman's coming, Grant would closely follow. Yet Grant expected that by the time Pemberton reached Vicksburg, Sherman, whose mixed force of veterans and recruits was expected to top forty thousand, would have possession of the place.

Sherman thought the plan had merit. After all, it closely matched his own conception of a river-based raid deep into the enemy's country. As expeditiously as possible, he transferred the divisions of James Denver and Brig. Gen. Jacob G. Lauman (a newcomer to Sherman's command) to Grant, then hastened north with Morgan Smith's division. Reaching Memphis on the twelfth, he found that the recently arrived recruits had been formed into two "irregular divisions" under Brigadier Generals Andrew Jackson Smith and George W. Morgan. The newcomers were fewer than Grant and Sherman had expected; added to Smith's and Steele's divisions, they would give Sherman a field force of approximately thirty-two thousand. As soon as enough transports were on hand at the landing, he was off for Vicksburg, only a few days ahead of McClernand's anticipated arrival.[11]

In his memoirs, Sherman claims that "I did not dream that General McClernand, or anybody else, was scheming for the mere honor of capturing Vicksburg." This was hardly the case; by now he was well aware of McClernand's efforts to usurp command of the Vicksburg expedition. In addition to resenting McClernand's assignment to independent command, which he viewed as a slap at Grant, Sherman thought little of McClernand's abilities as a field commander and feared the result of his interference in such a complex and difficult undertaking. Thus he betrayed no qualms about co-opting the troops the politician-general had helped enlist.[12]

Sherman's force set sail on the nineteenth, conveyed by a gunboat fleet. Two days later it lay off the landing at Helena while Steele's men filed aboard transports of their own, giving Sherman a combined force of four divisions. One of these he left at Milliken's Bend, a few miles upriver from Vicksburg, which the flotilla reached on Christmas Day. The following day the rest of the expedition sailed into the mouth of the Yazoo toward a landing at Johnson's Plantation on the Vicksburg side of the river.[13]

Sherman had no way of knowing that the coming offensive would be a solo act. On the day he left Memphis, Grant learned that his supply lines, which stretched almost two hundred miles north to Columbus, had come under attack. A raiding force under Nathan Bedford Forrest had destroyed long stretches of track, numerous bridges, and some depots in northern Tennessee and southern Kentucky, while downing miles of telegraph line, an action that would prevent Grant from communicating with Sherman except indirectly and belatedly.[14]

Forrest's blow was difficult enough to withstand, but on October 20 a second raiding column, under Earl Van Dorn—who after his defeat at Corinth had been demoted to a supernumerary command under Pemberton—looped around Grant's left flank and sacked the newly established depot at Holly Springs. The resources Van Dorn destroyed or confiscated—an estimated one million dollars worth of weapons, equipment, rations, and forage—convinced Grant that he must cut short his overland drive and return north to regroup and refit. Not only would he be unable to coordinate operations with a river expedition, he could no longer keep Pemberton's troops apart from Vicksburg. Worse still, he had no way of notifying Sherman of this radical change in plans.[15]

<hr />

Not until the second week in November did Johnston consider himself physically able to return to active duty. Much had happened in both of the major theaters of the war since he fell with a bullet wound and shell fragments in his upper body. In the West, not only had Van Dorn and Price been beaten by Rosecrans and other subordinates of Grant, but Bragg's invasion of Kentucky had been curtailed at Perryville on October 8, and his army had sought refuge in Middle Tennessee. Bragg's troops were now scattered throughout the rich farming country around Murfreesboro. Bragg's opponent, Buell, had fared even less well despite gaining the credit for evicting the Confederates from Kentucky. A sluggish retreat had done in Buell, who had lost command of the Army of the Ohio (when given to Rosecrans, its name was changed to the Army of the Cumberland). By mid-November, Washington was urging Rosecrans to engage Bragg and complete the job of destruction only begun by Buell.[16]

In Virginia, Johnston's successor in command of the Army of Northern Virginia had been busy although not uniformly successful. After forcing McClellan's withdrawal to the James, Lee ranged westward to confront the army under Pope that had occupied the Culpeper Court House vicinity. Jackson's corps, sent in advance to engage the new Union commander, pitched into him and held him at bay until Lee came up with the rest of the army, under Longstreet. On August 29 and 30, Lee reunited Jackson and Longstreet on the Bull Run battlefield, where he surprised and throttled Pope's command, sending it back to Washington in defeat reminiscent of Irvin McDowell's debacle little more than a year earlier.[17]

Now free to execute a cherished plan, Lee rode the tide of victory into Maryland, whose lower reaches he invaded early in September. Followed at a respectful distance by McClellan, who had assimilated Pope's survivors into his own army, Lee finally gave battle at Sharpsburg, along Antietam Creek. Following a day of almost unimaginable carnage that ended as a tactical draw, Lee felt constrained to cross the Potomac into the Shenandoah Valley, ending his attempt to relieve Virginia of the ravages of war. McClellan could not be made to move as quickly. Only days before Johnston fled his sickroom, McClellan finally returned to Virginia, where he followed Lee to the line of the Rappahannock. Like Buell after Perryville, Little Mac's pursuit was so sluggish that it cost him his command (if his earlier, less-than-brilliant generalship had not already done so). He was replaced by Ambrose Burnside, an officer with victories to his credit but who appeared to be no more of a match for Robert E. Lee's skill, agility, and daring.[18]

When Johnston reported for duty to Jefferson Davis, the president was not convinced his health had been sufficiently restored. Nevertheless, he offered him what appeared to be a major command, a new department that encompassed Confederate forces between the Alleghenies and the Mississippi River. As commander of the Department of the West, Johnston would exercise authority over no fewer than three armies, Bragg's in Middle Tennessee, Kirby Smith's in the eastern portion of the state, and Pemberton's at Vicksburg and in northern Mississippi. Although the assignment was sufficiently prestigious to win Johnston's approval, it was a geographical rather than an army command, a distinction that, at least at the outset, seemed lost on him. In time, he would come to consider it "big in name, empty in reality" because, as one of his colleagues remarked, while on paper commanding three armies, in reality Johnston "commanded nobody."[19]

In creating this vast fiefdom, Davis, who clung to his conviction that every sector of the Confederacy must be defended against invasion and occupation, envisioned it as a means of quickly and efficiently shuttling forces from one theater to another. If Johnston learned that Rosecrans was preparing to move against Bragg's army, he could order Pemberton or Smith to augment him before "Old Rosy" could strike. Conversely, Bragg could be pressed into service to counter a threat to either of his colleagues by Grant, Sherman, or some other Union leader. Johnston, as overall commander, would have the power to order troop movements as he saw fit. Moreover, when it was deemed advantageous he

180

could leave his headquarters in Chattanooga and assume direct command of any of these armies.

The philosophy that underlay the creation of the Department of the West stirred concerns in Johnston's mind. He would not feel comfortable usurping a senior subordinate's prerogatives by taking over his army, especially considering that he would lack an appreciation of the strategic situation locally. Second, Tennessee and Mississippi were so widely separated that it seemed unlikely troops could be transported quickly enough from one to the other to counter threats, let alone preempt them, especially in view of the chronic inadequacies of the Confederacy's rail system. Third, the grouping of forces within the department appeared flawed. Rather than bracketing Bragg's and Pemberton's forces, the subdivision should have linked Pemberton's department with the Arkansas enclave of Theophilus H. Holmes. Since Holmes's troops were operating directly across the Mississippi from Vicksburg, they ought to be considered the preferred source of reinforcement for Pemberton.[20]

On this last point, Johnston's thinking was flawed, too, for Holmes's force was too small and too scattered to serve as a ready source of augmentation. Even so, Johnston displayed a clearer understanding of strategic issues than Davis, who would never order Holmes to augment Pemberton no matter how dire the necessity. One day after reporting to the War Department for assignment, the general tried to impress on Secretary of War Randolph the logic of placing Holmes and Pemberton under the same umbrella. The secretary stopped his visitor in mid-sentence and read him a letter that made that same point, recently sent by Randolph to Holmes. Then he showed Johnston an order from Davis rescinding Randolph's directive. The dispute highlighted the frustrating relationship of president and cabinet officer, one that ended only two days later when Randolph submitted his resignation. He would be replaced by James A. Seddon, a professional politician more accepting of Davis's proclivity to micromanage the War Office.

Another conceptual stumbling block did not become evident to Johnston until he had taken up his new post. Although he was empowered to give orders to three army leaders, under the existing system none would report to him; each would communicate directly with the president and his war secretary. The arrangement would further weaken Johnston's knowledge of his subordinates' wants, needs, capabilities, plans, and intentions.[21]

With misgivings but also in the hope that he could make a go of his new assignment, Johnston prepared to take sorrowful leave of his friends in Richmond, including the Wigfalls, and head for southeastern Tennessee. A gracious gesture preceded his departure. Friends and associates, including many lawmakers who shared Johnston's antipathy toward Davis and by extension Robert E. Lee, attended a farewell breakfast in Johnston's honor, held at a posh restaurant in downtown Richmond. Although many of the diners made merry, the guest of honor, perhaps contemplating what lay ahead, appeared unusually quiet and somber. As the occasion was ending, Sen. William L. Yancey of Alabama, one of Davis's bitterest adversaries, proposed a champagne toast to "the only man who can save the Confederacy—General Joseph E. Johnston." When everyone had drunk, they began to applaud their hero, who only then stood and raised his glass. "Mr. Yancey," he replied, "the man you describe is now in the field—in the person of Robert E. Lee. I will drink to his health." And he did.[22]

Within days, General and Mrs. Johnston were heading west as rapidly as an aged and overburdened railroad would permit. On December 4, 1862, having been delayed by several breakdowns and accidents, none of them life-threatening, they reached Chattanooga. After seeing Lydia settled in circumstances as comfortable as could be had, the general and his staff established departmental headquarters in a large house in the city. Johnston barely had time to take a seat at his desk when confronted by a dilemma stemming from the impracticality of the geographical department system. A report reached him that Pemberton's forces were falling back under pressure from Grant along the line of the Mississippi Central. A subsequent dispatch from General Cooper's office urged Johnston to send reinforcements from Bragg's theater. Johnston demurred, arguing that Bragg was himself facing pressure from Rosecrans's army in and near Nashville. He pointed out that Holmes was in the best position to assist the army near Grenada. But when Holmes complained to Richmond that he could not cross the river without opening strategic Little Rock to enemy occupation, the administration did not press him to aid Pemberton. Although Johnston on December 5 traveled to Bragg's headquarters at Murfreesboro, he refused to order the army leader to deplete his main body in support of Pemberton. He did, however, request Bragg to send cavalry to operate in the enemy's rear—a move that produced the devastating raids on Grant's communications.[23]

A week after reaching Murfreesboro, Johnston had to curtail his inspection tour of Bragg's army and hasten back to Chattanooga. Upon arriving he was greeted by Jefferson Davis, who, concerned about the strategic situation in Tennessee and Mississippi, had left Richmond on the eighth to inspect the Confederacy's western defenses. The president seemed more anxious about the situation in Pemberton's theater and asked Johnston's opinion about transferring troops from Murfreesboro to Vicksburg. Johnston's response, the same one he had given General Cooper, did not satisfy the president, who ultimately ordered nine thousand of Bragg's infantry—one division and an attached brigade—to start for Mississippi, almost six hundred miles away via the meandering railroad. Davis believed the reinforcements would enable Pemberton to deal successfully not only with Grant but with any other force moving against Vicksburg, such as the one Sherman would launch via the Yazoo River.

The upshot of Davis's decision appeared to validate Johnston's conviction that troop transfers over such long distances could not be advantageously timed. The enforced augmentation of Pemberton deprived Bragg of manpower just as Rosecrans prepared to leave Nashville, advance on Murfreesboro, and initiate battle. Moreover, the last of the troops sent to Mississippi did not reach Pemberton until January 7, ten days after Sherman launched his attack on the Confederate stronghold.[24]

Sherman landed his expeditionary force on a spit of land surrounded by the Yazoo River and several obstructive waterways, including Chickasaw Bayou, which bordered the landing site on the east and south before joining the Mississippi a few miles above Vicksburg. When Sherman began to move his troops southward toward a long and steep ridgeline known as Chickasaw Bluffs or Walnut Hills, he moved in four columns. His left flank was covered by Steele's division, which moved up on the east side of Chickasaw Bayou. Advancing on the other side of the morass were the divisions of Morgan, M. L. Smith, and, farthest to the right, A. J. Smith. As the troops advanced, they were shelled by Confederate artillery on the heights. The guns, and their infantry supports, had been placed in position by Brig. Gen. Martin Luther Smith but were now commanded by Pemberton, who had reached Vicksburg from Grenada along with heavy reinforcements freed up by Grant's withdrawal from north Mississippi. Sherman believed he was opposed by fifteen thousand defenders, although before the operation ended that force would swell to twenty-five thousand, including the first wave of reinforcements from Bragg's army.[25]

Following a bombardment that did little to soften the Confederate defenses, on December 27 and 28 Sherman's men skirmished with the troops atop Chickasaw Bluffs and reconnoitered their positions. Their leader considered the latter position "strong by nature and by art"—i.e., through the erection of breastworks and the digging of trenches. As far as he could tell, the bluffs were accessible only at two points. In actuality, the bayou could be crossed at five places, including upon a "corduroy" bridge (a causeway fashioned from split logs) barely ten feet wide. Both of these access points, however, were obstructed by earthworks and an abatis of felled trees and were commanded by artillery. One of these approaches was in Steele's sector, the other a mile to the south, in front of the troops of Morgan L. Smith. Smith was severely wounded on the twenty-eighth by sharpshooter fire and was replaced by David Stuart, who had served under Sherman at Shiloh. Steele, however, reported himself unable to reach the bluffs from his position, and Sherman had him redeploy all but one of his brigades on the west side of the bayou, a cumbersome and time-consuming process that required a long counter-march and a run down the Yazoo aboard transports.[26]

On the evening of December 28, 1862, Sherman put last touches to his plan of attack. Next morning, at his order, every unit made a noisy demonstration, as if an attack was coming all along the line. The only men to advance, however, were those closest to the points where Sherman believed Chickasaw Bayou accessible. When Sherman had shown General Morgan the place at which his troops should cross, the division commander promised that "in ten minutes after you give the signal I'll be on those hills." The man would be in a position to know because he was supposed to lead his troops into the thick of the action.[27]

Morgan promised too much. His superior had a more realistic appreciation of the difficulties that lay ahead. Just before Sherman gave the signal to attack, he delivered to Morgan, via a staff officer, a sobering observation: "We will lose 5,000 men before we take Vicksburg, and may as well lose them here as anywhere else." Apparently Morgan was determined not to be one of the five thousand; when his men went forward shortly after noon, they did so without him. Absent his leadership, only one of his brigades, Col. John F. DeCourcy's, passed the treacherous bayou. Pounded by artillery as soon as it crossed the corduroy bridge, the brigade took cover behind the south bank of the bayou and refused to go farther. In his memoirs Sherman gives the impression that the brigade went to earth too quickly. Morgan, in a postwar account of the fight, claimed that DeCourcy's fifteen hundred men rushed forward only to be "mowed down by a storm of shells, grape and canister, and minié balls which swept our front like a hurricane of fire. Never did troops bear themselves with greater intrepidity. They were terribly repulsed, but not beaten." No attackers, whether veterans or rookies, could have withstood such treatment for long without giving into survival instincts and breaking for cover.[28]

Sherman would criticize Morgan not only for his aborted advance but also for failing to provide a covering fire for the single brigade of Steele's division on the other side of the bayou, which was moving up gamely on DeCourcy's left. Led by Brig. Gen. Frank Blair, the ex-congressman who had helped Nathaniel Lyon hold St. Louis for the Union, the eighteen-hundred-man force struggled across the bayou. Blair himself was on foot after his horse became inextricably mired in the ooze, but they finally gained firm ground. To advance further, Blair's men would have to scale a ten-foot-high embankment topped by an abatis and rifle pits, although both of these defenses had been abandoned when their occupants sought higher ground. Showered by Pemberton's artillery and bereft of flank support, Blair's men fell back, leaving about five hundred wounded behind, most of whom would fall into the enemy's hands.[29]

By 2:00 P.M., with Sherman's assault in dire trouble, another of Steele's brigades, Col. John M. Thayer's, attempted to cross the causeway in support of DeCourcy's men farther to the left. But the movement went awry when an order from Steele based on faulty intelligence brought most of the advancing men to a halt in front of an impassable slashing of felled trees. Although Sherman did not choose to make an issue of Steele's error, Thayer never forgave the division commander for interfering with his brigade.[30]

Gen. Frank P. Blair, USA

When Thayer's scattered command turned about and withdrew, the fight effectively ended. "Our loss had been pretty heavy," Sherman admitted, "and we had accomplished nothing, and had inflicted little loss on our enemy." At first he considered resuming the attack with fresh troops, but after scrutinizing Pemberton's defenses and the narrowness of the approach to Chickasaw Bluffs, he gave it up. The next day he had a change of heart. After reembarking most of his troops, he had David Porter convoy Steele's division up the Yazoo to a point below Haynes's Bluff from which he might attack the northern flank of Pemberton's defenses. But fog on the Yazoo, accompanied by a heavy rain, persuaded Sherman to call off the effort before it was fairly under way. He was also influenced by the sight of reinforcements from Vicksburg hastening up the other side of the Yazoo toward Haynes's Bluff.[31]

Although painfully aware of the field day his newspaper critics would have at his expense (he imagined a typical headline: "Repulse, Failure, and Bungling"), he retraced his path down the Yazoo and into the Mississippi. En route, he pondered why he had heard nothing, and gained no support, from Grant. "Most assuredly," he explained, "I had listened for days for the sound of his guns in the direction of Yazoo City," north of Pemberton's stronghold. On December 21 Sherman had learned of Van Dorn's attack on Holly Springs, but he failed to envision its effects on Grant's offensive.[32]

He finally learned the reason for Grant's silence on January 2, when he reached the mouth of the Yazoo and was met by the steamer *Tigress*, aboard which was John McClernand and his staff. Sherman must have felt a bit sheepish when confronted by the officer whose troops he had commandeered for a mission other than the one they had been organized for. If McClernand berated his junior colleague, however, neither man ever mentioned it. The politician-general informed Sherman that Forrest and Van Dorn had ruined Grant's plans, pointed out where Grant could be found (near La Grange, Tennessee), and explained why Sherman had encountered a much larger force atop Chickasaw Bluffs than he had anticipated.

McClernand followed his summary of recent events by announcing that he was assuming command of Sherman's expeditionary force. Two days later he issued an order establishing the Army of the Mississippi and placing himself in command of it. The army was to consist of two corps, each of two divisions, to be led by Sherman and Morgan. The latter's assignment to so high a command did not sit well with Sherman, who considered Morgan primarily responsible for the fiasco of the twenty-ninth. He was, however, powerless to influence McClernand's thinking.[33]

On the third, McClernand led the entire force up the Mississippi to Milliken's Bend, ten miles north of the mouth of the Yazoo. But the debarkation that was intended to take place there was put on hold when Sherman suggested to his new superior a target of opportunity along the Arkansas River, fifty-some miles north of its confluence with the Mississippi. This was Fort Hindman, a square, full-bastioned work mounting three 9-inch Columbiad rifles and numerous lesser artillery pieces, which sat adjacent to the village of Post of Arkansas. It was manned by five thousand troops, mostly dismounted cavalry, under Brig. Gen. Thomas J. Churchill. Perched on the left bank of the Arkansas around a horseshoe-shaped bend, Fort Hindman menaced the Union base at Helena, while shielding General Holmes's headquarters at Little Rock. Attacks by Rebel gunboats launched from Fort Hindman had damaged Union shipping on the Mississippi. An expeditionary force heading for Vicksburg would find its right flank and rear threatened by Churchill's fort.[34]

Sherman's attack on Fort Hindman

Operating against Hindman was a logical enough step that McClernand himself had considered taking it once he caught up with the army that had been stolen from him. Sherman, however, claimed that the politician-general argued against attacking the post until David Porter, despite his less-than-cordial feelings for McClernand—he mistrusted all nonprofessional soldiers, especially those that bragged and strutted as McClernand did—not only endorsed the operation but agreed to support it with a small fleet of warships. His involvement sold McClernand on the project. Sherman had supposed that he would be selected to command the expedition, but McClernand declared his intention to accompany and lead it. He had been looking for a manageable project with which to begin his maiden stint in independent command. He considered an early attack on Vicksburg "too big a boot" to try on, but an attack on Fort Hindman, which should prove no match for the Union army and navy, appeared "a boot of the right size."[35]

On January 8, 1863, McClernand and Porter went up the Mississippi past the mouth of the Arkansas. To disguise their objective, gunboats and transports continued north until entering the mouth of the White River. They ran up that stream for twenty miles, then took an old cutoff back to the Arkansas. Nearing the bend in which the fort nestled, late on the ninth the army debarked at a landing three miles below and the next day moved inland. Against light resistance, they invested Churchill's garrison on the north and west.

Late in the morning of the tenth, Sherman's and Morgan's troops rushed forward and overran a line of rifle pits in advance of Hindman's land faces. As they did, Porter's ships blasted the fort at a distance of twenty-three hundred yards. Eventually, three ironclads pulled to within four hundred yards of the east face, which their guns damaged heavily. The next day, shortly before McClernand—who would direct the battle from the deck of the gunboat *Black Hawk*—nerved himself to attack, the navy again ran in close to the fort, finishing off the east face and disabling all but one of Hindman's guns. At one o'clock the troops of Sherman and Morgan again leapt to the attack but made slow progress against Churchill's main works. With the fort's Columbiads silenced, Porter's gunners soon enfiladed the entire position, leaving the garrison helpless to defend itself. Soon after 4:00 P.M., white flags began to go up all along the works.

Perceiving that resistance was at an end, Porter left his flagship by yawl and entered the fort from its water side to receive the surrender of one of Churchill's subordinates, who happened to be a former seaman. Soon afterward, Sherman sought out General Churchill, received his sword as a gesture of capitulation, and set his men to disarming the garrison. When one of Churchill's colonels sulkily refused to surrender, Sherman told him to submit on peril of his life and the lives of his surrounded command. Muttering and grumbling, the officer handed over his saber.[36]

When Sherman repaired to the *Black Hawk* to report the garrison's capture, he found McClernand prancing about the deck, giddy with euphoria, exclaiming, "Glorious! glorious! my star is ever in the ascendant!" The self-congratulatory display did not impress the tired and hungry Sherman. One imagines he would have liked to slap the citizen-soldier into silence.[37]

Soon enough, McClernand was brought down to earth, although not by Sherman. When he learned of the operation on the Arkansas, Grant blasted what he called McClernand's "wild-goose chase." He fumed not because he thought the assault a bad idea but because it had tied up almost half the troops in the entire Department of the Mississippi. Unwilling to entrust precious resources to McClernand, Grant determined to take personal command of the entire Vicksburg project. On January 18, one day after leaving his rear supply base at Memphis, he ran down to the mouth of the Arkansas River, where he met McClernand returning from Fort Hindman. In short words he informed his fellow Illinoisan that he was no longer in charge of operations on the Mississippi or any of its tributaries.

McClernand received the announcement more or less respectfully, but he bristled when, less than two weeks later, Grant issued a general order dissolving the Army of the Mississippi and reducing its erstwhile leader to command of the Thirteenth Corps, Army of the Tennessee. The same order placed Sherman—who heartily approved of Grant's assertion of power—in command of the Fifteenth Corps. McClernand lodged a strident protest with Lincoln, reminding the president that he had been granted an independent command and describing Grant's usurpation as an act of professional jealousy. The successes achieved by citizen-soldiers like himself, he contended, were "gall and wormwood" to regular army veterans like Grant.[38]

Clearly, McClernand expected reinstatement. Thus he was shocked and dismayed when Lincoln proved unwilling to intervene in his behalf. Although praising McClernand for his recent success, Lincoln claimed that "I have too many family controversies (so to speak) already on my hands, to voluntarily, or so long as I can avoid it, take up another." With these words—gall and wormwood to John McClernand—the president fixed the parameters of the campaign to conquer the Gibraltar of the Confederacy.[39]

While Sherman had been operating against Chickasaw Bluffs, William S. Rosecrans had ended months of inactivity in Middle Tennessee by advancing against Bragg's army to the south. On the last day of 1862 and again two days later, the Army of the Cumberland and the Army of Tennessee grappled fiercely, at times desperately, along the banks of Stones River west of Murfreesboro. Although the Confederates opened the battle with a nearly overwhelming attack and appeared to hold the advantage during much of the first day, setbacks encountered on January 2, many the result of poor tactical decisions by Bragg, prompted the army leader to disengage and commence a retreat that would end five days and almost forty miles later in the Duck River valley north of Tullahoma.[40]

Braxton Bragg was not a people person—even his closest associates admitted that he could be cold, abrupt, and rude to his subordinates, even to members of his staff. Like Jefferson Davis, whose close friendship he retained despite his miscues in Kentucky and Tennessee, Bragg had an imperious, autocratic manner, and he was wont to regard anyone who criticized or opposed his rule as his mortal enemy. After Perryville and especially in the wake of Stones River, he found numerous critics and opponents within his own ranks, especially among his inner circle. These included his senior lieutenants, Leonidas Polk and William Hardee, both of whom believed the army had lost confidence in Bragg's leadership (though at first only Hardee would say so openly). Other high-ranking officers including Maj. Gens. John C. Breckinridge and Frank Cheatham echoed this sentiment. Cheatham went so far as to insist he would never fight again under Bragg's command.[41]

When Jefferson Davis became aware of the extent of Bragg's unpopularity and the magnitude of the dissent and unrest plaguing his army, he decided to send to Tullahoma someone who could render an impartial judgment on his ability to retain command of the army. Davis chose Johnston, who, being new to the theater, might be said to possess an outsider's objectivity. He was also considered a perceptive evaluator

Gen. Braxton Bragg, CSA

of military talent, and he certainly had the rank and authority to implement any changes he deemed critical to the effective functioning of the command. On January 22 Johnston was ordered to visit Bragg's headquarters for the third time in ten weeks, this time to inspect Bragg rather than any of his units.[42]

The assignment capped an especially busy period for the new department commander. After greeting Davis on his arrival in Chattanooga following Johnston's first tour of Bragg's army, the general had accompanied the president back to Murfreesboro, where Davis reviewed the army. What Davis observed made him agree with Johnston's assessment that the Army of Tennessee had recovered its strength and fighting spirit since departing Kentucky at the behest of the enemy.

When the visit to Tennessee ended, Johnston accompanied Davis on a tour of the western reaches of the department. They stopped first in Jackson, where

Davis addressed the recently convened legislature, then moved on to Vicksburg, where, in Pemberton's absence, Martin L. Smith commanded a garrison of six thousand—about half the strength, Smith calculated, that was needed to hold the place against attack. Johnston agreed with this analysis and opined to Davis that Port Hudson was also undermanned. Johnston advised the chief executive to order General Holmes to ship twenty thousand of his troops across the river to bolster both garrisons. Instead of acquainting his subordinate with the fact that Holmes could not have laid his hands on that many men had he stripped every guard shack and picket post in the state, Davis pledged to request him to supply the asked-for troops. This accomplished nothing. "Very properly," Johnston observed, Holmes refused to act until ordered do so.[43]

From Vicksburg, Davis and Johnston traveled north to Grenada, inspecting Pemberton's defenses on the south side of the Yalobusha only days before Grant, feeling the loss of his supply lines, withdrew from the other side of the stream. This happy event followed by a week the news—conveyed by Davis upon his arrival in Chattanooga—that Robert E. Lee had won a smashing victory over General Burnside outside Fredericksburg, Virginia, on December 13, 1862. It was in an atmosphere of rising spirits that Pemberton accompanied his president and his departmental superior on their return to Jackson. They arrived in the capital on Christmas Day, which Johnston spent regretting his separation from Lydia, who remained at Chattanooga. Davis, meanwhile, prepared to address the state legislature once again, this time to exhort the lawmakers to assist Gov. John J. Pettus in turning out every able-bodied male to resist the evil invader.[44]

From Jackson, Davis started on the long journey back to Virginia. Before he left, Johnston made one final attempt to persuade him of the impossibility of commanding within a single geographical sphere armies as far apart as Bragg's and Pemberton's. He also tried to make Davis see that such a command was "little more than nominal." But when Johnston respectfully asked to be reassigned to a more substantial and manageable post, Davis shook his head. While aware of the distance that separated the components of Johnston's command, he stressed that Richmond lay much farther from either of them and "he thought it necessary to have an officer nearer, with authority to transfer troops from one army to the other in an emergency."[45]

Johnston regarded as terribly shortsighted Davis's view of what could be accomplished with the meager resources available in the department. A few weeks later, however, the president effectively made his point by transferring one resource—Johnston himself—from Mobile, Alabama, where he had gone to inspect the local defenses, to Bragg's headquarters to assess its commander's prospects. Having twice visited the Army of Tennessee, Johnston believed he knew pretty much all there was to know about the command's wants, needs, and problems. Now he spent another three weeks inspecting its hierarchy. He was received enthusiastically enough. On January 27 one of Bragg's enlisted men noted that "Genl Joseph E. Johnston arrived at this place today. His presence will no doubt put fresh zeal into the troops. He is regarded as one of the great chieftains of the age."[46]

In turn, Johnston came away impressed by what he had observed. He reported to Davis his strong conviction that Bragg should be sustained in his present position. He cited the army leader's "recent operations, which in my opinion evince great vigor & skill. It would be very unfortunate to remove him at this juncture, when he has just earned if not won the gratitude of the country." Any survivor of Stones River might have taken exception with this pronouncement; reading it, he would have supposed that Johnston was referring to another battle, or to a commander other than the one who had just wrested defeat from the jaws of victory.[47]

While pleasing some of its recipients, notably Davis, Johnston's report disappointed Bragg's critics and opponents of the administration such as Louis Wigfall. The senator believed his friend had cast aside a gilt-edged opportunity not only to jettison an incompetent officer sustained only by the president's penchant for favoritism but also to gain for himself a position that Wigfall knew Johnston greatly desired.

His finding in Bragg's favor may have turned, as many historians believe, on Johnston's perception that by issuing a negative report he would appear to be intriguing for Bragg's job. Johnston's sense of integrity would not permit him to give rise to charges of self-interest. As he explained to Wigfall, "to remove the officer and put me in his place, & upon my investigation and report would not look well & would certainly expose me, injure me." And yet Johnston's own explanation, given in his memoirs, for rendering a favorable verdict suggests that rather than assess Bragg's standing among his subordinates, Johnston sought the opinion of lower-ranking officers as to the army's morale. These opinions persuaded him that the rank and file "were in high spirits, and as ready as ever for [a] fight; such a condition seeming to me incompatible with the alleged want of confidence in their general's ability." A determination on this point was not what Davis had been seeking. Yet, however flawed its methodology, Johnston's report ensured that Braxton Bragg would remain in command of the principal Confederate army in the West for months—and many defeats, setbacks, and disasters—to come.[48]

THIRTEEN

"I AM TOO LATE"

As Sherman anticipated, the newspapers pilloried him for the failure at Chickasaw Bluffs. The reporters who covered the operation not only failed to note that his attack was to have been supported by a cooperative offensive; they assumed that Sherman's subsequent subordination to McClernand was proof that he had blundered and been relieved of command. In articles and editorials across the country he was attacked as a bungler, a menace to the lives of his troops. The *Cincinnati Gazette* and the *St. Louis Republican*, among other journals, revived the accusations that he was insane, adding the new charge that his troops were mutinying against him. Again Sherman railed against his tormentors. Every brickbat they took to him had the power to hurt, but "none has given me more pain than the assertion that my troops are disaffected, mutinous, and personally opposed to me. This is false, false as hell. My own division will follow me anywhere. . . ."[1]

This time he was able to reply to his critics in a material—and drastic—way. Before his troops left Memphis for the Yazoo, he had issued an order barring from the expedition all civilians except transport crews. The order also declared that any participant who wrote anything for publication would be arrested and tried as a spy. After the battle Sherman learned that several reporters had defied his ban. The infuriated general decided to make an example of one of them, Thomas W. Knox of the *New York Herald,* who had written an especially condemnatory piece about Sherman's conduct during December 26–29, much of it derived, as the journalist claimed, from a bitter critique of the battle by one of Sherman's own generals, Frank Blair.

Three weeks after returning from the attack on Fort Hindman, Sherman had Knox arrested and court-martialed on charges that included spying. Sherman believed, or at least claimed, that the information Knox had caused to be published, especially that concerning the army's plans and numbers, would have been of great value to the enemy. As Sherman informed his naval colleague D. D. Porter, his intention was not to see the reporter hung or shot but "to establish the principle that such people cannot attend our armies, in violation of orders, and defy us, publishing their garbled statements and defaming officers who are doing their best." He intended to set a legal precedent affirming a commander's jurisdiction over those who reported on military matters, especially field operations.[2]

The tribunal convened on February 5, 1863, at Sherman's headquarters at Young's Point, Louisiana. The proceedings, which lasted nearly two weeks, ended with the reporter's acquittal on most of the charges against him—principally because the prosecution could not prove that any Confederates had read Knox's article, and thereby profited from it. The defendant was found guilty of violating Sherman's ban on civilians accompanying the expedition and of a similar decree issued by the War Department. Though the court attached no criminality to the violation, it ordered Knox expelled from the army under penalty of rearrest and imprisonment.

The verdict infuriated Sherman, but his temper cooled once he realized that, by ridding himself of Knox, he had fashioned a powerful weapon to use against other "buzzards of the press." He vowed not to exclude them from his ranks, but he and his staff would work zealously and continuously to keep them in line— they had been warned.[3]

Sherman had the time to indulge his fear and loathing of journalists because throughout the first three months of 1863 his command, like the rest of Grant's sixty-three-thousand-man army, had time on its hands as it waited for winter weather to abate, roads to dry, and supplies to arrive from the North in quantity sufficient to support a return to active campaigning. Having learned much from Sherman's failure north of Vicksburg, Grant desired, when he retook the field, to find some way to approach the fortified city from another direction. He considered operating east of the city, retracing his steps down the Mississippi Central to Jackson and then turning toward the river.

Sherman favored this course and recommended it to Grant, but the commanding general eventually discarded it as politically infeasible. To operate east of Vicksburg, he would have to return the army to Memphis, move his supplies there, and turn the town into a fortress capable of resisting a raid like the one on Holly Springs. But hauling the army so far from its current base would look like a retreat in the eyes of the Northern public, a large portion of which was already disheartened by the lack of substantial military progress anywhere in the war zone. Grant would not take that chance for fear of leaving the Lincoln administration open to condemnation and jeopardizing its chances in this fall's state and national elections. Sherman, never a political animal, did not agree with Grant's reasoning, but he abided by it nonetheless.[4]

Grant, convinced that the downpours and high waters that were regular features of a Louisiana winter would hamper both land and river movements against Vicksburg, decided that the army must wait out the rainy season in its present position. He was right to be patient. The rains that came down inundated the encampments of McClernand's corps at Young's Point, forcing it to move to higher ground at Milliken's Landing. Sherman held his ground, "laid off a due proportion of the levee for each subdivision of my command, and assigned other parts to such steamboats as lay at the levee."[5]

To keep his troops occupied and conditioned, Grant launched a succession of efforts, none of which he truly believed would succeed, to reach Vicksburg by an indirect route. His intent was to limit the army's exposure to Pemberton's defenses, which included long-range cannons capable of hurling a devastating fire to any force approaching on the river. The first of these make-work projects involved cutting a canal across De Soto Point, a peninsula opposite Vicksburg, to allow Porter's ships to pass through it and avoid exposure to the enemy's batteries. The second effort was aimed at clearing an existing but narrow route through waterways north of Vicksburg, including Lake Providence, to a point sixty miles below the city. The third was an attempt to reach Vicksburg from above via the Yazoo River, two of its tributaries, and an abandoned cotton canal near Helena, the Yazoo Pass. The fourth effort, an offshoot of the Yazoo Pass expedition, sought an inland water route that would enable the army to reach Vicksburg west of Chickasaw Bluffs via a spiderwork of waterways: the Yazoo, Steele's Bayou, Cypress Lake, Black Bayou, Deer Creek, Rolling Fork, and the Sunflower River.

Work on these projects lasted from late January to mid-March and involved large detachments of the army, mostly members of General McPherson's Seventeenth Corps. The troops labored under a tropical sun and torrential downpours amid lowlands where malaria and typhoid fever flourished. Despite the great exertions required of the fatigue parties and their losses due to sickness and accidents, none of the efforts provided effective access to Vicksburg. For this reason, Sherman was glad that his corps was involved mainly in the fourth and final effort, although also committed to the work at DeSoto Point.[6]

At Grant's direction, on March 16 Sherman placed the men of one of his divisions aboard two steamboats and led them up Steele's Bayou in company with a fleet of ironclads and mortar boats under David Porter. Floating debris severely limited the steamers' progress, but the more rugged ships of the navy pushed on ahead. Chagrined to fall so far behind, Sherman commandeered a tugboat and pushed on in advance of his vessels. He caught up with Porter near the point at which Steele's Bayou emptied into Deer Creek. On the sixteenth, the flag officer asked his army comrade to secure another debris-clogged waterway, Black Bayou, clearing the stream of flotsam and its banks of low-hanging trees that would obstruct the navy's passage should it have to use the bayou to return to home base. Though the job would be both tedious and arduous, Sherman agreed. Returning to his steamers, he led the way to Black Bayou and put elements of three regiments to work, some in the water, others on land. As Sherman predicted, the work was difficult in the extreme, the laborers muttering and grumbling their way through it. But under the watchful eye of the man they had begun to call "Uncle Billy," out of admiration for him and because he gave the impression of an old geezer, they dared not lay off it except during rest breaks.

The job was well under way but far from complete when, on March 19, Sherman heard Porter's guns booming with unusual regularity. That night a local African-American entered the division's bivouac carrying a plea for help entrusted to him by Porter. The message explained that his fleet, now many miles in advance of Sherman's troops, had been ambushed by Confederate infantry and artillery along both sides of Deer Creek. Some of his seamen had been stuck down, and the Rebels were felling trees to block his passage in either direction. Porter needed help, and he needed it right away.

Sherman lost no time in complying. He dispatched one of his brigades, the only troops within his immediate reach, up the east bank of Deer Creek. After they started off, he located a canoe and paddled down Black Bayou until he reached the steamboat carrying the balance of his command. He had it make all speed to Porter's rescue. Under his goading, the vessel plowed through the still-obstructed waterway, "crashing through the trees, carrying away pilot-house, smoke-stacks, and every thing above-deck." Reaching the entrance to Deer Creek near dark, beyond which the transport could not proceed, Sherman disembarked the troops and started them up the levee, a battalion of the Thirteenth United States Infantry—the regiment he had been commissioned to command but had never led into battle—in the vanguard.[7]

The journey that ensued was not only exhausting but also dangerous. In places where the road crossed a swamp, the water was hip-deep or higher. Some of the shorter men had to swim and the drummer boys had to carry their instruments on their heads. Despite the obstacles, the troops covered twenty miles by the following afternoon. "Our speed." Sherman wrote, "was accelerated by the sounds of the navy-guns, which became more and more distinct, though we could see nothing."[8]

Commandeering a subordinate's horse, Sherman departed the moving column at dawn and galloped up the levee unaccompanied by staff or escort. Several miles onward he overtook Porter's fleet, which was backing down Deer Creek under fire from infantry and cannoneers. One party of Rebels that had gotten below the ships was perilously close to damming up the channel. As Sherman raced past on his borrowed horse, Porter's seamen, seeing that their rescue was at hand, poked their heads out of their port holes and cheered "most vociferously."[9]

Sherman found their commander on the deck of one of his gunboats, attempting to direct defensive efforts while shielding himself with a plate from a smokestack. A relieved Porter explained that he had almost made up his mind to abandon ship and lead his crews through the swamps toward the Mississippi, a drastic resort. Sherman doubted that his naval counterpart "was ever more glad to meet a friend than he was to see me."[10]

Within a few hours, enough of Sherman's troops had come up to begin the task of clearing out the snipers, whom Sherman suspected had been sent down from Haynes's Bluff by General Pemberton. It was a simple task for land troops; when the last of the ambushers had been chased away, Porter resumed backing his ships down Deer Creek and into Black Bayou, an operation that consumed four days. Not until the twenty-seventh were Sherman's men back in their camps at Young's Point, where their leader was reporting the failure of the operation to his visibly disappointed superior. So ended Grant's fourth and final attempt to reach Vicksburg via a body of water other than the Mississippi.

In his memoirs, Joseph Johnston claims that "no military event worth mentioning occurred in either department [Bragg's or Pemberton's] in February 1863." Indeed, in the middle of that month he wrote Louis Wigfall that "I have been very busy for some time looking for something to do—to little purpose. Each of the three departments assigned to me [i.e., including the Department of East Tennessee, command of which Edmund Kirby Smith had just vacated] has its general and as there is no room for two, and I can't remove him. . . . nothing but the post of Inspector General is left to me. I wrote to the President on the subject—trying to explain that I am virtually laid upon the shelf with the responsibility of command, but he has not replied, perhaps because he has no better place for me. I should much prefer the *command* of fifty men."[11]

Indeed, Johnston had sent his civilian superiors a number of letters of complaint and, not only regarding his unsatisfying command situation. Days before, one of Secretary Seddon's subordinates, Robert G. H. Kean, head of the Bureau of War, had commented that Johnston "has written another of his brief unsatisfactory, almost captious letters," arguing, among other things, that Bragg required an additional twenty thousand men "to meet Rosecrans with confidence." A few weeks later Kean noted the receipt of another "sharp" missive from the department commander, this time complaining that an operation undertaken by the forces in East Tennessee had not been referred to him. Kean observed: "In substance he is clearly right; yet the letter in manner and spirit is of a piece with his jejune and ice tempered character of correspondence."[12]

One of the subjects on which Johnston unburdened himself was his conviction that Braxton Bragg deserved the government's support against his many critics. Such a comment, in the face of Bragg's flagrant mishandling of his command, makes it difficult to gauge the depth of Johnston's discontent at his seemingly anomalous position. He had rejected more than one opportunity to take over Bragg's army, a post he claimed to desire and to be willing to accept if formally offered him. Johnston gained yet another chance to displace Bragg when, in early March, the president ordered him back to Tullahoma, this time to take temporary command of the Army of Tennessee. Since Johnston's inspection tour, Davis had been the recipient of a steady flow of anti-Bragg sentiment; critics included the now-outspoken Polk, whom Davis liked and whose opinion he valued. The president had also heard the pleas of soldiers, politicians, and ordinary citizens that Johnston be given command of the army. Concerned that Bragg could no longer function in an atmosphere of rampant distrust and disapproval, Davis instructed Johnston, once he returned to Tennessee, to send Bragg to Richmond for consultation.

The subtext of Davis's directive—that he was looking for a discreet way of shouldering Bragg aside—could hardly have been lost on such a keen observer of the military-political scene as Joseph Johnston. Yet when he reached Tullahoma on March 18, he decided he must disobey Davis. Supposedly Elise Bragg, who had accompanied her husband into the field, was dangerously ill with typhoid. So that Bragg might stay with her, Johnston relieved him as ordered but deferred sending him to Richmond until Elise survived her crisis or succumbed to it. Mrs. Bragg did recover, but by the time the general returned to the army, Johnston himself had fallen ill. On April 10, he informed Davis that he could no longer serve in Bragg's stead; thus the latter was restored to command. He would retain it for the next nine months.[13]

One wonders if Johnston truly wished to take over a field army as he claimed or whether he was interested only in registering his dissatisfaction with the condition of affairs in his department. He was so troubled by the numerical inferiority of the armies within his purview that he doubted any of them could prevail in battle. If and when they were defeated, he feared that the stigma of failure would cling to him as well as to their immediate commanders. Viewed in this light, the vocal support he gave Bragg after Stones River may be seen as an effort to defend his actions as Bragg's superior. Furthermore, if a negative report by him forced Bragg's ouster and he replaced the man, he would inherit a command too weak by twenty thousand men to succeed. Here was a situation that invited disaster—disaster to the army, to the cause, and to Johnston's carefully cultivated reputation. No matter how he comported himself in this theater, whether as departmental head or army commander, he appeared predisposed to fail. Thus he could tell himself—as Lydia told him when her ire was up—that by placing him in an impossible position Jefferson Davis had set him up as the scapegoat for Confederate defeat in the West.[14]

Johnston remained in bed, "seriously sick" with fever and debility (possibly a flare-up of his battle wounds) through March and well into April. As before, throughout his recuperation he kept abreast of the war news, following Grant's progress—or lack of progress—in locating a water route to Vicksburg. Early in April he received a report from Pemberton that Grant was placing troops on transports and preparing to ship them to points unknown, perhaps to Middle Tennessee to support a new offensive by Rosecrans. By the eleventh of the month, Pemberton suspected Grant was heading for Memphis; if so, his leave-taking would enable Pemberton to gratify Johnston's desire that he return to Bragg the troops borrowed from him in December.[15]

The situation began to change on the sixteenth, when Pemberton informed departmental headquarters that most of Grant's army appeared destined to remain in front of Vicksburg. Later in the month, Johnston learned of a pair of raids against Confederate targets in Mississippi and Alabama. One was conducted by infantry mounted on mules and led by Col. Abel D. Streight of Rosecrans's army. Streight's incongruous force was pursued, overtaken, and captured whole by the redoubtable Bedford Forrest. The objective of the other column, about seventeen hundred cavalry under Col. Benjamin H. Grierson dispatched by Stephen Hurlbut at Grant's behest, was still undetermined, but the fast-moving troopers had attracted the attention of Pemberton's headquarters.[16]

More ominous news reached Tullahoma late on April 16, when Pemberton reported that a fleet of gunboats and transports had run past the Vicksburg batteries under cover of darkness. Six nights later a second such maneuver was also successful, few of the vessels involved being struck by Confederate salvos. Then, on the twenty-ninth, the warships that had slipped below Vicksburg began to shell the defenses at Grand Gulf, twenty-two miles from the city. By the following afternoon, Pemberton was warning Johnston via the telegraph that "the enemy is at Hard Times [Landing, opposite Grand Gulf] in huge force, with barges and transports, indicating a purpose to attack Grand Gulf, with a view to Vicksburg. Very heavy firing at Grand Gulf; enemy shelling our batteries from above and below."[17]

It appeared that Grant had made up his mind to attack Vicksburg not on the north or east but from the south, running empty transports past the city's defenses and, once out of range, using them to ferry across the river troops who had marched down its west bank. It was a formidable plan, but one Johnston believed Pemberton capable of defeating if he deployed properly and acted aggressively. As he would learn, however, Pemberton permitted himself to be led astray by clever feints, including a major diversion toward Haynes's Bluff by a subordinate whom Johnston had come to know by reputation, William T. Sherman. Grierson's foray through central Mississippi had likewise distracted Pemberton, preventing his troops from meeting Grant's people at the only point at which an amphibious invasion can be turned back, its landing site—in this case, the area around the village of Bruinsburg.[18]

Over the next two weeks, as Johnston struggled to regain his health, Grant's troops pushed inland. Fighting erupted on May 1 at Port Gibson, where the evacuees of Grand Gulf tried mightily but futilely to halt the northeastward advance of the invader. On this occasion and more than once thereafter, Pemberton's troops slowed the Yankees and even brought them to a halt, but the latter regrouped and muscled their way forward, seeking a decisive victory before Pemberton could take refuge inside Vicksburg. At least a portion of Grant's army appeared to be aiming for the railroad that connected Vicksburg to the state capital, with another poised to strike Jackson itself, where large quantities of matériel had been collected for Pemberton's use. Having failed to prevent the Federals from gaining their foothold south of Vicksburg, the defenders' situation was increasingly perilous, perhaps hopeless.[19]

On May 9, Johnston received from Richmond the message he had been expecting and also dreading, ordering him to Mississippi without further delay. Although still feeling the effects of his illness, he quit his sickroom, collected his staff, and boarded a westbound train. Four nights later he was in Jackson, squarely in the path of Grant's army. On hand to defend the place were two understrength brigades: the Tennessee and Texas infantry of Brig. Gen. John Gregg and the Georgia sharpshooters and artillerymen of Brig. Gen. William H. T. Walker, no more than six thousand officers and men. The day after Johnston's arrival, Gregg and Walker would be joined by an equally small brigade of Georgia and Mississippi troops commanded by Col. Peyton H. Colquitt. On the twelfth, farther east at Raymond, many of these soldiers had given a strong account of themselves despite facing twice as many Yankees, members of McPherson's corps. In the end, their heroics went for naught when they fell back to the capital in obedience to instructions from Pemberton.

Johnston wondered how, with so few troops, he could hold a city whose defenses consisted of an incomplete set of entrenchments thrown up only ten days earlier. He could expect little or no support from Pemberton's main body, which was scattered along the railroad west of Jackson, with a Yankee column between it and the city. En route to Mississippi, Johnston had received a dispatch from Pemberton indicating that Grant was moving toward Edwards's Station, fourteen miles from Vicksburg, and stating that Pemberton, "with my limited force," would attempt to block him. Pemberton feared, however, that he lacked the manpower to do so; he petitioned Johnston to send him reinforcements, including three thousand cavalry. "I urge this," he added, "as a positive necessity." Reading the dispatch, Johnston must have wondered where on the face of the earth—to say nothing of where in Mississippi—he would find so many troops. With heavy forces bearing down on him from the northwest and southwest, including a reported twenty-five thousand infantry under General Sherman only ten miles off, Johnston had all he could do to defend himself; augmenting Pemberton was out of the question.[20]

In the small hours of May 14, he decided that he had no recourse but to evacuate the capital, saving as many war goods as possible. He advised John Gregg, in overall command of the local forces, that when the Yankees arrived he should hold them off as long as possible with his foot troops, supported by a small force of cavalry and a few artillery pieces. Meanwhile, Johnston would evacuate the stores, to be hauled north of the city over the New Orleans, Jackson, & Great Northern Railroad.

His instructions imparted, Johnston sent a telegraph to Richmond, informing

Secretary Seddon of his lamentable but unalterable situation: "I arrived this evening, finding the enemy's force between this place and General Pemberton, cutting off communication. I am too late."[21]

<hr>

When Grant had made known, late in April, that he was considering running the Vicksburg batteries and ferrying troops across the river, Sherman vociferously opposed the idea. He believed, as he had made known several times over the months, that Grant's proper course was to return the army to Memphis, then resume the movement down the Mississippi Central that had been halted prematurely by Forrest and Van Dorn. Sherman thought a new movement by water too risky, and he argued the point with Grant's aides, especially Lt. Col. John A. Rawlins, Grant's adjutant general, who believed he had put the run-down-the-river scheme into his boss's head.

Sherman favored other operations as well, including attacking Pemberton's forces at Grenada; fortifying Yazoo Pass, the Tallahatchie River, and other important water routes; and threatening Holmes's enclave at Little Rock. Early in April he asked Rawlins to present these ideas, along with any that other senior officers wished to advance, before the commanding general. Sherman was attempting not only to broaden the strategic discussion but also to uncover the intentions of McClernand, who was widely believed to be intriguing against Grant in hopes of supplanting him. Sherman feared that if McClernand were permitted to keep his plans to himself, should the coming operation fail he could claim that his own more mature, more viable proposals had been ignored. Rawlins refused, however, to call a council of war, mainly because he knew Grant had made up his mind. When Grant announced that the army would execute his plan of campaign, Sherman understood that the debate was over. Saluting smartly, he readied his corps for the momentous operation ahead.[22]

If the Grant-Sherman relationship had been strained by this difference of opinion, neither man showed it. Any modicum of resentment Sherman might have felt was swept away by the success that attended Porter's run past the batteries, the ferry operation from Hard Times, and the landings near Bruinsburg. Moreover, just before the offensive got under way, Grant made a gesture that showed consideration for Sherman's feelings, an act the latter much appreciated. Grant's orders for the general movement, dated April 20, called for McClernand's troops to lead the move across the Mississippi followed by McPherson's corps, with Sherman's command bringing up the rear. To disguise the landing sites and deceive the enemy, Grant desired Sherman to feint north of the city near Haynes's Bluff. He was reluctant to order the maneuver, however, for fear that Sherman would incur the criticism of reporters who mistook the feint for another botched offensive at Chickasaw Bluffs.

Sherman saw behind Grant's reticence the unhappy truth that "we had to fight a senseless clamor at the North, as well as a determined foe and the obstacles of Nature. Of course, I answered him that I would make the 'feint,' regardless of public clamor at a distance." He did so on the twenty-ninth, when he led Blair's division (which included a brigade recently assigned to Sherman's brother-in-law, Brig. Gen. Hugh Boyle Ewing) up the Mississippi and into the Yazoo River. In the Yazoo he picked up a small flotilla commanded by Comdr. R. K. Breese and that night lay over at the mouth of Chickasaw Bayou. Near evening on the thirtieth, under cover of the navy's guns, Sherman landed Blair's troops in full view of the gunners on Haynes's Bluff. After "keeping up appearances all night," he reembarked and moved a short distance upriver. Through much of the next day, "similar movements were made, accompanied by reconnaissances of all the country on both sides of the Yazoo."[23]

On May 1 he received a communiqué from Grant calling him to Hard Times Landing preparatory to crossing the Mississippi. Via a courier-borne message he got the two divisions he had left behind, Steele's and Brig. Gen. James Madison Tuttle's, moving to Grand Gulf via Richmond. Sherman, with Blair's men, quickly joined them on the west bank. By noon of the sixth, all three divisions had crossed, and within another two days they had pushed as far inland as Hankinson's Ferry on the Big Black River, fifteen miles south of Vicksburg and forty-four miles west of Jackson. On the twelfth, along Fourteen Mile Creek east of Auburn, Mississippi, Sherman made contact with the enemy for the first time in this campaign. After a three-hour fight, his opposition, which consisted mostly of Col. Wirt Allen's dismounted cavalry, fell back and dispersed. By then, however, Adams's men had burned a bridge over the creek that Sherman's pioneers had to rebuild to keep the advance going. The next morning, as per Grant's on-scene direction, Sherman moved to Raymond, which hours earlier McPherson's corps had wrested from the outgunned Confederates of John Gregg.[24]

On May 14 Grant ordered Sherman and McPherson to converge on Jackson, the former from the southwest on the road from Mississippi Springs, the latter from the northwest via the Clinton Road. McPherson got there first and engaged Gregg's Tennesseans and Texans in a driving rain. Despite moving over roads turned into soup and across fields that were now lagoons, Sherman hastened to his colleague's support. Three miles from Jackson, Tuttle's division, leading the column, came under fire from a battery at the lower end of the town. While Tuttle deployed his foot soldiers, Sherman brought up guns of his own including those of Waterhouse's battery, which had performed so effectively at Shiloh. As soon as Waterhouse got the range of the enemy, their guns fell silent, and they wheeled to the rear. Moving up, the attackers encountered a line of scary-looking entrenchments that had been dug out of the bed of a deep stream and which were shielded by guns—perhaps those that had just withdrawn. Sherman ordered a flanking movement by his right, only to discover that the trenches had been vacated. Before Tuttle could resume his movement, Steele closed up on his right, and the divisions advanced side-by-side into the town. They learned that most of Jackson's men, including Gregg's division, had fled. Even so, Sherman reported capturing 250 defenders, "with all the enemy's artillery (eighteen guns), with much ammunition and valuable public stores."[25]

With Jackson in his grasp, Sherman, at about four o'clock, joined McPherson and the recently arrived Grant in a jubilant reunion at the Bowman House hotel, adjacent to the state capitol. One result of the meeting was that the following day, while Grant and McPherson headed north toward a confrontation with Pemberton's main body, Sherman's men wrecked the railroad and public property for miles around the town. Items that fell prey to the occupiers included the Pearl River bridge; a government foundry; a gun-carriage manufactory; a cotton factory; twenty miles' worth of tracks and ties on the Southern Railroad and the New Orleans, Jackson & Great Northern; and a few structures that Sherman admitted were destroyed pursuant to no order, including a Catholic church and the unfortunately named Confederate Hotel, "the former resulting from accidental circumstances and the latter from malice." He summed up the demolition by claiming, not inaccurately, that "Jackson, as a railroad center or Government depot of stores and military factories, can be of little use to the enemy for six months."[26]

Sherman's troops destroying Jackson, Miss.

The only item of interest that Sherman left out of his report was that in advancing on Jackson he had engaged for the first time Joseph E. Johnston, who, nominally at least, had commanded the forces defending the town. It had been an uneven contest from start to finish, one Johnston could not possibly have won. But there would be more confrontations to come, and not all would end with the premature departure of one of the antagonists.

———※◇※———

By 2:00 P.M. on the fourteenth, the supplies removed from Jackson were on their way to Canton, and the defenders north of town, who had done a remarkable job of holding off McPherson's corps, were disengaging and falling back. Johnston called in Gregg's, Walker's, and Colquitt's troops and led them five miles north of town along a road he believed would enable him to join forces with Pemberton. The latter, whose troops Johnston estimated at thirty-two thousand (in actuality, he had ten thousand fewer), had concentrated at Edwards's Station on the railroad east of Vicksburg. As soon as they were beyond pursuit by McPherson or Sherman, Johnston sent a dispatch to Pemberton, informing him of what had transpired at Jackson, explaining that a large enemy force—perhaps half of Grant's army—occupied the place, and opining that "it would decide the campaign to beat it." He desired Pemberton to join him and help him inflict "a heavy blow upon the enemy." But Johnston failed to receive a prompt reply, which worried him. Time was fast slipping away; Pemberton and he needed to unite before Grant managed to block them.[27]

The next day Johnston led his meager force to Calhoun Station, fourteen miles north of Jackson. He received there a dispatch from Pemberton—but not in answer to his of the previous day—stating that he intended to march from Edwards's Station in a southwesterly direction in hopes of coming in behind Grant's main force and cutting its line of communications. In making this move, however, Pemberton was seeking a phantom objective, for Grant had already taken steps to cut his own line of supply. He wished his troops to live off the country and thus be independent of a base the enemy could attack in hopes of duplicating Van Dorn's success.

Pemberton's message was disheartening, for it told Johnston that his subordinate was moving away from, not toward, a junction of forces. Johnston rushed a courier toward Edwards's Station with a message urging Pemberton to march, instead, to Clinton, where they could link. This was substantially the same advice he had given Pemberton late on the thirteenth, upon arriving in Jackson.

Hopeful that the second order had done the trick, Johnston remained at Calhoun throughout the sixteenth, giving the troops under him, who were exhausted from marching and fighting, essential rest.

That afternoon he received Pemberton's reply to his communiqué of the thirteenth. Now his subordinate indicated a willingness to move in Johnston's direction although disliking the idea of straying from Vicksburg, which only one week earlier Jefferson Davis, true to his determination to hold every point on the Confederate map, had urged Pemberton to hold at all costs. "In directing this move," Pemberton told Johnston, "I do not think you fully comprehend the position that Vicksburg will be left in."[28]

Reading this, Johnston may have suspected that he would fail to dissuade his subordinate from a disastrous course. As befit his philosophy of husbanding manpower, Johnston considered it much more important to preserve an army than occupy a position, especially one so vulnerable to attack or siege. Even before he arrived in Mississippi, he had considered Vicksburg a death trap, one he hoped Pemberton would avoid at all costs. But even as Johnston waited hopefully for a union of forces, Pemberton was being brought to battle southeast of Edwards's Station on terms favorable to his opponent.

Johnston would not learn until much later how this had happened. It turned out that on the fourteenth Pemberton called his senior subordinates into council to frame a response to Johnston's dispatch calling them to Clinton. After a discussion of the situation, Pemberton took a vote. A majority ruled in favor of obeying the summons, but two of Pemberton's generals called for a shift westward to locate and sever Grant's communications with the Mississippi. Although favoring neither alternative—he preferred a fall-back to Vicksburg—Pemberton adopted the minority view.[29]

The next day, the fifteenth, Pemberton marched his army across Baker's Creek, aiming for Grant's nonexistent line of communications. Failing to locate it, he countermarched through Edwards's Station in a belated attempt to comply with Johnston's directive. By then, it was too late; his movements had attracted Grant's attention, and early on the sixteenth the forces of McPherson and McClernand, supported by Blair's division, detached from Sherman, advanced against the Confederate position atop eighty-foot-high Champion Hill. During a savage, day-long succession of attack and counterattack, Pemberton suffered almost four thousand casualties to fewer than twenty-five hundred for Grant; he was barely able to bring off the rest of his army and cross Baker's Creek to temporary safety.[30]

The next day, Pemberton put his weary and disgruntled troops on the roads to

Vicksburg, his place of sanctuary, while his rear guard, the division of Brig. Gen. John Stevens Bowen (which had fought gamely at Port Gibson and Champion Hill), attempted to block the crossings of the Big Black River nine miles east of the city. Yet within an hour of making contact, elements of McClernand's and McPherson's corps routed Bowen's men, killing or capturing more than seventeen hundred and sending the rest scurrying across the stream over bridges that other Rebels then burned. Undaunted by the roadblock, early on the eighteenth Grant began crossing his troops, including Sherman's command, on pontoon bridges.[31]

Ignorant of what had transpired at Champion Hill and the Big Black, on the seventeenth Johnston moved with Gregg's, Walker's, and Colquitt's men in the direction he believed Pemberton was heading, ready for a junction. That night he bivouacked along the road from Livingston, several miles to the north and east of Edwards's Station. After midnight, Johnston was awakened by one of Pemberton's scouts, bearing a message that his commander had composed that morning. In it Pemberton recounted the events that had followed the recent council of war. He described briefly the fight at Champion Hill, although refusing to describe it as the debacle it truly was, and announced his fall-back to the Big Black. Soon after digesting the disturbing news, Johnston heard from "good but unofficial sources" that Pemberton had left the river, heading for Vicksburg.[32]

With a sinking feeling Johnston dashed off a warning to his subordinate: "Vicksburg is of no value and cannot be held; if, therefore, you are invested in Vicksburg, you must ultimately surrender." Early on the nineteenth, he received Pemberton's reply, written from a city already under siege. Pemberton regretted to inform Johnston that he had convened another council to discuss the best way to respond to the order to evacuate Vicksburg. The unanimous decision of his subordinates was that it was impossible to do so without ruining the morale of the army and panicking the civilian population. Therefore, "I have decided to hold Vicksburg as long as possible, with the firm hope that the Government may yet be able to assist me in keeping this obstruction to the enemy's navigation of the Mississippi River. I still conceive it to be the most important point in the Confederacy."[33]

With these words, Pemberton effectively sealed the fate of his army, and of his nation.

On the morning of May 16 Sherman, in response to Grant's order, moved Steele's and Tuttle's divisions from Jackson to Bolton's Station on the railroad northeast of Champion Hill. The next day, after driving defenders from the east bank near Bridgeport, he crossed the river on one of the army's floating bridges and took a road leading to points north of Vicksburg. When he bivouacked that night, Grant joined him by the campfire. Sherman recalled that "we sat on a log, looking at the passage of the troops by the light of those fires; the bridge swayed to and fro under the passing feet, and made a fine war-picture."[34]

The next morning, the two rode together in the direction of the bluffs that overlooked Vicksburg. All around them, the army was moving briskly, confidently, even jubilantly, toward its ultimate objective, Sherman's corps on the right, McPherson's in the center, McClernand's on the left. Sherman's route of march led him over familiar ground, albeit from a different direction than before—one he thus observed from an entirely new perspective. Before the afternoon was over, his forward echelon had gained the crest of Walnut Hills, toward which many of the same troops had fruitlessly maneuvered less than five months before. This feat, critical to clamping a death grip on Pemberton's garrison, moved the corps commander to make a solemn admission to his superior. As Grant later recalled, Sherman confessed that until that moment he had felt "no positive assurance of success. This, however, he said was the end of one of the greatest campaigns in history. . . . Vicksburg was not yet captured, and there was no telling what might happen before it was taken; but whether captured or not, this was a complete and successful campaign."[35]

Sherman's imputation of historical significance was justified, but so was his acknowledgment that much work remained before the city was in Grant's hands and the Mississippi flowed freely from source to mouth. Grant got right to it. The following day, acting on the supposition that the weakness Pemberton's troops had displayed on the Big Black signified widespread demoralization, he ordered a general attack on Vicksburg, Sherman's corps from the north, McPherson's from the east, and McClernand's from the southeast.

The assault was spearheaded by Frank Blair's division, which included not only Hugh Ewing's brigade but also the First Battalion, Thirteenth United States Infantry, one of whose company officers was Capt. Charles Ewing. At 2:00 P.M., Blair's men went forward, their target a vulnerable-looking salient called the Stockade Redan. As Sherman reported, the troops gained the top of the parapet but were prevented from crossing it by a blizzard of shot and shell. Each of Blair's brigades suffered terribly, the Thirteenth United States taking especially heavy losses. Charles Ewing, who survived the storm, won this day so much praise for his conduct that he was soon on the road to promotion. His advancement would culminate in his March 1865 appointment to brigadier general of volunteers. Prior to that he would gain a coveted position on the staff of his brother-in-law, an occurrence that generated accusations of nepotism but one justified both by leadership potential and subsequent results. Charles's elevation, coupled with Hugh's brigadier generalcy and the brevet of major general their brother Tom would earn (the latter was serving as commander of the District of the Border, comprising Kansas and western Missouri) would make the Ewings close competitors to the "Fighting McCooks" of Ohio—six brothers and cousins who became general officers—as the most star-studded family in the Union.[36]

(from left) Hugh, Philemon, Thomas, and Charles Ewing

The Ewing tradition was also upheld this day by Hugh, whose brigade achieved the deepest penetration of any of the attacking units. In the end, however, even Hugh's stalwarts fell short of a breakthrough, though only by a matter of yards. So close had Blair's men gotten to the Rebel works that when Sherman called off the attack, many could not withdraw until after dark. Elsewhere, McClernand's and McPherson's men captured picket posts in advance of Pemberton's main line but came up short of their objectives.[37]

The results opened the eyes of Grant's troops to the strength of Pemberton's works and the tenacity of their occupants. The next day, Grant called his corps commanders together. Sherman recalled that "we compared notes, and agreed that the assault of the day before had failed, by reason of the natural strength of the position, and because we were forced by the nature of the ground to limit our attacks to the strongest parts of the enemy's line." They decided to try again, aiming for some of the same works as well as others thought to be more weakly manned. Two days later, at 10:00 A.M., May 22, the army went forward, this time preceded by an hour-long bombardment. Blair's division, supported closely by Tuttle's, advanced down the ominously named Graveyard Road toward the Stockade Redan. From a vantage point two hundred yards from the point of attack, Sherman had a clear view of the proceedings: "The rebel line, concealed by the parapet, showed no sign of unusual activity; but as our troops came in fair view, the enemy rose behind the parapet and poured a furious fire upon our lines; and, for about two hours, we had a severe and bloody battle, but at every point we were repulsed."[38]

As the attackers hastened back to their starting point, some of them badly wounded, crawling on hands and knees to avoid the rain of missiles overhead, Grant arrived at Sherman's field headquarters. Sherman frankly admitted that his assault had failed. Grant explained that McPherson's effort had also fallen short. While they talked a courier arrived from McClernand's headquarters with a message in which the corps commander claimed his men had seized the Rebel parapet in their front. He urged Grant to order Sherman and McPherson to resume their assault; if they did, McClernand implied, he would achieve a breakthrough that would fatally weaken Pemberton's entire position.

Sherman recalled Grant as scoffing at McClernand's claim, declaring, "I don't believe a word of it!" Sherman, however, persuaded him to give McClernand the benefit of the doubt. Grant eventually agreed to ride to McClernand's headquarters and ascertain for himself the state of affairs. He told Sherman that if he did not return by 3:00 P.M., to renew the attack. Three o'clock came but Grant did not, so Sherman sent four of his brigades back into action. The effort, he noted ruefully, "was a repetition of the first, equally unsuccessful and bloody." The brigades had failed to coordinate their movements, with the result that they were repulsed in succession. Their exertions, and those of McPherson's men on the left, went for naught; McClernand gained nothing despite having committed his entire command to a do-or-die assault.[39]

Two lopsided defeats three days apart convinced Grant to forgo the quick route to victory and take the long but more predictable road, siege warfare. It was a practical decision, adopted with regret. Grant was aware that Northern morale was sagging under the weight of a recent defeat in Virginia where the Army of the Potomac, now under Maj. Gen. Joseph Hooker, had been outmaneuvered, outfought, and outwitted by Robert E. Lee's Army of Northern Virginia near a

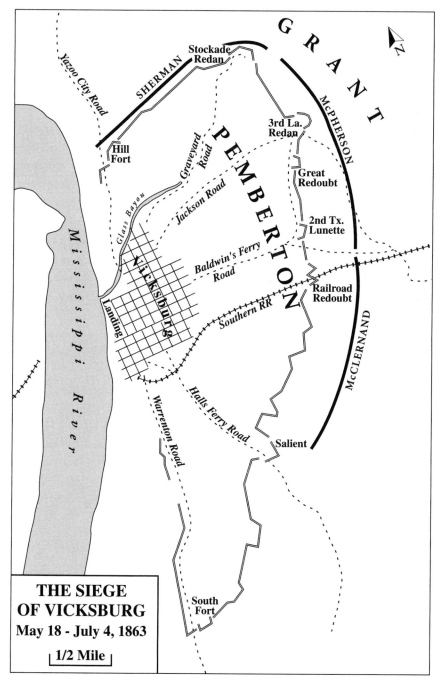

The Siege of Vicksburg, May 18-July 14, 1863

crossroads west of Fredericksburg known as Chancellorsville. The only benefit accruing from the battle was the mortal wounding of the irreplaceable Stonewall Jackson. Supporters of the Union badly needed a triumph in some theater, and Grant feared he would need weeks, if not months, to give it to them.

His single consolation was his permanent separation from John McClernand. The thorn in Grant's flesh had been plucked as a result of McClernand's late-May publication, in violation of departmental orders, of his official report of the fighting on the twenty-second. In it the politician-general claimed credit for single-handedly turning the tide of battle but being forced to retreat because of Sherman's and McPherson's failure to support him. Grant used the weapon thus given him to relieve the politician-general from command, an act that Abraham Lincoln declined to overturn.

Sherman, for one, was not sorry to see the man go. There was no place in the army for a glory seeker whose troops were mere stepping stones to success in the political realm. For Sherman—as he would pungently declare many years in the future—war was hell. For McClernand and too many others like him, war was opportunity.[40]

FOURTEEN
WAR
IN EARNEST

Upon receiving Pemberton's message of May 19 revealing his intention to occupy Vicksburg, Johnston wrote him that "I am trying to gather a force which may attempt to relieve you. Hold out." Over the next several days he cobbled together a small army consisting of the forces that had helped him defend Jackson, plus the divisions of John C. Breckinridge (the 1860 presidential candidate of the southern wing of the Democratic Party) and William Wing Loring (Stonewall Jackson's disgruntled subordinate in the Shenandoah Valley), the infantry brigades of Brig. Gens. Nathan G. Evans, Matthew D. Ector, Evander McNair, Samuel Bell Maxey, Albert Rust, and a small division of cavalry under Brig. Gen. William H. Jackson.

Johnston estimated his force at less than thirty thousand troops of all arms. This was not nearly enough to oppose effectively Grant's vast host, which Johnston feared outnumbered his more than two-to-one. The disparity gave him no realistic prospect of evicting the Federals who had invested Vicksburg. He could neither lift the siege, nor—because he lacked an efficient means of communication with Pemberton—could he strike Grant from the rear in conjunction with a sortie by the Vicksburg garrison. Believing these daunting obstacles insurmountable, Johnston made no serious attempt to relieve Pemberton's army, nor did he develop a plan capable of doing so. Although he always maintained that he intended somehow to save his trapped subordinate, his actions and intentions as revealed in his correspondence with Pemberton and the Confederate government between late May and early July 1863 fail to bear him out.

From the outset, Pemberton hoped and believed Johnston would fight his way through to rescue him. As he informed Johnston on May 21, "the men credit and are encouraged by a report that you are near with a large force. They are fighting in good spirits. . . ." On the twenty-ninth Johnston, who at the time was at Canton, well east of Pemberton, attempted to lower his subordinate's expectations: "I am too weak to save Vicksburg." Already he had pled an inability to reinforce Maj. Gen. Franklin Gardner, whose garrison at Port Hudson was besieged by Maj. Gen. Nathaniel P. Banks's Nineteenth Army Corps, a command that Grant was expected to support but with whom he had been unable to coordinate operations. All Johnston could do for Gardner was offer the faint hope that Edmund Kirby Smith, now in command of the Confederate Trans-Mississippi Department, would send troops across the river to strike Banks from the rear. In the end, Smith did nothing to help. For his part, Johnston cited an insufficiency of field transportation as his reason for being unable to assist Gardner, although he was also concerned that any move toward Louisiana would leave his communications open to attack by Grant.[1]

Over the next six weeks Johnston repeated his "I am too weak" mantra to anyone who urged him to rescue Pemberton. Occasionally, however, he held out the prospect that he would find a way to save Vicksburg and, by extension, Port Hudson. Even as he cited manpower inadequacies, he suggested that Pemberton and he "co-operate" through "mutually supporting movements." As late as June 14 he informed Pemberton that he hoped to "save you and your garrison" through "exact co-operation" of movements. These indirect pledges of support served no purpose except a temporary lift to morale inside Vicksburg, for Johnston made no effort to keep any of them.[2]

Beginning in early June, Johnston sparred verbally with his superiors in Richmond, all of whom—Davis, Seddon, Cooper—considered Vicksburg too valuable a possession to be given up and believed that, at the very least, a substantial effort should be made to save it. As he did when communicating with Pemberton, Johnston gave the government officials mixed signals as to his intentions. Although in early June he complained that he had "not . . . half the troops necessary" to fight through to Pemberton, he also declared that his "only plan" was to relieve Vicksburg. He mixed his messages again later in the month by telling Secretary Seddon quite plainly that he considered saving Vicksburg a hopeless task. A week later he was hinting to Pemberton that there was still a chance they could cooperate to save the garrison; he went so far as to suggest that "in a day or two" he would make a diversion in Pemberton's favor and "open communications" with him.[3]

Troop strength became a bone of contention in Johnston's dealings with Richmond. Seddon seemed to believe his force numbered thirty-four thousand exclusive of militia forces, which, the secretary implied, ought to be added to this total. Johnston countered by explaining that not all the units he had expected to receive had reached him and that when or if they did the total would not exceed twenty-six thousand. Then Johnston seized on the secretary's comment as suggesting that the government intended to send him enough additions to meet the figure Seddon had mentioned. Johnston must have realized the secretary had meant no such thing, but he wanted to put Seddon on the defensive.[4]

Johnston hoped to receive at least some reinforcements, and he asked Richmond's help in obtaining them. Davis and Seddon declared that no troops were available outside Johnston's own department, but on June 8 they solicited his opinion about detaching from Bragg's army. Johnston stunned them by pleading ignorance of Bragg's troop strength, even suggesting that they were in a better position to know. Furthermore, whether to detach troops from Bragg was the government's call: "I have not considered myself commanding in Tennessee since assignment here, and should not have felt authorized to take troops from that department after having been informed by the Executive that no more could be spared."

Johnston's admission suggested that he lacked a fundamental knowledge of conditions in his own command. It also bespoke an effort to evade the responsibility of making a major strategic decision—and not for the first time. Davis considered Johnston's profession of ignorance "extraordinary," coming as it did from Bragg's immediate superior. He also reacted incredulously to Johnston's June 12 warning that "to take from Bragg a force that would make this army fit to oppose Grant's, would involve yielding Tennessee. It is for the Government to decide between this State and Tennessee. . . . Without some great blunder of the enemy, we cannot hold both."[5]

Upset and angry at Johnston's attempted abdication, by June 16 his superiors began to press him to attack Grant's army. "Vicksburg," Seddon lectured him, "must not be lost without a desperate struggle. The interest and honor of the Confederacy forbid it. I rely on you still to avert the loss. If better resources do not offer, you must attack. It may be made in concert with the garrison, if practicable, but otherwise, without—by day or night, as you think best." Johnston replied blandly that the secretary did not realize what he was asking: "You do not appreciate the difficulties in the course you direct, nor the probability and consequences of failure." In saying this Johnston was refusing to obey a direct order. Quite properly, he could have been cashiered for insubordination. Instead, Seddon merely repeated his instructions, albeit in less direct language, explaining rather defensively that "only the conviction of almost imperative necessity for action, induces the official dispatch I have just sent you."[6]

An unmoved Johnston stood his ground. Attack meant defeat, and defeat meant opening the rest of Mississippi and all of Alabama to Grant's hordes. That was a risk he was unwilling to take even when commanded to do so by his ordained superior. His recalcitrance had a predictable effect. By late June Robert Kean was reporting that "the President is said to be furious with Johnston." For his part, Kean was at a loss to understand "why some energy cannot be infused into the western department." One of Davis's closest confidants, Brig. Gen. Josiah Gorgas, chief of the Confederate ordnance department, hoped that "Johnston will soon move upon Grant. The public will never forgive Johnston if he allows the city to fall without an effort to relieve it."[7]

But Johnston made no such effort, although by the last days of June, to assure the government that he was not sitting idly by as the soldiers and civilians inside Vicksburg starved, he left his station north of Jackson. On June 29, he marched his command—now large enough to have been divided into divisions commanded by Generals Breckinridge, Loring, Walker, and Samuel Gibbs French—toward the east bank of the Big Black. Two days later, he took position between the river and the village of Brownsville. On July 2 and 3 he reconnoitered the area north of the nearby railroad, from which, he intimated to Richmond, he expected to launch a diversionary attack in behalf of the garrison. In the end he decided nothing could be accomplished in that sector, but he made plans to examine the other side of the tracks.

The opportunity never arose. On the fifth, he learned that Pemberton had surrendered the city and its defenders to Grant on Independence Day. The news could hardly have come as a shock; as early as June 22 Pemberton had suggested that his superior communicate with Grant about permitting the garrison to evacuate, retaining its arms but turning Vicksburg over to the invader. Perhaps reasoning that Grant would never agree, Johnston did not broach the proposal.

On the evening of the seventh, Johnston marched his command back to Jackson. Two days later, the day on which Franklin Gardner, having heard the news out of Mississippi, surrendered Port Hudson to Banks, Johnston found himself penned up in the capital by Sherman, at the head of an expedition comprising large elements of his own corps; the Thirteenth Corps, now under Edward Ord; and the Ninth Corps, recently arrived from Virginia under Maj. Gen. John G. Parke. By this time Johnston had the full complement of troops he had been expecting but which fell far short of Sherman's numbers. Johnston was further handicapped by the poor quality and unsuitable location of the rifle pits that constituted Jackson's only defenses. Hoping for the best, on July 8 Johnston placed his troops in these trenches and prepared to confront his enemy.

Historians cannot understand why a badly outnumbered Johnston would wish to defend a town without strong works that already had been stripped of military goods and whose communication lines had been thoroughly wrecked. He no longer needed to remain within supporting range of Vicksburg. Perhaps it was a face-saving gesture, one made for appearance's sake. Whatever the reason, he spent the next several days skirmishing with Sherman's people on all sides of the town and trying unsuccessfully to capture one of their ammunition trains. By July 12 Sherman was making a limited attack (easily repulsed) on Breckinridge's position. He was also shelling Jackson's outskirts and downtown, reducing so many houses to charred rubble that his men would dub the result "Chimneyville." Before the quasi-siege ended, Johnston would suffer seventy-one soldiers killed, more than five hundred wounded, and twenty-five missing.

At first puzzled why Sherman made no attempt to overwhelm him, Johnston eventually decided that his opponent was a shrewd and cautious man, qualities Johnston could appreciate in another. Sherman did not need to destroy Johnston's motley command, only prevent it from interfering with the operations of Grant's main force inside Vicksburg, where prisoners were being rounded up and issued paroles and local citizens were being succored by the Union commissary department.

On the fourteenth, Johnston discovered that Sherman was judiciously placing batteries of heavy-caliber guns around the town, reviving year-old memories of besieged Yorktown. Convinced that it would be "madness on our part to attack him," on the night of May 16–17 Johnston evacuated, his troops crossing the Pearl River in two columns and trooping west along the railroad in the direction of Morton. His retreat coincided with the reduction of his command. On the twenty-third, three days after he bivouacked near Morton, he received a terse message from General Cooper notifying him that the Department of East Tennessee had been merged into Bragg's department and that the latter was being removed from Johnston's authority. Johnston was now reduced to commanding the few forces operating in Mississippi, east Louisiana, and Alabama south of the Tennessee River. Ostensibly, as Cooper suggested, the change had been made in conformity with a suggestion from Johnston himself. This may have been true technically. The general suspected, however, that the action was a result of the disfavor into which he had fallen in Richmond, and he braced himself for penalties yet to come.[8]

Perhaps taking his cue from Grant, who admitted that Joseph Johnston "was about the only general on that side whom he feared," over the weeks following the assault of May 22 Sherman kept an eye peeled to the rear for a general who might attack the Army of the Tennessee as a diversion for a breakout by Pemberton. As soon as he got word of Pemberton's surrender, Sherman set out to eliminate the threat posed by Johnston and his force of unknown size near Jackson.

Sherman's marching orders enjoined his subordinates to "hold their troops in perfect [order] for battle at all times, and on encountering the enemy will engage him at once." The same directive stressed the penalties to be levied upon soldiers caught looting or destroying private property. This injunction—expressive of Sherman's distaste for violence done to the social order and yet at variance with his determination to carry the war to the enemy's civilian population—had little effect. En route to Jackson, hundreds of soldiers ran amuck, pillaging, burning, and assaulting noncombatants. One prominent target was the Hinds County plantation of Joseph Davis, whose home and fields were ravaged and his slaves spirited away by foragers enraged to learn that he was the older brother of the president of the Confederacy. Another victim was a ninety-five-year-old woman whose home and almost everything in it was torn apart as she watched. To a passing army surgeon she sobbed, "If you live to be as old as I am, pray never to see the like again as long as you live!"[9]

Sherman did not approve of these excesses, but he appreciated some of their effects. The march to Jackson illustrated the successful application of his policy of creating disaffection by waging what one of his soldiers called "war in earnest. Destruction, misery, devastation and everything that can be added to them make the sum of it." Sherman was delighted to hear that many locals, distraught over the loss of homes, livestock, and crops, had turned their wrath on the government that had failed to protect them, loudly uttering anti-Confederate sentiments. He was not surprised by their reaction. Most of those who cursed their public officials were members not of the planter aristocracy but of the South's middle class, a species Sherman analyzed when, in early June, he responded to an invitation from General Halleck to express his thoughts on the military and political reconstruction of the occupied South: "The smaller farmers, mechanics, merchants, and laborites . . . have, in fact, no real interest in the establishment of a Southern Confederacy, and have been led or driven into war on the false theory that they were to be benefited somehow—they know not how. They are essentially tired of the war. . . ."[10]

After he flushed Johnston's troops out of Jackson, Sherman opted to forgo a pursuit. But when Grant decreed one should be made, he sent a picked force from Steele's division, stripped for mobility, on Johnston's heels. The column caught up with the fugitives at Brandon, skirmishing with them and, once they withdrew farther east to Morton, contented itself with destroying public property. Meanwhile, Sherman resumed a job he had been forced to curtail when called to Vicksburg on May 16. His troops burned a vast quantity of matériel and railroad stock that Johnston had left behind in Jackson, goods that could have been carried off had the Confederate commander devoted some resources to repairing the badly damaged Pearl River trestle south of town. By the time Sherman and his men left to return to Vicksburg on July 27, the countryside within a thirty-mile radius of the capital had been systematically denuded, while the right-of-way of both of the local railroads had been torn up for forty miles above and sixty miles below the place. Sherman considered it a tough job well done: "Jackson, once the pride and boast of Mississippi, is a ruined town."[11]

By month's end Sherman had established his headquarters on the west bank of the Big Black about twenty miles from Vicksburg. His corps now consisted of four divisions, having added one formed for Hugh Ewing to those commanded by Steele, Blair, and Tuttle. Sherman and his men enjoyed the unbroken rest granted them after weeks of laboring in swamps and bayous, tramping across western Mississippi, charging enemy works, besieging towns, and destroying the war-sustaining resources of the enemy. Sherman was elated by the outcome of the campaign in this theater, which he dared believe would play a major role in bringing the war to a successful conclusion.

Recent events in the East promised to have the same effect. In early June Robert E. Lee had launched his second invasion of Northern territory, a campaign begun with great promise but cut short by the Army of the Potomac, now under Maj. Gen. George Gordon Meade, which had overtaken the Confederates in south-central Pennsylvania. One day before Vicksburg's fall, Lee had been decisively defeated on the fields and ridges outside Gettysburg and forced to return to Virginia minus several thousand casualties he could ill afford to lose. To further brighten Sherman's state of mind, while Lee was marching to his fateful confrontation with Meade and Pemberton's army was being starved into submission, General Rosecrans was completing a masterful series of advances, threats, and feints that eventually drove Bragg's army out of Middle Tennessee and into Chattanooga.[12]

Even as he read the promising news from distant theaters, Sherman learned that for their services throughout the campaign just ended, McPherson and he had been nominated to be brigadier generals in the regular army, Sherman's promotion to rank from July 4, McPherson's from August 1. Grant's support had been critical in gaining the promotions, and Sherman let his superior know how grateful he was. To round out Sherman's contentment, within days of the promotion announcement Ellen arrived from Ohio for a six-week visit along with twelve-year-old Minnie, eleven-year-old Lizzie, nine-year-old Willy, and six-year-old Tommy. Cump was delighted to see his wife and each of the children, but his heart leapt at the sight of the son who had inherited his name, his looks, and his love of the military. He glowed when his headquarters escort, the First Battalion, Thirteenth Infantry, adopted Willy as their mascot, dressed him in a junior version of a sergeant's uniform, and included him in many of their drills and ceremonies.[13]

Then, suddenly and crushingly, Sherman's peace of mind evaporated. On September 22 Grant, from Vicksburg, directed him to ready one of his divisions for shipment to Chattanooga. The next day he was summoned to Grant's side and shown dispatches from Halleck telling of a disaster to the Army of the Cumberland. In mid-August, under the prodding of Lincoln and Stanton—and in conjunction with an advance on Knoxville by the Army of the Ohio, now under Ambrose Burnside, the seemingly lethargic Rosecrans finally left Middle Tennessee to challenge Bragg's army in its new lair. He came on with such verve and brashness that Bragg on September 6 made the fateful decision to evacuate Chattanooga and retreat into Georgia.

Made overconfident by his enemy's drastic reaction, Rosecrans crossed the Georgia line in loose formation, expecting to meet little or no opposition. Instead, on September 19 Bragg, recently reinforced by two divisions sent by rail from Lee's army under James Longstreet, turned on his pursuer and attacked. On day two of a fierce, extended battle along Chickamauga Creek near Rossville, Longstreet penetrated Rosecrans's right flank, then moved north, rolling up the Union line—all except George Thomas's corps—and driving most of its troops from the field in disorder and panic.[14]

The fugitives took refuge in Chattanooga, where, although spared pursuit through Bragg's indecision, found themselves besieged by an enemy who took up commanding positions east and south of the city. Their supply lines cut, within days the Federals stood on the brink of starvation. Washington had petitioned Grant to go to Rosecrans's rescue with many of the troops who had taken

Vicksburg, to be joined at Chattanooga by the Eleventh and Twelfth Corps of Meade's army under the command of the supposedly discredited Joe Hooker.[15]

On the twenty-fifth, Sherman returned to his camps on the Big Black, orders in hand. As his command packed up to leave (all but Tuttle's division, which would remain at Vicksburg along with Ord's troops and most of McPherson's), Sherman and his family rode into the captured city. There they boarded a Mississippi River steamer heading north. Sherman would accompany his wife and children to Memphis before rejoining his corps for the journey to Chattanooga.

When the ship prepared to cast off, Willy was suddenly found to be missing. As Cump and Ellen edged toward panic, a sergeant from the Thirteenth regulars went looking for the boy and some minutes later came back to the boat, leading Willy by the hand. The boy was all smiles, having appropriated a double-barrel shotgun he had found lying around; his relieved father joked with him about decamping with stolen property. But the merriment ended when, as the steamer churned upriver under a torrid sun, Willy complained of feeling ill. Ellen put him to bed, but his condition rapidly worsened. A surgeon on board examined the boy and diagnosed him as suffering from a virulent strain of typhoid. As soon as they reached Memphis, the family took rooms in the Gayoso House and sent for the city's leading physician, who confirmed the army doctor's diagnosis.

Willy Sherman

According to all who gathered around his bedside, Willy bore his suffering without complaint, but he sank quickly away. On October 3, twenty-four hours after the family reached the city, he died. "The blow was a terrible one to us all," his father recalled years later, "so sudden and so unexpected, that I could not help reproaching myself for having consented to his visit in that sickly region in the summer-time. Of all my children, he seemed the most precious. . . . I had watched with intense interest his development, and he seemed more than any of the children to take an interest in my special profession." Willy was the son Sherman had hoped to give to the army as a legacy of his own pride and devotion. Now he was gone, and the hope gone with him.[16]

It was a blow from which the father would never fully recover and one that put additional strain on a marriage that had endured more than its share of trials and burdens. Willy's passing may have brought Ellen and Cump together in a way that no pleasant experience could have, but shared grief did not make the tragedy easier to bear, and for a time the pain was insupportable. The night after Willy's death, Cump wrote to thank the commander of the headquarters escort and, through him, every member of the Thirteenth Infantry, for " their kind behavior to my poor child." In words almost poetic in their mournful cadence, he poured out his cup of misery: "The child who bore my name, and in whose future I reposed with more confidence than I did in my own . . . now floats a mere corpse, seeking a grave in a distant land, with a weeping mother, brother, and sisters clustered about him. . . . Child as he was, he had the enthusiasm, the pure love of truth, honor, and love of country, which should animate all soldiers. God only knows why he should die this young. He is dead, but will not be forgotten till those who knew him in life have followed him to that same mysterious end."[17]

As a soldier himself, he could not let personal tragedy interfere with duty and responsibility: "For myself I can ask no sympathy. On, on I must go till I meet a soldier's fate, or see my country rise superior to all factions, till its flag is adored and respected by ourselves and all the Powers of Earth." Going on meant leaving his distraught wife and sobbing children at Memphis and hastening to join his troops on the water and on the march. His ultimate destination was Chattanooga, where Grant was also headed although via a later start and a roundabout route through Louisville and Nashville. Preparing his troops for the trip consumed most of his daylight hours, leaving him little time for anything but his duties, yet it failed to still the workings of his tormented mind. As he wrote Ellen, "sleeping—waking—everywhere I see poor little Willy. Why should I ever have taken them [the children] to that dread climate?" Unknown to either of them, when she left Cump at Memphis Ellen was again pregnant. But the son she bore the following June would not fill the void of Willy's passing. Sickly from birth, Charles Celestine Sherman died at six months, an event that only deepened the aura of tragedy that had enveloped the family.[18]

Not till October 11 was Sherman ready to leave Memphis via the railroad to Charleston. His orders called on him to repair that southeastward-running line as he traveled, as extensive sections had fallen prey to Confederate raiders. He would follow the Memphis & Charleston through Corinth, Mississippi, to

Athens, Alabama. Via that line he was also to draw supplies for his corps, obviating the need to use the overtaxed railroads that connected the armies with the great supply depot at Nashville.

By the time he departed Memphis, two of his four divisions, those led by Brig. Gens. Peter J. Osterhaus (a veteran of the Prussian army who had replaced General Steele, now commanding the Department of Arkansas at Little Rock) and John Eugene Smith, had already left by the same route for Athens. After Sherman got off, the rest of his command would follow him eastward.

Almost from the start, he encountered delays and troubles large and small. At Collierville, only a few miles out of Memphis, Rebel horsemen under Brig. Gen. James R. Chalmers—sent by Joe Johnston to wreck the Memphis & Charleston—attacked the depot just as Sherman's train pulled in. For four hours the raiders battled the small guard at the station. Until finally chased off by Brig. Gen. John M. Corse's division, Chalmers created considerable havoc and destruction, bombarding Sherman's train with artillery, setting sections of it on fire, even stealing one of the general's horses from a rear boxcar.[19]

After the journey resumed, Sherman and his troops halted time and again to repair tracks and ties wrecked by troopers led by Maj. Gen. Stephen D. Lee. It was a vexation for every traveler, as it was for General Grant, who eventually put a stop to it. When he reached Iuka, Mississippi, on October 27, Sherman received a dispatch directing him to leave the repairs to the Sixteenth Corps, which was commanded by an experienced railroad engineer, Maj. Gen. Grenville M. Dodge. Sherman and his troops were to push on by foot and horseback across south-central Tennessee to the supply base at Stevenson, Alabama. They were to cross the Tennessee River at neighboring Bridgeport, then hasten north to Chattanooga.[20]

En route to Iuka, Sherman had seen a copy of a general order from Halleck naming Grant commander of the Military Division of the Mississippi, encompassing the Army of the Tennessee and the forces of Rosecrans and Burnside. The same order gave Grant the power to replace Rosecrans, if he chose, with the general already known as the "Rock of Chickamauga." Grant made the change without hesitation. He and George Thomas were far from bosom friends. A coolness in their relationship, the precise origin of which remains unknown, dated at least to the Corinth campaign. Thomas, however, was an old-school type, dignified, proud, a bit stuffy, as well as frustratingly slow to move, but he was a reliable and trustworthy subordinate, something Grant had never accused William Rosecrans of being.[21]

The elevation of his friend Thomas pleased Sherman no end, as did the concurrent news that he himself was Grant's hand-picked successor in command of the Army of the Tennessee. As currently organized, that army consisted of Osterhaus's, Smith's, and Ewing's divisions of the Fifteenth Corps and the Second Division of McPherson's Seventeenth Corps, under John Smith. Thomas's army comprised Maj. Gen. Gordon Granger's Fourth Corps, Maj. Gen. John M. Palmer's Fourteenth Corps, and the two corps sent from the Army of the Potomac under Hooker, the Eleventh, whose immediate commander was Maj. Gen. Oliver Otis Howard, and the Twelfth, under the direct command of Maj. Gen. Henry W. Slocum. At present Slocum was detached from the body of his corps, having accompanied a division that was guarding the railroad between Nashville and Chattanooga. In Slocum's absence—which had been arranged as a result of his well-known antipathy toward Hooker, dating from the fiasco at Chancellorsville—his senior subordinate, Brig. Gen. John W. Geary, had charge of the corps.

Sherman, having ridden on ahead of his troops, reached Chattanooga, at the end of his 330-mile journey from Memphis, on the evening of November 14. He was greeted warmly by both Grant and Thomas. The two had spent the past three weeks in each other's company, but it was obvious to everyone at army headquarters that Grant felt much more at ease in Cump Sherman's presence. General Howard, one of the witnesses to Sherman's arrival, could see that plainly. A pious teetotaler who had attended a theological sem-

Gen. Oliver Otis Howard, USA

inary back home in Maine before graduating from West Point and had lost an arm during the battle of Fair Oaks, Howard recalled that upon Sherman's entrance, Grant rose ceremoniously from the rocking chair in which he had been sitting, perhaps to ease the pain of a deep body bruise suffered weeks before during a riding accident in Louisiana. Sherman's host "extended his hand, and, while his face lighted up with its characteristic smile, paid Sherman some compliment on his promptitude; then being about to resort to his habitual cigar, offered one to his new guest. Sherman took the cigar, lighted it, and never ceased to talk in that offhand, hearty, manly way which everybody who knew him will remember. He had not even stopped to take a seat. Grant pointed to an old high-back rocking chair and said, 'Take the chair of honor, Sherman.' 'Oh, no,' the latter rejoined; 'that belongs to you, General!' Grant humorously remarked, 'I don't forget, Sherman, to give proper respect to age.' Sherman instantly took the proffered chair and laughingly said: 'Well, then, if you put it on that ground, I must accept.'"[22]

Grant never engaged in such banter with any other subordinate. Those who knew them well never tired of observing that the two seemed close enough to be brothers. Sherman felt the same way. He wrote after the war, "[W]e were brothers—I the older man in years, he the higher in rank. We both believed in our heart of hearts that the success of the Union cause was not only necessary to the then generation of Americans, but to all future generations. We both professed to be gentlemen and professional soldiers, educated in the science of war by our generous Government for the very occasion which had arisen. . . ."

Brothers they might be, but not twins. Their differences of appearance, manner, and temperament were striking: One was short and squat, well-kempt, solid-stolid, quiet almost to shyness, who drew his inspiration from practical know-how and common sense. The other was tall, rawboned, ill-dressed and poorly coiffured, who talked and gestured as if animated by a constant charge of nervous energy, a scholar deeply versed in warfare, politics, history, and psychology. Theirs was a relationship that, as Howard observed, "did not grow from likeness, but from unlikeness. They appeared rather the complements of each other—where the one was especially strong, the other was less so, and *vice-versa*. It was a marriage of characters, in sympathy, by the adjustment of differences."[23]

As soon as the introductions had been completed and the small talk expended, "Sherman," Howard wrote, "quickly took the lead of the whole party and brought on a discussion of the military situation. . . ." That situation appeared so bleak that it was a wonder the troops under the now-deposed Rosecrans had not starved in the manner of Vicksburg's defenders. All supply lines to Chattanooga—which lay on the south side of the Tennessee where the river bent to the south and then severely to the north, enclosing a peninsula known as Moccasin Point—had been severed. For sustenance the garrison had to rely on a fragile, tenuous wagon route from the railroad at Stevenson, Alabama, over rocky crests, steep ridges, and through a valley ripe for ambushing. Late in September and early in October Bragg's cavalry commander, Maj. Gen. Joseph Wheeler, had attacked a wagon train, ten miles in length, that had been trundling over this roundabout circuit to bring essential goods to Rosecrans's army. Wheeler's troopers burned more than one thousand vehicles and destroyed or confiscated millions of dollars worth of rations, forage, and matériel.[24]

Chattanooga continued to be denied easy access to the goods it needed to sustain life and fighting spirit. The Confederate blockade was kept effective, if not airtight, by the dispositions Bragg had made to maintain his siege. What remained to him of the troops he had led at Chickamauga were deployed on top of a series of commanding ridges: broad Raccoon Mountain, west of Chattanooga; rugged Lookout Mountain, on the southwest; and five-hundred-foot-high, fifteen-mile-long Missionary Ridge, which overlooked the city on its east side. Each of these positions was occupied by the infantry of William Hardee and John Breckinridge and a portion of Wheeler's cavalry.

Bragg's high-altitude positions were so inaccessible to attackers that they required relatively few troops to hold them. This was fortunate, for Bragg had lost thousands of the troops and two of the subordinates who had served him at Chickamauga. Late in October 1863, Jefferson Davis had decided to keep Bragg in command of the army despite renewed, and intensified, criticism by his subordinates following his refusal to press Rosecrans's retreat to Chattanooga. The president then ordered General Polk—who had quarreled openly and bitterly with Bragg after Chickamauga and for his temerity had been dismissed by his superior—to go to Mississippi as Joe Johnston's second in command. Polk replaced William Hardee, who in late July had happily left Bragg's army for the same subordinate position under Johnston but was now cajoled by Davis into returning to the Army of Tennessee to command Polk's corps.[25]

The second disaffected subordinate, Longstreet, who had broken with Bragg after Chickamauga, had been permitted to leave the Army of Tennessee on his own terms. Concerned that Bragg and Longstreet could not cooperate, early in November the president gave the latter what he had long wanted, an independent command. Lee's Old War Horse was permitted to take the divisions he had brought from Virginia, along with additional artillery and most of Wheeler's horsemen, to East Tennessee, there to attack or besiege Burnside's small army at Knoxville. Thus, soon after Grant reached Chattanooga and ten days before Sherman arrived, Bragg's siege lines had been depleted of some seventeen thousand infantry and cavalry. A loss of that magnitude, no matter how important the mission Longstreet had been entrusted with, appeared to be a major blunder. It was the job of Grant, Sherman, and Thomas to make sure it was.[26]

The truncated command to which Johnston was assigned in the wake of his controversial service in the Vicksburg campaign, although encompassing most of Alabama, was known as the Department of Mississippi and East Louisiana. By lessening the amount of territory and the number of troops for which he was responsible, the reorganization gave him a position that more closely matched his ideas of what a theater command should be. This, however, was not the intent of his civilian overlords. After Vicksburg's loss, Davis and Seddon left no doubt that Johnston had been punished for his passive response to Pemberton's pleas for help.

Their comments about Johnston's perceived shortcomings, once guarded, had become blatantly denunciatory. Shortly after the general evacuated Jackson to escape Sherman's siege, Davis complained to Robert E. Lee that all Johnston seemed good for was to "retreat . . . to the pine woods of Mississippi, and if he has any other plan than that . . . it has not been communicated." When, a few days later, Josiah Gorgas suggested to Davis that Pemberton's stronghold fell to the enemy due to a lack of provisions, the president replied, "Yes, from want of provisions inside and a general outside who wouldn't fight."[27]

If Davis had had his way, he would have forced Johnston out of the army or relegated him to staff duties. But the general's congressional support remained strong, and the public had a generally high estimation of his ability. Robert Kean expressed this point when in his diary entry for July 26 he wrote, "While I do not trust him [Johnston] because he is timid and because he hates Davis and Lee, I have a high opinion of his military coup d'oeil, derived however mainly from public reputation. . . ."[28]

Despite Johnston's continued popularity, Davis decided to go public with his dissatisfaction. When Hardee arrived at Morton to begin serving under Johnston, the latter felt able to leave Mississippi to complete the inspection tour of Mobile's defenses cut short in March by his temporary posting to Tennessee. Shortly before he left the Gulf Coast to return to Morton, he received a fifteen-page letter in Davis's handwriting that constituted a set of charges against Johnston for numerous alleged crimes of commission and omission dating back eight months. Most revolved around Davis's conviction that Johnston had abdicated his responsibilities by claiming, when sent to Vicksburg in May, that he had relinquished authority over Bragg's department and army and therefore could give Bragg no orders.[29]

Johnston would claim that Davis's charges did not faze him; he professed to believe that anyone who perused them would regard them as patently false. Lydia Johnston wrote that the general "laughs at [Davis's] rebukes," and she quoted her husband as declaring that "no indignity from Davis could drive him from the service." Other observers believed that Johnston deeply resented Davis's action. "The president detests Joe Johnston for all the trouble he has given him," Mary Chesnut opined. "And General Joe returns the compliment with compound interest. His hatred of Jeff Davis amounts to a religion. With him it colors all things."[30]

Johnston's actions belied his claim of indifference toward Davis's treatment of him. Early in August, back in Morton, he composed a detailed and lengthy rebuttal of the president's accusations. It seemed to do him little good; while Davis's supporters in the Congress secured the dissemination of his dispatches to Johnston during the Vicksburg campaign, as well as the list of charges, neither Johnston's communications with Richmond nor his point-by-point refutation was included in the public record. As the general argued persuasively, "[I]t would have been as consistent with propriety to transmit my defense with his accusations, and certainly as much so with fairness." His congressional friends repeatedly called for the publication of Johnston's effort at self-defense, but to no effect.[31]

Davis's attempts to condemn publicly Johnston's performance at Vicksburg did not end with the release of that sixteen-page indictment. Davis saw to it that General Pemberton's report of the Vicksburg operations, a voluminous condemnation of Johnston's failure to lift Grant's siege despite repeated pledges to do so, was transmitted to the War Department on August 25 and at once leaked to the press. Having learned of the report's availability, Johnston repeatedly sought a copy for himself. Although as Pemberton's superior it should have been submitted to him before anyone else, a copy did not reach him until the end of October. Johnston immediately denounced it as a tissue of misstatements, inaccuracies, false accusations, and evasions. Pemberton's mistake, however, was in "regarding accusation of me, whom he had selected for an adversary, as defense of himself."[32]

Deciding that written criticism was insufficient to convince the public that Johnston was to blame for the loss of Vicksburg, Davis called for a court of inquiry into the fiasco of May–July 1863. When he learned of the pending tribunal, Johnston was initially pleased; he believed it would give him the opportunity to present evidence that would vindicate his conduct and silence his critics. When he had the chance to think it over, however, he feared that the court, to be held in Atlanta during the first week in September, would permit only testimony unfavorable to his case. Recently Johnston had given the president a new reason to find fault with him, and this too might influence the judges against him. On August 21, when Rosecrans began to move against Chattanooga, Bragg had importuned Johnston for assistance. Several weeks earlier Johnston had promised the government that in such an event he would dispatch nine of his eleven infantry brigades to Chattanooga; instead he sent only six, retaining some nine thousand infantry and six thousand horsemen despite the studied lack of activity in his area of operations.[33]

Some of Johnston's congressional supporters wrote to warn him that the president did indeed intend to stack the proceedings against him and in such a way as to destroy his military career. Put on notice, Johnston made sure he was in Atlanta on the day appointed for the court's convening, only to discover that it had been indefinitely suspended. The outcome left him with mixed feelings. He was glad he did not have to fight to have his story told before a panel of judges disposed to uphold Davis's claims against him, yet he also regretted being denied that opportunity. His only recourse was to amend his own Vicksburg report to include a point-by-point rebuttal of charges by an adversary seeking to rehabilitate his own reputation at the expense of his superior's.[34]

It was a disagreeable business, for while Johnston did not fear tangling with his civilian bosses he disliked attacking a fellow officer, especially on grounds of prevarication. Nevertheless, his revised report hammered home his theme that the disasters that overtook Pemberton "were due not merely to his entangling himself with the advancing columns of a superior and unobserved enemy, but to his evident determination to be besieged in Vicksburg, instead of maneuvering to prevent a siege. . . . Vicksburg was greatly imperiled when my instructions from Tullahoma to concentrate were neglected. It was lost when my orders of May 13 and 15 were disobeyed. To this loss were added the labor, privations, and certain capture of a gallant army when my orders for its evacuation were set aside."[35]

———— ⋙•⋘ ————

Once Sherman's weary, footsore, mud-spattered troops slogged through to Chattanooga, Grant made short work of the siege Braxton Bragg had imposed on Chattanooga. The first step in the process had already been taken. Its success was due primarily to Brig. Gen. William Farrar Smith, chief engineer of the Army of the Cumberland, who devised a deceptively simple way of restoring the garrison's supply lines. Under Smith's guidance, early on October 27 troops had laid pontoons across both prongs of Moccasin Point. Once the prongs were secured by the troops under Hooker and other commanders, and the pontoons had been laid, sup-plies were carted into the city by wagons crossing both bridges and the peninsula in between. The wagon trail lay beyond range of the artillery Bragg had placed atop Lookout Mountain to prevent the delivery of supplies by steamboat. When the new route was opened for use on October 30, it was dubbed "the Cracker Line" by soldiers who had gone for weeks without their ration of hard bread.[36]

Following preliminary actions in Lookout Valley, Grant was ready to advance on Bragg's siege lines by having Sherman attack the Confederate right flank on Missionary Ridge, with supporting efforts by Hooker and Thomas against other units of Bragg's army. The operation, scheduled for the twenty-first but held up by the late arrival of Sherman's column because of abominable weather and bot-tomless roads, began two days later when Thomas's army attacked Orchard Knob, a spur of Missionary Ridge, and drove its defenders back on their main force. Sherman's role began next day before dawn, with the crossing of Moccasin Point by the heterogeneous force entrusted to him. Its composition, dictated largely by the positions of the troops in relation to their objectives, included elements of his and Thomas's armies: Morgan Smith's and Hugh Ewing's divisions of the Fifteenth Corps, John Smith's Seventeenth Corps division, Howard's Eleventh

Corps, and the Second Division, Fourteenth Corps, commanded by the ironically named Brig. Gen. Jefferson C. Davis.[37]

Gen. Joseph Hooker, USA

Scheduled to begin at first light, Sherman's assault, slowed by the instability of the pontoons linking Moccasin Point and Chattanooga, did not go forward until around one thirty. Sherman intended to seize the summit of Tunnel Hill at the north-ern end of the ridge, so named because it rose above the tunnel that carried the tracks of the Chattanooga & Cleveland Railroad through the mountain. Once he secured this posi-tion, which he judged to be the key point on Bragg's right flank, Sherman would turn south and attack all along the crest, rolling up the Army of Tennessee, cut-ting its communications, and choking off its escape route.

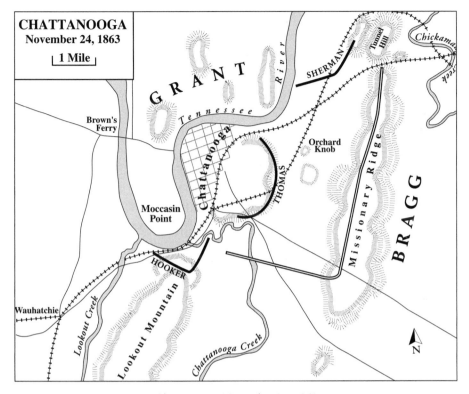

CHATTANOOGA
November 24, 1863

| 1 Mile |

Chattanooga, November 24, 1863

At first, the advance went smoothly. For two hours or more the Federals, with the troops of Sherman's own army in the lead, advanced against light opposition, driving skirmishers from the northern tip of the crest. At about three-thirty, however, the head of the column, Brig. Gen. Joseph A. J. Lightburn's brigade of Morgan Smith's division, reached the high ground toward which Sherman had aimed and found itself on a hill separated from the rest of the ridge by a deep and wide saddle. When Lightburn's troops crossed the low ridge to the next crest, they found that it too was separated by a saddle from the main portion of Missionary Ridge.

The surprise was largely Sherman's, as was the blame. As he wrote in his after-action report, "from studying all the maps, I had inferred that Missionary Ridge was a continuous hill; but we found ourselves on two high points, with a deep depression between us and the one immediately over the tunnel which was my chief objective point." He tried to gloss over the error—the result of his failure to make a pre-attack reconnaissance—by claiming that the ground taken when moving across the first saddle was strategically important. But he could not disguise the fact that he had blundered, causing a major delay in turning the Rebel right. The lapse was suggestive of the same careless approach to tactics that had caused the second assault of May 22 at Vicksburg to fail so signally.[38]

Refusing to regroup or fall back, Sherman's divisions converged on the second saddle and eventually drove its occupants—members of the division of Maj. Gen. Pat Cleburne, who had opened the first day at Shiloh by nearly overrunning Sherman's camps—back to the slope at the end of Missionary Ridge proper, the real Tunnel Hill. The attack having faltered due to Sherman's miscue, gathering darkness prevented its completion until the morning of the twenty-fifth, which dawned clear and cool after an all-night rain mixed with sleet and snow.

Although the rugged, ravine-infested ground made coordination among participants difficult, Sherman's attack rolled forward just before sunrise, Hugh Ewing's division in the advance. It was a two-pronged operation, Corse's brigade attacking straight down the ridge while the brigade of Col. John M. Loomis struck the west flank of the high ground. As Sherman looked on anxiously from the rear, Corse's troops thudded into Cleburne's breastworks-shielded position and were thrown back. A second and then a third charge also met repulse. After several hours of inconclusive fighting, both sides appeared exhausted. Sherman kept the pressure on Cleburne by throwing in fresh brigades and gaining some ground, but a determined counterattack late in the afternoon stabilized the hard-pressed Confederate line. Soon it became apparent that Sherman could not maneuver enough troops up the rugged peaks around Tunnel Hill to carry the position within the hour or so of daylight remaining this day.[39]

As it turned out, he did not have to. Although sent forward late because of Sherman's slow progress, the soldiers of Thomas's army finally attacked the western face of Missionary Ridge, captured the works at its base and then, to avoid the fire being poured down on them from the guns at the summit, began to ascend the sheer wall face of the ridge in groups large and small, without given orders. Reaching the crest, they drove away its flabbergasted defenders. When Sherman learned of Thomas's success, he renewed his pressure on the works in his front— and found them empty. Cleburne's men, having witnessed the rout of their comrades, had fallen back to mount a rear-guard action that would spare Bragg's beaten army from annihilation. Sherman regretted his adversary's escape, but he gloried in the fact that Bragg's grip on the high ground commanding Chattanooga had been irrevocably broken.[40]

Sherman was proud of his army's service this day, as inconclusive as it had been due to the rugged, broken terrain and the supreme difficulty of coordinating offensive operations. He was not one to acknowledge mistakes readily, and he would admit to none this day. Even so, he was quick to credit the contribution to victory of his friend George Thomas, without which Sherman's and Cleburne's troops might have grappled to doomsday without breaking their stalemate.

FIFTEEN

"I'VE GOT JOE JOHNSTON DEAD!"

The rout of November 25, 1863, accomplished what no effort by the government in Richmond had succeeded in doing—it ended the reign of Braxton Bragg as commander of the Army of Tennessee. Like Sherman, Bragg would not admit error. In his report of the fighting outside Chattanooga he maintained that "no satisfactory excuse can possibly be given for the shameful conduct of the troops on the left [on Missionary Ridge] in allowing their line to be penetrated. The position was one which ought to have been held by a line of skirmishers against any assaulting column. . . ." Try as he might to evade accountability, however, he knew that in the mind of the public, as well as in the minds of most of his troops, the blame would accrue to him. It was yet another blow to his pride, prestige, and reputation, one he doubted he could overcome. On the evening of November 28, after informing General Cooper of his new position at Dalton, Georgia, atop the sheltering wall of Rocky Face Ridge, Bragg added, "I deem it due to the cause and to myself to ask relief from command."[1]

Jefferson Davis, who believed that Bragg's ability to lead had been shattered, was inclined to grant the request but only if a suitable replacement was available. He offered the position to Hardee, Bragg's senior subordinate. The Georgian, fearing the responsibility and wishing to remain in a subordinate position, declined the command on a permanent basis but agreed to take it until a successor was named. A disappointed Davis then sounded out Robert E. Lee, who recommended Beauregard, then at Charleston supervising the defenses of the Carolina and Georgia coast. But Davis and Beauregard had been on icy terms dating from First Manassas, and since then their relationship had frozen over completely. Davis refused to offer the post to the prickly Creole.

After failing to persuade Lee to accept the command, Davis found himself in

234

the unhappy position of having to consider Joe Johnston. Knowing the president's feelings against his West Point classmate, Lee did not recommend him until certain that Davis had rejected Beauregard. By then Davis was under pressure from the Confederate Congress, especially from Senator Wigfall and his supporters, as well as from high-ranking officers whom he trusted such as Leonidas Polk, to appoint Johnston. Seeing no viable alternative, on December 16 Davis took a long dose of bitter medicine and announced his decision to appoint Johnston commander of the principal Confederate army in the western theater. Polk would take over Johnston's command in Mississippi, while Bragg would move to Richmond to fill the post of chief military advisor that Lee had held prior to June 1862. In his new position, Bragg, his recent disgrace notwithstanding, would wield a great deal of power, not only by advising Davis on field appointments but also by helping to shape grand strategy. From Richmond, in fact, he would exert almost as much influence on the movements of the Army of Tennessee as he had when leading it in the field.[2]

On December 18, when he received telegraphic orders to report to Dalton and take command of the army huddling there, Joe Johnston was several months into a relatively quiet term as head of a small department. Lydia, who had joined him in October, had turned his Meridian, Mississippi, headquarters into a home whose comforts and amenities they both enjoyed. One month before receiving his summons to Georgia, Johnston had written Senator Wigfall that "I have been having a very quiet time since July. Almost a peace establishment so we have gone to house keeping. . . ." Although convinced that he had been exiled to this backwater command as the result of Davis's animus, Johnston was reluctant to trade a tranquil home for the headaches that went with commanding a large army.[3]

Still, the prestige of the job attracted him, as did the prospect of rejuvenating a command abused and misused by another. Then, too, he felt he owed it to his congressional friends to take the job, and he wished to gratify the officers and men who hoped he would restore the strength and spirit they had lost under Bragg. In early December, Brig. Gen. William W. Mackall, an old friend of Johnston's who had served as Bragg's chief of staff until relieved at his own request after Chickamauga, informed Johnston that "almost every one expects you to take the command and consider H. [Hardee] a *locum tenens*." Mackall added enthusiastically that "the army wants you. . . . I have even heard Bragg's friends say that your presence would be worth ten thousand men to the army. . . ."[4]

Such sentiment made Johnston believe he had a fair chance of succeeding in his new position even given the lack of support and the outright hostility he could expect from the administration. He may have reasoned that if he could not get along with the president, he could work with Davis's chief advisor. By openly praising Bragg's leadership on more than one occasion, Johnston assumed he had cultivated the man's goodwill. If Bragg had a modicum of gratitude in him, he would happily serve as a buffer between Johnston and his civilian overlords.

Johnston arrived in Dalton by train on the day after Christmas 1863 and assumed command the next morning. He found waiting for him a letter from Secretary Seddon, giving the War Department's view of the situation Johnston faced. "It is apprehended," the secretary wrote, "the army may have been, by recent events, somewhat disheartened, and deprived of ordnance and material. Your presence, it is hoped, will do much to reestablish hope and inspire confidence." Richmond expected Johnston not only to revive the army physically but also to restore its will to fight and in so doing recruit volunteers and entice the many veterans who had deserted to return to the ranks. Once the transformation had been made, Johnston should take the offensive, especially if he learned that Grant was depleting his forces to reinforce other commands. Seddon stressed that Johnston could not afford to sit idle while the enemy added to its considerable strength and stocked provisions to support a renewal of active operations in the spring.[5]

None of these points impressed Johnston, who considered Seddon's advice not only elementary and self-evident but also an implied gesture of disrespect to "one thought competent, apparently, to the second military position in importance in the Confederacy." Ignoring most of the secretary's "instructions," Johnston set about to review the army and take notes on what needed to be done to revive it. He quickly discovered, as he took pains to inform Seddon, that "this army is now far from being in condition to 'resume the offensive'." The results of his early inspections caused him to dispute the opinion of Davis, who wrote Johnston not long after Seddon did, that the Army of Tennessee was in good spirits and tolerable physical condition. The president added his belief that the command was, or would soon be, stronger in terms of manpower than any fighting force "actually engaged in any battle on the Confederate side during the present war." Johnston, however, estimated the army's strength at forty-three thousand officers and men, less than half as many as Grant could call on. Even with the addition of the reinforcements—mostly cavalry—that Davis subsequently promised him, Johnston would remain handily outnumbered. Davis's cockeyed analysis confirmed Johnston's suspicion that the president had lost touch with the condition of the Confederacy's military forces.[6]

Johnston's early reviews produced some worrisome findings. The army's supply system was totally inadequate to its needs; the men were deficient in food, blankets, tents, and cold-weather clothes; and the dead of winter found an alarming number of them barefoot. Firearms, especially rifles, were in short supply, as was ammunition. The army's horses, mainly its artillery teams, were few and in poor health. In some ways the most troubling deficiency was in transportation. Hundreds of wagons and ambulances were needed to put the army in a condition to march and fight.

Although historians generally consider Johnston a poor administrator, he threw himself wholeheartedly into the task of rebuilding this army, and he achieved marked results in a brief time. Throughout that winter and into the spring of 1864 he secured large quantities of replacement clothing including many thousands of shoes, sometimes by commandeering trains and ships whose cargo had been earmarked for civilian use. He worked closely and agreeably with Georgia's touchy governor Joseph E. Brown and secured his cooperation in persuading the state-owned Western & Atlantic Railroad, which linked Chattanooga and Atlanta, to be more regular and efficient in shipping matériel to the army from supply depots in the rear. He also improved the army's diet, increasing the variety of the rations issued to the men, and he worked hard to resolve the chronic deficiency of such vital foodstuffs as fruits and vegetables.[7]

From personal experience, Johnston appreciated the importance of quick and effective treatment of wounds and disease. Therefore he strove to upgrade the quality of hospital care, to increase the availability of medical stores, and to fill vacancies in the army's surgical ranks. He importuned the Confederate ordnance department to increase his allocation of small arms, rifle ammunition, and artillery projectiles. He made only modest gains in reducing the transportation problem, but when spring came the army was more mobile and more capable of being supplied on the march than it had been for months. He also gave his support to a religious revival that swept through the army's winter camps, which served to strengthen the men's spiritual commitment to the war and to the Confederate cause. Before the coming campaign was over, Johnston would join in this outpouring of religious zeal by acceding to Lydia's wishes that he participate in a ritualized cleansing of his sins. At her request, Leonidas Polk doffed his lieutenant general's uniform, donned his bishop's robe, and, with Generals Hood and Hardee standing witness, baptized Johnston in the Episcopalian rite.[8]

Finally, Johnston won the gratitude of his soldiers through a liberal issuance of furloughs, something unheard of under his predecessor, and by reorganizing the army along lines that bolstered state pride. One of Bragg's most unpopular administrative actions had been to break up General Cheatham's division of Tennessee infantry by transferring some of its brigades to other commands. Johnston restored the division's all-Tennessee orientation by ordering the return of the lost units, an act that won him the devotion of Cheatham and every officer and man under him.[9]

Such wide-ranging efforts at rebuilding the army's physical and spiritual strength appear to have raised considerably the corporate morale. A company officer opined that by his reforms Johnston gained the confidence of "nine-tenths of the army." Another soldier, writing to his local newspaper, claimed that the "old army spirit" had been rekindled throughout the ranks. A chaplain agreed: "The enthusiastic spirit of 1861 is spreading abroad." By early March, General Mackall, whom Johnston had returned to his former post of army chief of staff, was observing that "our army is in fine spirits and everyone seems pleased" with the condition of affairs. At the same time, Johnston himself was writing that "the tone and temper of this army has certainly improved greatly since the beginning of 1864, and I would now freely meet odds of three to two." He did not believe those odds were available to him, although by the time he wrote, the army had been bulked up to an "aggregate present" strength of almost fifty thousand, about seven hundred of whom were deserters lured back to the ranks by Johnston's well-received amnesty policy. Johnston would claim that by spring more than five thousand absentees, most of whom had been on detached service, had returned to the army.[10]

Cheatham was not the only subordinate whose trust and loyalty Johnston gained. He maintained cordial relations with his senior subordinates including Hardee and Polk (who would return to the army, with his small corps, in mid-May), as well as with most of the army's seven division commanders. Johnston may well have won the special loyalty of Pat Cleburne, who had created a storm of controversy and protest among his colleagues when in December 1863 he drafted and circulated a proposal to recruit slaves into the Confederate ranks upon promise of emancipation. When feeling began to rise against Cleburne, Johnston, working for once in tandem with Richmond, suppressed the controversy, keeping it from leaking into the press and political circles and salvaging Cleburne's career, if not his prospects for advancement.

One who reacted indignantly to Cleburne's proposal was Joseph Wheeler. The cavalry leader, a confirmed Negrophobe, not only condemned the temerity of his Irish-born colleague but held Johnston responsible for failing to punish the culprit. He also faulted Johnston's own race-based plan, under which the number of slaves traveling with the army would be increased so they could substitute for soldiers employed behind the lines but critically needed at the front. Although beholden to Johnston for augmenting and resupplying his horsemen, as well as for protecting him against politicians who called for his demotion on grounds of incompetence, the cavalryman had been a close supporter of Braxton Bragg, who was responsible for Wheeler's January 1863 promotion to major general. After Bragg left the army for his new post in Richmond, Wheeler covertly opened a correspondence with him, praising Bragg's abilities as an army leader and disparaging Johnston's.[11]

Gen. Joseph Wheeler, CSA

Wheeler's criticisms of his new commander paled in comparison with those sent to Jefferson Davis by John Bell Hood, recently promoted to lieutenant general and in late February 1864 assigned to the Army of Tennessee. Hood, a bold and aggressive commander who had lost the use of an arm at Gettysburg and his right leg to amputation after Chickamauga, had just recuperated from the latter wound when Johnston agreed to take him on as one of his corps commanders. Recent historians have questioned the long-popular assumption that Hood came west in the unofficial role as a spy at army headquarters through whom Jefferson Davis could learn the plans and intentions of a commander he did not trust to keep him informed of such matters. In fact, almost from the day he arrived in Georgia, Hood sent the president damaging assessments of Johnston's leadership. Hood contradicted his superior's vocal opinion that the army was in no condition to launch and sustain an offensive. He also disputed Johnston's assertions that he was handily outnumbered, declaring that "the enemy is weak, and we are strong." Even so, nothing proves that Davis sent Hood to undermine Johnston or elicit grounds for his removal, as the latter and his partisans would contend.

In sending Hood to Georgia, Davis appears to have been motivated by the hope that the younger man's enthusiasm and aggressiveness would activate the same qualities in Johnston. Nor does it seem to be true, as Johnston implied in his postwar writings, that from the start he considered Hood unworthy of his trust. For the first three months of Hood's connection with the army, Johnston and he were on close, even intimate, terms. Other generals such as Hardee appear to have viewed Hood as Johnston's favorite subordinate, the one on whom the army leader relied for counsel and support.[12]

Whether or not Davis intended so, Hood performed a valuable and necessary service for the president and his subordinates. When Johnston commented, as he often did, that anything he sent over the telegraph might fall into the wrong hands, he appears to have been referring not only to the Yankees but to Davis, Seddon, and Bragg, the triumvirate that constituted, as one of Johnston's staff officers put it, "the *enemy* at Richmond." To some extent, his distrust of the president and his subordinates derived from Johnston's increasing prominence as leader of the antiadministra-

Gen. John Bell Hood, CSA

tion bloc in the field forces of the Confederacy. As Thomas L. Connelly (one of the many modern-day historians of the Army of Tennessee) has observed, when Johnston arrived at Dalton "under the banner of the anti-Davis forces in the Congress, Confederate politics was at last imbedded in the army's command system. Bragg's operations had been more of a matter within the army. Now, any support of Johnston was to be linked with opposition to the administration. . . ."[13]

One aspect of Johnston's opposition was his refusal to accept Richmond's vision of the strategy that should guide him when active campaigning resumed. His intention, perfectly in keeping with his personal proclivities and in tune with his belief that he was almost prohibitively outnumbered, was to remain on the defensive until his enemy made a miscue that invited a counterattack. His superiors, however, favored a proactive strategy. In large measure the brainchild of Robert E. Lee, this plan revolved around a junction of Johnston's army and Longstreet's forces in East Tennessee. The siege of Burnside's garrison had been lifted in early December 1863 and since then Longstreet had been wintering in the mountains above Knoxville. Early in March Davis sent an aide to Longstreet's headquarters with a copy of the plan, which the general acknowledged but did not necessarily accept. Longstreet favored a more radical (and less viable) plan to unite his cavalry with the horsemen available to Johnston and Polk in a mounted invasion of Kentucky aimed at wrecking the vital Louisville & Nashville Railroad.[14]

Undaunted, the war lords of Richmond fleshed out and fine-tuned the plan, which they formally adopted. It called for Johnston to abandon his communications line, the Western & Atlantic, march to Tennessee, link with Longstreet at a point about forty miles south of Knoxville, then cross the Tennessee River and the Cumberland Mountains and capture Nashville. The authorities believed this possible if Johnston were reinforced with five thousand troops from Polk's command—infantry as well as horsemen—and another ten thousand sent up from Charleston by Beauregard.

In advocating this strategy to Johnston, his superiors were every bit as uncommunicative as he was with them. Early in March, when Bragg ordered him to prepare to put in motion the agreed-upon plan of campaign, Johnston had no idea what he was talking about. When the concept was finally laid before him, Johnston protested that he was far from ready to assume an offensive in any direction. His army remained only partially restored to its pre-Chattanooga condition; he lacked the necessary manpower; he continued to be hamstrung by transportation shortages; and his supply lines remained fragile and tenuous. Some of Johnston's subordinates believed he was exaggerating the army's deficiencies to avoid having to carry the battle to Grant's legions. But Johnston remained fixed in his conviction that it was preferable to keep his troops in place and well concentrated until the Federals attacked. After they were defeated, his troops could move into Tennessee. He even hinted that it might be necessary to fall back from Dalton to a better defensive position. The prospect appalled Davis, the consummate defender of Confederate territory, who feared a retreat would open the underbelly of Georgia and central Alabama to the claws of the enemy.[15]

The impasse between Dalton and Richmond would never be broken. After this initial exchange of conflicting views, neither side made an effort to agree on a plan of action. Over the winter both Johnston and his superiors sent emissaries to explain their preferences and argue against the other's views, but nothing was resolved and no common ground was staked out. Historian Richard M. McMurry lays the blame for this lack of consensus on Johnston, arguing that "rarely did he provide the Richmond authorities with alternative proposals or with precise information concerning either his army or the strength and activities of the enemy in his front. . . . Johnston seems simply to have given up efforts to discuss strategy with the government and to have taken refuge in a hope that events would move in the direction he foresaw and that he would be vindicated. Because of this impasse, the Confederates began the 1864 campaign with no understanding of what they were trying to do."[16]

———————

Sherman's difficulties on Tunnel Hill notwithstanding, Grant, who caught up with him at Ringgold, Georgia, where the pursuit of Bragg effectively ended, was grateful for the Army of the Tennessee's hard-driving offensive on November 25, 1863, and he made sure his favorite subordinate knew it. He intended to permit Sherman's men to return to Chattanooga by a leisurely march, asking only that they destroy, as they went, the railroad north of Dalton. Meanwhile, Grant directed George Thomas to send Granger's Fourth Corps to the relief of Burnside, who had reported his garrison besieged by Longstreet and down to three days' rations. But when Grant returned to Chattanooga on the twenty-ninth, he found that Granger, who doubted the advisability of marching to Knoxville in weather Sherman called "bitter cold," had yet to start. An angry Grant got the corps commander moving, but to make sure he kept up the pace he added Sherman's troops to the relief expedition and put their commander in charge of it.[17]

Sherman made preparations to march promptly enough, but it was December 2 before he could recall everyone and start them northward. From the start, the long, cold journey was an ordeal. Sherman's men were ill equipped for the march, having been "stripped for the fight," low on rations and carrying a single coat or blanket per man. All their suffering appeared to go for naught when late on the fifth they reached the outskirts of Knoxville, to discover that Longstreet, fearing their arrival, had cleared out, and to learn that Burnside's troops were not as hard up for provisions as the troops who had marched to their relief.

Leaving Granger's corps to augment the garrison, Sherman returned his own troops to Chattanooga. Grant, again grateful for his friend's prompt and effective service, had him return Howard's and Davis's units to Thomas, then permitted the Army of the Tennessee to go into winter quarters across the line in Alabama. Sherman concentrated most of his command at Bridgeport, although numerous detachments were scattered through southern and western Tennessee as well as along the Mississippi from Natchez to the mouth of the Ohio River.

Neither Sherman nor Grant wished the troops to remain idle until the return of spring permitted them to take on the enemy at Dalton now commanded by Joe Johnston. When an opportunity came to resume active operations in a more moderate clime, Sherman seized it. Reports from General Halleck had suggested that enemy forces in western Tennessee were planning to attack supply lines and outposts on the Mississippi and perhaps attempt to close the river to Union ship-ping. That prospect was daunting, for it threatened to undo everything the cap-ture of Vicksburg and Port Hudson had achieved.

Sherman was not about to let that happen. He saw in the situation a chance to apply his policy of raiding enemy territory with large columns independent of estab-lished lines of supply. With his characteristic flair for hyperbole, on December 21 he informed Maj. Gen. John A. Logan, McPherson's ranking lieutenant, that "to secure the safety of navigation of the Mississippi River, I would slay millions. . . . I think I see one or two quick blows that will convince them [the Confederates] that, though to stand behind a big cotton-wood and shoot at a passing boat is good sport and safe, it may still reach and kill their families hundreds of miles off. . . . I think in all January and part of February I can do something in this line."[18]

Grant approved Sherman's proposal and gave him free rein to carry it out. The result was Cump's late-January return to Vicksburg, from which point he planned to march on Johnston's erstwhile headquarters at Meridian, where the Southern Mississippi Railroad crossed the Mobile & Ohio. He intended to lay waste to extensive stretches of both lines, making it difficult, if not impossible, for the Rebels to move quickly enough to disrupt supply lines and attack isolated posts. The devastation of the local countryside would also deprive the enemy of a region that supplied him with grain, cattle, and other war-sustaining resources.

Although scheduled to start sooner, Sherman's expedition did not get under way until February 3, 1864, following weeks of planning and supply stockpiling. He moved out of Vicksburg at the head of two divisions of the Sixteenth Corps, under Hurlbut; McPherson's Seventeenth Corps, also two divisions strong; and a small force of cavalry, a total of about twenty-five thousand officers and men. A support-ing operation had been gotten up, consisting of seven thousand troopers under Brig. Gen. William Sooy Smith who on February 11, more than a week behind sched-ule, rode south from Memphis with the intention of meeting Forrest's cavalry and keeping it out of Sherman's path. Sherman had put in motion other diversionary operations including an amphibious advance up the Yazoo River and a movement by infantry under General Logan from northern Alabama toward Rome, Georgia.[19]

The expedition achieved substantial, but not complete, success. Sherman reached Meridian with minimal difficulty, having skirmished with Wirt Adams's cavalry and elements of Polk's infantry on much of the same ground fought over during the Vicksburg campaign, including the Big Black River, Clinton, Jackson, and Morton. For the most part, however, Polk allowed his enemy to come on; his nine thousand foot soldiers under Loring and French were shoved east into Alabama, while S. D. Lee's horsemen were cut off from their supports and forced to retreat north of Sherman's route of advance.

Given easy access to Meridian, the raiders reached their objective on February fifteenth. They spent days wrecking the railroads in all four directions, Hurlbut's men tearing up tracks and ties north and east of the town, McPherson's mangling those to the south and west. The Federals also destroyed or carried off every item of conceivable utility to the enemy. As during the Vicksburg campaign, a great amount of private property was violated, and much of it went up in smoke. Without commenting on the vandalism, Sherman wrote that "10,000 men worked hard and with a will in the work of destruction, with axes, crowbars, sledges, claw-bars, and with fire, and I have no hesitation in pronouncing the work as well done." Resources rendered unserviceable to the enemy included 150 miles of rail-road, 67 bridges, 700 trestles, 20 locomotives, 28 boxcars and flatcars, and boun-tiful quantities of foodstuffs, cotton, and lumber.[20]

Sherman had expected to be joined near Meridian on or about the tenth by Smith's column, but, having heard nothing from it, on the twentieth he decamped for points north. By March 6, having outdistanced angry pursuers, he was back at Vicksburg, having suffered 170 casualties on the journey while inflicting upwards of 600 on his foe. At Vicksburg, Sherman learned that Smith had met overwhelming defeat on February 21 near West Point at the hands of Forrest and his much smaller command. Smith had suffered further damage when he retreated and Forrest pur-sued with a wild fury. In light of Smith's failure, the expedition was not the over-whelming success Sherman had claimed in his report. Still, he had inflicted enough damage to Confederate resources in western Mississippi to justify the time and effort that had gone into the project. The operation had also furnished another illustration of the effectiveness of Sherman's policy of bringing the war home to the civilian population of the South in a way not to be forgotten, or forgiven.[21]

Grant praised Sherman's accomplishments, which he viewed as having pre-empted a spring offensive in Polk's department. He expressed his thanks from Washington, where he had gone on March 4 to accept, at a White House ceremony, the revived rank of lieutenant general, last held by George Washington, and to assume command of all the armies of the United States. It was an honor richly deserved, thought Sherman, but it also posed a danger. At first Grant intended to maintain his headquarters in the West, a course favored by Sherman, who believed that anywhere else he would find himself hamstrung by politicians attempting to dictate strategy. Grant tended to agree, but after taking the pulse of the war in the East he decided that "here was the point for the commanding general to be. No one else could, probably, resist the pressure that would be brought to bear upon him to desist from his own plans and pursue others." In the coming campaign Grant would travel with Meade, proscribing grand strategy for the Army of the Potomac while its commander handled the tactical details. This effort at dual-control command would prove an unwieldy arrangement, but Grant and Meade would make it work through their shared commitment to final victory. Thus Grant fended off Sherman's plea, "For God's sake and for your country's sake, come out of Washington!"[22]

Grant willingly shared the credit for his rise to overall command. He expressed his gratitude in a letter sent jointly to Sherman and McPherson, the subordinates who "above all others, I feel indebted for whatever I have had of success." As the senior of the two, Sherman received the command that Grant was leaving behind, the Military Division of the Mississippi. "I determined," Grant wrote, "to have Sherman advanced to my late position, McPherson to Sherman's in command of the department [of the Tennessee], and Logan to the command of McPherson's corps. These changes were all made on my recommendation and without hesitation."[23]

Sherman was proud to accept Grant's mantle and humble enough to wear it without fanfare or self-congratulation. He knew how much of his own success was

Gen. John M. Schofield, USA

due to the support and encouragement of the new general-in-chief (Halleck's title had been changed to army chief of staff). Had the assignment been offered him a year before, Sherman might have done his best to refuse it, considering himself unworthy of it and unable to do it justice. But in the months that he had served as Grant's right hand, he had acquired an enormous amount of self-confidence. Now, especially given the support he could expect from Thomas, McPherson, and Maj. Gen. John McAllister Schofield, successor to Ambrose Burnside as commander of the Army of the Ohio—an experienced brigade, division, and department commander whose war service dated from Wilson's Creek, in August 1861—Sherman experienced no pangs of inadequacy when accepting this high position.

The timing of his promotion, which took effect on March 18, left him less than two months to prepare his vast command for field service. Fortunately, the armies were so well organized, so well officered, armed, and equipped, and their soldiers—most of them two- and three-year veterans—so well versed in the business of war, that those two months were principally devoted to concentrating their well-scattered components and estimating their supply needs, tasks Sherman supervised from his rear headquarters at Nashville. He also spent the time conferring with his commanders. To do so he traveled to such distant points as Pulaski, Tennessee; Huntsville, Alabama; Chattanooga, and Knoxville.[24]

Logistical issues claimed an increasing amount of his time as winter drew to a close. Working with commissary's and quartermaster's officers and railroad officials, he determined that in order to provide the precampaign stockpile his armies required, 130 boxcars, each carrying ten tons of rations, forage, and matériel, would have to make a daily run from Louisville and Nashville to the forward depot at Chattanooga. From there, the provisions would be carted to the front by a fleet of canvas-topped wagons. It appeared a Herculean task, but Sherman tackled it with characteristic energy and produced results. By late April, the Chattanooga-bound traffic had increased from between sixty-five to eighty cars a day to nearly two hundred. This had been achieved by many expedients including limiting car space to cargo. Would-be passengers, including soldiers on detached duty or returning from furlough, were forced to reach the front on foot. When, as he had anticipated, officers and enlisted men began to complain, Sherman had a ready rejoinder: "Show me that your presence at the front is more valuable than two hundred pounds of powder, bread, or oats."[25]

Although Grant left all considerations of strategy and tactics to Sherman, the two consulted at some length after the general-in-chief's journey to Nashville in mid-March, and later at Cincinnati where Sherman accompanied his superior on Grant's return to the East. The main point Grant made during these sessions was that Sherman's operations were to be coordinated, as closely as possible, with those of Meade in middle Virginia; with those of Maj. Gen. Benjamin F. Butler's smaller Army of the James, which was to attack Richmond from below while Meade engaged Lee's Confederates north of the enemy capital; and with those of Maj. Gens. Franz Sigel and George Crook in the Shenandoah Valley and the new state of West Virginia, respectively. Grant had hoped to add to this wide-ranging strategy an offensive against Mobile by the troops of Nathaniel Banks, but political considerations of the kind Sherman feared Grant might bow to had decreed that the commander of the Ninteenth Corps move up the Red River from New Orleans to occupy Texas, an ill-considered venture that was already well on its way to failure.

At Nashville and Cincinnati, Grant gave Sherman carte blanche, as he repeated in a formal letter of instruction dated April 4, 1864, to "move against Johnston's army, to break it up, and to get into the interior of the enemy's country as far as you can, inflicting all the damage you can against their war resources." While the Army of Tennessee was to be Sherman's primary objective, due consideration was given to geographical targets, especially Atlanta, the rail and industrial center of the Deep South. Whether or not Sherman moved directly against that major source of Confederate military sustenance, it was supposed that Johnston would do his utmost to defend it. Thus, whatever road Sherman took, he expected it to lead, eventually, to the Gate City.[26]

On paper, at least, he had the wherewithal to go wherever he pleased, carrying his enemy along by the force of his momentum. His ninety-nine thousand officers and men were distributed among seven infantry corps and one corps of cavalry: McPherson's Army of the Tennessee consisting of Logan's Fifteenth Corps; Dodge's so-called Left Wing, Sixteenth Corps (two divisions strong); two divisions of Blair's Seventeenth Corps, who were at their homes on leave as a reward for reenlisting for the war and would not join Sherman on campaign for more than a month; Thomas's Army of the Cumberland comprising the Fourth Corps, now commanded by Howard; Palmer's Fourteenth Corps; the Twentieth Corps (the former Eleventh and Twelfth Corps, Army of the Potomac) under Hooker; a cavalry corps led by Brig. Gen. Washington L. Elliott; and Schofield's Army of the Ohio, by far the smallest component of Sherman's force, embracing only the Twenty-Third Corps and the cavalry division of George Stoneman.[27]

By the first week of May, Sherman's unavoidably hasty preparations for the march were complete, and he was ready to see what he could accomplish at the head of a multitude of seasoned warriors. He had no illusion that the coming journey would be a pleasure excursion. As he wrote Ellen on the fourth, "I go to Ringgold tomorrow and will then be within Four miles of the enemy. We may have some of the most desperate fighting of the war, but it cannot be avoided deferred or modified[.] I will as heretofore do my best and trust in the troops. All my dispositions thus far are good."[28]

247

When he learned that Sherman had taken over for Grant, Johnston hoped that the man who, when a corps commander, had avoided direct encounters with him would prove, as an army group leader, more forthcoming and direct. Specifically, Johnston hoped Sherman would attack him frontally, striking his main line of defense west of Dalton. This line, which generally faced to the west, was anchored atop Rocky Face Ridge, a pine-covered series of heights rising eight hundred feet from the valley floor and extending several miles to the south, where it merged into Chattanooga Ridge. Cut up by a series of defiles including Mill Creek Gap (or Buzzard Roost) and, farther south, Dug and Snake Creek Gaps, it was a formidable position, especially if struck head-on.

That is what Sherman appeared to do on May 7, following days of ever-intensifying skirmishing along a broad front northwest of Dalton. That morning, Thomas's army advanced on Johnston from the direction of Ringgold, across Tunnel Hill, immediately west of Rocky Face Ridge and toward Mill Creek Gap. Schofield's army, on Thomas's left, angled south from Varnell's Station toward the Confederate right flank, its movements monitored by Wheeler's cavalry, the bulk of which was deployed in Crow Valley, directly east of Rocky Face. Johnston knew that Sherman's force contained a third army—McPherson's—but that command was not to be seen this morning. The Army of the Tennessee had started its march from a point in rear of Sherman's other components, near Chattanooga. Moreover, McPherson had a special role to play, of which Johnston was unaware.[29]

Johnston responded to Sherman's movements by making what he considered thorough and judicious dispositions. He placed Maj. Gen. Alexander P. Stewart's division of Hood's corps and Maj. Gen. William B. Bate's division of Hardee's corps in Mill Creek Gap, while deploying Cheatham's division on the northern end of Rocky Face Ridge. Two more of Hood's divisions, under Maj. Gens. Carter L. Stevenson and Thomas C. Hindman, were deployed in Crow Valley, where they connected with a picket line maintained by Wheeler's cavalry. In reserve near Dalton were the divisions of Pat Cleburne and William H. T. Walker, of Hardee's corps. Johnston would soon have additional troops to deploy. He had recently gained Jefferson Davis's permission to add at least one division of Polk's command in Mississippi. Soon afterward, Polk had given Johnston the good news that he was bringing to Georgia almost all of his infantry and cavalry. His fourteen thousand troops would increase Johnston's army to fifty-seven thousand.[30]

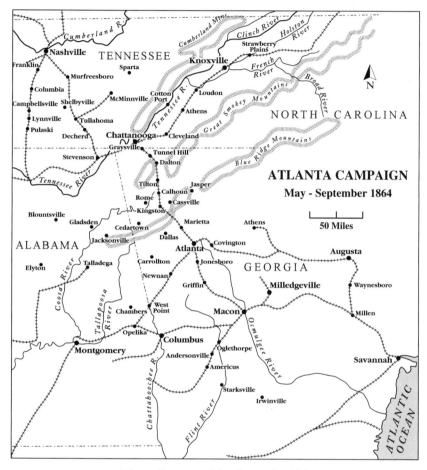

Atlanta Campaign, May-September 1864

Johnston's defenses held strong through the fighting on the seventh and again the next day. His troops threw back several limited attacks by Thomas against Rocky Face and by Schofield in Crow Valley, although none appeared to be strongly pressed. At midday, however, Johnston heard from cavalry scouts well south of his main position near Rome that at least one division of McPherson's army was heading toward Villanow, twelve miles to the southwest, perhaps aiming for Snake Creek Gap, well beyond Johnston's lower flank. Then, on the eighth, Hooker's corps assaulted Dug Gap, which was lightly guarded. Troops that had rushed up from the rear under Cleburne prevented the skeleton force of defenders from being overwhelmed. By nightfall, Johnston was relieved to hear that Hooker had withdrawn from the gap, preserving the integrity of the Confederate left.[31]

By the close of May 8, Johnston's line on Rocky Face and in Crow Valley remained intact. This was comforting news, but the army leader was concerned by McPherson's approach well to the south. Later Johnston would blame his cavalry chief for allowing the Yankees to outflank him by that route. Wheeler had placed his troopers too far to the north and east to cover the strategic defile, which gave access to the town of Resaca, on the Western & Atlantic north of its crossing of the Oostenaula River. Historians picked up Johnston's criticism, and to this day Wheeler's reputation remains blighted by his performance in the opening days of the campaign. In the main, however, the fault was Johnston's. Despite his career-long experience in topographical engineering, he virtually ignored the gap at the lower end of Rocky Face, nor did he call Wheeler's attention to it. On the other hand, Sherman's attention had been directed to the gap late in February, when a part of Thomas's army skirmished with the Confederates near the lower end of Taylor's Ridge, the high ground west of and parallel to Rocky Face.[32]

On the ninth, at last persuaded he must counter McPherson's advance, Johnston ordered some of the detached cavalry near Rome to plug Snake Creek Gap. Soon after the troopers arrived, however, they were driven back by a large column of Yankee infantry. The vital pass was already in enemy hands as was, perhaps, the fate of the Army of Tennessee.

The attacks of May 7 and 8 on Johnston's main line had confirmed Sherman's preconceived belief that the position was too strongly held to be taken by a head-on assault. "I had no purpose to attack Johnston's position in front," he later wrote, "but marched from Chattanooga to feign at his front and to make a lodgment in Resaca, eighteen miles to the rear," where he planned to cut both his opponent's communications and his route of retreat. Sherman added: "The movement was partly, not wholly, successful." At the outset, however, he believed it stood an excellent chance of succeeding. On the morning of the ninth, when he learned that the head of McPherson's column had penetrated Snake Creek Gap and was moving toward the railroad in the enemy's rear, Sherman exulted: "I've got Joe Johnston dead!"[33]

He spoke too soon. He had never thought of his subordinate and friend James B. McPherson as a timid man, but McPherson acted timidly on May 9. His scouts had informed him that Resaca was held at least in divisional strength, the advance of Polk's Army of Mississippi having arrived by rail from Mississippi. McPherson feared that once on the east side of the gap, he might be squeezed between this force and Johnston's main body coming down from Dalton. Thus he hesitated, engaged at long range Resaca's defenders, whom he found well posted behind fieldworks, then ordered a withdrawal although he had failed to reach the railroad Sherman had sent him to disrupt.[34]

Sherman was bitterly disappointed by his lieutenant's uncharacteristic faint-heartedness, which he believed had cost him the element of surprise. He was correct. On the tenth, Johnston had dispatched Hood with three divisions to Resaca. Arriving there after McPherson pulled back, Hood returned, as ordered, one-third of his force to Dalton but gained Johnston's permission to leave two divisions at Tilton, on the railroad six miles north of Resaca. That was a small defense force for so important a target, and, realizing this, Sherman decided to return to Snake Creek Gap, this time with his main body. With the Rebels now on alert, only overwhelming force would ensure a breakthrough in that sector. Leaving Howard's infantry and a portion of Elliott's cavalry to hold Johnston's attention, he placed Schofield's command and the remainder of Thomas's in rear of the Army of the Tennessee and started for Snake Creek Gap early on the eleventh. A day and a half later, the vanguard of this gigantic column had reached the head of the defile and was pushing through it.

At first the path to the railroad looked clear, but by morning of the thirteenth McPherson's advance found the area west of Resaca occupied in force. The previous night Johnston had finally left Dalton for points south. It had taken him that long to determine, with Wheeler's help, that the force attacking Rocky Face Ridge had been so diminished that Sherman's main body must have moved toward his left and rear. Johnston was able to put off evacuating until the last minute because he enjoyed interior lines of movement and could count on the good roads south of Dalton.[35]

The stage was thus set for the first sizable confrontation of the campaign. On the fourteenth, at Sherman's behest, McPherson ordered the Sixteenth Corps division of feisty, one-armed Brig. Gen. Thomas W. Sweeny to force its way over the Oostenaula. Late in the day Sweeny succeeded in crossing near the mouth of Snake Creek, but before his men could threaten either the railroad or Johnston's lower flank, a large force of Rebel infantry crossed the stream above Lay's Ferry. Fearing he would be cut off, Sweeny pulled back to the north side, close to Sherman's right flank.[36]

While McPherson's flanking force moved out, Sherman pressed Johnston's main body along Camp Creek, which flowed parallel to and a mile west of the Western & Atlantic. Polk's recently arrived corps held the left of the defense line in this area, near the point where the creek flowed into the Oostenaula. Hardee's corps had taken position in the center of the line and Hood's was on the right, close upon the banks of the Connasauga River. Throughout May 13 and well into the next day, Sherman attacked the length of this perimeter, making little headway. While the infantry and artillery slugged it out, Wheeler's horsemen held back Howard's corps, which was approaching via Mill Creek Gap. The Rebel horsemen spent hours fighting, falling back, halting and fighting again—tactics they had perfected while covering the many retreats of Braxton Bragg.[37]

The Battle of Resaca

Wheeler also aided Johnston through reconnaissance. In midafternoon of the fourteenth, just after Hindman, on the Rebel right, repulsed an attack by a portion of Schofield's army, Wheeler's scouts noticed that the Union left flank appeared unanchored and vulnerable. Johnston promptly ordered Hood to strike with the divisions of Stewart and Stevenson, supported by four brigades drawn from the center and left of the battle line. The assault, which swept forward at about 4:00 P.M., was initially successful. Hood drove in the Fourth Corps division of Maj. Gen. David Sloane Stanley, exposing a battery to capture. The Union gunners nevertheless held to their posts despite mounting pressure, hurling case-shot at the advancing Confederates. Just before Hood's regrouped divisions could overwhelm them, reinforcements from Hooker's corps stanched the gray wave. Shortly after, darkness came down to close the day's action.[38]

When skirmishing resumed early on May 15, Sherman determined on another effort to reach and cut the railroad; to start it off, he sent Sweeny back to the south bank of the Oostenaula, then ordered Hooker, supported by Howard, to assault the right-center of Johnston's line. Due to the complex logistical preparations, the attack was late in starting and when launched was easily repelled by the divisions of Hindman and Stevenson. The Federals gained a small advantage, however, when Hooker seized, after a desperate fight, an earthwork in front of Stevenson's position that mounted four field pieces.[39]

Late in the day Johnston counterattacked, throwing Hood's troops, supported by forces elsewhere on the Confederate line, against Sherman's fragile left flank. The effort ended prematurely when Johnston discovered that Sweeny's Federals had crossed the river in flatboats near Lay's Ferry, this time moving to within striking distance of the railroad. For some reason, although Johnston canceled the attack, Stewart's division charged, unsupported, and was thrown back with heavy loss. Even though he challenged Sweeny's crossing with troops stripped from his attack column, Johnston found he could not dislodge the foothold the Yankees gained on the south bank.[40]

His position suddenly untenable, Johnston called off all offensive operations and made plans to evacuate Resaca. After nightfall, Hood's corps began crossing the river at the railroad bridge as well as on pontoons, followed by the men of Hardee and Polk. So ended a battle that had cost Sherman almost seven thousand casualties and Johnston as many as fifty-two hundred, the difference being the advantage the Rebels enjoyed in fighting on the defensive. By opting to strike his enemy indirectly, not frontally, Sherman had hoped to minimize casualties, but the two-day slugging match that resulted from McPherson's unwillingness to hasten from Snake Creek Gap to Resaca had decreed a much bloodier outcome than he or any of his subordinates had anticipated. Even so, Sherman had taken and maintained the initiative throughout the fight, and his inspired tactics had forced his enemy to retreat not only from Dalton but from Resaca as well.

Sherman had not "gotten" Joe Johnston as he had predicted, but he had come very close. As one of the latter's soldiers wrote of the desperate fighting at Resaca, "I consider Gen. Johnston the best General in the Confederacy, not even excepting Robt. E. Lee, but this is one time that old Sherman came near over-reaching him."[41]

SIXTEEN
A FAILURE TO COMMUNICATE

Joe Johnston had not intended to start his campaign this way: forced out of Dalton, then compelled to evacuate an equally strong position at Resaca. Johnston desperately needed a new line of operations, but when he crossed the Oostenaula he found himself in a country not conducive to defense. The precipitous, thickly timbered ridges characteristic of the terrain north of the river were gone, replaced by gently rolling hills with minimal forest cover. In such a country, he would succeed only if he could divide his pursuers and take on a portion at a time. He felt compelled, however, to follow the line of the Western & Atlantic in the direction of Atlanta. The chances of finding a place to make a stand on either side of the right-of-way seemed remote.[1]

When he reached Calhoun, five miles south of Resaca, on May 16, 1864, he expected to reach a position that covered the several roads he believed Sherman's army was using to pursue him. He was disappointed to find Oothcaloga Creek so wide that it posed an obstacle to maneuvering his forces. After a brief stopover to give his men a chance to rest and consume their meager rations, he headed on to Adairsville, some seven or eight miles closer to the Etowah River. About two miles above that town, the meandering creek narrowed so much that it made Johnston believe he could fit his army into the valley formed by the stream. But when he reached there on the seventeenth, he was again frustrated by the local topography. Near Adairsville the valley widened so much that it would extend beyond any position the army took up, leaving its flanks "in the air." Once more forced to travel on, Johnston put additional distance between himself and the hounds baying at his heels, held back not only by Wheeler's horsemen but also by Polk's cavalry, the division of Brig. Gen. W. H. ("Red") Jackson. In moving south, Johnston rejected the advice of Hardee, who believed that the country around Adairsville offered a suitable defensive position. Hood, however, disagreed (or so Johnston later claimed), calling for a withdrawal below the Etowah, twelve miles to the south. Johnston agreed to continue the retreat, but he held out the hope of striking Sherman somewhere north of the river.[2]

As he resumed the movement south, Johnston studied the roads that diverged from Adairsville. One led almost straight south to Kingston, where it crossed the railroad to Rome. The other ran southeastward across a barren country to Cassville. Johnston believed that Sherman would take both trails, dividing his force and thus leaving it vulnerable to an attack in detail. He decided to set a trap that would enable him to take the offensive for the first time in the campaign. He sent the army's highly conspicuous wagon train, accompanied by Hardee's corps, to Kingston. Since Hardee had the rear of the column, Sherman would naturally assume that Johnston's entire army had proceeded in that same direction and would follow it with his main body. Johnston arranged for Hardee, once he reached Kingston, to shift eastward to join Hood and Polk in pitching into the smaller column that came down the road to Cassville.[3]

It was an enterprising plan, and it might have succeeded had not a chance intrusion by the enemy and a lack of communication between Johnston and Hood, who was to deliver the principal assault, served to scuttle the entire operation. Late on the morning of the nineteenth Sherman's column approached the ambush site, blissfully ignorant of Hood's concealed presence opposite its left flank. But Hood's trap never closed. At the last minute the corps commander, although supposedly a devotee of offensive warfare, withheld the blow he was to deliver, then withdrew from his position of ambush.

Hood's action had come in response to the approach of a second, unexpected enemy force bearing down on his rear via the more easterly road from Canton. Johnston, of course, was bitterly disappointed by the turn of events as well as chagrined by Hood's decision to leave his original position without the permission of his superior. Hood's shift so disarranged Johnston's plans that he called off the offensive in a fit of anger. Johnston himself had failed to detect the advance of the Yankee column, a large detachment of one of Hooker's divisions that had gotten separated from its corps and had blundered onto the wrong road at the right time—the right time for William T. Sherman.

Later Johnston accused Hood of overreacting to a false report. The army leader never acknowledged the presence of an intruder, perhaps because Hood failed to make contact with it, ensuring that no sounds of fighting reached Johnston's ears. The lost opportunity was so upsetting to Johnston that it overshadowed the cheerful news from Virginia he had received earlier that day: Lee's army, having battled Meade's to a bloody stalemate in the heavily forested area west of Fredericksburg known as the Wilderness, had inflicted substantial casualties on its enemy farther south and east near Spotsylvania Court House. The glad tidings had prompted Johnston to predict openly that the Confederacy had won its independence. Now he feared he had been premature.[4]

His intention to strike Sherman thwarted, Johnston fell back on his preferred strategy, the offensive-defensive. Expecting to be attacked next morning by Sherman's reunited columns, he moved his troops onto a shallow ridge southeast of Cassville, deploying Hood's men on the right, Polk's in the center, and Hardee's on the left, the latter's flank extending across the railroad. Johnston considered the position a formidable one, especially on the right and on Polk's front. That night as he repaired to his tent, expecting at dawn to engage the Federals whose cannons were already playing on his lines, Johnston was asked to visit General Polk at his field headquarters. Puzzled by the summons, Johnston hurried there to find Hood in the bishop's company. They had some bad news for their superior.

Hood took the lead in explaining the problem: neither he nor Polk was confident of holding his position in the morning, sections of which were liable to be enfiladed by the enemy's artillery. Both generals urged Johnston to pull up stakes and relocate south of the Etowah. Johnston was surprised and confused by their findings, which did not gibe with the information he had received from his artillery chief, Brig. Gen. Francis A. Shoup. "A discussion of more than two hours followed," Johnston recalled, but his subordinates remained adamant that a quick withdrawal was imperative. It would appear that some harsh words were exchanged, for after the war Johnston admitted to having accused Hood and Polk not only of banding together to thwart him but of "being beaten before battle." That attitude would only ensure defeat. He added, regretfully, "although the position was the best we had occupied, I yielded at last, in the belief that the confidence of the commanders of two of the three corps of the army, of their inability to resist the enemy, would inevitably be communicated to their troops, and produce that inability."[5]

The decision was especially painful in light of the army's earlier retreats. Johnston was greatly concerned about the impact on morale of another full-scale withdrawal. It would also be personally embarrassing to Johnston, who that morning had issued an order proclaiming that the army's retreating days were over: "You will now turn and march to meet his [the enemy's] advancing columns. Fully confiding in the conflict of the officers, the courage of the soldiers, I lead you into battle. . . ."[6]

Johnston's frame of mind was not improved when General Hardee, who had not joined the gathering at Polk's headquarters until after a decision had been made, argued vociferously against it, believing the army's position entirely defensible. It was too late. The withdrawal was already under way.[7]

Once again, what had appeared a gleaming opportunity to bring Sherman to battle on terms favorable to his undermanned but determined opponent had gone by the boards. In addition to disappointing his soldiers, Johnston's policy of avoiding battle was making him a target of criticism and derision throughout the Confederacy. Mary Chesnut, now living in Camden, South Carolina, noted in her diary: "Every newspaper (except some Georgia ones) in the Confederacy is busy as a bee, excusing Joe Johnston's retreats. He gives up one after another of those mountain passes where one must think he could fight and is hastening down in the plain."

Gen. William J. Hardee, CSA

Mrs. Chesnut believed that Johnston's Fabian policies, which were producing discontent not only among the authorities in Richmond but also among the Confederate people at large, portended disaster. So too did Johnston's continuing, and highly public, squabbles with Jefferson Davis, which the diarist and many in her circle ascribed to the general's selfishness and conceit. She quoted a like-minded friend as complaining that "if the president had sent him [Johnston] then out of the Confederacy—sent him to Sherman and McClellan, who admire him so much—he would have saved us in all probability. For Joe Johnston's disaffection has been the core round which all restless halfhearted disappointed people consolidated, and Joe Johnston's dissatisfaction with our president and our policy has acted like a dry rot in our armies."[8]

During the night of May 19, Sherman, traveling with Thomas's army, communicated by courier with each of his commanders. McPherson was then some five miles behind Thomas, while Schofield had taken up a more isolated position six miles to the north. Fully expecting a battle in the morning, Sherman ordered his armies to converge on Cassville at daylight. They were in position, or nearly so, by the appointed hour, only to find the enemy gone. At once Sherman dispatched cavalry in pursuit. Their leader reported that Johnston had passed the Etowah. Sherman was plainly surprised. It was true that his opponent was heavily outnumbered, but he had also been during the Vicksburg campaign when he hunkered down to hold Jackson in defiance of the odds against him. Why this latest retreat? Had Johnston lost his nerve? Or was it the doing of an overly cautious subordinate?

After the war Sherman had the opportunity to find the answers to those questions, at least to his own satisfaction. His postwar contacts with Johnston being frequent, Sherman received a full account of his version of why he had abandoned Cassville. But Sherman also had a postwar interview with Hood, whose recollection of the event was greatly at variance with Johnston's. Hood told Sherman that he had not argued against holding his artillery-enfiladed position; he had merely objected to fighting the coming battle on the defensive. Hood claimed to have "asked General Johnston to permit him with his own corps and part of Polk's to quit their lines, and to march rapidly to attack and overwhelm Schofield." Johnston, Hood contended, had taken offense at this characterization of his tactics and in a huff had ordered a retreat. Sherman could not decide whose story was more credible, but "it was sufficient for us that the rebel army did retreat that night, leaving us masters of all the country above the Etowah River."[9]

After securing good crossing points, Sherman decided to give his hard-marching soldiers a few days' respite. They rested in place, Thomas's army at and around Cassville, Schofield's a couple of miles farther south at Cassville Station, and McPherson's eight miles to the west at Kingston, where the Western & Atlantic joined the railroad to Rome. The break from marching permitted a couple thousand laborers under the direction of Col. W. W. Knight, Sherman's superintendent of railroad repairs, to mend broken sections of the Western & Atlantic, which had become the Federals' line of supply as well as Johnston's. Repairs complete, trains came down with enough supplies to enable the advance to resume.

Johnston's latest retreat had placed his army in a secluded section of central Georgia whose main geographic feature was the Allatoona Mountains. Since the railroad ran through one of the passes in the mountain range, Johnston undoubt-edly expected his opponent to follow him into the narrow defile. But Sherman knew better. Twenty years earlier, when investigating wartime claims by Georgia militiamen, he had spent days studying the local topography: "I therefore knew that the Allatoona Pass was very strong, would be hard to force," and provided opportunities for an ambush.[10]

Rather than taking the bait dangling before him, Sherman planned to turn Johnston's left flank via a wide circuit to the south and west with a return to the railroad at or near Marietta. The move would require the men to be supplied for as long as a week by wagon train instead of rail cars. Therefore, when his troops resumed the march on the twenty-third, they carried twenty days' prepared rations. McPherson's army crossed the Etowah near Kingston, Thomas's southeast of that point, and Schofield's a few miles farther upstream.

Once on the south bank, the armies moved on parallel lines, heading gener-ally southeastward. The soldiers had benefited from their recent rest, for the march was rapid and strenuous. Sherman knew that if he could pass Johnston's flank without the enemy's knowledge, he would be closer to Atlanta than Johnston was. But Sherman was beginning to see just how deft his opponent was in discerning his intentions and moving to foil them. Thanks to a reconnaissance north of the Etowah by Wheeler, Johnston learned of the flank drive. Late on May 23, he placed Hardee's corps in a blocking position several miles south of Dallas. At first Hood's troops were held at Allatoona and Polk's close to the local pass, but on the twenty-fourth, when it became clear that Sherman's destination was Dallas, Johnston ordered a junction of forces. He deployed Hardee's corps west of the town, astride the road between Dallas and Powder Springs. The next day Polk's soldiers took position on Hardee's right, while Hood extended the gray line northward to cover a vital crossroads near a Methodist meetinghouse known as New Hope Church.[11]

At midday on the twenty-fourth, cavalry in advance of Hooker's Twentieth Corps under Brig. Gen. Edward M. McCook approached Dallas from the north-east and took note of the Confederate buildup. Later the horsemen intercepted a message from Johnston, confirming that he was lying in wait for Sherman. Apprised of Johnston's intentions, Sherman, fearing he had lost the advantage of surprise, moved forward with caution. About 11:00 A.M. on the twenty-fifth the Union vanguard, the Twentieth Corps, encountered Rebel cavalry in front of a bridge over Pumpkinvine Creek. Withdrawing under fire, the troopers torched the bridge. Before the structure could collapse, however, General

Geary put out the flames and crossed his division over the stream. His men proceeded for perhaps four miles before being halted by a sizable body of infantry. Bringing up all three of his brigades, Geary pushed the Rebels back, then stopped to await instructions.

Geary's immediate superior, Hooker, came up to the firing lines, studied the situation, and decided he was facing a formidable line of defense, an opinion shared by George Thomas. They failed to convince Sherman, however, who believed Geary had struck Johnston's far left, which was weak enough to be driven in or turned. He did not know that the Twentieth Corps had encountered Stewart's division in full strength and well entrenched.

Refusing to consider any suggestion that he might be a making a mistake, Sherman had Hooker order up his remaining divisions, Maj. Gen. Daniel Butterfield's and Brig. Gen. Alpheus S. Williams's. Late in the afternoon, Geary's men left their works and joined their comrades in a headlong assault on Stewart's position. They quickly encountered what Williams called "a most effective and murderous fire that came from all directions except the rear," which dropped men by the dozen. Able to make no headway against such a storm, after dark the attackers disengaged and fell back, having suffered more than one thousand casualties. By then the battlefield had acquired an enduring nickname from Federals who would retain vivid memories of the carnage there: the "Hell Hole."[12]

Sherman, disappointed but not chastened by his miscalculation, hoped to recoup his losses on the twenty-sixth, but fate, and the elements, conspired against him. As he wrote, "[T]he night was pitch-dark, it rained hard, and the convergence of our armies toward Dallas produced much confusion. . . . I slept on the ground, without cover, alongside of a log, got little sleep, resolved at daylight to renew the battle, and to make a lodgment on the Dallas and Allatoona Road if possible, but the morning revealed a strong line of intrenchments facing us, with a heavy force of infantry and guns." He spent much of that day getting his forces, especially the just-arriving troops of McPherson and Schofield, in position for another effort to break through to the railroad. While the opposing sides traded skirmish fire, Sherman scrutinized the line facing him and finally admitted that Johnston was in heavy force, barring his path.[13]

Planning anew, Sherman determined to envelop his opponent's right and to attack from the rear, preceded by demonstrations elsewhere along the line. His chosen instrument, once again, was Thomas's army: specifically, Brig. Gen. Thomas J. Wood's division of Howard's Fourth Corps, supported by Brig. Gen. Richard W. Johnson's division of the Fourteenth Corps as well as by one of Schofield's brigades, and preceded by demonstrations elsewhere on the line. The preattack preparations were sufficiently complex and the terrain on which they were made was difficult enough that the movement did not get under way until some time after 4:00 P.M. on May 26. Sherman feared that the late start would be an impediment to success. An even greater handicap, although one unknown to him, was that Pat Cleburne detected the movement soon after it began, moved his men across the Federals' path near the village of Pickett's Mill, and had them construct breastworks. Upon the approach of Wood's leading brigades under Brig. Gen. William B. Hazen and Col. William H. Gibson, Cleburne's riflemen blasted them from many angles. Hazen's men, then Gibson's, began to fall back, their flanks exposed by the late arrival of supports. When the reinforcements finally appeared, they too were savaged, not only by rifle fire but by shell and canister. After suffering heavy casualties that included the severe wounding of General Johnson, the latecomers were forced to the rear, their formations irretrievably broken. Many attackers, however, had taken refuge in a hollow beyond range of Cleburne's guns. So close were they to the enemy position that they could not withdraw until after dark. But as they began to pull out, Brig. Gen. Hiram Granbury's brigade attacked the ravine and captured two hundred of its luckless occupants. All told, Sherman's losses at Pickett's Mill topped two thousand; Cleburne's were less than one-fourth as many.[14]

Satisfied that Johnston's left flank was unassailable and concerned about the three-mile gap that separated Davis's division near Dallas and Hooker's corps at New Hope Church, Sherman believed he had no recourse to evacuating the area and seeking a new line to occupy. Early on the twenty-eighth he began shifting to the left. Thomas's and Schofield's forces moved first, while McPherson's army remained in its trenches outside Dallas. Johnston detected the movement, but at first believed it included the Army of the Tennessee. He ordered Hardee to send a force to probe the area believed to be under evacuation. In response, Bate's division pushed west over open ground, its only support a small force of cavalry on its left. Through miscommunication, Bate's troops believed the horsemen, some of whom ranged ahead of the infantry, had found McPherson's trenches abandoned. Bate's men leapt to the attack, hoping to cut off or at least harass the enemy's withdrawal. They came on shouting, as one of their opponents wrote, "a yell the devil ought to copyright." McPherson's men waited for the misguided attackers to come within effective range and then methodically mowed them down. For half an hour or more they took a fearful toll of the unsupported division, most of whose men nevertheless refused to flee until they had exhausted every possibility of breaching the blue line. At last they fell back, broken and bleeding, having sacrificed themselves terribly but having kept McPherson's troops penned to their rifle pits. It would be June 1 before the Army of the Tennessee could safely disengage and follow Thomas and Schofield toward the Western & Atlantic Railroad, Marietta, and Atlanta.[15]

~•~

When most of Sherman's troops pulled out of the Dallas area on the twenty-eighth, their enemy closely monitored the operation. During a conference at army headquarters that afternoon, Hood suggested to Johnston that Sherman should be attacked while shifting position, beginning with his left flank. Johnston agreed and gave the necessary orders for Hood's corps to pull out of line, pass behind the rest of the army and around its right flank, and to take position to waylay the Yankees in transit. When Hood attacked, Hardee and Polk would lash the enemy in their front.

The next morning the other commanders waited for the sound of musketry from Hood's new position, the signal to launch an all-out attack. They waited in vain. At about 10:00 A.M., several hours after the operation was to have begun, Johnston was met by a courier from Hood who explained that his superior had discovered a division of the Army of the Cumberland entrenching at right angles to his path of attack. The corps leader wanted to know what he should do under these circumstances. Believing that the delay in attacking would prove fatal, Johnston, fuming that his subordinate had found a new way to frustrate him, recalled him to his starting-point.[16]

Johnston's latest fall-back enabled Sherman to gain his immediate objectives. On June 1, as a heavy, steady rain began to drench north Georgia, cavalry under Stoneman and Brig. Gen. Kenner Garrard rode to Allatoona Pass ready for a fight, but found it unoccupied. Two days later and five miles farther on, Sherman's infantry returned to the railroad at Acworth. Sherman halted to allow his supply trains to catch up with him and to rebuild the trestlework over the Etowah.

As soon as the men fell out of their marching columns they began to dig rifle pits and construct breastworks, just as they had at frequent intervals since leaving Ringgold. In fact, the wholesale construction of fieldworks had become a defining aspect of the campaign. The adjutant of the Twentieth Ohio Volunteers, noting the trend, explained that "wherever the army moves, either in gaining the enemy's works or in forming a new line of attack, the first duty after the halt is to create defensive fieldworks—rude indeed, but enabling us to hold our ground

Sherman's troops building fieldworks

against counterattack. . . . Though this year's campaigns have seen more such close combat than any other war, when men can kill one another at six hundred yards, that is what they prefer."[17]

During this respite from combat, the Federals paid avid attention to reports and rumors of the progress of the war in other theaters. For the most part, the news was not good. By early June, some of the operations that Grant had set in motion concurrent with Sherman's campaign had failed signally; others had degenerated into static warfare; still others remained in progress and thus inconclusive. In middle Virginia, Grant and Meade had driven Lee through the Wilderness, then south from Spotsylvania Court House, en route suffering thousands of casualties, most of them the result of head-on attacks against Lee's entrenched lines. Now the antagonists were converging on an area about ten miles north of Richmond, Cold Harbor. To the south, meanwhile, Butler's army had not only failed to take the Confederate capital by storm but had retreated to a peninsula between the James and Appomattox Rivers where it had been "bottled up" by troops rushed up from the Carolinas under General Beauregard. Well to the west, Sigel's attempt to sweep the Shenandoah Valley of organized Confederates had failed miserably at New Market, although General Crook had managed to destroy railroads and supply caches that enemy forces beyond the Alleghenies relied on to sustain themselves. In Louisiana, the so-called Red River campaign had ended after a series of ignominious defeats and retreats that Nathaniel Banks's reputation would never survive.

For his part, Joe Johnston used the lull in operations to review the effectiveness of his responses to Sherman's movements. The assessment depressed him as much as the news from distant fields disheartened the troops on the other side of the firing lines. He had been unable to prevent his opponent from flanking him out of one position after another, nor had he brought the invaders to battle on terms favorable to the defenders. He vented his frustration in a letter to his wife, who was now residing with friends in Atlanta. "Sherman," he complained, "is the most Cautious [officer] who ever Commanded troops . . . so Cautious that I can find no opportunity to attack him except behind intrenchments." On a past occasion he had admitted to Lydia that "I have never been so little Satisfied with Myself." Reviewing the many occasions on which he had deferred to his subordinates' preferences, he added: "[I] have never been so weak—so little governed by my own opinions."[18]

Unable to find an opening for a telling blow from the front, Johnston gave increasing thought to striking Sherman in the rear, breaking his communications link to Chattanooga by wrecking strategic portions of the Western & Atlantic. He believed his adversary so dependent on his railroad line that any disruption might make him halt and pull back—perhaps all the way back to Tennessee. Ordinarily, Wheeler's cavalry would be the means to this end, but Johnston, who put too much reliance in the imprecise and incomplete returns provided by his cavalry leader, considered his mounted arm too weak to send a significant portion of it so far from the rest of the army. He refused to reconsider his stance even when Governor Brown began to petition him to attack Sherman's railroad as a means of lessening the havoc the Yankees were wreaking on his state. On this issue Johnston clashed with Wheeler himself, who in one of his covert letters to Braxton Bragg argued that "if my command or only a portion of it could be detached, I could promise good results. . . . I am certain I could materially change the aspect of the campaign."[19]

At Brown's urging, President Davis and Secretary Seddon added their voices to his. Johnston replied with the bromide that he needed every cavalryman at his disposal to protect his flanks and front and to provide him with timely intelligence. He could not spare even a small detachment to target the railroads in the enemy's rear. Instead, beginning in early June, he began to urge Richmond to assign that job to Nathan Bedford Forrest, then in northern Mississippi. Johnston argued that Forrest, an experienced raider, did not face the formidable opposition that Wheeler did. The idea went nowhere because unlike Johnston, Davis and Seddon had to think in terms of what was best for the Confederacy as a whole. Mississippi could not be sacrificed for the sake of Georgia. Forrest would remain where he was for the foreseeable future.[20]

The possibility of a raid against his communications troubled Sherman, who anticipated such an effort by Forrest if not by Wheeler. To preempt it, Sherman, with Grant's approval, ordered a succession of cavalry advances into Forrest's department calculated to immobilize and, if possible, to cripple his command. Sherman's deterrent concept would prove highly effective. Every operation he launched would be met and defeated by the "Wizard of the Saddle," but by having to counter so many movements Forrest was prevented from threatening Sherman's supply lines until too late to achieve anything of lasting value.[21]

By the second week in June 1864, with the rain still coming down in buckets, the railroad bridge on the Etowah had been put in operation and supplies were again flowing to Sherman's armies. Another event that raised the general's spirits was his receipt of the two divisions of the Seventeenth Corps that had been on veteran furlough in the North. Fortified physically and morally by the additions, on the tenth Sherman's armies moved out of Acworth and down the muddy right-of-way of the railroad, past Big Shanty, toward a series of commanding eminences—Brush, Pine, Lost, and Kennesaw Mountains—and, farther south, the town of Marietta. As the Federals came on, Johnston the Predictable fell back.[22]

Two days after leaving Acworth, Thomas's army, in the center of Sherman's formation, had grouped near the base of Pine Mountain, on top of which Hardee had posted General Bate's division. The rains having slackened at last, Sherman spent the fourteenth at the front, for a part of that time close up on the firing line. At one point he came under a shelling from a Rebel battery on the crest of Pine Mountain, supporting a line of entrenched infantry. He directed a Fourth Corps gun crew to return fire, concentrating on a small party of Confederates at the summit who appeared to be monitoring General Howard's dispositions through field glasses.

As Sherman rode off, the cannoneers began to comply. One shell exploded directly in front of the enemy party, tearing through the upper body of Leonidas Polk and killing him instantly. Johnston, who had accompanied Polk on a personal reconnaissance, was shocked and saddened by the bishop's horrific demise. When able to return his mind to operational affairs, he named General Loring to be Polk's temporary successor. Eventually, A. P. Stewart would move over from Hood's corps to fill the position on a permanent basis.[23]

On June 16, when a portion of Schofield's army took up an advanced position threatening Hardee's place on the left of the Pine Mountain line, Johnston ordered yet another fall-back, this time to high ground along Mud Creek, near the base of Kennesaw Mountain. On the evening of June 18, after Thomas's artillery managed to enfilade the new position, the Confederates pulled back still closer to Kennesaw. Sherman believed Johnston intended to withdraw all the way to the Chattahoochee River, the last water barrier before Atlanta.[24]

The Gate City was a prize that Sherman was becoming increasingly interested in acquiring. Whether he fully appreciated the publicity that would accrue from its capture is not known, but Sherman had a solid understanding of Atlanta's lofty place in Confederacy strategy. He hungered for the opportunity to reduce to cinders and rubble the city's war-sustaining resources, believing their loss would exert a major influence on the outcome of the war.

The government in Washington had an even greater appreciation of Atlanta's worth to the Confederacy and the void its capture and occupation would create in the hearts of Southerners. Especially for Abraham Lincoln, Atlanta's fall could not come soon enough. By late June not only had Union operations elsewhere gone to smash, Grant's once-promising offensive had bogged down outside Petersburg, Virginia, twenty-two miles south of Richmond, where the Army of the Potomac had been forced to lay siege to Lee's Confederates. The investment was destined to drag on for months, lowering morale in the war-weary North and imperiling Lincoln's reelection chances. In August the president would pen a gloomy memorandum on the likelihood of his defeat at the hands of his former military favorite, George McClellan, the candidate of the peace wing of the Democratic Party.[25]

Without intending to, Sherman added to Lincoln's military woes. On June 20, believing Johnston in rapid retreat to the Chattahoochee, he pushed Schofield's command, in advance of the rest of his army group, eastward across Noyes Creek toward Sandtown. The following day Schofield, unaware that the enemy had halted and fortified, incautiously neared Johnston's new line, which was anchored on the Kennesaw Mountain range. Perceiving a chance to lash out at his pursuers, after dark on the twenty-first Johnston had Hood move his troops from the right of this line, east of Kennesaw, to the left, where they confronted the unsuspecting oncomers. Early the next day, however, Schofield captured some Rebel stragglers who alerted him to Hood's shift of position, which suggested an impending assault.

Forewarned, Schofield's men probed Hood's new line, then fell back and took position behind works they had built across the Powder Springs Road near the house of a farmer named Kolb. Hood took the withdrawal as an invitation to attack, which he did, advancing over open ground that crossed the line of fire of Hooker's corps, on Schofield's left. The Twentieth Corps artillery and infantry broke up the attack almost before it began, making casualties of one thousand Rebels. Repenting of his rashness, Hood recalled the survivors to his new position on the left of the line that extended northeastward to Kennesaw.[26]

After the fight of the twenty-second, Sherman pondered his next move. He had finally come to see that Johnston, far from retreating, was blocking the Federals' access to the railroad. Sherman's lines had become dangerously extended, Schofield's troops on the right being fully eight miles from the Western & Atlantic. The rain that had fallen almost continuously for more than three weeks had ceased entirely, but the ground south and west of Kennesaw, Sherman's only viable route of advance, was so saturated that it might not support an extended movement.[27]

Most historians credit the condition of the roads for prompting Sherman to take the drastic step of plowing ahead against Johnston's well-entrenched, artillery-shielded line along the craggy slopes of Kennesaw Mountain. In the main, however, Sherman acted out of sheer frustration—frustration over being stymied wherever he turned. He was weary of flanking and sidestepping only to be beaten to his next destination by a wily and agile opponent exploiting to the fullest the advantage of interior lines of movement.[27]

Thus it was that on the morning of June 27 Sherman ordered McPherson's army to assault the southwestern end of the Kennesaw range while Schofield's command moved up the Powder Springs Road to and across Olley's Creek, holding in place the troops on Johnston's far left. Sherman entrusted the main effort to the Army of the Cumberland, specifically to Jefferson Davis's division of the Fourteenth Corps and Maj. Gen. John Newton's Fourth Corps division. Both units were to attack south of the Dallas Road. Farther north, Morgan Smith's division of Logan's Fifteenth Corps, Army of the Tennessee, would charge up Burnt Hickory Road, supported by elements of the Sixteenth and Seventeenth Corps. Davis's attack would be directed at Cheatham's Hill, named for the commander of the Confederate division that occupied the position; Newton's assault would target the trench lines held by Cleburne's division. Meanwhile, Smith's troops would advance against a salient in the enemy's center, where the left flank of French's division of Loring's (formerly Polk's) corps joined the right flank of Walker's division of Hardee's corps.[28]

Following long-range skirmishing and a brief artillery bombardment, Sherman's attacks began at about 8:00 A.M. His men went forward in sweltering heat, the temperature already climbing toward 100 degrees Fahrenheit, but they encountered a fire that was even hotter. Cut up by musketry coming at them from many points along the steep, boulder-strewn hills and showered with rounds from batteries that had a clear view of their coming, the attackers did not stand a chance. Only the short distance to the Rebel position prevented them from being annihilated. Reaching the first line of works, they grappled fiercely with the defenders, shooting and being shot at point-blank range, slashing each other with bayonets, hammering one another with clubbed muskets.

The fighting was ghastly but also brief, anywhere from forty-five minutes (Johnston's estimate) to two and a half hours (as most historians claim). Then it was time for the attackers, those who remained upright, to turn and race for the rear. Many held back, however, fearful of the gauntlet of fire they would have to run. Frantically they scooped out rifle pits in which they huddled to escape the steady stream of missiles overhead. As on many previous fields, the trapped men had to remain under the enemy's guns until darkness enabled them to crawl homeward. By then twenty-five hundred of their comrades lay on the shell-scorched field, including two of the Army of the Cumberland's most capable brigade leaders, Brig. Gen. Charles G. Harker and Col. Daniel McCook, the latter Sherman's prewar law partner from Kansas. Johnston would estimate his losses at slightly more than eight hundred killed, wounded, and missing.[29]

The decision to assault well-entrenched positions on commanding ground had been a disastrous one. Not surprisingly, however, Sherman, at least at the time, refused to accept any blame. He would claim that each of his army commanders had approved of the attack, but this seems highly unlikely. Later General Schofield stated he had not favored it and in fact had argued against it. Sherman also ascribed the defeat to the loss of Harker, McCook, and numerous regimental commanders. At one point he even blamed his troops, asserting that the position would have been carried had the attackers displayed "one-fourth more vigor." In private, he keenly regretted the loss of life his misguided strategy had caused. It appears that he never forgave himself for the death of Dan McCook, to whose family he sent an emotional letter of apology.[30]

After the war, he continued to defend his reasons for attacking Kennesaw: his belief that Johnston's line, which stretched from Marietta all the way to Olley's Creek, was so thin as to be vulnerable to a quick, highly concentrated attack. In his after-action report he also justified the attack on the ground that he had to show Johnston he could not be counted on to sidestep forever. When conditions warranted, he would attack frontally and unreservedly. This was the same message that Grant had served Robert E. Lee three weeks earlier at Cold Harbor. After trying unsuccessfully for a month to pass the flank of the Army of Northern Virginia, Grant had committed Meade's army to direct assaults against strong positions, the result being a casualty count almost three times the size of Sherman's at Kennesaw Mountain.[31]

Johnston was pleased to inform Richmond of Sherman's defeat on the twenty-seventh. Within days, however, he realized how fleeting his triumph had been. Schofield's gains across Olley's Creek had put the Confederate left in such peril that by July 1, when the roads had dried sufficiently for Sherman to resume his flanking movement, Johnston had to abandon the Kennesaw line. By July 3, he occupied a position near Smyrna Camp Ground, less than twelve miles from the suburbs of Atlanta. By Independence Day Sherman's troops were again in contact with him, and when the Army of the Tennessee crossed Nickajack Creek in the face of Hood's inability to stop it, Johnston's left was again in jeopardy. That night he evacuated his newest position, falling back to a line of detached log redoubts, each large enough to be occupied by eighty soldiers, along the west (upper) bank of the Chattahoochee near where the Western & Atlantic crossed it on a high trestle. Packed with earth, entirely enclosed, and interconnected by a heavy stockade, the works were the brainchild of Johnston's chief artillerist, General Shoup. A great amount of work had gone into erecting these unconventional but formidable defenses. Although his superior had authorized their construction, Shoup perceived that "the spirit of my design was not understood or not heeded by Gen. Johnston." Nor was it appreciated by Hood, who, almost as soon as his corps occupied these works began to complain that his position was untenable and to urge a retreat to the east (lower) side of the river.[32]

To Shoup's chagrin, by July 9 Johnston was considering abandoning the works he had designed. The previous day, while McPherson's army feinted toward Turner's Ferry, opposite the Confederate left, Schofield's troops had forded the river by the mouth of Soap Creek, well north of Johnston's right, occupying a stretch of high ground from which they could not be driven. That ended Johnston's defense of the Chattahoochee. On the tenth he left the river behind and headed for Atlanta. He established a new perimeter in the valley of Peachtree Creek, midway between that stream and the fortifications that ringed the city to the south.[33]

Johnston's latest retreat was also his last. The authorities in Richmond no longer had faith in his ability to hold the line and halt Sherman. Over the weeks Johnston had pledged, either directly or by implication, that he would stand and fight above the Oostenaula, the Etowah, and the Chattahoochee. He had kept none of those promises. Late in June, Johnston had been visited by Louis Wigfall, then en route to Texas for some home-state politicking. The senator with his finger on the pulse of the Confederate capital warned his friend that because of his inability to arrest Sherman's progress, Davis was seriously considering relieving him of his command. If Johnston's position was shaky then, it was now precarious in the extreme. On the thirteenth, General Gorgas expressed the prevailing wisdom in Richmond: "Everybody has at last come to the conclusion that Johnston has retreated far enough." Gorgas had already written that "I fully expect to hear of his [Johnston's] retreat behind Atlanta." Pro-Davis newspapers in the capital and elsewhere echoed this fear and urged that Johnston be heavily reinforced so that he could force a showdown with Sherman, or be removed.[34]

Though the civilians in the capital had lost faith in him, Johnston could tell himself that his troops maintained confidence in his ability and judgment, understood the need to withdraw in the face of a much stronger enemy, and were keeping their courage up. This was the view of General Mackall, who noted in his diary on July 8 that "the army keeps up in spirits and health most wonderfully. . . ." Historians have generally held this to be true. A dissenting view, however, has emerged in recent years, offered by such chroniclers of the Army of Tennessee as Richard McMurry and Larry J. Daniel. McMurry has concluded, from a study of soldiers' recorded comments, that although "many, perhaps most . . . maintained their confidence in Johnston . . . feelings were nowhere near unanimous one way or the other." He quotes at some length the views of soldiers opposed to the army's continual retreats. A typical comment came from a Georgia infantry captain writing to his sister after the withdrawal from the Chattahoochee: "I don't like giving up so much territory, it looks to me like the beginning of the end as though we were going right straight down to the Gulf of Mexico."[35]

Having conducted a wider sampling of soldiers' writings, Daniel agrees with McMurry's findings. He observes that although there was an upsurge of support for their commander in June 1864, "by July, the men not only had become more opinionated one way or the other . . . but also there was a noticeable decline in confidence in Johnston's leadership. Clearly, those who claim that Johnston's retreats did not adversely affect morale do so in the face of significant evidence to the contrary."[36]

Johnston might have survived this crisis of confidence had he worked harder to gain the goodwill of his superiors. But, as had been true of him since the start of the war, he continued to alienate Davis, Seddon, and Bragg by failing to divulge his plans and intentions. He refused to give direct answers to direct questions, thus leaving the impression that he had no real plan to defend Atlanta. His well-known aversion to holding territory at the cost of manpower militated against the possibility that he would fight to the last to defend a city he believed had no hope of survival.

Failing to secure a statement of intent from Johnston, Davis all but made up his mind to relieve him. But he did not want to do so unless absolutely necessary, and if he did he wanted to be certain a viable successor was available. Hood had been writing unflattering opinions of Johnston's generalship since early March, and his condemnation of his superior's unwillingness to assume the offensive struck a chord with the president. Davis considered Hood the type of commander—aggressive, confident, courageous—who could prevail in the face of heavy odds. At least Hood would give the offensive a fair trial. That was all that Davis had asked of Johnston.

Desiring to give his ranking general one last chance, the day the army left the Chattahoochee Davis dispatched Braxton Bragg to Atlanta to learn Johnston's plans and report back to him. Unbeknownst to Davis, when Bragg reported at army headquarters on July 13 he was predisposed to call for Johnston's ouster. Bragg intimated to Johnston, however, that the visit was less an official errand than a courtesy call while he was on his way to inspect S. D. Lee's forces in Mississippi. On the thirteenth, he had a long talk with Johnston but, remarkably, never asked him about his plans. Johnston, for reasons of his own, divulged nothing. When Bragg left Atlanta, he was ready to recommend Johnston's dismissal. Johnston, however, got the impression they had parted on good terms, Bragg having "left me impressed with the belief that he was pleased with all my operations & what he learned of the condition of the army."[37]

Before departing, Bragg wired Davis that, in his opinion, Johnston had no intention of defending the city ("I cannot learn that he has any more plan for the future than he has in the past"). In a long letter, to be hand-delivered to Davis, Bragg elaborated on his conviction that Johnston would never resort to the offensive, the only method of saving the Army of Tennessee from utter ruin. He added some critical comments about Johnston that Hood had given him in a private interview, and he urged that if a change in command was desired, Hood should replace Johnston. "Hood would give unlimited satisfaction," Bragg wrote, "and my estimate of him, always high, has been raised by his conduct in this campaign." Bragg made no mention of Johnston's grievances against his corps commander, nor did he cite those occasions when Hood, rather than seeking battle, had urged disengagement and withdrawal.[38]

Although Bragg's letter did not reach Davis in time to influence his final decision, the president had a good idea of his emissary's opinion. When, on July 17, Johnston refused a final request to specify his plans for defending Atlanta, Davis consulted with his cabinet about removing the general. Receiving unanimous consent for an action he had already resolved to take, Davis ordered General Cooper to wire a message to Johnston's headquarters, notifying him that for his failure "to arrest the advance of the enemy to the vicinity of Atlanta" and for his refusal to express confidence in his ability to defeat or repel Sherman, "you are hereby relieved from command of the Army and Department of Tennessee." These responsibilities were to be handed over, without delay, to John Bell Hood.[39]

SEVENTEEN

AND FAIRLY WON

On the morning of July 19, 1864, by which time Hood was in command and Johnston was on his way by train to exile in Macon, Sherman was informed of the change of opponents. In his memoirs he claims to have taken little notice of the event beyond the fact that the new commander, as his West Point classmate Schofield was quick to point out, had a reputation as an aggressive fighter. In a postwar article, however, Sherman wrote that his response to the news of Hood's promotion was that "the Confederate Government rendered us most valuable service." Sherman was fully aware that he could keep forcing Johnston out of one position after another but that defeating him decisively would take months and cost additional thousands of lives. Some of Sherman's subordinates were likewise relieved to know that Johnston was out. General Hooker noted that the word "was received by our officers with universal rejoicing." Maj. Gen. Jacob D. Cox, one of Schofield's division commanders, who admired Johnston's "patient skill and watchful intelligence and courage," felt that his removal was "equivalent as a victory to us."[1]

With Hood in command, the Army of Tennessee could be counted on to be more offensive-minded. "I inferred," Sherman wrote, "that the change of commander meant 'fight'." While perhaps bloodier and more violent, the battles to come were likely to be more decisive and thus more satisfying. In all likelihood, they would also be more susceptible of being influenced by Sherman's advantage in strength. "This was just what we wanted," he declared, "to fight in open ground, on any thing like equal terms, instead of being forced to run up against prepared intrenchments." Years after the war, General Corse quoted Sherman as exclaiming, "Boys, we've got 'em. . . . Hood is in command. We will have our fight to-morrow."[2]

If Sherman made this prediction, he was off by only one day. Early on the twentieth, while the Union leader began to cross Peachtree Creek, three miles north of Atlanta, Hood came out swinging. Adopting a plan supposedly developed by his predecessor, the new commander concentrated against Thomas's army, advancing on Sherman's right flank and separated by two miles from Schofield and McPherson. The attacking force consisted of Hardee's and Stewart's corps. The third corps, formerly Hood's, had been temporarily entrusted to Frank Cheatham, who, along with some three thousand Georgia militia under Johnston's 1862 subordinate Gustavus W. Smith, manned the eastern sector of Atlanta's twelve-mile line of fortifications, toward which Schofield and McPherson were advancing.

At about 3:00 P.M., at least two hours behind Hood's timetable, Hardee initiated the attack on the Confederate right, striking the Fourth Corps division of John Newton. Stewart's corps, deployed west of Hardee, then made contact with the right flank of Geary's division of the Twentieth Corps, which had become isolated from its designated support force, the troops of Alpheus Williams. When the latter came up they, too, came under attack, as did the unit on the far right of the Union line, Col. Anson McCook's brigade of the Fourteenth Corps. Although surprised by the aggressive assault, the Federals reacted swiftly and effectively. Because Geary had faced his battle line to the right, the Confederates crossed its path at an oblique angle to the west, exposing themselves to a devastating enfilade. When General Thomas rushed to the front to take personal command, he brought with him several batteries that, moving quickly into position north of the creek, added greatly to the firestorm that engulfed the attackers and caused most of them to race to the rear. Another reason for the failure of Hardee's attack was that it lacked the participation of Cleburne's division, which Hood had reluctantly pulled out of the fight to reinforce comrades hard-pressed by McPherson's advance northeast of Atlanta.[3]

While Geary fought farther west, Newton's division dug in atop a high ridge along the Collier's Bridge Road, where it, too, leveled a heavy fire at Hardee's attackers. Other Confederates, however, assailed Newton's left flank, nearly breaking it, until driven back by a fresh Union brigade that came up just in time. A Confederate assault on Newton's right flank also failed through the timely appearance of Brig. Gen. William T. Ward's division. Before the afternoon ended, Hood's drive had stalled. After dark he withdrew Hardee and Stewart, who reported a combined loss of about forty-eight hundred as against fewer than two thousand in Thomas's ranks.[4]

Sherman, who had accompanied Schofield's column throughout the fight

(Hood had not been on the field of battle, either) summed up what the day meant for him and his men. Thomas's army had been taken by surprise and for a time roughly handled. "We had, however, met successfully a bold sally, had repelled it handsomely, and were also put on our guard and the event illustrated the future tactics of our enemy."[5]

After the fighting on Peachtree Creek died out, Sherman advanced his armies up to the enemy's entrenchments north and east of the city. The proximity of the antagonists made another confrontation inevitable. Relatively small-scale fighting consumed the twenty-first, during which Brig. Gen. Mortimer D. Leggett's division of the Seventeenth Corps drove Cleburne's defenders from the tree-cleared crest known as Bald Hill, two and a half miles southeast of downtown Atlanta. Leggett's success, achieved only after what Cleburne called the hardest fighting he had ever witnessed, resulted in the hill being renamed in the division commander's honor.[6]

The day after Leggett's Hill was secured, Hood launched his second sortie, this aimed at McPherson's army, which had shifted into position near Decatur, due east of Atlanta along the Georgia Railroad. Confirming Sherman's belief that Hood could be lured into attacking impulsively, the Confederate commander planned an open-ground assault, one that would prove that his army had not lost the will to fight everywhere except behind breastworks. While Stewart occupied the rest of Sherman's force above the city, Cheatham and Hardee would take on McPherson, the former by a frontal assault, the latter via a long march around the enemy's southern flank.

The operation got under way on the night of the twenty-first, when Hardee began his fifteen-mile trek toward the Union left rear. At the same time, Hood withdrew some forces from the city's outer works and placed them inside the city itself, making McPherson believe, or at least hope, that the city was being evacuated. McPherson's subsequent advance, which drew him farther from Schofield's army on his right, concerned Sherman, who decided that the Army of the Tennessee should halt, tear up the railroad toward Decatur, then shift to the far right by passing around the rear of Schofield and Thomas. That morning, McPherson rode to Sherman's headquarters to discuss this matter and other topics including their adversary's affinity for bold, if not necessarily well-reasoned, maneuvers (McPherson had also been a classmate of Hood's). "We agreed," wrote Sherman, "that we ought to be unusually cautious and prepared at all times for hard fighting, because Hood, though not deemed much of a scholar, or of great mental capacity, was undoubtedly a brave, determined, and rash man. . . ."[7]

Sherman described McPherson as "in excellent spirits, well pleased at the progress of events so far." As they talked, the sounds of "lively skirmishing" became audible not far off, and McPherson decided to see for himself what it meant. Sherman recalled that the army leader "jumped on his horse, saying he would hurry down his line and send me back word what these sounds meant." That was the last Sherman spoke to his trusted subordinate and close friend.[8]

Gen. James B. McPherson, USA

As Sherman quickly learned, the skirmish fire signaled the start of a major engagement, later christened the Battle of Atlanta. Two and a half miles outside the city Hardee's attackers had struck McPherson's army from the west and south. The Georgian had intended to attack much earlier but constrictive terrain and errors by the officers at the head of his two columns had slowed the march. By the time his advance was detected, Hardee had yet to clear the front of McPherson's line. Instead of the left rear of the Army of the Tennessee, he had struck its left-center, held by Dodge's Left Wing, Sixteenth Corps.

Dodge's men, whom many of their comrades thought of as railroad repair men rather than combat veterans, this day gave an outstanding account of themselves in the latter role. They stubbornly held their embattled line, repulsing two attacks and killing General Walker, who led the effort against their right flank. A few minutes later, James McPherson rushed to the front, a single orderly by his side. Hoping to reestablish contact between Dodge's troops and Frank Blair's farther to the right, he stumbled upon one of Cleburne's skirmish lines, turned to flee, and was shot dead.

The fighting then shifted to Blair's position, which the divisions of Cleburne and Brig. Gen. George E. Maney struck in close coordination. The attack temporarily dislodged the Seventeenth Corps and threatened to isolate Dodge's troops as well. When all seemed lost, a fresh brigade that McPherson had ordered up shortly before his death filled the gap and, in a display of eleventh-hour heroics, repulsed the attackers. Dodge then sidled toward his right, sealing the breach. Unable to make further headway, Hardee quit the field, having come within an ace of victory only to taste defeat for what must have seemed the thousandth time in this campaign.[9]

Hood was largely to blame for Hardee's failure, having remained in the rear throughout the fight. With no superior to hasten him, Cheatham had delayed his assault on Logan's Fifteenth Corps, on Blair's right, until too late to be of material support to Hardee. When Cheatham finally moved out, augmented by Smith's less-than-reliable militia, he penetrated Union positions along the south side of the railroad, displacing the Fifteenth Corps division of Morgan Smith, routing Lightburn's brigade, and capturing a battery of 20-pounder Parrott rifles. The Tennessean's drive was finally halted by Logan, who, having succeeded McPherson, rushed up

Gen. Benjamin F. Cheatham, CSA

one of Dodge's brigades, supported by a portion of a Fifteenth Corps division.

The reinforcements sent Cheatham's men reeling to the rear, dazed and bloody. Along with the demoralized militia who had been of little assistance to them, they took refuge inside the fortifications of the city. The losses in Cheatham's and Hardee's ranks had been enormous—almost eight thousand killed, wounded, or missing, more than twice the number the Army of the Tennessee had absorbed.[10]

———— ◆ ————

Sherman was pleased by his army's response to yet another surprise assault by his overly aggressive opponent. At the same time, he was saddened and distressed by the loss of McPherson, whose body he had undergo a brief autopsy so he might inform the man's family of the exact cause of death before its removal to Marietta for shipment to Ohio under escort. Four days later Sherman named General Howard to be McPherson's permanent successor and assigned the Fourth Corps to General Stanley. Sherman desired his armies to be commanded by West Pointers, but his decision to go with Howard gave offense to John Logan, a citizen-soldier who had performed well in army command following McPherson's fall, as he had in the role to which he now returned, that of Fifteenth Corps commander. Logan suppressed his disappointment for the duration of the war, but he continued to resent Sherman's action. Years later, as a powerful senator and congressman, he would take his revenge by publicly criticizing West Point and the regular army (which Sherman then commanded) and imposing reductions in military appropriations that provoked Sherman's ire and indignation. Late in life, the two men would reconcile, brought together at a gathering of their old veterans.[11]

Even before Howard took the reins, his new army was moving into the position on the far right that Sherman had assigned it days before. By July 28, it had deployed one and a half miles west of Atlanta. Dodge's corps faced toward the city, with Logan's and Blair's farther to the right. Having already damaged the railroad to Decatur, Howard's command was now poised to threaten the Atlanta & West Point Railroad and the Macon & Western, which united a couple of miles southwest of Atlanta. These lines of movement and supply were critical to the continued existence of Atlanta as a Confederate stronghold. Doubtful that the Yankees would relinquish their lodgment unless pushed, Hood decided to move against them with the corps of Stewart and S. D. Lee, the latter recently promoted to lieutenant general and assigned to the permanent command of Hood's corps.[12]

Enjoined by Sherman to proceed cautiously while so far from his comrades, Howard strengthened the line he had taken up near Ezra Church and scouted the country to the south, early on July 28 detecting the enemy's approach. The advancing troops intended to skirt Howard's right flank and flail the Union rear. Instead, they struck Logan's position, which was "refused" (i.e., at a right angle to the rest of Howard's line) and heavily entrenched. Attacking as soon as he came within range without waiting for Stewart to move up in support, S. D. Lee, inexperienced in corps command, hurled his brigades recklessly at Logan's barricades and suffered one repulse after another. When Stewart finally got into the fight, he could commit only two of his divisions. Those, too, suffered heavily, while Stewart and his senior subordinate, General Loring, were both severely wounded.

Once again Hood had attempted to supervise operations from his headquarters inside Atlanta, causing a predictable breakdown in command communications.

S. D. Lee's futile attacks had been made in ignorance of what his superior expected of him. After dark, Hood withdrew both corps to Atlanta, their effective strength having been reduced by five thousand. These latest losses only exacerbated a man-power situation that had become acute since Hood's assumption of command. At the end of June, Johnston's army had included forty-five thousand effective infantry. Since then, this number had shrunk to thirty-two thousand. That kind of arithmetic appeared to spell disaster for Hood's army and the city it defended. Already there was talk in Richmond that Hood, who had replaced Johnston in order to make the Army of Tennessee fight, would have to be relieved because he had fought it too often.[13]

The successful retention of his foothold west of Atlanta was heartening to Sherman, as was the behavior of Howard and Logan, who not only showed courage and skill throughout the fight but also a disposition to get along. "To this fact," Sherman wrote, "I at this time attached much importance, for it put me at ease as to the future conduct of that most important army." The fighting of the twenty-eighth also encouraged Sherman's soldiers to believe that they could lure Hood out of his works and fight him to their advantage.[14]

So believing, Sherman pushed ahead with his plan to envelop Hood's left flank. While the fighting at Ezra Church was in progress, he had sent the cavalry divisions of Stoneman, McCook, and Garrard to sever the railroads southwest and south of Atlanta. Stoneman had taken on the additional mission of raiding Macon and its vicinity in order to liberate, if possible, the inmates of the notori-ous Andersonville prison camp. In the end, the cavalry attained only a few of its objectives, breaking sections of the Atlanta & West Point Railroad but bypassing other targets once Hood sent his own horse soldiers in pursuit. Wheeler's men, supported by Red Jackson's understrength division, attacked and uprooted two of the three forces, preventing further damage to the lines. Then they pursued, over-took, surrounded, and captured Stoneman's force virtually intact more than twenty miles short of Macon.[15]

Sherman may have been stymied but not stopped. Before July was over, he had moved close enough to Atlanta to begin shelling it. Though the distance to target was considerable, the artillery fire, which continued throughout August—several hours each day, often well into the night—did considerable damage and claimed the lives of many occupants, soldiers and civilians. By August 2 Hood's scouts were reporting that Sherman's right wing was beginning to move even farther west of

Atlanta. That day Sherman had Schofield's troops take position on the right of Howard's army and force a crossing of the north fork of Utoy Creek near Herring's Mill, three and a half miles southwest of Atlanta. Schofield's objective was East Point, four miles to the southeast, where the railroads running into Atlanta met. Although ordered to coordinate his movements with those of the Fourteenth Corps division of Brig. Gen. Absolom Baird, Schofield failed to do so, mainly due to a conflict over rank and seniority with Baird's superior, John Palmer. He also failed to crack the formidable works, which included entanglements of felled trees, that had been erected on ridges south of the Sandtown Road by S. D. Lee. Despite the setback, Sherman ordered the troops involved to hold their most advanced positions until he was ready to launch his climactic offensive against the Gate City.[16]

Sherman's recent movements had forced Hood to alter his defensive formations. By mid-August, Hardee had been shifted from the east side of Atlanta to the southwest. Lee now held the center of the line of defense, which covered Ezra Church. The infantry and artillery of Stewart and the militia of Smith extended the line across the Marietta Road to the northern outskirts of the city. Having been advised by Jefferson Davis to refrain from committing the main army to offensive operations unless success seemed certain, Hood opted to send his cavalry on a mission that his predecessor had studiously avoided. On August 10 Joe Wheeler and four thousand of his troopers rode north around the contending forces to strike and destroy the railroad that linked Sherman's armies to their supply bases in other states.

On paper, the results of Wheeler's expedition were impressive: the Western & Atlantic torn up and railroad bridges downed near Marietta, Cassville, Calhoun, and elsewhere; similar if lesser damage done to the railroad between Chattanooga and Nashville; foodstuffs and beef on the hoof seized and sent to Hood's commissariat. Yet the raid achieved nothing in the strategic sense, for it came too late to stop Sherman's final drive against Atlanta. Moreover, specially trained and equipped railroad crews repaired the damage to the W & A with such speed and efficiency as to demoralize the raiders. Errors in judgment cost Wheeler fifteen hundred troopers whom he detached for an unsuccessful (and unauthorized) attack on Knoxville. They were never seen again. Furthermore, Union cavalry along his route tore into his column at several points, inflicting many casualties.[17]

In addition to these setbacks, the raid gave Sherman an opportunity to complete his envelopment of his enemy's left flank. With most of Hood's cavalry off the board, Sherman dispatched the mounted division of Brig. Gen. H. Judson Kilpatrick to reach and wreck the railroad to Macon. Sherman was not an aficionado of cavalry warfare, and the recent failures of Stoneman, McCook, and Garrard seemed to confirm his low opinion of raiding. But he considered Kilpatrick more enterprising than any of the others and believed he had the killer instinct they lacked (he would later call the brigadier "a hell of a damned fool," but given Sherman's flair for irony this was not necessarily a putdown).[18]

On this occasion, however, the division leader failed to meet his commander's standards of performance. On the day he started out, August 18, Kilpatrick's troopers tore up a section of the West Point Railroad before marching to Jonesboro, on the Macon & Western sixteen miles south of the city. There his men levered up more track and destroyed much matériel, but presently they were set upon by Rebel infantry and Jackson's cavalry and chased back to home base. Though Kilpatrick assured Sherman that it would take ten days to repair the damage, trains were running on those tracks two days after his return.[19]

Convinced that his horsemen "could not or would not work hard enough to disable a railroad prop-

Gen. H. Judson Kilpatrick, USA

erly," Sherman determined to descend upon the Macon line with thousands of foot soldiers. On the evening of the twenty-fifth he sent back to the Chattahoochee the Twentieth Corps, now led by Henry Slocum (Joe Hooker was gone, having been relieved at his own request when passed over for McPherson's replacement). While Slocum's men covered the railroad bridge as well as two of the armies' pontoon spans, the rest of Sherman's force marched southwest of the city toward sites named for the sacred and the inane, Mt. Gilead Church and Lick Skillet. As they came on, Schofield pulled out of his position near Utoy Creek to cover his comrade's left flank and wagon trains.[20]

Because Wheeler's departure had deprived him of his "eyes and ears," Hood had to depend on less reliable sources of information on Sherman's movements. When scouts reported Slocum's fallback to the Chattahoochee, the Confederate

Sherman's troops destroying a railroad

commander believed it signaled a retreat by all of Sherman's forces. Lacking cav-alry to penetrate the enemy's counterreconnaissance screen, Hood had no way of verifying the news. He appears to have accepted it because he wished it to be so. His willing self-deception was emulated by his soldiers, who reacted joyously to the report of Sherman's retreat. So did Atlanta's civilian population, who dared believe that the hated invader was gone and their beloved city safe.[21]

Early on August 28, Kilpatrick's horsemen, covering the right of the Army of the Cumberland as it moved toward the West Point Railroad, seized a section of that line, which they held until infantry comrades joined them. In the afternoon, Thomas's foot soldiers reached the railroad at Red Oak and Fairburn, where, working in teams, they tackled the job of demolition with energy and enthusi-asm. Sherman described the process: "The track was heaved up in sections the length of a regiment, then separated rail by rail; bonfires were made of the ties and of fence-rails on which the rails were heated, carried to trees or telegraph-poles, wrapped around and left to cool. Such rails could not be used again; and, to be still more certain, we filled up many deep cuts with trees, brush, and earth, and commingled with them loaded shells, so arranged that they would explode on an attempt to haul out the bushes."[22]

Only when he learned the West Point line was under attack did Hood realize that his opponent had not cleared out. Even so, as late as the thirtieth he believed that only two Union corps were moving around the city's west side. Late that day he sent Hardee, with his own corps, under Pat Cleburne, and Lee's troops, to chase the Yankees away. Cleburne was to assail Thomas's south flank while Lee struck frontally. The march was long and taxing, and not till the morning of the thirty-first did the rear of Hardee's column reach Jonesboro.

On the last day of August, while the work of destruction continued on the Atlanta & West Point Railroad, the main bodies of all three of Sherman's armies moved cross-country toward the Macon line. Schofield's troops reached it at the depot known as Rough and Ready, eight and a half miles above Jonesboro; the Army of the Cumberland struck the tracks at two points farther south. Riding with Thomas at the head of one of his columns, Sherman was aware that Hood must be waiting for him up ahead, and he felt uneasy about the "ominous silence" that surrounded the advancing troops: "I was expecting at each moment to hear the sound of battle."[23]

He heard it shortly before 3:00 P.M., as Logan's corps neared Jonesboro from the northwest and Cleburne's corps attacked its right flank, which was covered by Kilpatrick's cavalry. Misinterpreting this affair as a prearranged signal to attack, S. D. Lee charged on Cleburne' right, breaking Logan's skirmish line and capturing a nest of rifle pits. Once it hit Logan's main position, however, Lee's attack appeared to lose momentum. Although it took a toll of the division on Logan's left, under William B. Hazen, it was thrown back with heavy loss by reinforcements from the Seventeenth Corps. As per orders from Hood, Lee pieced together his broken ranks and in the early hours of September 1 led them back to Atlanta. Cleburne, meanwhile, had failed to envelop Logan's other flank, held by a division recently assigned to John Corse, and was likewise forced into retreat.[24]

Believing that Sherman was preparing to attack the southern fortifications of Atlanta while the fighting raged at Jonesboro, Hood evacuated the city and marched to meet Lee's corps, which he assigned to guard duty on his right flank. These movements left Hardee's corps isolated at Jonesboro, and Sherman decided to trap and annihilate it. The operation began with an attack by Davis's Fourteenth Corps (General Palmer, like Hooker, had been relieved at his own request following his clash with Schofield at Utoy Creek). Davis's men, attacking from the north, smashed through the middle of Hardee's attenuated position, capturing two Confederate brigades. Late in the afternoon, Stanley's Fourth Corps, slowed by unfamiliar terrain, got into position to hit the Rebel right flank northeast of the depot, but night came on before it could strike. In the meantime, Sherman had Frank Blair send the Seventeenth Corps around to the right and below Jonesboro to prevent Hardee's retreat, which appeared imminent. But because Stanley had been so late getting into his position, Hardee withdrew his remaining troops through the Fourth Corps' sector and led them to safety along the railroad. At Lovejoy's Station, ten miles below Jonesboro, he halted and dug in, waiting for Hood, Lee, and Stewart to join him.[25]

With the coming of night on September 1, Sherman awaited word from Slocum, whose corps had been dispatched to "feel forward occasionally toward Atlanta," to determine if rumors that the city was being evacuated were true. "That night," he wrote, "I was so restless and impatient that I could not sleep, and about midnight there arose toward Atlanta sounds of shells exploding," and perhaps also of musketry. The noise made him fear for the safety of the Twentieth Corps: "An interval of quiet then ensued, when again, about 4 a.m. arose other similar explosions, but I still remained in doubt whether the enemy was engaged in blowing up his own magazines, or whether General Slocum had . . . become engaged in a real battle."[26]

In the morning Sherman led the pursuit of Hardee, whom he encountered near Lovejoy's Station. Fighting broke out there, but while it raged, Sherman began to receive reports that the city was in Slocum's hands. A few hours later a note from the corps commander confirmed that the explosions Sherman had heard signaled the destruction of matériel, including heavy ordnance, by Hood's rear guard as the last of Atlanta's defenders evacuated shortly after dawn. Slocum's troops had entered the city unopposed. "His letter was dated inside the city," Sherman recalled, "so there was no doubt of the fact." He shared the news with Thomas, who at first feared it was too good to be true. Presently, however, the staid old general gave vent to his emotions: "He snapped his fingers, whistled, and almost danced, and, as the news spread to the army, the shouts that arose from our men, the wild hallooing and glorious laughter, were to us a full recompense for the labor and toils and hardships through which we had passed in the previous three months."[27]

It was fair compensation, as well, for the administration in Washington, which had weathered so many storms arising from its handling of the war, a good many of them in the weeks since Sherman had left Ringgold to do battle with Joe Johnston. When Sherman's telegram of September 2, announcing that "Atlanta is ours, and fairly won," was received in the capital, the rejoicing may have been less raucous than that of Sherman's troops, but it was no less heartfelt. As the president himself later admitted in an interview with Sherman, "he had previously felt in doubt, for the summer was fast passing away; that General Grant seemed to be checkmated about Richmond and Petersburg, and my army seemed to have run up against an impassable barrier, when, suddenly and unexpectedly, came the news" that changed everything. Two months after Atlanta's fall, Lincoln would win reelection, soundly defeating the so-called Peace Democrats and ending the Confederacy's last, faint hope of survival.[28]

Lincoln must have foreseen this outcome when he sat down on September 3 to convey to Sherman and, through him, to every officer and enlisted man in the Military Division of the Mississippi the government's thanks and gratitude for their "distinguished ability and perseverance" in the face of a stubborn foe. Then the president turned historian: "The marches, battles, sieges, and other military operations, that have signalized the campaign, must render it famous in the annals of war, and have entitled those who have participated therein to the applause and thanks of the nation."[29]

Joseph and Lydia Johnston took the train from Atlanta to Macon at six-thirty in the evening of July 19. Senator Wigfall's son, Halsey, an officer on Hood's staff, saw the general off on his sad journey. He was surprised to discover that "no one could ever have told from his countenance or manner that anything unusual had occurred. Indeed he seemed in rather better spirits than usual though it must have been at the cost of much exertion." In fact, what Halsey Wigfall beheld was the reaction of a man from whose shoulders a crushing burden had been lifted.[30]

The Johnstons spent two and a half months in Macon before relocating, early in October, to the "attractive suburb" of Vineville, where they moved into a vacant house owned by the brother-in-law of General Mackall, Johnston's faithful subordinate. Mackall and his family soon joined the new arrivals. After Johnston's departure from Atlanta, Hood had asked Mackall to stay on as army chief of staff. However, the brigadier quickly ran afoul of Hood and his patron, Bragg, whom Mackall, having learned of the latter's role in Johnston's dismissal, considered a backstabber. For the second time in his career, Mackall was relieved of command at his own request, whereupon he headed for Vineville.[31]

Johnston enjoyed his stay in the Macon area, where people treated him with deference and respect, many openly regretting his difficulties with the authorities in Richmond and decrying his treatment at their hands. Johnston spent the time writing his report of the Atlanta campaign and corresponding with former subordinates, political supporters, and old friends like Dabney Maury. To Maury he poured out some of the bitterness his relief had occasioned. He was especially upset over the unflattering public comparisons that had been made of him and Robert E. Lee, who had been forced to retreat at least as often and as far as Johnston but who continued to be regarded as a warrior god. As Johnston put it, "Why, then, should I be condemned for the defensive while General Lee was adding to his great fame by the same course?"[32]

Far from the sound of guns, he continued to fight the war and to lash out at his enemies. Having come to understand something of the role Bragg had played in his downfall, Johnston condemned him as well as the civilian superiors who had assigned him an impossible task, had criticized him for fighting in the only way that would preserve the army they had entrusted to his care, and had replaced him with a general whose only claim to army command was the oft-repeated boast that he could do a better job than the man above him. As Johnston had observed when acknowledging the notice of his own relief, "confident language by a military commander is not usually regarded as an evidence of competence."[33]

To Maury he made no attempt to answer the question of whether he would have fought to defend Atlanta, although in correspondence with Wigfall, Beverly Johnston, and others, he vehemently denied the charge, given much play in the newspapers, that at the time of his dismissal he was prepared to abandon the city to Sherman. In his memoirs and in other postwar writings Johnston claimed that he never considered giving up Atlanta without a fight. He probably meant what he said, at least in retrospect. But based on his record of retreating in the face of adversity and his prejudice against holding territory for political reasons or to prop up morale, most historians believe that Johnston would have surrendered the city after making what he considered a good-faith effort to defend it. In other words, he would have fought off Sherman until he judged the effort to be hopeless. Then he would have evacuated to save his army.[34]

Given his highly publicized penchant for retrograde operations and his thorny relationship with the administration in Richmond, Johnston at first doubted that he would be granted another chance to lead an army in the field. On the other hand, despite the critical coverage he had received in proadministration organs, his public image remained that of an experienced and, in many ways, a skillful and perceptive leader. The Confederacy did not have at its disposal many of this species, especially with the rank and seniority that Johnston commanded.

Then, too, he was not the only officer in Georgia to be tarred with the brush of failure. During the weeks following his relief he read of the defeats that Hood's strategy had heaped on the Army of Tennessee. After early September he must have taken a measure of satisfaction in the fact that the man who had vowed to hold Atlanta to the last had been forced to give it up.

In fact, even before he sacrificed the army to his passion for the offensive, Johnston's successor had been unpopular with the rank and file. After Peachtree Creek, the battle of Atlanta, and Ezra Church, the army's disenchantment with their new commander had grown geometrically. In late September, when President Davis visited Hood's new headquarters at Palmetto, Georgia, twenty-five miles southwest of Atlanta, his speeches to the troops were interrupted by cries of "Give us General Johnston!"[35]

In these events the politically astute Johnston may have sensed a trend in his favor. Perhaps he had been too hasty in supposing he would never have the opportunity to correct Hood's mistakes—and his own.

As soon as Sherman took possession of Atlanta, he strove to destroy its war-making capacity. To do so effectively, he believed the city's civilian population had to be removed. This was carried out under terms of a special field order Sherman issued on September 8. The decree, which affected women and children as well as able-bodied males, provoked an outcry from local politicians and national officials, as well as from General Hood, with whom Sherman exchanged vituperative letters on the subject, Hood criticizing Sherman for wanton cruelty and Sherman responding with a charge of self-righteous hypocrisy.[36]

The Union commander was unmoved by criticism that he was violating the ethics of warfare. As he wrote to General Halleck, "I am not willing to have Atlanta encumbered by the families of our enemies. I want it a pure Gibraltar." His correspondent assured him that despite the mournful wail of outraged Rebels, his policy was "justified by the laws and usages of war." Northern newspapers, including those who two years before had branded him crazy, incompetent, or both, applauded Sherman's gloves-off approach to civil-military relations. Even Ellen Sherman, who had begun the war as a moderate Democrat with sympathetic feelings toward Southerners, wrote approvingly of his course, "as it has always seemed to me preposterous to have our Government feeding so many of their people—their insolent women particularly for they are responsible for the war and should be made to feel that it exists in sternest reality."[37]

As soon as Atlanta had been depopulated, Sherman set his legions to destroying factories, foundries, rolling mills, armories, arsenals, warehouses, depots, rolling stock, and whatever railroad track his agents of destruction had failed to mangle before Atlanta's fall. Explosions loud and small, the crackle of flames gutting public buildings, and the resounding thud of wood and masonry structures collapsing in a heap were daily reminders of Sherman's relentless determination to raze as much of this city as he thought necessary to ensure its inability to support the field forces of his nation's enemy.[38]

His army was so vast that only small portions of it were kept busy demolishing war resources and keeping tabs on Hood's refugees, who showed little inclination to challenge the armies that had run them out of town. The majority of Sherman's soldiers lolled in their camps, enjoying a rest they once doubted would ever be granted them. Sherman disliked the prospect that these veterans might grow soft from a lack of hard marching and hard labor, especially with so much yet to be done before a just peace could be won.

Grant thought the same way. From his siege lines around Petersburg, where he and Lee remained locked in static but steady combat, he sent Lt. Col. Horace Porter of his staff to confer with Sherman on future strategy. Arriving at Sherman's headquarters on September 20, Porter was immediately impressed with his host, whom he considered "one of the most dramatic and picturesque characters of the war." When Sherman got down to cases, he explained that thus far he had been unable to bring Hood's fugitives to bay, and he doubted he ever would. He expressed, therefore, an intention to wage a campaign in another direction. After ensuring that Hood would not interfere with his movements, "I want to strike out for the sea." He sent Porter back to Grant with a half-jocular proposal to a fellow family man: "If you can whip Lee and I can march to the Atlantic, I think Uncle Abe will give us a twenty days' leave of absence to see the young folks."[39]

Sherman's idea intrigued Grant, who also saw risks in it. He raised some objections, as did Lincoln, mainly relating to the damage Hood could do to Union outposts, communications, and supply depots if left unchecked. While waiting for a final decision, Sherman took steps to assuage his superiors' concerns. Early in October he left Slocum's troops to hold Atlanta, then began a pursuit of Hood's suddenly mobile army. He could not prevent his opponent from attacking the outpost at Allatoona on the sixth, but he rushed to the threatened point reinforcements under General Corse. Supposedly Corse was responding to an order from Sherman that became the basis of story, song, and legend ("Hold the fort, I am coming!"). Whatever the nature of his summons, Corse successfully defended the post until larger forces arrived to lift Hood's siege.[40]

As Sherman came on, Hood moved briskly from point to point, keeping ahead of his pursuers and doing considerable damage to the Federal supply line. A frustrated Sherman soon tired of the chase and gave ever more serious thought to marching to the coast—to Savannah, Jacksonville, Charleston, or some other major port where he could make contact with the blockading squadrons of the U. S. Navy and from them replenish his supply coffers. Until then, a matter of a few weeks, he surmised, his men would have to live off the land. This was a stratagem Sherman had given a great deal of thought to since Grant resorted to it when advancing against Vicksburg. Sherman believed the tactic a viable one, since his armies would be crossing a portion of Georgia that had been largely spared the rod of war and thus was relatively fecund. The main attraction of such a campaign would be the opportunity to apply, on a grand scale, the hard-war policies Sherman had advocated ever since his days in command in West Tennessee.

After much prodding from Sherman, late in October Grant gave conditional approval to his ambitious scheme. In later weeks the general-in-chief's support for the plan appeared to waver, especially after Lincoln expressed concern that when Sherman turned away from Hood, nothing would stop him from invading Tennessee, and perhaps Kentucky. Though neither Lincoln, Grant, nor Sherman knew it at the time, this is exactly what the Confederate leader intended to do. By mid-October he had evolved a plan, one reluctantly approved by his newly installed departmental commander, Beauregard, to head for the Ohio River, en route collecting supplies, attacking outposts, and making life dangerous for the Unionists in his path.[41]

In the end, Sherman overcame Grant's objections by proposing to send George Thomas to Nashville, where he could block any attempt by Hood to invade the Bluegrass State. Sherman would augment Thomas with Schofield's corps, plus all of the cavalry except Kilpatrick's division, as well as with forces shifted from inactive theaters, including a corps under Maj. Gen. A. J. Smith, currently stationed in Missouri. Sherman calculated that Thomas would have at least forty thousand troops with which to confront an approximately equal number of Rebels. In the meantime, Sherman would march to the coast at the head of sixty-two thousand veterans divided between a right wing under General Howard, consisting of the Fifteenth and Twentieth Corps, Army of the Tennessee, and a left wing (the "Army of Georgia") comprising the Fourteenth and Twentieth Corps and led by Slocum.[42]

At the head of such an army—seasoned veterans well versed in every aspect of soldiering and fully in tune with Sherman's policy of bringing the war home to the enemy's populace—their leader was certain, as he assured Grant, that "I can make this march, and make Georgia howl!"[43]

EIGHTEEN
REUNION IN THE CAROLINAS

The March to the Sea is often regarded as a major military campaign even apart from the strategy that underlay it. In truth, it was of relatively short duration—barely five weeks all told—and it featured almost no fighting of any consequence. Because Hood did not attempt to follow Sherman's hordes, they had virtually free access to Georgia's eastern midsection, which they crossed along a route almost 250 miles long and 60 miles wide. The only defenders they encountered were the cavalrymen of Joe Wheeler, whom Beauregard had convinced Hood to leave behind when he started for Tennessee (Hood would be compensated by the temporary addition of Forrest's troopers) and the amateur soldiers of the Georgia militia.[1]

The true importance of Sherman's march lies not in its duration or its itinerary but in the philosophy behind it. Never in the annals of American military operations, and rarely in foreign wars, had an army cut loose from its supply base to cross so extensive a tract of enemy territory for the dual purpose of severing communications connecting a fertile source of supply (in this case, the farmlands of east-central Georgia) and a military force operating in a distant theater (Lee's Army of Northern Virginia) and of eroding the enemy's will to fight by assaulting his societal base, destroying his homes and fields, and confiscating his property. In concept and execution, the operation embodied the hard-war themes of its creator and director. Sherman knew, or should have known, that his men would leave devastation and misery in their wake, giving rise to charges of cruelty and barbarism. He viewed these possibilities as the just desserts of a people who had dared to meddle with the most perfect form of government known to the modern world, who had shattered the sacred compact between God and man that had produced the American Union. Moreover, he believed that the severity of his military policy would serve to bring an unjust and unholy conflict to as rapid a conclusion as possible. The war had gone on too long, had consumed far too much blood and treasure. He believed himself justified in ending it by any means short of outright genocide.

The march got under way on November 14, 1864, two and a half months after Atlanta's occupation began. The troops who marched out of the city where ware-houses and supply dumps continued to smolder were stripped for fast movement and, if necessary, hard fighting. The men had been provided with twenty days' rations, while other supplies, mainly weapons and ammunition, accompanied them aboard wagons. A herd of beef cattle driven along in the rear of each column would supplement the daily diet. The rest of their rations, the men would have to procure from the land. At Sherman's order, every brigade leader had formed foraging squads commanded by one or more officers. But these parties, which could go forth mounted if they acquired horses and mules, would prove too small to provide for so large a command. As a result, as the march progressed, foraging became more and more decentralized. Eventually one or two companies out of every regiment were assigned foraging duties, and the foodstuffs they gathered no longer went to the brigade commissariat but directly to the foragers and their comrades.[2]

Sherman laid down strict rules governing the conduct of his "bummers" (a term of opprobrium coined by Georgians, probably derived from the German word for idler or vagrant). From the first, however, the restrictions were either relaxed by the officers or ignored by the foragers themselves. When sent out to obtain food and fodder, the men considered themselves free agents, licensed to do as they thought best in the interests of feeding themselves and their com-rades. If they should inflict suffering or privation on the civilians whose property they intruded upon, that was so much to the good. A typical for-ager in Slocum's column, who would continue in South Carolina the regi-men he had adopted in Georgia, wrote his sister back home in Illinois to ask how she would like it if hun-gry, angry soldiers were rummaging through her house on a daily basis,

Gen. Henry W. Slocum, USA

robbing chicken coops, spring-houses, and corncribs, spiriting away the family herd, and, given an ounce of provocation, setting fire to everything in sight. "It is a disagreeable business," the volunteer admitted, "but I feel some degree of consolation in the knowledge that I never went beyond my duty" to take from the land and the people of the enemy.[3]

Even before the march began, Sherman's men had adapted nicely to his concept of living off the country—they had practiced it during their fruitless, short-lived pursuit of Hood through northern Georgia. "They take it to like ducks to water," was Sherman's verdict. To be sure, foraging had a certain allure for almost every soldier under his command. It was an exhilarating experience to loot and vandalize without fear of serious penalty. An Iowa soldier informed his parents that he was happy to help Georgia's farmers "to market with their produce." A New York enlisted man wrote home that "you better believe we lived bully" on the march. These men and their comrades justified their behavior in terms Sherman would have appreciated. "It is but right," an Indiana officer mused, "that these people should feel some of the hardships of the war, they will better appreciate peace when it does come, and be not so ready to rush wildly into the same vortex again."[4]

Georgia yielded up to Sherman a fantastic cache of provender. All told, his bummers confiscated almost seven thousand horses and mules, more than thirteen thousand head of cattle, a half million pounds of grain, and nearly eleven million pounds of fodder. These were the legitimate spoils of military operations. Other proper targets included supply depots, stockpiles of contraband goods such as cotton and medical stores, and, especially, rail lines. On their journey through Georgia, Sherman's troops wrecked 317 miles of track on the state's two major east-west railroads, the Central Railroad (which ran from Macon to Augusta) and the Georgia Railroad (connecting Atlanta and Augusta, before veering north toward Charleston, South Carolina). One historian has proclaimed that "no command on either side . . . had the knack for destroying railroads like Sherman's army."

Having honed their craft on the journey to Atlanta and during the work of demolition after the city's occupation, the soldiers had become adept at fashioning rails, heated over burning ties, into "Sherman's neckties." Mere burning failed to prevent a displaced rail from being reused. According to General Slocum, "no rail should be regarded as properly treated till it has assumed the shape of doughnut; it must not only be bent but twisted." Referring to techniques developed by Sherman's chief engineer, Bvt. Lt. Col. Orlando M. Poe, Slocum added that "with Poe's hooks a double twist can be given to a rail, which precludes all hope of restoring it to its former shape except by re-rolling." Sherman's troops applied themselves so conscientiously to this endeavor that local officials estimated it would be February 1865 before either of the mangled lines could be returned to service, and then only if railroads of lesser importance were cannibalized of tracks and ties and every laborer in the state was forced to join in the repairs.[5]

Although aware that only token forces were available to challenge him, when Sherman left Atlanta he marched his columns in directions calculated to deceive the enemy as to his destination. When Howard's wing started out, Kilpatrick's horsemen, in its van, moved down the railroad to Macon, prompting the cavalry of Wheeler and the old men and boys of Gustavus Smith's militia to withdraw toward that city. While Kilpatrick tangled with the few Rebels who remained on the railroad and also demonstrated southward, Howard's infantry and artillery turned toward the east, heading for the rail junction at Gordon, south of Milledgeville. After the ruse had had its effect, Kilpatrick withdrew and followed the infantry. Recovering his bearings, Wheeler started off after Howard, overtaking and skirmishing with units of the Fifteenth Corps near Griswoldville. But Wheeler failed to reach that town before Kilpatrick did. When he arrived the place was a mass of burning ruins.

The damage was to be expected, for Kilpatrick's troopers were little more than arsonists. Their leader, who shared Sherman's view of how Southerners, including noncombatants, should be treated, had issued packs of sulphur matches to his division at the start of the march. Every trooper carried them in his saddlebags. Kilpatrick encouraged their use; his oft-articulated vision of postwar Georgia included miles of "chimney stacks without houses."[6]

After bypassing Macon, Howard's men reached Milledgeville, Georgia's capital, from the south just as Slocum's wing, with which Sherman was traveling, closed up on the north and west. The new arrivals found that Governor Brown and most of the legislature had "ignominiously fled," as Sherman put it, "in the utmost disorder and confusion." Brown had spirited away the furnishings of the governor's mansion—carpets, curtains, furniture, "even the cabbages and vegetables from his kitchen and cellar—leaving behind muskets, ammunition, and the public archives."[7]

During the time they spent in the city, November 22–24, the soldiers systematically destroyed all forms of public property, ransacking the state arsenal, penitentiary, and library, while torching caches of contraband goods including warehouses crammed with cotton. Companies and regiments invaded the statehouse, where their officers, some of whom had been imbibing confiscated spirits, held a mock legislative session during which they voted to rescind Georgia's ordinance of secession. When the last troops decamped, they left behind mangled railroad track, smoldering buildings, streets littered with books with pages torn out and miscellaneous legal documents, broken crockery, empty bottles, and, at St. Stephen's Episcopal Church, a pipe organ that had been stuffed with molasses.[8]

Sherman's columns again split up as they moved east of Milledgeville, crossing a marshy countryside watered by the Oconee and Ogeechee Rivers. To keep up his deception, Sherman had Kilpatrick demonstrate toward Augusta, sixty miles to the northeast. The tactic only partially disrupted the defensive plans of General Hardee, who had been detached from Hood's army to take command of the Department of South Carolina, Georgia, and Florida. Hardee suspected that Sherman was as likely to move against Savannah as against Augusta. While he headed for Savannah to take command of that fortified city's garrison, he ordered Smith's militia to move eastward as quickly as possible, although to what purpose remains obscure.

Certainly the citizen-soldiers had no chance of bringing the invaders to bay. They had proved as much on November 22 when, near Griswoldville, a large detachment made contact with the veteran infantry of Brig. Gen. Charles Carroll Walcutt's brigade, part of the right flank of Howard's wing. At first believing the Yankees were in small force, the militia foolishly charged them. After recovering from the shock of the attack, the Federals trained their repeating rifles on the militiamen and methodically cut them down. When the shooting stopped, Walcutt's men crossed the field of battle to survey the results. The dead—hundreds of them—lay in piles. The sight moved one of Walcutt's officers to tears: "Old grey haired and weakly looking men and little boys, not over 15 years old, lay dead or writhing in pain. I did pity those boys. . . ."[9]

On the rest of their excursion through Georgia, Kilpatrick's and Wheeler's cavalries engaged in a running battle at points including Waynesborough, Millen Grove, Rocky Creek Church, Thomas's Station, Brier Creek, and Ebenezer Creek. Along Ebenezer Creek on December 8 Wheeler rounded up and returned to their masters two thousand fugitive slaves, including women and children, who had attached themselves to General Davis's Fourteenth Corps in the hope of being led out of bondage. The chattels had been callously abandoned, left stranded on the south side of the stream when Davis abruptly took up the pontoon bridge upon which his troops had crossed.[10]

This incident, which brought the army some adverse publicity in the North, pointed up Sherman's Negrophobia. When newspaper reporters criticized both Davis and him, he defended his subordinate's action as military necessity and brushed off the criticism of himself. By early 1865, his belief in the inherent inferiority of African Americans was well entrenched. Moreover, he would not waver in his determination to bar all-black units from serving in his armies. As he wrote Ellen the following month, on the so-called Negro Question, "I am right and won't change."[11]

Soon after Ebenezer Creek, however—whether from a growing appreciation of military politics or from genuine sympathy—some of his more callous attitudes toward black people appeared to moderate, and he began to express concern for the welfare of the liberated slaves in his domain. When his army was on occupation duty in Savannah, Sherman drafted a field order that won the glowing approval of the visiting secretary of war. With Edwin Stanton's support, Sherman declared that the sea islands of South Carolina and Georgia, as well as the abandoned rice plantations along a thirty-mile stretch of the Carolina coast and the country bordering Florida's St. John's River "were reserved and set apart for the settlement of the negroes now made free by the acts of war and the proclamation of the President of the United States."[12]

Sherman biographer John Marszalek observes that "it was a revolutionary document, and it is ironic that someone with Sherman's antiblack attitudes should have issued it." But once promulgated, the decree received little support from him. He always claimed that it was a wartime measure. Thus, in 1866, when President Andrew Johnson ended the so-called Port Royal Experiment, Sherman tacitly acquiesced in the action.[13]

Two days after Ebenezer Creek, Sherman's advance reached Savannah, which he thought of as defended by a "mongrel" force. After rebuilding a ruined bridge, he sent Hazen's division over the Ogeechee River to storm Fort McAllister, Savannah's foremost work. On the thirteenth Sherman observed Hazen's successful assault from the roof of a rice mill. McAllister's fall opened Ossabaw Sound, permitting Sherman to establish communications with the ships of Adm. John A. B. Dahlgren's blockading fleet.[14]

His line of communications having been secured, Sherman sent Hardee a surrender demand, hinting strongly that unless it was accepted he would allow his troops, once inside Savannah, to run amuck. Hardee refused the demand, but on the evening of December 21 he evacuated his nine-thousand-man garrison and most of his light artillery via a makeshift bridge across the Savannah River to South Carolina. Immediately upon their departure, Sherman's troops took full possession. On the twenty-second Sherman, who had been on Hilton Head Island, South Carolina, conferring with officers of the army and navy on ways to cut off Hardee's escape, learned of the city's occupation and hastened there. Upon arriving he took steps to restrict the looting and vandalism with which he had threatened Hardee. Then he sent a telegram to Abraham Lincoln offering him, "as a Christmas gift, the city of Savannah, with 150 heavy guns and plenty of ammunition, and also about 25,000 bales of cotton."[15]

At this time, Grant was still facing Lee at Petersburg, having made little outwardly visible progress in evicting the Confederates. Through systematic gains on both ends of the siege lines, however, the general-in-chief was slowly but steadily stretching the enemy's defenses to their breaking point. Meanwhile, all was serene in Tennessee, where George Thomas had, as Sherman put it, "so nobly fulfilled his promise to ruin Hood." After characteristically deliberate preparations, during December 15–16 Thomas had attacked and routed Hood's army outside Nashville, sending it in headlong retreat to the Tennessee River, closely pursued by cavalry and infantry. Hood's overwhelming defeat would lead to his removal from command and to the breakup of the once-proud, once-powerful Army of Tennessee. Any observer with a modicum of perceptivity could see, as Sherman had seen for some time, that as 1864 rushed toward an end, so did the war for Confederate independence.[16]

Along with Lincoln, Stanton, and Halleck, Grant sent hearty congratulations for "the splendid results" of Sherman's campaign, "the like of which is not read of in past history." Their voices added to a swelling chorus of praise from all quarters of the nation as well as from abroad. Even the lords of the Fourth Estate, with whom Sherman had jousted so long and so sharply, showered him with compliments. Typical was the reaction of the *Chicago Tribune*, which, noting Sherman's message to Lincoln, called him "our Military Santa Claus" and declared that his march deserved a "place parallel with the Anabasis and the best efforts of Marlborough, Napoleon, and Wellington." The *London Herald* expected Sherman's name to be "written on the tablet of fame, side by side with that of Napoleon and Hannibal." Even the enemy expressed admiration for the feat. "Sherman's march through Georgia," wrote Robert Kean, "has been conducted with consummate skill. He has so directed it as to induce the collection of troops at points at which he seemed to be aiming and then he has passed them by, leaving the troops useless and unavailable. . . . I give up all as lost, so far as opposing Sherman was concerned."[17]

All of this was music to Cump's ears, but he did not like the sound of Grant's subsequent suggestion that he place his troops aboard transports and sail up the coast to Virginia. Sherman wished very much to get in on the kill at Petersburg, but he favored an overland movement through the Carolinas. As he stressed to Grant, "[T]ransportation by sea would very much disturb the unity and *morale* of my army, now so perfect." Fortunately, by the time those troops were sufficiently rested to resume active campaigning, Grant had changed his mind, doubtful that he could procure the necessary shipping in less than two months.[18]

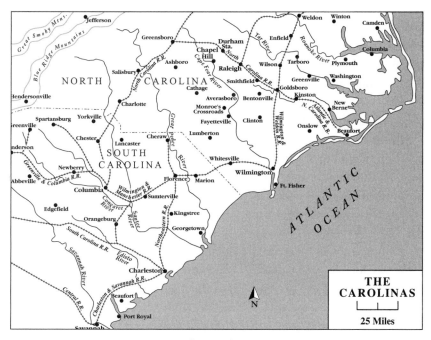

The Carolinas

Relieved of the unhappy prospect of bypassing the state that was, in his mind and in the minds of most of his men, the cradle of secession, on January 14, 1865, Sherman started his army north by land, securing a foothold on the South Carolina side of the Savannah. Howard's wing sailed aboard small vessels to Beaufort, where it debarked and marched to Pocotaligo, on the railroad between Savannah and Charleston. At about the same time, the left wing, Slocum's infantry and Kilpatrick's cavalry, crossed the Savannah on a causeway, landing at Coosawhatchie. Sherman wanted Howard to feint toward, but not attack, Charleston, which he considered "a mere desolated wreck . . . hardly worth the time it would take to starve it out."

Slocum's wing would also engage in misdirection, advancing toward Augusta, Georgia, before turning north in earnest.[19]

When the march through South Carolina got fully under way on February 1, Sherman knew where he was heading: Columbia. On the way to the state capital his men ran roughshod, paying back in fire and fury those who had precipitated the holocaust by declaring their state out of the Union. When his men finally crossed the Pee Dee River into North Carolina in the first week of March, one of Sherman's bummers observed proudly, "We left a black track in South Carolina." Another declared that he did not believe "there was a man in the army but has set fire to one or more buildings" in the Palmetto State.[20]

This last claim was an exaggeration, but Sherman's troops had put to the torch a long list of villages and towns, including Barnwell (christened "Burnwell" by the soldiers), Gillisonville, Hardeeville, Lawtonville, Lexington, McPhersonville, Midway, Orangeburg, Robertsville, and Springfield. Columbia came in for the most memorable treatment; it went up in flames soon after the first troops entered on February 17. Bummers were responsible for most of the devastation, but the garrison's unfortunate decision to place cotton bales in the streets in a futile attempt to bar the invaders' way contributed to the spread of the flames when the material caught fire, quite possibly by accident. Whatever the degree of the soldiers' involvement, by the time the conflagration burned itself out, about a third of the city lay in charred ruins.[21]

North Carolina did not share the fate of her neighbor to the south. As the last state to secede, one that boasted a large Unionist population, she was treated much less harshly by the invaders. To be sure, pantries were emptied of edibles and farm animals were lassoed and led away from fields and barns and a certain number of homes—especially if Rebel regulars or guerrillas fired on Sherman's columns from adjacent property—were put to the torch, but the destruction wrought here paled in comparison to the devastation visited on the first state to leave the Union.

During the early days of Sherman's excursion through the Old Line State, his men faced light opposition. However, on March 10, Wade Hampton, recently sent from Virginia to command all Confederate cavalry in the state, teamed with Wheeler in a predawn assault on Kilpatrick's camps at Monroe's Cross Roads, northwest of Fayetteville. Kilpatrick's sleep-befogged troopers were put on the defensive for hours before infantry arrived to chase off the attackers. Their leader, meanwhile, had been forced to run for his life clad only in nightshirt and boots. "Kilpatrick's Shirttail Skedaddle," as the affair became known, furnished humor not only for the men of Hampton and Wheeler but also for Sherman's foot soldiers, most of whom regarded their mounted comrades as comic-opera warriors.[22]

In marked contrast, the army's infantrymen, hard-bitten and cynical as many of them had become, treated Sherman as a hero. They appear to have grasped the significance of the campaign on which he was leading them, and when he rode past they thanked him with cheers and applause for the honor of participating in so historic an undertaking. Stories about his remarkable personal habits began to sweep the ranks. He hardly ate, he almost never slept, he knew the name of every soldier in the ranks, and when he stopped to speak to them, first removing the well-chewed cigar always in his mouth, he treated them like back-home friends or relatives.

Gen. Wade Hampton, CSA

Soldiers found Uncle Billy to be both approachable and egalitarian. "His customary appearance," wrote an admiring bummer, "was to walk along the roadside with his hands in his trousers' pockets . . . and talk good earnest common sense with the person nearest him, regardless of rank. This was delightful for a subordinate, knowing his exalted position and yet feeling at ease."[23]

Here was a compliment that a soldier could not apply to a great many commanding officers. But it was one that those in gray had long paid to one of their more down-to-earth generals, Joseph E. Johnston.

———◦◦◦———

As much as possible, Johnston followed the course of Sherman's march from his temporary home in Georgia and then, after the late fall of 1864, in Columbia, South Carolina, where Lydia's sister and some family friends resided. They found they could not stay there indefinitely, because the cost of living was prohibitively high, but the general himself left prematurely a week before Christmas to renew battle with the civilian superiors he believed had undermined his command of the army in north Georgia.[24]

At the urging of congressional friends and his brother Beverly, Johnston visited Richmond to ascertain why his report of the campaign to Atlanta had not been published as he, Wigfall, and other friends and supporters had called for. He also hoped to forestall rumored efforts by the administration to discredit the assertions contained in that report, many of which were highly critical of Davis and his subordinates. Johnston's ire was aroused when he learned that Davis had appended to his unpublished report an endorsement that pronounced many of Johnston's statements at variance with "the impression created by other communications contemporaneous with the events referred to." Johnston was incensed by the government's failure to respond to his subsequent demand to reveal the source of that impression.[25]

Unable to obtain any satisfaction in the capital, Johnston returned to Columbia to spend a bleak Christmas with Lydia and her relatives. Early in the new year, when it appeared that Sherman was set to turn north from Savannah, Johnston offered his services to the local defense forces, but apparently nothing came of it. Fearing for Lydia's safety, in January he sent her to live in North Carolina and late in the month he joined her in Lincolnton, a hill country town in the southwestern corner of the state. There, presumably well removed from Sherman's path, Johnston devoted his attention to the war news. He was quietly pleased by Hood's fall from grace but concerned by the condition of the command the man had led to ruin. According to reports, what remained of the Army of Tennessee had congregated in northern Mississippi, desirous of opposing Sherman's invasion of the Carolinas but lacking transportation to that theater. There seemed to be no directing head capable of resolving the impasse.[26]

Johnston began to wonder if he might become that person. As Hood's reputation sank, his own rose steadily. By Christmas, Robert Kean was observing that "a great pressure has been brought to bear, since Hood's overthrow, for the reassignment of Johnston." On January 14, the Senate in Richmond not only voted to make Robert E. Lee general-in-chief of the Confederacy's armies but recommended Johnston's assignment as commander of the Army of Tennessee, an action in which the House concurred four days later.[27]

The drive to reinstate the only general besides Lee in whom the Congress had any faith quickly grew to irresistible proportions, but Johnston refused to say he would accept the position if offered to him. As he wrote to William Mackall, "I think deliberately that while Mr. Davis is President, no friend of mine or of the

country ought to wish to see me restored to the command." In addition to doubt-
ing that the administration would lend him greater support than it had on earlier occasions, Johnston feared that it was too late to stop Sherman's inexorable
march. Should he be returned to the field, it would be to preside over an
inevitable defeat. As Lydia had warned him numerous times over the years, if
Davis offered him the command it was only to set him up as a scapegoat for military failure.[28]

To the last, Davis was loath to appoint Johnston to anything. In an effort to
answer the congressional clamor in his behalf, on February 18 the president sat
down and composed a four-thousand-word memorandum, detailing the basis of
his lack of trust in Johnston's leadership. The memo reviewed every instance of
friction and conflict between the two dating to Johnston's first field assignment
at Harpers Ferry. "My opinion of Genl. Johnston's unfitness for command," Davis
emphasized, "has ripened slowly and against my inclination into a conviction so
settled, that it would be impossible for me again to feel confidence in him as the
commander of an army in the field." Yet only days after Davis completed this
litany of misdeeds, Robert E. Lee requested him to endorse Johnston's reinstatement, which the general-in-chief described as the only way to appease the mush-
rooming sentiment in Congress and among the public at large. Undoubtedly
against his better judgment as well as his strong conviction, Davis allowed Lee to
talk him into making the appointment, which he signed with the utmost reluctance and regret.[29]

Johnston would not learn of the existence of Davis's caustic memo until more
than a year after war's end. In late February 1865, he was outraged when Wigfall
presented him with a summary of the contents of John Bell Hood's report of the
Georgia campaign that had recently been submitted to John C. Breckinridge,
Seddon's successor as war secretary. In that self-serving document, Hood flayed
his predecessor for numerous sins of commission and omission but chiefly for
destroying the morale of the Army of Tennessee even as he spared its physical
health by withholding it from offensives and leading it on retreat after retreat.[30]

But Johnston was not too bitter or too proud to ignore the call of duty. When,
on the twenty-third, Davis and Lee offered to return him to command of his old
army, he repressed his misgivings and announced his availability. As soon as his
reinstatement became fact, he kissed Lydia farewell and traveled to Charlotte.
There he conferred with General Beauregard, whose ill health prevented him from
personally assuming command and who wished his colleague well with his new/old
army. From Beauregard, Johnston learned that his field force would comprise

approximately five thousand troops of the Army of Tennessee, now under A. P. Stewart, some eleven thousand other members of Beauregard's command including Hardee's garrison (most recently stationed at Charleston but now heading to join Johnston via Cheraw, South Carolina), and the undersized cavalry corps of Hampton and Wheeler.[31]

Johnston was to be augmented by a few thousand North Carolina troops that had been placed under Braxton Bragg for the defense of Fort Fisher, the huge earthwork that controlled access to the city of Wilmington. These troops had been freed for service elsewhere following the fort's mid-January capture by a large contingent from the Army of the James under Bvt. Maj. Gen. Alfred Terry. The following month Terry had teamed with troops sent from Tennessee under John Schofield to seize and occupy Wilmington, the last open Confederate sea-port of any value. Bragg's latest assignment was an embarrassment to the man who had played a leading if covert role in Johnston's relief. Fearing Johnston's wrath, Bragg asked to be relieved, only to have his request summarily denied by Jefferson Davis. He need not have worried, for Johnston, to his credit, refused to allow personal feelings to color his military relationship with Bragg.[32]

All told, Johnston would exercise command over some twenty-one thousand officers and men, scattered from Charlotte to Augusta on the southwest and Charleston on the southeast. These were too few, in his estimation, to gain a lasting advantage over Sherman's legions, whose strength he estimated as above seventy thousand. Johnston was nevertheless heartened by the fighting spirit his old veterans displayed despite their ordeal under Hood. When the army's thinned ranks passed on review at Charlotte, one Alabamian remarked, "Three cheers were given in a very joyous tone and manner expressive of great satisfaction. The old general looks as usual hearty and soldier like. . . . He is as well loved in this army among the men, as an officer can be. They have every confidence in him. . . ."[33]

Johnston, however, had no confidence in his ability to do more than maneuver long enough to buy time for negotiations toward "fair terms of peace." Reminiscent of the pessimistic outlook he had expressed when taking command in Jackson, Mississippi, almost two years earlier, he informed Lee that "it is too late to expect me to concentrate troops capable of driving back Sherman." His command—what there was of it—was simply "too weak to cope" with the Yankees who had descended upon the Carolinas like so many blue-tinged locusts. Still, he would give it his best effort, if for no other reason than because he was a soldier, and a soldier fought to the last for a cause he believed in.[34]

By mid-March, as the disparate elements of his force began to come together in the countryside south of Raleigh, the state capital, Johnston had transferred his headquarters to Smithfield, a central location more conducive to concentration. By this juncture Sherman's troops were surging north from Fayetteville, scene of Kilpatrick's embarrassing encounter with Hampton and Wheeler, en route to the coast at Goldsboro, there to link with Schofield and Terry. Sherman was in a bit of a hurry, for "I then knew that my special antagonist, General Jos. Johnston, was back, with part of his old army; that he would not be misled by feints and false reports, and would somehow compel me to exercise more caution than I had hitherto done." On the fifteenth Sherman pushed his army across the Cape Fear River. Howard's Fifteenth and Seventeenth Corps were on his right, and Slocum's Fourteenth and Twentieth Corps were on the extreme left, so Sherman marched warily, "with almost a certainty of being attacked" on the left.[35]

The Battle of Bentonville

He was not being unduly cautious. On the seventeenth, Johnston, new to this part of the state, requested General Hampton, who was conversant with the local geography, to select a suitable venue in which to surprise Sherman. Working from maps that made the distance between the enemy's wings seem longer than it was,

Johnston decided to attack Slocum near Bentonville, cutting him off from his comrades and beating him in detail before supports could reach him. Based on a plan of battle submitted by Hampton, Johnston on the eighteenth placed Bragg's troops, screened by Hampton's own cavalry, across the road to Goldsboro, there to block Slocum's progress while the forces of Hardee and Stewart attacked from tree-shielded positions to the northwest. When Slocum neared the area accompanied by Davis's Fourteenth Corps and with the Twentieth Corps, now led by Alpheus Williams, lagging well behind, he was set upon by Hampton's troopers, who fought and then fell back. In this manner, the corps commander was lured into a confrontation with Bragg's troops, occupying heavy breastworks farther east, bolstered by the only cannons at Johnston's disposal. Surprised by the power in the gray line opposite him, Slocum fell back and began to entrench.

Five miles from Bentonville, Sherman, approaching Goldsboro at the head of Howard's column, heard the sounds of musketry and cannons in the west. Suddenly a courier galloped up with a message from Slocum announcing that he was tangling with what appeared to be Johnston's entire force. At once Sherman turned Howard's column around, sending Logan's corps, followed by Blair's, to Slocum's assistance. Sherman hoped that Slocum had been attacked from the east; in that event, the enemy's back would be turned toward the Federals who hoped to take them in rear.[36]

The proposed pincers never closed, but it did not matter. Hardee had been late getting into his assigned position and once there his movements were slowed by a dense thicket in which he formed for his attack. By the time he charged, around 3:00 P.M., almost five hours behind schedule, part of his force had been shifted to Bragg's embattled line by Johnston, who once again yielded to the entreaties of a fearful subordinate. By then, too, the delay had given the Fourteenth Corps time to batten down and the Twentieth Corps time to hustle up from the rear and provide support.

Two of Davis's brigades had been mauled, but the corps' line remained essentially intact. When Williams arrived, he extended that line and joined with Davis in repulsing a series of attacks, each delivered with less strength and spirit than the previous one. By evening, realizing that his badly depleted ranks were no longer capable of sustaining an offensive, Johnston recalled his exhausted troops. Despite the fact that they had run out of steam, he was gratified by the all-out effort his battered veterans had put forth, which showed that despite the travail they had been subjected to, they were still capable of impressive, if relatively short-lived, performances.[37]

306

Around noon the next day, Howard's wing came up to unite with Slocum's from a direction that threatened the rear of Bragg's command. Sherman might have crushed Johnston's much smaller force between his mighty columns, but his respect for his opponent's ability to exploit any opening stayed his hand. As he admitted in his memoirs, "[I]n the uncertainty of General Johnston's strength, I did not feel disposed to invite a general battle." He also plead concern for the staying-power of his men, who had gone days without regular rations; thus, "during the 20th we simply held our ground and started our trains back to Kinston for provisions, which would be needed in the event of being forced to fight a general battle at Bentonville."[38]

On the twenty-first a heavy rain fell, preventing Sherman from advancing against his enemy directly, although he almost scored a breakthrough in the Rebel left rear when Maj. Gen. Joseph A. Mower's division of the Seventeenth Corps attacked and dented a portion of Johnston's line, threatening his route of retreat. Fighting hard and long, Johnston shored up the position, but then, noting the precarious condition of his line, which ran along the south side of a deep stream, he decided to withdraw under cover of night. His retreat across Mill Creek Bridge was ably covered by the troopers of Hampton and Wheeler, who early on the twenty-second made several saber charges in order to keep back the nearest pursuers.[39]

Sherman was content to let Johnston go. Had he exploited Mower's breakthrough by throwing in additions, he might have finished off his enemy, but "I preferred to make [a] junction with Generals Terry and Schofield, before engaging Johnston's army, the strength of which was utterly unknown. The next day he was gone, and had retreated on Smithfield; and, the roads all being clear, our army moved to Goldsboro."[40]

Despite Sherman's expectations, he would not engage Johnston again. Their battles were behind them, as was, for all intents and purposes, the war itself.

———◆———

During March 22–24, Sherman united with Terry and Schofield at Goldsboro, where his men enjoyed ready access to rations. He gave them plenty of time to consume them. While they partook, he sailed up the coast to City Point, Virginia, where, on the twenty-seventh and twenty-eighth, he met with President Lincoln, General Grant, and Admiral Porter (whose fleet had helped take Fort Fisher and Wilmington) for a strategy session aboard the presidential yacht *River Queen*, berthed in the Appomattox River. With spring on the land, Grant was poised to launch a final effort to drive Lee from Petersburg. Lincoln, while hopeful that this would bring an end to the fighting in Virginia, wished aloud that peace might be achieved without a final bloodletting.

Sherman got the distinct impression that the president wished to work out an honorable peace, one consistent with the fulfillment of the war aims of the North but without causing the Southern people, and especially its soldiery, needless humiliation and resentment. Lincoln went so far as to imply that he would not be averse to Jefferson Davis's escaping the country to exile into some foreign land. Lincoln's overriding aim appeared to be "to end the war speedily, without more bloodshed or devastation, and to restore all the men of both sections to their homes."[41]

Sherman would claim that Lincoln specifically asked him to assure North Carolina governor Zebulon B. Vance, with whom Sherman was in contact with a view to a cease-fire throughout his state, "that, as soon as the rebel armies laid down their arms, and resumed their civil pursuits, they would at once be guaranteed all their rights as citizens of a common country; and that to avoid anarchy the State governments then in existence, with their civil functionaries, would be recognized by him as the government *de facto* till Congress could provide others." Although Sherman was no politician, Lincoln's view of a postwar South tallied with his own vision of a desirable future. Once the war was over, he, like Lincoln, would be willing to let the Southern people reestablish their legal and political institutions as a means of guaranteeing the preservation of social order, a condition Sherman considered integral to national harmony and prosperity.[42]

When the shipborne conference broke up, Sherman returned quickly to the Carolina coast, from which, as he had promised Grant, he would be prepared to start north by forced marches on April 10 with the objective of corraling Johnston's army, capturing and paroling its men, then cooperating with Meade against the Army of Northern Virginia. On the appointed date, he advanced on Johnston's army, now encamped near Raleigh. Sherman moved at the forefront of almost ninety thousand officers and men divided among Howard's Army of the Tennessee, Slocum's Army of Georgia, and the reconstituted Army of the Ohio under Schofield, consisting of the latter's own Twenty-Third Corps, now under Maj. Gen. Jacob D. Cox, and General Terry's Tenth Corps, with Kilpatrick's cavalry attached.

The massive column did not get far from Goldsboro before news was received on the twelfth that Grant had in fact pried Lee's army out of its works around Petersburg, had sent the Confederates on a long march to the west, and had overtaken and brought them to bay. On the ninth, at Appomattox Court House, Lee had surrendered the principal fighting force of the Confederacy. By then Sherman's men had also learned that Richmond was finally in Union hands, the Confederate government having evacuated on the second. Jefferson Davis and a large entourage, thought to be heading for the Carolina coast, were still at large. "Of course," wrote Sherman, the intelligence "created a perfect *furore* of rejoicing," but it did not mean the war was over. His troops had yet to snare a highly mobile army led by a shrewd and savvy commander.[43]

That proved to be a daunting task. Without much impedimenta to slow him down, Johnston covered great distances in quick time, leaving Sherman's larger, heavier, wagon-impeded column in his dust. Kilpatrick's cavalry skirmished with Hampton's on a daily basis, but the slow-footed infantry seemed to have no hope of overtaking its foe. Unsurprisingly, when Sherman entered Raleigh on the thirteenth, Johnston was long gone.

As when following Hood after the fall of Atlanta, Sherman quickly tired of the pursuit. Thus on the fourteenth he was overjoyed to receive a message from Johnston under a flag of truce. The Confederate commander, in view of the recent events in Virginia, proposed a suspension of hostilities, "to permit the civil authorities to enter into the needful arrangements to terminate the existing war." With an almost audible sigh of relief, Sherman offered to meet and "arrange with you any terms for the suspension of further hostilities between the armies. . . ." On the sixteenth Johnston wrote again, agreeing to meet Sherman the following morning at a point between Sherman's advance position at Durham Station and Johnston's rear echelon at Hillsboro. At the appointed hour on the seventeenth, Sherman started for the meeting site, only to be hailed by a civilian telegrapher who reported that an important message was coming through.[44]

As of April 11, Johnston knew only that Lee had evacuated Richmond and Petersburg. He had no idea if the commander of the Army of Northern Virginia might be heading his way for a joint confrontation with Sherman, as some rumors had it, or whether he was being driven in an entirely different direction. Thus he was ignorant of momentous events unfolding off to the north when, that evening near midnight, he took a train to Greensboro, sixty-five miles west of Raleigh, in response to a summons from the fugitive president of the Confederate States of America.

At Greensboro, following an all-night ride, he met with Davis in a private railroad car. Also in attendance were General Beauregard, Secretary of State Benjamin, Secretary of the Navy Stephen Mallory, and Postmaster General John H. Reagan. Davis wanted a progress report on Johnston's forces, which he believed were capable of carrying on the fight against Sherman. Johnston, who was convinced that the war was lost, tried to acquaint the superior he despised with the hard facts, but without success. He tried again that evening, after Secretary of War Breckinridge joined the group with positive confirmation of what till then had been only a rumor, that Lee had laid down his arms at Appomattox Court House. With that crushing news as a backdrop and with the vocal support of Beauregard, on April 13 Johnston finally won Davis's approval for a face-to-face meeting with Sherman to attempt to build a peace proposal acceptable to both sides.[45]

Thus it was that Johnston returned to his field headquarters at Hillsboro and arranged the armistice with Sherman. On the seventeenth, while their staff officers mingled outside, two men who had been exchanging missiles for the past two years sat across from each other at a table in a cabin near Durham Station owned by one James Bennett, and exchanged words and ideas. "We had never met before," wrote Sherman, "though we had been in the regular army together for thirteen years; but it so happened that we had never before come together. He was some twelve or more years my senior; but we knew enough of each other to be well acquainted at once."[46]

When the introductions ceased, Sherman showed his opponent the telegram he had been handed as he left Raleigh. It contained the news of Abraham Lincoln's assassination and death, a near-fatal attack on Secretary of State Seward, and other acts attributed to a conspiracy of Southern sympathizers. Sherman watched Johnston closely as he perused the cable: "The perspiration came out in large drops on his forehead, and he did not attempt to conceal his distress. He denounced the act as a disgrace to the age, and hoped I did not charge it to the Confederate Government. I told him I could not believe that he or General Lee, or the officers of the Confederate army, could possibly be privy to acts of assassination; but I would not say as much for Jeff. Davis. . . ."[47]

After decrying the heinous acts that had occurred in Washington, the two talked surrender. At Sherman's insistence that his opponent must consider his army beaten and ready to be surrendered, Johnston expressed his conviction that any further bloodshed "would be *murder*," but he believed arrangements could be reached to surrender all forces in rebellion against the United States, not merely his own. He intimated that while he lacked the power to make this happen, he could procure the requisite authority from Davis. Sherman mentioned that he had spoken recently to both Lincoln and Grant, "and that I was possessed of their views," and was also conversant with the "most generous and liberal terms" that Grant had extended to Lee.[48]

The two agreed to meet again the next day at the same place, and they did, this time with Secretary of War Breckinridge present in his capacity as a representative of both the military establishment and the civil government of the Confederacy. By now Sherman had conferred with most of his generals, who had advised him to agree to some terms, "for they all dreaded the long and harassing march in pursuit of a dissolving and fleeing army—a march that might carry us back again over the thousand miles that we had just accomplished." Bearing this in mind as well as Lincoln's sentiments in favor of quick restoration of civil government in the South, on the afternoon of the eighteenth Sherman worked with his adversary to hammer out a peace proposal embodying substantially the same terms as offered at Appomattox but with additional considerations.[49]

Johnston had brought with him a memorandum drafted by Postmaster General Reagan as the basis for an agreement, one covering various civil as well as military issues. Sherman found the document "so general and verbose" that he claimed to ignore it. The terms he wrote out, however, bore enough resemblance to Reagan's that they must have been influenced by the memorandum. The final document provided for the surrender of all Southern armies but also for the recognition of existing state governments in the South once their officials had taken the oath of allegiance to the government of the United States. It also allowed disbanded Confederate units to deposit their arms in state arsenals, and it guaranteed to Southerners their political rights and franchises, as well as rights of person and property. "The papers were duly signed," Sherman wrote, "we parted about dark, and my party returned to Raleigh."[50]

The next morning Sherman dispatched copies of the signed document to Washington via a trusted staff officer. He professed not to care whether the agreement was "approved, modified, or disapproved in toto, only I wanted instructions." Instead he got General Grant, who arrived by boat on the twenty-fourth with word that Stanton and President Andrew Johnson had abrogated the treaty and advising him, as Sherman put it, that "I had no authority to make final terms involving civil or political questions." Sherman's superiors saw in the agreement what he had not: that it could be construed as recognizing insurgent governments, guaranteeing slaveholders' rights, and removing from Congress and the president the power to administer reconstruction in the conquered South. A new agreement had to be negotiated, one that confined itself to the surrender of Johnston's army.[51]

So displeased were the Washington officials that Grant had come to North Carolina with authority to relieve Sherman for having overstepped his bounds. Grant would not do that to so trusted a subordinate, but he did accompany Sherman back to the Bennett house for yet another round of talks. Initially, Sherman did not bristle at the rebuke dealt him, but then he learned that Stanton had leaked the story to the newspapers and had publicly insinuated that Sherman had not tried hard to corral fugitive members of the Confederate government—and may even have taken a bribe to allow Davis to flee the country. Mortally offended, Sherman vowed to resent Stanton's insult, come what may. The next time he saw Stanton was at a major public gathering in late May, a gala review of the armies of Meade and Sherman through the streets of Washington before thousands of spectators. In the presence of President Johnson and other high officials, Sherman snubbed the war secretary by refusing to shake his hand.[52]

With Grant on hand, Johnston and Sherman revised their agreement. They worked with a sense of urgency, for the armistice they had agreed to was to expire in forty-eight hours, whereupon the armies would resume hostilities, something neither commander wished to see. In the end, Johnston agreed to surrender on the basis of the terms offered at Appomattox, thus defying Davis's insistence that, the initial treaty having been voided, the fighting should go on.[53]

This attitude was acceptable to neither general. In their minds there had already been too much death and suffering. They would not allow a chance for a viable peace to slip through their fingers. After signing the document, they shook hands in a gesture of mutual respect and agreed to part—perhaps forever—on a note of hope and optimism, believing that what they had fashioned this day would restore health to a nation sickened almost to death from four years of internecine strife.

EPILOGUE
WARRIORS
IN PEACETIME

Joseph Eggleston Johnston bade his "matchless soldiers" a final goodbye on May 2, 1865, the day the last members of his surrendered command received their parole papers and prepared to march for home. "I now part with you with deep regret," he told them in General Orders No. 22, ". . . and bid you farewell with feelings of cordial friendship; and with earnest wishes that you may have hereafter all the prosperity and happiness to be found in the world."[1]

Joseph E. Johnston in later years

As Johnston soon found out, prosperity and happiness were not easy to come by in the conquered South. For the first several months after he left the field, Lydia and he resided in Greensboro. The area, like most of the former Confederacy, was under military occupation, but Johnston had few quarrels with either the volunteer troops who did local duty or with the regulars who replaced them when the Civil War army disbanded. Like most ex-Confederates, he was distressed by the devastation of the Southern economy, although he welcomed the demise of slavery, an institution he believed retarded rather than advanced prosperity.

Finding gainful occupation in that dismal economic climate was a major concern, especially for an ex-soldier with little civilian professional experience. He tried but failed to gain an engineering position in Richmond, then lost a bid to become president of the Mobile & Ohio Railroad. By the fall of 1865, he and Lydia were residing in Baltimore, where he took an executive position with the National Express Company, one of many transportation firms that sprang up in the South to take the place of rail lines that had been put out of commission, some permanently, during the war. That October, recalling his days as quartermaster general, he wrote to one of his nephews that "it is needless to tell you that I am not as flush as when the U.S. gave me $6000 a year in gold." Even his latest, low-paying enterprise dried up, and a partnership in a stock-raising business failed to pan out.[2]

The following spring he gained the presidency of a small local railroad, the Alabama & Tennessee, but the road was soon verging on bankruptcy and he bailed out. He landed on his feet by taking a position as an American agent for a London-based insurance firm, in which capacity he managed more than one hundred agents in three southern states. The position left him sufficiently secure financially to devote much time to his primary interest, his war memoirs. Although handicapped by the loss of most of his personal papers, he worked tirelessly on the book, which was published in 1874 under the title *Narrative of Military Operations Directed during the Late War Between the States*.[3]

The book was not a financial success, but it permitted him to settle scores with old enemies, chiefly Jefferson Davis. In fact, Johnston's memoirs read like a detailed summary of his bitterly contentious relationship with the Confederate president. Long passages are devoted to a point-by-point rebuttal of Davis's criticism of Johnston's leadership. An entire chapter details and refutes the charges contained in the "Unsent Message" that Davis composed in February 1865 to silence congressmen who were clamoring for Johnston's reinstatement to field service but which he suppressed when forced to sanction the appointment.[4]

In other postwar writings, including several articles published in the 1880s in the compilation *Battles and Leaders of the Civil War*, Johnston again refought his wartime battles with the president. In too many instances, his efforts to exonerate himself of miscues and defeats and to condemn Davis for mismanaging the war make the author appear petty, carping, and mean-spirited, hardly the impression Johnston wished to present. His least attractive contribution to anti-Davis lore was his unfounded suggestion, given heavy newspaper coverage in 1881, that at war's close the president had absconded with almost two million dollars in gold from the Confederate treasury.[5]

314

Johnston took an active part in organizations and ceremonies designed to disseminate the Southern view of the war and to honor the stalwarts of the Confederacy. In 1873 he raised funds for a memorial to his old colleague Robert E. Lee, who had died three years earlier but not before the two paved over the sometimes rocky road their relationship had traveled. Two years later Johnston was an honored guest at the unveiling of a monument to Stonewall Jackson in Richmond. In 1883 he was invited to speak at the dedication of the Lee mausoleum on the campus of Washington University, of which "Marse Robert" had been president during the last five years of his life—a ceremony Jefferson Davis refused to attend after learning that Johnston would be present. In May 1889 he was chosen to unveil the equestrian statue of Lee that continues to grace Richmond's Monument Avenue. Johnston himself would be honored by a full-length statue erected in 1912 at Dalton, Georgia, site of his headquarters during the winter of 1863–64, and by a bust unveiled in February 1933 in the Old Hall of the Virginia House of Delegates, in Richmond.[6]

Although a private person to the end of his years, Johnston always maintained a keen interest in politics. Eventually he was enticed to make forays into public life. In 1876 he was seriously considered for the post of secretary of war under Rutherford B. Hayes, an Ohioan who curried the support of southerners and who was responsible for ending military reconstruction in the former Confederacy. That same year Johnston made headlines by criticizing a pending treaty between the United States and the Hawaiian kingdom which, if passed, would hurt the farmers of the Deep South by removing the tariff on imported sugar and rice.[7]

Johnston's growing involvement in politics suffered a setback when he failed to win election as a delegate to the Democratic national convention in 1876, but two years later, having returned to Virginia after an eight-year residence in Savannah, Georgia, he accepted the nomination of the state Democratic Party for Congress. Although reluctant to mix it up on the political stump, he ran an effective campaign, won the election, and served an undistinguished single term in the House of Representatives. After leaving Congress he tried to reenter commercial life, with minimal success. Early in 1884 he admitted to a friend that "my employments are rather small and unprofitable." The following year, during the first administration of Grover Cleveland, he was again considered for a cabinet post. Although Johnston failed to secure the position, Cleveland named him U.S. commissioner of railroads, a position he held for several years.[8]

By the time Johnston stepped down from this post, his life seemed to be drawing rapidly to a close. He suffered a blow from which he never recovered when

Lydia, who for years had been in failing health, died in February 1887 at their Washington, D. C., home. Her passing left him spiritually bereft and contributed heavily to his physical decline. He joined her in death on March 21, 1891. Following a funeral in the capital—at which his coffin was escorted by an honor guard of aged veterans of the Army of Tennessee—he was laid to rest beside Lydia and his beloved nephew, Pres, in Baltimore's Greenmount Cemetery.[9]

His refusal to shake hands with his civilian superior at the Grand Review of the Union Armies on May 24, 1865, would seem an inauspicious way to begin a postwar military career, but William Tecumseh Sherman rebounded nicely, perhaps because in his dispute with Edwin Stanton public sentiment appeared to be on his side. In truth, his national prominence, especially that accruing from his capture of Atlanta and his remarkable anabasis through Georgia, had rendered his stature heroic and his reputation unassailable. His role as Ulysses Grant's coadjutor in victory assured him of a major command in the postwar army. In fact, he had his choice of assignments.

William T. Sherman in later years

One thing Sherman knew: he wanted nothing to do with military reconstruction. He believed it both morally wrong and utterly impossible to reform the conquered South by the imposition of penalties and recriminations. Having done everything he could to devastate the military and economic capacity of the Confederacy, Sherman wanted nothing so much as to restore the region to prosperity and strengthen its commitment to American political values. To his brother John, who would ally himself with the radical faction of the Republican Party that wished to postpone readmission of the South until major social and political adjustments were institutionalized, Cump argued: "We cannot keep the South out long, [nor] can we change opinions by force."[10]

Instead, he opted to administer the other major postwar mission of the army, the pacification of the frontier. In his eyes, Native Americans, by rejecting the ways of white civilization, retarded national progress and diluted American hegemony. In the summer of 1865 he accepted command of the Military Division of the Mississippi (later the Military Division of the Missouri), headquartered at St. Louis, which included the territory from Canada to Texas and from the Mississippi River to the Rockies. Over the next four years he supervised the army's efforts to remove hostile tribes from the path of westward settlement.

Although he served on peace commissions charged with making treaties and administering the reservation system, Sherman's assessment of the situation in his domain was characteristically blunt: Indians had to be segregated from white society, and "all who cling to their old hunting grounds are hostile and will remain so till killed off." To his brother he expressed an even harsher view: "The more we can kill this year, the less will have to be killed the next year, for the more I see of these Indians the more convinced I am that all have to be killed or maintained as a species of pauper. Their attempts at civilization are simply ridiculous."[11]

Sherman zealously defended the army against the eastern reformers who charged it with committing atrocities and starving reservation-bound tribes, and he reacted violently to Indian "massacres." In December 1866, when Sioux warriors wiped out a woodcutter party near Fort Phil Kearny, Nebraska Territory, Sherman exploded: "We must act with vindictive earnestness against the Sioux, even to their extermination, men, women, and children. Nothing else will reach the root of this case." He was a vocal proponent of the transcontinental railroad, which he viewed as a means not only of spreading civilization but also of increasing military mobility and curtailing the Indians' freedom to roam the West.[12]

A major reason why Sherman had rejected a reconstruction command was his desire that the army be kept out of partisan politics. Yet he himself could not always escape political involvement, especially after October 1866, when Andrew Johnson summoned him to Washington. Although he supported many of the president's conservative policies, he resisted involvement in Johnson's extended and bitter conflicts with Ulysses S. Grant, Edwin Stanton, and the Congress, conflicts that eventually brought on Johnson's impeachment. Despite his dislike of Stanton, Sherman rejected numerous overtures to replace the war secretary, mainly because it would elevate him above his friend and mentor Grant, then the commanding general of the army.[13]

When Grant entered the White House in March 1869, he named Sherman as his successor. Initially Sherman took pride and pleasure in his status as commanding general and he strove to meet his obligations as "Father of the Army." Over time, however, he grew disenchanted with the position, which lost some of its prestige and much of its influence upon the ascendancy of Grant's second secretary of war, William Worth Belknap. A volunteer officer who had risen to brigade command in the Army of the Tennessee, Belknap stripped Sherman's office of the power to make military assignments and to command the chiefs of the various War Department bureaus, who thereafter reported directly to the secretary. Sherman believed that Belknap failed to oppose effectively the efforts of legislators such as John Logan to cut the pay and strength of the peacetime army. His power struggle with Belknap strained Sherman's personal relations with Grant, who, mired in scandals that demanded his attention, refused to support his old subordinate against his civilian superior.[14]

Although he championed the military reforms of Emory Upton, William Hazen, and others and established a system of postgraduate education for the army, Sherman found his duties reduced to the point that in 1871 he left the country for ten months to tour the military establishments of Europe and Asia. His discontent over his supernumerary status peaked in September 1874, when he gained permission to move army headquarters to his favorite city, St. Louis. Far from the political intrigues of the capital, he spent a leisurely year and a half. His hegira invited charges that he had abdicated his responsibility to support and protect the army, but it gave him the time to write his memoirs, which were published in two volumes one year after Joseph E. Johnston's appeared (and under the same imprint).[15]

Like his wartime opponent's, Sherman's reminiscences contain blunt and sometimes harsh commentary on men and events of the Civil War, but they are less contentious and more readable than Johnston's. The venture into publication prompted Sherman to author numerous articles on his war experiences, his relations with Grant and other heroes of the conflict, and general military matters, published in prominent periodicals including *Century Magazine* and the *North American Review*. He worked many of these same themes into the hundreds of talks he gave before military, fraternal, and patriotic organizations. He especially enjoyed addressing the veterans who had served under him, to whom he emphasized that war was perdition and to be avoided at all costs.

In April 1876, after Belknap was implicated in one of the many scandals of Grant's administration and resigned his office, Sherman consented to return army headquarters to Washington. The restoration of his former power, however, was never complete, and when he retired from the army in November 1884, handing over the post to Gen. Philip H. Sheridan, he considered his tenure characterized more by confrontation and conflict than by solid, sustained achievement. The experience only sharpened his inherent aversion to politics, an impulse that motivated him to reject numerous possibilities for public office, including, in 1884, the Republican presidential nomination.[16]

Throughout his term as commanding general and well into his retirement, Sherman's domestic life was largely one of turmoil. He became a doting father, especially to the daughters he determinedly spoiled, and he became a father in fact for the final time in January 1867 with the birth of his eighth child and fourth son, Philemon Tecumseh ("Cumpy") Sherman. He took tremendous pride in his children and was a major influence in their lives, but his often stormy relationship with Ellen continued almost unabated until her death in November 1888.

Although Cump and Ellen loved and respected each other in their own way, numerous disputes roiled the marriage waters and led him into at least a couple of sexual affairs, one with the young widow of his favorite staff officer, Joseph C. Audenreid. In the late 1870s the strains upon the marriage caused a lengthy separation and nearly a divorce. Ellen's constant nagging that he become a practicing Catholic drove them ever farther apart, especially after May 1878, when their oldest living son, Tommy, whom Sherman had groomed to head the family when he passed on, entered the Jesuit priesthood.

For Tommy's attempt to set his own course in life, which the father considered an act of betrayal, Sherman severed ties with his son. They never fully reconciled, nor did Sherman completely forgive Ellen, whom he suspected of encouraging Tommy to abandon his familial responsibilities. Relieved by Ellen's passing and yet regretful that he had contributed much to their contentious union, he spent his last years in a modest house in New York City, where he died from pneumonia, aggravated by his lifelong asthmatic condition, on February 14, 1891.[17]

The first postwar meeting of Sherman and Johnston occurred only a few months after the latter's surrender, when Sherman, then commander of the Division of the Missouri, took a steamer from St. Louis to Memphis and met on board his old antagonist. As Sherman noted in his memoirs, "[W]e were, of course, on the most friendly terms, and on our way up we talked over our battles again, played cards, and questioned each other as to particular parts of our mutual conduct in the game of war." They spoke animatedly of the battles of the Atlanta campaign, especially of Sherman's indirect role in the death of General Polk, and of the day at Cassville when Sherman, having intercepted a copy of Johnston's memo declaring that his army's retreating days were over, expected to be attacked, only to have Johnston turn away and retreat. Following this shipboard meeting, the two kept up an intermittent correspondence, which at one point seems to have lapsed. They would not meet again, face-to-face, for some years.[18]

By the early 1870s they were in contact, through the intercession of mutual friends. They exchanged letters touching on the political situation North and South, including the rise of vigilantism in the old Confederacy in the guise of the Ku Klux Klan, a fact that both men deprecated. Sherman occasionally presented Johnston with copies of government publications relating to the war, including a complete set of the proceedings of the congressional panel known as the Joint Committee on the Conduct of the War, before which Sherman had testified in May 1865.[19]

Assuredly, each presented the other with a copy of his memoirs. In print Johnston portrayed Sherman not only as a hard fighter but as an innovative tactician; Sherman described Johnston as a wily foe who in retreat could be more dangerous than generals given to attacking. Sherman also pleased Johnston by downgrading the performances of John Pemberton and John Bell Hood. Then, too, his estimation of Jefferson Davis as a war leader was almost as low as Johnston's, and although he mentions the Rebel president infrequently, Sherman makes his feelings about him quite clear.

In the late 1870s, the generals became quite close. For several years, Johnson, as congressman and then as railroad commissioner, and Sherman, as commanding general of the army, maintained homes in the nation's capital. Their families exchanged dinner invitations and attended many of the same social gatherings. In time, the Johnstons became a fixture at the Shermans' home, and "General Joe" became a favorite of the Sherman children and grandchildren. One of Minnie Sherman's daughters retained throughout her life "a most vivid impression of her grandfather and the Confederate general bending low over Civil War maps as they refought their mutual battles, General Johnston's bald head still shining in her memory."[20]

The two lost touch after Sherman moved army headquarters, and his family, to St. Louis, but they reestablished contact upon Sherman's return to the capital after Secretary Belknap's fall from power. Upon Sherman's retirement and return to St. Louis, they were estranged for the better part of two years although together in New York in July 1885 when both served as pallbearers at the funeral of Ulysses S. Grant, another Union hero whom Johnston had come to respect. The following year the Shermans were back in the East, residing at New York's Fifth Avenue Hotel; they and the Johnstons saw each other socially when General Joe was in town on business. Following the deaths of their wives, the old men did all in their power to console one another, but with indifferent success.

After Cleveland lost the White House to Republican Benjamin Harrison in 1888, Johnston feared losing his position as railroad commissioner, his only source of income at the time. Although four years removed from his commanding general's post, Sherman retained a certain amount of influence in government circles; he used it to make a "friendly interposition" on Johnston's behalf with Harrison's secretary of the interior. By March 1889, as Harrison took office, Sherman was able to assure friends of Johnston's that the general "will not be disturbed in his present office." Johnston, when he learned of Sherman's involvement, wrote him a heartfelt letter of thanks, noting that his old antagonist's "friendly interest gave me infinite pleasure and high gratification."[21]

While often estranged by divergent business interests, the two continued to paper the distance between them with a regular correspondence, exchanging good wishes, reviewing political and economic issues, and planning opportunities to meet at veterans' gatherings, an increasing number of which, by the 1880s, were attended by both Yankees and Rebels. Writing to Johnston not long before his death, Sherman alluded to those blue-gray veterans' associations and to a growing interest in forming a combined Union and Confederate organization known as the Order of United American Veterans.

Sherman doubted the need for such a group—certainly he and Johnston had not required one to cement their friendship. As he noted in his final letter to his Confederate friend, "[Y]ou and I became reconciled in April 1865, [and] have remained so ever since with no apologies or concealments." They had "shaken hands across the bloody chasm," a chasm that was finally closing for every American who retained vivid memories of their war. "The cause which made you and me enemies in 1861," Sherman observed, "is as dead as the rule of King George in 1776. . . . all [others] who are willing to be reconciled can do it by simply becoming good American citizens."[22]

Six weeks after penning these words, Sherman was dead. Though frail from years and suffering from a heart condition, the eighty-four-year old Johnston insisted on fulfilling a request the Sherman family had made of him, serving as an honorary pallbearer at the general's funeral service in New York City. Despite the rawness of the season, the old Confederate made the journey from Sherman's residence to the church along with thirty thousand other members of the funeral procession including President Harrison, members of his cabinet, congressmen, justices of the Supreme Court, foreign dignitaries, and old soldiers North and South.

As Sherman's casket was readied for the procession, the pallbearers stood, heads uncovered, in the morning chill. Someone leaned close to Johnston and whispered, "General, put on your hat, you will take cold." Johnston was resolute in his reply: "If I were in his place and he standing here in mine, he would not put on his hat."[23]

A month later, he was truly in Sherman's place, having caught a severe chill that fatally weakened his heart. His final assessment of his friend had undoubtedly been correct. Had he been in Johnston's place—even had he foreseen the consequences—Sherman would have made the same gesture of respect and admiration for the man who had become the worthiest opponent of his career in arms.

NOTES

Abbreviations Used in Notes:

B&L	*Battles and Leaders of the Civil War*
CV	*Confederate Veteran*
CWH	*Civil War History*
CWTI	*Civil War Times Illustrated*
DUL	Duke University Library
EES	Ellen Ewing Sherman
GLC	Gilder Lehrman Collection
JEJ	Joseph E. Johnston
LC	Library of Congress
MoC	Museum of the Confederacy
MSS	Manuscripts, Papers
OHS	Ohio Historical Society
OR	*War of the Rebellion: A Compilation of the Official Records of the Union and Confederate Armies*
ORN	*Official Records of the Union and Confederate Navies*
SFMSS	Sherman Family Papers
SHSP	*Southern Historical Society Papers*
UNDL	University of Notre Dame Library
USAMHI	U.S. Army Military History Institute
USMA	United States Military Academy
UVL	Alderman Library, University of Virginia
VHS	Virginia Historical Society
W&ML	College of William and Mary Library
WTS	William T. Sherman

One:

1. A. L. Jordan, *Gen. Jos. E. Johnston: A Review of His Military Career* . . . (Pulaski, Va., n. d.), 4; Bradley T. Johnson, *A Memoir of the Life and Public Service of Joseph E. Johnston* . . . (Baltimore, 1891), 2–7; Robert M. Hughes, *General Johnston* (New York, 1893), 6–8; Gilbert E. Govan and James W. Livingood, *A Different Valor: The Story of General Joseph E. Johnston, C.S.A.* (Indianapolis, 1956), 12–13; Craig L. Symonds, *Joseph E. Johnston: A Civil War Biography* (New York, 1992), 10–11.

2. Symonds, *Joseph E. Johnston*, 11; Hughes, *General Johnston*, 10.

3. Hughes, *General Johnston*, 11–12.

4. Ibid., 12.

5. Ibid., 13; Mary Boykin Chesnut, *Mary Chesnut's Civil War*, ed. by C. Vann Woodward (New Haven, Conn., 1981), 382.

6. Hughes, *General Johnston*, 13.

7. Ibid., 14; Symonds, *Joseph E. Johnston*, 13.

8. Peter Johnston to JEJ, July 17, 1825; Benjamin R. Johnston to JEJ, Dec. 4, 1825; both, JEJ MSS, UVL; JEJ to Louisa S. Johnston, June 30, 1825, JEJ MSS, W&ML.

9. Symonds, *Joseph E. Johnston*, 13; *Official Register of the Officers and Cadets of the U.S. Military Academy, West Point, New York* (West Point, N.Y.), 1826, 13; 1827, 10; 1828, 8; 1829, 6.

10. Hughes, *General Johnston*, 16; Byron Stinson, "Night Blindness in CW Soldiers," *CWTI* 4 (Jan. 1966): 33.

11. *Roll of the Cadets [of the United States Military Academy] Arranged According to Merit in Conduct, for the Year Ending 30th June, 1826* (West Point, N.Y., 1826), 3; *Official Register of the U.S. Military Academy*, 1827, 19; 1828, 19; 1829, 19; Symonds, *Joseph E. Johnston*, 16; Joseph T. Glatthaar, *Partners in Command: The Relationships between Leaders in the Civil War* (New York, 1994), 105; Extract from Delinquency Log of JEJ, n. d., USMA Archives, West Point, N.Y.

12. Francis B. Heitman, comp., *Historical Register and Dictionary of the United States Army* (2 vols. Washington, D.C., 1903), 1: 259, 262, 394, 539, 577–78, 715, 796; Ezra J. Warner, *Generals in Blue: Lives of the Union Commanders* (Baton Rouge, La., 1964), 49–50, 327; Ezra J. Warner, *Generals in Gray: Lives of the Confederate Commanders* (Baton Rouge, La., 1959), 141, 159–60, 242–43.

13. Symonds, *Joseph E. Johnston*, 19; Douglas Southall Freeman, *R. E. Lee: A Biography* (4 vols. New York, 1934–35), 1: 55, 82–83; A. L. Long, *Memoirs of Robert E. Lee: His Military and Personal History* . . . (Philadelphia, 1886), 71.

14. Symonds, *Joseph E. Johnston*, 16; Robert Maddox, "The Grog Mutiny: One Merry Christmas at West Point," *American History Illustrated* 16 (Dec. 1981): 32–36; Thomas J. Fleming, *West Point: The Men and Times of the United States Military Academy* (New York, 1969), 58.

15. Maddox, "Grog Mutiny," 36–37; Govan and Livingood, *Different Valor*, 14.

16. Symonds, *Joseph E. Johnston*, 21; JEJ to Louisa S. Johnston, Jan. 25, 1829, JEJ MSS, W&ML; Robert M. Hughes, ed., "Some Letters from the Papers of General Joseph E. Johnston," *William & Mary Quarterly Historical Magazine* 11 (1931): 319–20.

17. Symonds, *Joseph E. Johnston*, 23.

18. Ibid., 23, 27–29; James M. McPherson, *Ordeal by Fire: The Civil War and Reconstruction* (New York, 1982), 51.

19. Symonds, *Joseph E. Johnston*, 23–24; McPherson, *Ordeal by Fire*, 46n.

20. Symonds, *Joseph E. Johnston*, 24, 86, 93.

21. George B. Johnston to Beverly B. Munford, Apr. 17, 1907, Beverly Bland Munford MSS, VHS.

22. JEJ to Louisa S. Johnston, Nov. 18, 1831; JEJ to Beverly R. Johnston, Nov. 13, 1832; both, JEJ MSS, W&ML; Symonds, *Joseph E. Johnston*, 25, 46.

23. Symonds, *Joseph E. Johnston*, 25–27; George W. Cullum, comp., *Biographical Register of the Officers and Graduates of the U.S. Military Academy* (3 vols. Boston, 1891), 1: 427; Hughes, *General Johnston*, 17; Russell F. Weigley, *History of the United States Army* (New York, 1967), 159.

Two:

1. WTS, *Memoirs of General William T. Sherman: Second Edition, Revised and Corrected* (2 vols. New York, 1886), 1: 9–10; E. V. Smalley, "General Sherman," *Century Illustrated Monthly Magazine,* n. s. 5 (1884): 451; Manning F. Force, *General Sherman* (New York, 1899), 1; John F. Marszalek, *Sherman: A Soldier's Passion for Order* (New York, 1993), 2; Lee Kennett, *Sherman: A Soldier's Life* (New York, 2001), 6–7; Lloyd Lewis, *Sherman, Fighting Prophet* (New York, 1932), 20–21; B. H. Liddell Hart, *Sherman, Soldier, Realist, American* (New York, 1993),1–2; Stanley P. Hirshon, *The White Tecumseh: A Biography of William T. Sherman* (New York, 1997), 1–4; John Sherman, *John Sherman's Recollections of Forty Years in the House, Senate and Cabinet: An Autobiography* (2 vols. Chicago, 1895), 1: 15–24.

2. Force, *General Sherman,* 2; James M. Merrill, *William Tecumseh Sherman* (Chicago, 1971), 15; WTS, *Memoirs, Second Edition,* 1: 10–11.

3. WTS, *Memoirs, Second Edition* 1: 11; Smalley, "General Sherman," 452; Sherman, *John Sherman's Recollections,* 24.

4. Sherman, *John Sherman's Recollections,* 24.

5. Weigley, *History of the United States Army,* 121; WTS, *Memoirs, Second Edition,* 1: 11; Merrill, *William Tecumseh Sherman,* 16.

6. WTS, *Memoirs, Second Edition,* 1: 13–14; Merrill, *William Tecumseh Sherman,* 18–19; Marszalek, *Sherman,* 3–6.

7. EES, *Memorial of Thomas Ewing of Ohio* (New York, 1873), 1–29; Marszalek, *Sherman,* 7–9; WTS, *Sherman at War: The Thirty-two Newly-Found Sherman Letters,* ed. by Joseph H. Ewing (Dayton, Ohio, 1992), 20; Michael Fellman, *Citizen Sherman: A Life of William Tecumseh Sherman* (New York, 1995), 5–6.

8. Lewis, *Fighting Prophet,* 32–33; Merrill, *William Tecumseh Sherman,* 19; Kennett, *Sherman,* 9.

9. Marszalek, *Sherman,* 10; Fellman, *Citizen Sherman,* 5.

10. Lewis, *Fighting Prophet,* 33–34; Fellman, *Citizen Sherman,* 6–8; Merrill, *William Tecumseh Sherman,* 19–21; Marszalek, *Sherman,* 9–10.

11. Merrill, *William Tecumseh Sherman,* 21.

12. Anthony Gannon, "A Consistent Deist: Sherman and Religion," *CWH* 42 (1996): 307–21; Charles Royster, *The Destructive War: William Tecumseh Sherman, Stonewall Jackson, and the Americans* (New York, 1991), 269–70.

13. Marszalek, *Sherman,* xv–xvi, 8–9.

14. WTS, *Memoirs, Second Edition,* 1: 14.

15. Ibid., 14–15.

16. Ibid.; Lewis, *Fighting Prophet,* 42–44; Fellman, *Citizen Sherman,* 7.

17. WTS, *Memoirs, Second Edition,* 1: 15–16; Force, *General Sherman,* 3–4; Warner, *Generals in Blue,* 170–71, 224–25, 349–50, 500–02, 524; Warner, *Generals in Gray,* 84–85, 131–32, 157–58, 167–68, 213–14; Freeman Cleaves, *Rock of Chickamauga: The Life of General George H. Thomas* (Norman, Okla., 1948), 9; Bernarr Cresap, *Appomattox Commander: The Story of General E. O. C. Ord* (San Diego, Calif., 1981), 14; John F. Marszalek, "'A Full Share of All the Credit': Sherman and Grant to the Fall of Vicksburg," in Steven E. Woodworth, ed., *Grant's Lieutenants: From Cairo to Vicksburg* (Lawrence, Kan., 2001): 5–6.

18. WTS, *Memoirs, Second Edition,* 1: 17; WTS and John Sherman, *The Sherman Letters: Correspondence between General Sherman and Senator Sherman from 1837 to 1891,* ed. by Rachel Sherman Thorndike (New York, 1969), 8–13; O. O. Howard, *Autobiography of Oliver Otis Howard, Major General, United States Army* (2 vols. New York, 1907), 1: 57.

19. WTS, *Sherman at War,* 2; *Official Register of the U.S. Military Academy,* 1837, 14, 22; 1840, 9, 24; Delinquency Log of WTS, n. d., USMA Archives.

20. WTS, *Memoirs, Second Edition,* 1: 17; Fleming, *West Point,* 100; WTS, *Home Letters of General Sherman,* ed. by M. A. DeWolfe Howe (New York, 1909), 5–6; James L. Morrison, Jr., *"The Best School in the World": West Point, the Pre-Civil War Years, 1833–1866* (Kent, Ohio, 1986), 85.

21. WTS, *Memoirs, Second Edition*, 1: 17.

22. Morrison, *"Best School in the World,"* 217n.; Merrill, *William Tecumseh Sherman*, 287.

23. WTS, *Memoirs, Second Edition*, 1: 17.

24. Marszalek, *Sherman*, 30–31.

25. WTS, *Memoirs, Second Edition*, 1: 17–20; Fellman, *Citizen Sherman*, 16; Jane F. Lancaster, "William Tecumseh Sherman's Introduction to War, 1840–1842: Lesson for Action," *Florida Historical Quarterly* 72 (1993): 56–64; Katherine Burton, *Three Generations: Maria Boyle Ewing (1801–1864), Ellen Ewing Sherman (1824–1888), Minnie Sherman Fitch (1851–1913)* (New York, 1947), 62.

26. WTS and John Sherman, *Sherman Letters*, 13–15.

27. WTS, *Memoirs, Second Edition*, 1: 23–24; WTS, *Home Letters of General Sherman*, 19–20, 24–25.

28. WTS, *Memoirs, Second Edition*, 1: 27–30; WTS, *Memoirs of General William T. Sherman, by Himself* (2 vols. New York, 1875), 1: 9; WTS, *Home Letters of General Sherman*, 19–33; WTS and John Sherman, *Sherman Letters*, 22–24; Force, *General Sherman*, 6–7; Smalley, "General Sherman," 453; E. Merton Coulter, "Sherman and the South," *North Carolina Historical Review* 8 (1931): 41–44; Marszalek, *Sherman*, 38–46; Kennett, *Sherman*, 28–32; Fellman, *Citizen Sherman*, 19–20.

Three:

1. Symonds, *Joseph E. Johnston*, 27–29; Cullum, *Officers and Graduates of the U.S. Military Academy*, 1: 427–28.

2. JEJ to Beverly R. Johnston, Jan. 9, Mar. 25, 1834; both, JEJ MSS, W&ML.

3. Cullum, *Officers and Graduates of the U.S. Military Academy*, 1: 428; E. D. Keyes, *Fifty Years' Observation of Men and Events, Civil and Military* (New York, 1884), 163.

4. Symonds, *Joseph E. Johnston*, 30; JEJ to Beverly R. Johnston, Feb. 18, 1836, JEJ MSS, W&ML.

5. Hughes, *General Johnston*, 17–18; Symonds, *Joseph E. Johnston*, 31; John K. Mahon, *History of the Second Seminole War, 1835–1842* (Gainesville, Fla., 1967), 135–57.

6. Hughes, *General Johnston*, 18–19; Symonds, *Joseph E. Johnston*, 31–34; Mahon, *Second Seminole War*, 157–62.

7. Symonds, *Joseph E. Johnston*, 34; JEJ to Beverly R. Johnston, June 13, 1837, JEJ MSS, W&ML.

8. Hughes, *General Johnston*, 19; Symonds, *Joseph E. Johnston*, 34; Heitman, *Historical Register and Dictionary*, 1: 578; JEJ to "My Dear Little Lizzie," Apr. 15, 1837, Floyd–Johnston-Preston MSS, W&ML.

9. George E. Buker, *Swamp Sailors in the Second Seminole War* (Gainesville, Fla., 1997), 60–62; Symonds, *Joseph E. Johnston*, 37–39; Mahon, *Second Seminole War*, 219–20.

10. Hughes, *General Johnston*, 20–21; Johnson, *Memoir of Joseph E. Johnston*, 10–11.

11. Buker, *Swamp Sailors*, 62–63; Symonds, *Joseph E. Johnston*, 40–41.

12. Hughes, *General Johnston*, 21; Heitman, *Historical Register and Dictionary*, 1: 578.

13. Cullum, *Officers and Graduates of the U.S. Military Academy*, 1: 428; JEJ to J. Preston Johnstone, May 30, Aug. 31, Oct. 17, 1839, Mar. 11, 16, July 12, Nov. 19, 1840, May 13, 21, June 2, Sept. 16, 1841; all, JEJ MSS, W&ML.

14. JEJ to J. Preston Johnstone, May 13, 1842, JEJ MSS, W&ML; Hughes, *General Johnston*, 22–23; Johnson, *Memoir of Joseph E. Johnston*, 262–63; Symonds, *Joseph E. Johnston*, 48–52; John A. Munroe, *Louis McLane, Federalist and Jacksonian* (New Brunswick, N.J., 1973), 125, 488, 510.

15. Dabney H. Mary, *Recollections of a Virginian in the Mexican, Indian and Civil Wars* (New York, 1894), 152.

16. JEJ to J. Preston Johnstone, Mar. 23, 1839, Mar. 16, July 12, 1840; all, JEJ MSS, W&ML.

17. K. Jack Bauer, *The Mexican War, 1846–1848* (New York, 1974), 8–9, 16–17.

18. Ibid., 46–48, 52–63, 86–101, 209–17.

19. Ibid., 232–42.

20. Heitman, *Historical Register and Dictionary*, 1: 578; Symonds, *Joseph E. Johnston*, 54–56; Charles Winslow Elliott, *Winfield Scott, the Soldier and the Man* (New York, 1937), 455.

21. Bauer, *Mexican War*, 261–74; Symonds, *Joseph E. Johnston*, 59; Elliott, *Winfield Scott*, 464.

22. Hughes, *General Johnston*, 25–26; Maury, *Recollections of a Virginian*, 38, 40; Dabney H. Maury, "Interesting Reminiscences of General Johnston," *SHSP* 18 (1890–91): 172; Symonds, *Joseph E. Johnston*, 59; Pierre G. T. Beauregard, *With Beauregard in Mexico: The Mexican War Reminiscences of P. G. T Beauregard*, ed. by T. Harry Williams (Baton Rouge, La., 1956), 32–33; James I. Robertson, Jr., *Stonewall Jackson, the Man, the Soldier, the Legend* (New York, 1997), 61.

23. Hughes, *General Johnston*, 25.

24. Robertson, *Stonewall Jackson*, 63; Symonds, *Joseph E. Johnston*, 65–66; Freeman, *R. E. Lee*, 1: 260, 266; JEJ to Beverly R. Johnston, Aug. 25, 1847, JEJ MSS, W&ML.

25. JEJ to Eliza Johnston, Jan. 12, 1848, JEJ MSS, W&ML.

26. Bauer, *Mexican War*, 306–11.

27. Ibid., 312–17; Justin H. Smith, *The War with Mexico* (2 vols. New York, 1919), 2: 154; Beauregard, *With Beauregard in Mexico*, 78–81; Johnson, *Memoir of Joseph E. Johnston*, 14–15; Hughes, *General Johnston*, 30–32; Symonds, *Joseph E. Johnston*, 67–70.

28. Hughes, *General Johnston*, 31–52; Heitman, *Historical Register and Dictionary*, 1: 578.

29. Heitman, *Historical Register and Dictionary*, 1: 578; Symonds, *Joseph E. Johnston*, 72–74; JEJ to Edward W. Johnston, Jan. 6, 1851, JEJ MSS, W&ML; Jeffrey N. Lash, *Destroyer of the Iron Horse: General Joseph E. Johnston and Confederate Rail Transport, 1861–1865* (Kent, Ohio, 1991), 2–3; Averam B. Bender, *The March of Empire: Frontier Defense in the Southwest, 1848–1860* (New York, 1968), 71–72, 94–95; William H. Goetzmann, *Army Exploration in the American West, 1803–1863* (New Haven, Conn., 1959), 226–38, 261, 268; William H. Goetzmann, *Exploration and Empire: The Explorer and the Scientist in the Winning of the American West* (New York, 1966), 273–74.

30. Cullum, *Officers and Graduates of the U.S. Military Academy*, 1: 428; Symonds, *Joseph E. Johnston*, 76–83; JEJ, Diary of the Survey of the Southern Border of Kansas, May 16–Oct. 29, 1857, JEJ MSS, W&ML; Nyle H. Miller, ed., "Surveying the Southern Boundary of Kansas: From the Private Journal of Col. Joseph E. Johnston," *Kansas Historical Quarterly* 1 (1932): 104–39; JEJ to Assistant Adjutant General, USA, May 27, 1858, JEJ MSS, GLC.

Four:

1. WTS, *Memoirs, Second Edition*, 1: 32.

2. WTS to Philemon B. Ewing, Aug. 22, 1842, WTS MSS, OHS; WTS to EES, Mar. 12, 1843, SFMSS, UNDL; Burton, *Three Generations*, 63–64; John F. Marszalek, "General and Mrs. William T. Sherman, A Contentious Union," in Carol K. Bleser and Leslie J. Gordon, eds., *Intimate Strategies of the Civil War: Military Commanders and Their Wives* (New York, 2001): 140–41.

3. Marszalek, *Sherman*, 48.

4. WTS, *Memoirs, Second Edition*, 1: 32–34; WTS, *Home Letters of General Sherman*, 29.

5. WTS, *Memoirs*, 1: 9–11; WTS, *Home Letters of General Sherman*, 34–35.

6. WTS, *Memoirs*, 1: 12–18; WTS, *Home Letters of General Sherman*, 38–82; WTS to Thomas Ewing, May 3, 1865 [recalling journey to California], WTS MSS, GLC; "W. T. Sherman's Journal of Monterey California & Discovery of Gold," WTS MSS, LC.

7. Bauer, *Mexican War*, 127–41, 164–200.

8. Ibid., 195; John F. Marszalek, *Commander of All Lincoln's Armies: A Life of General Henry W. Halleck* (Cambridge, Mass., 2004), 55.

9. Fellman, *Citizen Sherman*, 23–24; Marszalek, *Sherman*, 63–67; Kennett, *Sherman*, 39–43; WTS, *Home Letters of General Sherman*, 114.

10. Marszalek, *Sherman*, 67–68; Kennett, *Sherman*, 43–44; WTS, *Home Letters of General Sherman*, 109.

11. WTS, *Memoirs*, 1: 40–41; Marszalek, *Sherman*, 68–70; Kennett, *Sherman*, 45–46; Anna McAllister, *Ellen Ewing, Wife of General Sherman* (New York, 1936), 56.

12. Bauer, *Mexican War*, 368–84; WTS, *Memoirs*, 1: 70–72.

13. WTS, *Memoirs*, 1: 73–81; Kennett, *Sherman*, 47–49.

14. WTS, *Memoirs*, 1: 82–83.

15. Ibid., 84; Fellman, *Citizen Sherman*, 36; McAllister, *Ellen Ewing*, 62–63; Burton, *Three Generations*, 77; Merrill, *William Tecumseh Sherman*, 80–81; Roy F Nichols, ed., "William Tecumseh Sherman in 1850," *Pennsylvania Magazine of History and Biography* 75 (1951): 425.

16. WTS, *Memoirs*, 1: 84–85; Nichols, "William Tecumseh Sherman in 1850," 425–26; Burton, *Three Generations*, 79.

17. WTS, *Memoirs*, 1: 85–87.

18. Fellman, *Citizen Sherman*, 36–38; Merrill, *William Tecumseh Sherman*, 84–85; Marszalek, *Sherman*, 85–87.

19. Heitman, *Historical Register and Dictionary*, 1: 882; WTS, *Memoirs*, 1: 88–93; WTS to George Gibson, Sept. 1, 1851, WTS MSS, GLC; WTS, *Home Letters of General Sherman*, 120–32; Merrill, *William Tecumseh Sherman*, 85–92; Marszalek, *Sherman*, 86–91.

20. WTS, *Memoirs*, 1: 92–93.

21. Ibid., 93–94.

22. Ibid., 94–95.

23. Ibid., 95–99.

24. Kennett, *Sherman*, 63–65.

25. WTS, *Memoirs*, 1: 100–120; WTS, *Home Letters of General Sherman*, 133–42.

26. Heitman, *Historical Register and Dictionary*, 1: 882; WTS, *Memoirs*, 1: 101–02; Fellman, *Citizen Sherman*, 52–53; Marszalek, "General and Mrs. William T. Sherman," 143–44.

27. WTS, *Memoirs*, 1: 107; Marszalek, "General and Mrs. William T. Sherman," 144.

28. WTS, *Memoirs*, 1: 116–18, 132–33; WTS, *Home Letters of General Sherman*, 138–40; Marszalek, "General and Mrs. William T. Sherman," 144; Fellman, *Citizen Sherman*, 53.

29. WTS, *Memoirs*, 1: 103–16; WTS, *Home Letters of General Sherman*, 146–47; John F. Marszalek, *Sherman's Other War: The General and the Civil War Press* (Memphis, Tenn., 1981), 34–36; Kennett, *Sherman*, 70–71.

30. WTS, *Memoirs*, 1: 118–24; WTS and John Sherman, *Sherman Letters*, 60–62; WTS, "Sherman and the San Francisco Vigilantes: Unpublished Letters of General W. T. Sherman," *Century Illustrated Monthly Magazine*, n. s. 21 (1891): 296–300; Royster, *Destructive War*, 135–36; Marcus Cunliffe, *Soldiers & Civilians: The Martial Spirit in America, 1775–1865* (Boston, 1968), 87.

31. WTS, *Memoirs*, 1: 124–32; WTS, "Sherman and the San Francisco Vigilantes," 300–09; Fellman, *Citizen Sherman*, 57–59; Kennett, *Sherman*, 70–71; Marszalek, *Sherman*, 107–09.

32. WTS, *Memoirs*, 1: 131–32; Fellman, *Citizen Sherman*, 58–59.

33. WTS, *Memoirs*, 1: 103.

34. Ibid., 134–37; WTS, *Home Letters of General Sherman*, 147–52; WTS to EES, Feb. 13, 1860, SFMSS, UNDL.

35. WTS, *Memoirs*, 1: 138–39; Marszalek, *Sherman*, 112–13.

36. WTS, *Memoirs*, 1: 139.

37. *New York Times*, Sept. 10, 1885; William Conant Church, *Ulysses S. Grant and the Period of National Preservation and Reconstruction* (New York, 1926), 57n.; Lloyd Lewis, *Captain Sam Grant* (Boston, 1950), 347.

Five:

1. Symonds, *Joseph E. Johnston*, 90–91; JEJ to Assistant Adjutant General, USA, May 27, 1858, JEJ MSS, W&ML.

2. Ethan S. Rafuse, *McClellan's War: The Failure of Moderation in the Struggle for the Union* (Bloomington, Ind., 2005), 80; Symonds, *Joseph E. Johnston*, 45, 81, 87, 91; Warner, *Generals in Gray*, 89–90, 159–60; Warner, *Generals in Blue*, 455–56.

3. Freeman, *R. E. Lee*, 1: 411–12; Symonds, *Joseph E. Johnston*, 91.

4. R. E. Lee to JEJ, July 30, 1860; JEJ to "My dear Lizzie," Aug. 28, 1863; both, JEJ MSS, W&ML; Hughes, *General Johnston*, 33–34; JEJ to "My Dear Lizzie," June 30, 1860, Floyd-Johnston-Preston MSS, W&ML.

5. Symonds, *Joseph E. Johnston*, 91–92.

6. McPherson, *Ordeal by Fire*, 114–17; JEJ to Thomas T. Gantt, June 23, 1888, JEJ MSS, W&ML.

7. McPherson, *Ordeal by Fire*, 117–37.

8. Symonds, *Joseph E. Johnston*, 89–90; Hughes, *General Johnston*, 34; Jefferson Davis, "Report on the Claim of Lt. Colonel Johnston, 1st Cavalry, to the Rank of Brevet Colonel," Apr. 15, 1858; John B. Floyd to Adjutant General, USA, Mar. 6, 1860; both, JEJ MSS, W&ML.

9. Govan and Livingood, *Different Valor*, 28.

10. McPherson, *Ordeal by Fire*, 140–45, 149–51.

11. Peter C. Johnston to JEJ, Mar. 10, 1861, JEJ MSS, W&ML.

12. George F. Holmes to Johnston Family, Jan. 1, 1861, JEJ MSS, UVL; Symonds, *Joseph E. Johnston*, 96; Leslie J. Perry, "Davis and Johnston: Light Thrown on a Quarrel Among Confederate Leaders . . .," *SHSP* 20 (1892): 98.

13. Chesnut, *Mary Chesnut's Civil War*, 187.

14. JEJ, *Narrative of Military Operations Directed During the Late War Between the States* (New York, 1874), 10; Dispatch Book of JEJ, June 13, 1861–Aug. 3, 1862 [including copies of his resignation from USA and appointment in CSA], JEJ MSS, W&ML.

15. WTS, *Memoirs*, 1: 139–40; WTS, *Home Letters of General Sherman*, 153; Fellman, *Citizen Sherman*, 67–68.

16. WTS, *Memoirs*, 1: 140, 142–43; Kennett, *Sherman*, 82–83.

17. WTS, *Memoirs*, 1: 141.

18. Ibid., 141–42.

19. Ibid., 142–43; WTS, *Home Letters of General Sherman*, 160–62; WTS and John Sherman, *Sherman Letters*, 76–77; Walter L. Fleming, *General W. T. Sherman as College President: A Collection of Letters, Documents, and Other Material, Chiefly from Private Sources, Relating to the Life and Activities of General William Tecumseh Sherman, to the Early Years of Louisiana State University, and to the Stirring Conditions Existing in the South on the Eve of the Civil War, 1859–1861* (Cleveland, 1912), 19–30; Kennett, *Sherman*, 84–85.

20. WTS, *Memoirs*, 1: 144–45, 150–51.

21. Ibid., 145–47; Fleming, *Sherman as College President*, 64–65, 84–87, 97–100; Kennett, *Sherman*, 85–89; Liddell Hart, *Sherman*, 54.

22. WTS, *Home Letters of General Sherman*, 174–75; Fleming, *Sherman as College President*, 104–05, 137–41; John Bennett Walters, *Merchant of Terror: General Sherman and Total War* (Indianapolis, 1973), 3.

23. WTS, *Home Letters of General Sherman*, 162.

24. David French Boyd, "General William T. Sherman as a College President," *American College* 2 (1909–10): 6–7; Fleming, *West Point*, 160–61.

25. WTS, *Memoirs*, 1: 147–50; WTS, *Home Letters of General Sherman*, 167 and n–169; WTS and John Sherman, *Sherman Letters*, 77–78; Fleming, *Sherman as College President*, 118–20, 174–79.

26. WTS, *Memoirs*, 1: 151–59; Fleming, *Sherman as College President*, 305–64.

27. WTS, *Memoirs*, 1: 159–61; Fleming, *Sherman as College President*, 363, 375.

Six:

1. JEJ, *Narrative of Military Operations*, 12; Symonds, *Joseph E. Johnston*, 97; Govan and Livingood, *Different Valor*, 29; Alfred P. James, "General Joseph Eggleston Johnston, Storm Center of the Confederate Army," *Mississippi Valley Historical Review* 14 (1927): 347.

2. OR, I, 2: 783–84, 787; JEJ, *Narrative of Military Operations*, 12.

3. JEJ, *Narrative of Military Operations*, 13, 71–72; OR, I, 2: 844.

4. JEJ, *Narrative of Military Operations*, 13, 16; Perry, "Davis and Johnston," 93.

5. JEJ, *Narrative of Military Operations*, 13; OR, I, 2: 844–45; Symonds, *Joseph E. Johnston*, 102–03.

6. JEJ, *Narrative of Military Operations*, 13–16; Symonds, *Joseph E. Johnston*, 103–04; OR, I, 2: 871–72, 877; Copy of "Orders, No. ——, Harper's Ferry, [Virginia], May 24, 1861," Confederate Military Leaders Collection, MoC.

7. Govan and Livingood, *Different Valor*, 34–35; Symonds, *Joseph E. Johnston*, 104; Joseph Howard Parks, *General Edmund Kirby Smith, C.S.A.* (Baton Rouge, La., 1954), 127–28; Dennis Frye, *2nd Virginia Infantry* (Lynchburg, Va., 1984), 8.

8. Symonds, *Joseph E. Johnston*, 101; Govan and Livingood, *Different Valor*, 30, 40–41; Glatthaar, *Partners in Command*, 98; Chesnut, *Mary Chesnut's Civil War*, 800.

9. Govan and Livingood, *Different Valor*, 30–31.

10. Ibid., 31; John Cheves Haskell, *The Haskell Memoirs*, ed. by Gilbert E. Govan and James W. Livingood (New York, 1960), 6–7.

11. E. P. Alexander, *Fighting for the Confederacy: The Personal Recollections of General Edward Porter Alexander*, ed. by Gary Gallagher (Chapel Hill, N.C., 1989), 82.

12. Chesnut, *Mary Chesnut's Civil War*, 268.

13. Symonds, *Joseph E. Johnston*, 102–03.

14. JEJ, *Narrative of Military Operations*, 17–18; OR, I, 2: 880–81; William C. Davis, *Battle at Bull Run: A History of the First Major Campaign of the Civil War* (Garden City, N.Y., 1977), 5–7, 42–45.

15. OR, I, 2: 881, 910; JEJ, *Narrative of Military Operations*, 17–19.

16. WTS, *Memoirs*, 1: 166–69; Fleming, *Sherman as College President*, 375–78.

17. WTS, *Memoirs*, 1: 166–67.

18. Ibid., 167–68.

19. Ibid., 168; Kennett, *Sherman*, 112; Fellman, *Citizen Sherman*, 85–86.

20. WTS, *Memoirs*, 1: 170–71.

21. Ibid., 169–71; Fellman, *Citizen Sherman*, 86; Sherman, *John Sherman's Recollections*, 1: 244.

22. Sherman, *John Sherman's Recollections*, 244.

23. WTS, *Memoirs*, 1: 171–73.

24. Ibid., 173–74; William C. Winter, *The Civil War in St. Louis: A Guided Tour* (St. Louis, 1994), 34–55; Elden E. Billings, ed., "Letters and Diaries: The St. Louis Riots," *CWTI* 2 (June 1963): 39–40.

25. WTS, *Memoirs*, 1: 174; Sherman, *John Sherman's Recollections*, 1: 245; Fellman, *Citizen Sherman*, 88; Heitman, *Historical Register and Dictionary*, 1: 882.

26. WTS, *Memoirs*, 1: 175.

Seven:

1. Ethan S. Rafuse, *A Single Grand Victory: The First Campaign and Battle of Manassas* (Wilmington, Del., 2002), 69; OR, I, 2: 894–98.

2. OR, I, 2: 896; Davis, *Battle at Bull Run*, 49–51.

3. Davis, *Battle at Bull Run*, 51–52; OR, I, 2: 901–02, 922–23; T. Harry Williams, *P. G. T. Beauregard, Napoleon in Gray* (Baton Rouge, La., 1954), 70–71; Alfred Roman, *The Military Operations of General Beauregard in the War between the States, 1861 to 1865 . . .* (2 vols. New York, 1884), 1: 76–78.

4. OR, I, 2: 64–74, 123–24; JEJ, *Narrative of Military Operations*, 22; Symonds, *Joseph E. Johnston*, 107; Davis, *Battle at Bull Run*, 42–45; David Detzer, *Donnybrook: The Battle of Bull Run, 1861* (New York, 2004), 54–58.

5. OR, I, 2: 910, 923–25; Glatthaar, *Partners in Command*, 100–01.

6. OR, I, 2: 472, 929–30; JEJ, *Narrative of Military Operations*, 23; Detzer, *Donnybrook*, 59–60.

7. JEJ, *Narrative of Military Operations*, 23–25; OR, I, 2: 472; Davis, *Battle at Bull Run*, 45–48.

8. OR, I, 2: 934–35; JEJ, *Narrative of Military Operations*, 27.

9. JEJ, *Narrative of Military Operations*, 27–29; Jeffrey N. Lash, "Joseph E. Johnston and the Virginia Railways, 1861–62," *CWH* 35 (1989): 10–13.

10. OR, I, 2: 157, 179–87, 472; Davis, *Battle at Bull Run*, 84–85; Detzer, *Donnybrook*, 63–64.

11. WTS, *Memoirs*, 2: 385.

12. Ibid., 177–78.

13. Ibid., 178.

14. Ibid., 179–80; OR, I, 2: 368; Warner, *Generals in Blue*, 93–94, 514–15; WTS to EES, July 6, 1861, SFMSS, UNDL.

15. Marszalek, *Sherman*, 147.

16. WTS, *Memoirs*, 1: 180; WTS to EES, July 16, 1861, SFMSS, UNDL; Lewis, *Fighting Prophet*, 168–69; Detzer, *Donnybrook*, 125–30.

17. Davis, *Battle at Bull Run*, 77–78.

18. JEJ, *Narrative of Military Operations*, 31.

19. OR, I, 2: 473; JEJ, *Narrative of Military Operations*, 32–33.

20. Williams, *P. G. T. Beauregard*, 74; Roman, *Military Operations of Beauregard*, 1: 84–87.

21. OR, I, 2: 473, 980, 982; JEJ, *Narrative of Military Operations*, 33.

22. JEJ, *Narrative of Military Operations*, 33–35; OR, I, 2: 473.

23. WTS, *Memoirs*, 1: 181; WTS to EES, July 19, 1861, SFMSS, UNDL; Davis, *Battle at Bull Run*, 107–24; John Hennessy, *The First Battle of Manassas: An End to Innocence, July 18–21, 1861* (Lynchburg, Va., 1989), 12–25.

24. WTS, *Memoirs*, 1: 181.

25. Ibid.,181–82.

26. OR, I, 2: 473; JEJ, *Narrative of Military Operations*, 36–37, 58; Hughes, *General Johnston*, 53–55; Davis, *Battle at Bull Run*, 134–36; Robertson, *Stonewall Jackson*, 832n–33n; Lash, "Johnston and the Virginia Railways," 13–14.

27. OR, I, 2: 473; JEJ, *Narrative of Military Operations*, 37–38; Symonds, *Joseph E. Johnston*, 115; Hughes, *General Johnston*, 55–56; Davis, *Battle at Bull Run*, 136–39; John D. Imboden, "Incidents of the First [Battle of] Bull Run," *B&L* 1: 230.

28. OR, I, 2: 473; JEJ, *Narrative of Military Operations*, 38.

29. OR, I, 2: 473–74; JEJ, *Narrative of Military Operations*, 39–42; Symonds, *Joseph E. Johnston*, 116–17; Williams, *P. G. T. Beauregard*, 77–80; JEJ, "Responsibilities of the First [Battle of] Bull Run," *B&L* 1: 245–46.

30. Davis, *Battle at Bull Run*, 159–64; Hennessy, *First Battle of Manassas*, 35–40.

31. JEJ, *Narrative of Military Operations*, 42–46; Hennessy, *First Battle of Manassas*, 40–69; Davis, *Battle at Bull Run*, 165–97.

32. OR, I, 2: 474–75; JEJ, *Narrative of Military Operations*, 46–50; Rafuse, *Single Grand Victory*, 145–51; Davis, *Battle at Bull Run*, 197–200, 248; Hennessy, *First Battle of Manassas*, 70–77, 83.

33. Hennessy, *First Battle of Manassas*, 77–86; Davis, *Battle at Bull Run*, 20–13.

34. OR, I, 2: 369, 371–73; WTS, *Memoirs*, 1: 186.

35. OR, I, 2: 369–70; Davis, *Battle at Bull Run*, 217–18.; Hennessy, *First Battle of Manassas*, 103.

36. OR, I, 2: 370; WTS, *Memoirs*, 1: 187; Davis, *Battle at Bull Run*, 218; Rafuse, *Single Grand Victory*, 179; Hennessy, *First Battle of Manassas*, 103–04.

37. OR, I, 2: 370; WTS to EES, July 28, 1861, SFMSS, UNDL; Davis, *Battle at Bull Run*, 218; Warner, *Generals in Blue*, 93–94.

38. OR, I, 2: 370; WTS, *Memoirs,* 1: 187; WTS, *Home Letters of General Sherman,* 207–10.

39. OR, I, 2: 476; JEJ, *Narrative of Military Operations,* 50–51; Davis, *Battle at Bull Run,* 225–33; Hennessy, *First Battle of Manassas,* 111–16.

40. OR, I, 2: 476–77; JEJ, *Narrative of Military Operations,* 51–52.

Eight:

1. JEJ, *Narrative of Military Operations,* 52–53; Davis, *Battle at Bull Run,* 236–42; Detzer, *Donnybrook,* 408–24.

2. JEJ, *Narrative of Military Operations,* 53–56; Symonds, *Joseph E. Johnston,* 122–23; Jefferson Davis, *The Rise and Fall of the Confederate Government* (2 vols. New York, 1881), 1: 348–57.

3. JEJ, *Narrative of Military Operations,* 59–65; JEJ, "Responsibilities of First Bull Run," 252–53; Perry, "Davis and Johnston," 102–03; Symonds, *Joseph E. Johnston,* 124–26; Davis, *Rise and Fall of the Confederate Government,* 1: 357–66; Rafuse, *Single Grand Victory,* 202–03.

4. WTS to EES, July 24, 28, 1861; both, SFMSS, UNDL; Keyes, *Fifty Years' Observation,* 434–35.

5. WTS, *Memoirs,* 1: 187–88.

6. Ibid., 188; WTS to EES, July 28, Aug. 3, 1861; both, SFMSS, UNDL; WTS to Philemon Ewing, Sept. 30, 1861, WTS MSS, GLC.

7. WTS, *Memoirs,* 1: 188–89; WTS to EES, Aug. 19, 1861, SFMSS, UNDL.

8. OR, I, 2: 762, 766; Rafuse, *McClellan's War,* 131–32; WTS to EES, Aug. 3, 1861, SFMSS, UNDL.

9. WTS, *Memoirs,* 1: 191–92; WTS to EES, Aug. 3, 1861, SFMSS, UNDL.

10. WTS, *Memoirs,* 1: 189.

11. Ibid., 189–90.

12. Ibid., 190–91.

13. Ibid., 191; Heitman, *Historical Register and Dictionary,* 1: 882; WTS to EES, July 28, Aug. 3, 12, 1861; all, SFMSS, UNDL.

14. WTS, *Memoirs,* 1: 192–93; Clarence E. Macartney, *Lincoln and His Generals* (Freeport, N.Y., 1970), 102–03; Warner, *Generals in Blue,* 500–02.

15. WTS, *Memoirs,* 1: 192; WTS to EES, Aug. 17, 19, 1861; both, SFMSS, UNDL; R. M. Kelly, "Holding Kentucky for the Union," *B&L* 1: 373–75.

16. WTS, *Memoirs,* 1: 192–93.

17. R. E. Lee to JEJ, July 24, 1861, Letters of Confederate Generals Robert E. Lee, Stonewall Jackson, Jeb Stuart, and Joseph E. Johnston, 1861–64, Albert and Shirley Small Special Collections Library, University of Virginia, Charlottesville; JEJ, *Narrative of Military Operations,* 66–67.

18. Maury, *Recollections of a Virginian,* 144–45; Symonds, *Joseph E. Johnston,* 126; June I. Gow, "Military Administration in the Confederate Army of Tennessee," *Journal of Southern History* 40 (1974): 195–96; Douglas Southall Freeman, *Lee's Lieutenants: A Study in Command* (3 vols. New York, 1942–44), 1: 112.

19. Perry, "Davis and Johnston," 97–101; JEJ, *Narrative of Military Operations,* 70–72; Symonds, *Joseph E. Johnston,* 126–27; William J. Cooper, Jr. *Jefferson Davis, American* (New York, 2000), 363–64; William C. Davis, *The Cause Lost: Myths and Realities of the Confederacy* (Lawrence, Kan., 1996), 21–22; Richard M. McMurry, "'The Enemy at Richmond': Joseph E. Johnston and the Confederate Government," *CWH* 27 (1981): 6–7.

20. JEJ, *Narrative of Military Operations,* 72–73; Perry, "Davis and Johnston," 101; Symonds, *Joseph E. Johnston,* 127–29; Glatthaar, *Partners in Command,* 104–05; Chesnut, *Mary Chesnut's Civil War,* 608.

21. OR, IV, 1: 611; Freeman, *Lee's Lieutenants,* 1: 114–15; Rembert W. Patrick, *Jefferson Davis and His Cabinet* (Baton Rouge, La., 1961), 35–36.

22. Chesnut, *Mary Chesnut's Civil War,* 136; Symonds, *Joseph E. Johnston,* 129.

23. JEJ, *Narrative of Military Operations*, 73; OR, I, 5: 881–82; Robert Douthat Meade, "The Relations Between Judah P. Benjamin and Jefferson Davis: Some New Light on the Working of the Confederate Machine," *Journal of Southern History* 6 (1939): 472–73; Steven E. Woodworth, *Davis and Lee at War* (Lawrence, Kan., 1995), 52.

24. Symonds, *Joseph E. Johnston*, 132–35; OR, I, 5: 892–94, 987, 993–94, 1011–12.

25. JEJ to Judah P. Benjamin, Dec. 27, 1861, Confederate Military Leaders Collection, MoC; Symonds, *Joseph E. Johnston*, 135; OR, I, 5: 993–94, 1011–12, 1015–16, 1020–21, 1028, 1035; Freeman, *Lee's Lieutenants*, 1: 118–20.

26. Symonds, *Joseph E. Johnston*, 135–36; OR, I, 5: 1016, 1036–37, 1045, 1057–59, 1086–87, 1089; Steven H. Newton, *Joseph E. Johnston and the Defense of Richmond* (Lawrence, Kan., 1998), 21–24.

27. JEJ, *Narrative of Military Operations*, 87; Robertson, *Stonewall Jackson*, 311–13.

28. Robertson, *Stonewall Jackson*, 315–21; Patrick, *Davis and His Cabinet*, 168–70; Glatthaar, *Partners in Command*, 109–10.

29. JEJ, *Narrative of Military Operations*, 88–90; OR, I, 5: 1053, 1059–60.

30. Newton, *Johnston and the Defense of Richmond*, 37–38; Robert Douthat Meade, *Judah P. Benjamin, Confederate Statesman* (New York, 1943), 235; Glatthaar, *Partners in Command*, 111.

Nine:

1. WTS, *Memoirs*, 1: 193–94; Kelly, "Holding Kentucky for the Union," 373–78; WTS to J. Mora Gross, Sept. 9, 1861, WTS MSS, GLC; WTS to John Sherman, Sept. 9, 1861, WTS MSS, LC.

2. WTS, *Memoirs*, 1: 194–96; WTS to EES, Sept. 18, 1861, SFMSS, UNDL.

3. WTS, *Memoirs*, 1: 197; Kelly, "Holding Kentucky for the Union," 378–79; WTS to Thomas Ewing, Sept. 15, 1861, Thomas Ewing and Family MSS, LC.

4. WTS, *Memoirs*, 1: 197–98.

5. Ibid., 198–99; Merrill, *William Tecumseh Sherman*, 174; OR, I, 4: 296–97.

6. Fellman, *Citizen Sherman*, 92–93.

7. WTS, *Memoirs*, 1: 200–202.

8. Ibid., 202–03; Fellman, *Citizen Sherman*, 93–94; Marszalek, *Sherman*, 161–62.

9. WTS, *Memoirs*, 1: 204; Marszalek, *Sherman*, 162.

10. WTS, *Memoirs*, 1: 205; WTS to EES, Oct. 23, Nov. 1, 1861; both, SFMSS, UNDL; WTS to John Sherman, Oct. 26, 1861, WTS MSS, LC; "Recollections of Sherman," *Harper's New Monthly Magazine* 30 (1865): 641, 644.

11. Merrill, *William Tecumseh Sherman*, 177–79; Marszalek, *Sherman*, 162; EES to John Sherman, Nov. 10, 1861, WTS MSS, LC.

12. WTS, *Memoirs*, 1: 214–15; WTS to Robert Anderson, Nov. 21, 1861, Anderson MSS, LC; WTS to John Sherman, Nov. 21, 1861, WTS MSS, LC.

13. WTS, *Memoirs*, 1: 215; Fellman, *Citizen Sherman*, 99–100.

14. WTS, *Memoirs*, 1: 215.

15. Ibid., 215–16.

16. Ibid., 216.

17. JEJ, *Narrative of Military Operations*, 75–77, 83–84; Symonds, *Joseph E. Johnston*, 30–31; L. Van Loan Naisawald, "The Battle of Dranesville," *CWTI* 4 (May 1965): 5–10; Williams, *P. G. T. Beauregard*, 100–101; OR, I, 5: 885–86; Davis, *Rise and Fall of the Confederate Government*, 1: 449–52.

18. Roman, *Military Operations of Beauregard*, 1: 210–14; James, "Johnston, Storm Center of the Confederate Army," 350–51.

19. Symonds, *Joseph E. Johnston*, 141–43.

20. Ibid., 143, 145; JEJ, *Narrative of Military Operations*, 96–97; OR, I, 5: 1079; Newton, *Johnston and the Defense of Richmond*, 34–38; Stephen W. Sears, *To the Gates of Richmond: The Peninsula Campaign* (New York, 1992), 12–13.

21. JEJ, *Narrative of Military Operations*, 97; Symonds, *Joseph E. Johnston*, 145, 404n.

22. JEJ, *Narrative of Military Operations*, 102.

23. Ibid., 102–04; OR, I, 5: 528–31, 533–35, 1090–92, 1094; 51, pt. 2: 488; Symonds, *Joseph E. Johnston*, 145–46; Cooper, *Jefferson Davis, American*, 174; Glatthaar, *Partners in Command*, 112–13; Newton, *Johnston and the Defense of Richmond*, 55–58.

24. JEJ, *Narrative of Military Operations*, 97–101, 104–06; JEJ, "Responsibilities of First Bull Run," 256–58; Newton, *Johnston and Defense of Richmond*, 52–55.

25. Marszalek, "General and Mrs. William T. Sherman," 144–46.

26. Ibid., 153–56; Marszalek, *Sherman*, 403–04, 406–07, 413–14, 416–21, 492.

27. Fellman, *Citizen Sherman*, 49–50.

28. WTS, *Memoirs*, 1: 216; Fellman, *Citizen Sherman*, 100–01; Marszalek, *Sherman*, 164–65; Whitelaw Reid, *A Radical View: The "Agate" Dispatches of Whitelaw Reid, 1861–1865*, ed. by James G. Smart (2 vols. Memphis, Tenn., 1976), 1: 79–81.

29. Fellman, *Citizen Sherman*, 101; Merrill, *William Tecumseh Sherman*, 185; EES to John Sherman, Dec. 10, 12, 17, 1862; all, WTS MSS, LC.

30. John Sherman to EES, Dec. 14, 1861; WTS to EES, ca. Dec. 18, 1861; both, SFMSS, UNDL; WTS to John Sherman, Dec. 21, 1861, WTS MSS, LC; OR, I, 8: 819; Fellman, *Citizen Sherman*, 102–03; Merrill, *William Tecumseh Sherman*, 185–86.

31. WTS to Philemon Ewing, Jan. 20, 1862, WTS MSS, GLC; WTS, *Sherman at War*, 45–46.

32. WTS to Thomas Ewing, Dec. 21, 1861, Thomas Ewing and Family MSS, LC; EES to Abraham Lincoln, Jan. 10, 1862; WTS to EES, Jan. 16, 1862; EES to WTS, Jan. 29, 1862; all, SFMSS, UNDL; Fellman, *Citizen Sherman*, 102–03.

33. WTS, *Memoirs*, 1: 218–19; Fellman, *Citizen Sherman*, 104–05; Merrill, *William Tecumseh Sherman*, 191–92; EES to WTS, Jan. 29, 1862, SFMSS, UNDL.

34. WTS, *Memoirs*, 1: 219–20.

Ten:

1. WTS, *Memoirs*, 1: 220; Ulysses S. Grant, *Personal Memoirs of U. S. Grant*, ed. by E. B. Long (New York, 2001) 146.

2. Grant, *Memoirs*, 147; OR, I, 7: 575–77.

3. OR, I, 7: 120–30, 159–67, 170–82, 625; ORN, I, 22: 537–39, 547, 584–86, 590–91, 598; Grant, *Memoirs*, 148–57.

4. WTS, *Memoirs*, 1: 221; WTS to EES, Feb. 17, 1862, SFMSS, UNDL; WTS, *Sherman at War*, 47–48.

5. WTS, *Memoirs*, 1: 221.

6. Ulysses S. Grant, *The Papers of Ulysses S. Grant*, ed. by John Y. Simon et al. (28 vols. to date. Carbondale, Ill., 1967–), 5: 215–16; Marszalek, "'A Full Share of All the Credit'," 5–9.

7. OR, I, 7: 638; WTS, *Memoirs*, 1: 224–25.

8. WTS, *Memoirs*, 1: 225–26; WTS to EES, Mar. 12, Apr. 3, 1862; both, SFMSS, UNDL; WTS, *Sherman at War*, 47–48; OR, I, 10, pt. 1: 252.

9. WTS, *Memoirs*, 1: 227.

10. Ibid., 227–28; OR, I, 10, pt. 2: 31; WTS to EES, Mar. 17–18, 1862, SFMSS, UNDL; Wiley Sword, *Shiloh: Bloody April* (New York, 1974), 3–11.

11. WTS, *Memoirs*, 1: 228–29, 233; Wiley Sword, "The Battle of Shiloh," *CWTI* 17 (May 1978): 8.

12. OR, I, 8: 605; Sword, *Shiloh*, 21–22.

13. WTS, *Memoirs*, 1: 229; Larry J. Daniel, *Shiloh, The Battle That Changed the Civil War* (New York, 1997), 132.

14. Charles Shiels Wainwright, *A Diary of Battle: The Personal Journals of Colonel Charles S. Wainwright, 1861–1865*, ed. by Allan Nevins (New York, 1962), 23–24; JEJ, *Narrative of Military Operations*, 108; Symonds, *Joseph E. Johnston*, 146–47.

15. Davis, *Rise and Fall of the Confederate Government*, 1: 465–66; Freeman, *R. E. Lee*, 2: 4–7.

16. Symonds, *Joseph E. Johnston*, 147–48; Sears, *To the Gates of Richmond*, 21–24, 27–29.

17. JEJ, *Narrative of Military Operations*, 110; OR, I, 11, pt. 3: 408–09.

18. OR, I, 11, pt. 1: 8–17; JEJ, *Narrative of Military Operations*, 108–12; Sears, *To the Gates of Richmond*, 35–39, 46–47.

19. JEJ, *Narrative of Military Operations*, 112–15; JEJ, "Manassas to Seven Pines," *B&L* 2: 203–04; Freeman, *R. E. Lee*, 2: 21–23; Freeman, *Lee's Lieutenants*, 1: 148–51; Davis, *Rise and Fall of the Confederate Government*, 2: 70–71; Cooper, *Jefferson Davis, American*, 375.

20. JEJ, *Narrative of Military Operations*, 115–16.

21. Ibid., 117; Sears, *To the Gates of Richmond*, 40–41, 57.

22. JEJ, *Narrative of Military Operations*, 117–18.

23. Ibid., 118–19; OR, I, 11, pt. 3: 461, 464, 469–71, 476–78, 485–86.

24. JEJ, *Narrative of Military Operations*, 118–19; Symonds, *Joseph E. Johnston*, 151–55; F. Y. Dabney, "Anecdotes of the Peninsular Campaign. I.—General Johnston to the Rescue," *B&L* 2: 275–76.

25. OR, I, 7: 683; 10, pt. 2: 15, 21, 30, 32, 36.

26. WTS, *Memoirs*, 1: 229.

27. Ibid., 229–30; 234–35; OR, I, 10, pt. 2: 90, 93–94; Sword, *Shiloh*, 121–29.

28. OR, I, 10, pt. 1: 248–49; WTS to EES, Apr. 11, 1862, SFMSS, UNDL; Sword, *Shiloh*, 173–76; Daniel, *Shiloh*, 158–61.

29. OR, I, 10, pt. 1: 249.

30. Ibid.; Daniel, *Shiloh*, 202–14.

31. OR, I, 10, pt. 1: 249–50; WTS to Thomas Ewing, May 3, 1862, WTS MSS, GLC; Sword, *Shiloh*, 176–89; Daniel, *Shiloh*, 170–72; Reid, *Radical View*, 1: 133–35.

32. OR, I, 10, pt. 1: 250; Sword, *Shiloh*, 189; Daniel, *Shiloh*, 171–73; Marszalek, "'A Full Share of All the Credit',"12

33. Grant, *Memoirs*, 180–81.

34. OR, I, 10, pt. 1: 250; Daniel, *Shiloh*, 188–91, 238–41.

35. OR, I, 10, pt. 1: 250.

36. Daniel, *Shiloh*, 226–28, 243–44, 250–53.

37. OR, I, 10, pt. 1: 251–54; WTS to EES, Apr. 11, 1862, SFMSS, UNDL; WTS to Philemon Ewing, May 16, 1862, Thomas Ewing and Family MSS, LC; Daniel, *Shiloh*, 265–92; "Recollections of Sherman," 645.

Eleven:

1. JEJ, *Narrative of Military Operations*, 119–20; Sears, *To the Gates of Richmond*, 65–68.

2. JEJ, *Narrative of Military Operations*, 120–25; OR, I, 11, pt. 1: 448–70, 491–95, 533–48, 564–74; Alexander, *Fighting for the Confederacy*, 81–82; Sears, *To the Gates of Richmond*, 68–82.

3. OR, I, 11, pt. 1: 614–16, 626–33; Sears, *To the Gates of Richmond*, 84–86.

4. JEJ, *Narrative of Military Operations*, 126–28.

5. Ibid., 130–31; OR, I, 11, pt. 1: 25–30.

6. JEJ, *Narrative of Military Operations*, 128–32; OR, I, 11, pt. 1: 30–33; pt. 3: 194.

7. JEJ, *Narrative of Military Operations*, 132.

8. Ibid., 132–33.

9. Sears, *To the Gates of Richmond*, 117–20; Glatthaar, *Partners in Command*, 116; Charles F. Bryan, Jr., "Stalemate at Seven Pines," *CWTI* 12 (Aug. 1973): 8, 10.

10. JEJ, *Narrative of Military Operations*, 133–35; OR, I, 11, pt. 1: 933–34, 939–40, 943–44, 989–91; Sears, *To the Gates of Richmond*, 121–28; Joseph P. Cullen, *The Peninsula Campaign, 1862: McClellan & Lee Struggle for Richmond* (Harrisburg, Pa., 1973), 54–55; Bryan, "Stalemate at Seven Pines," 10–11, 39–43; James Longstreet, *From Manassas to Appomattox: Memoirs of the Civil War in America* (Philadelphia, 1896), 89–97; Jeffry D. Wert, *General James Longstreet, the Confederacy's Most Controversial Soldier: A Biography* (New York, 1993), 115–21.

11. Sears, *To the Gates of Richmond*, 128–38; Bryan, "Stalemate at Seven Pines," 43–47; Longstreet, *From Manassas to Appomattox*, 97–100; Wert, *General James Longstreet*, 121–24.

12. JEJ, *Narrative of Military Operations*, 136–38; OR, I, 11, pt. 1: 935–42; Symonds, *Joseph E. Johnston*, 171–74; Sears, *To the Gates of Richmond*, 150; Drury L. Armistead, "The Battle in Which General Johnston Was Wounded," *SHSP* 18 (1890–91): 187.

13. JEJ, *Narrative of Military Operations*, 138–39; OR, I, 11, pt. 1: 934; Johnson, *Memoir of Joseph E. Johnston*, 89–90; Armistead, "Battle in Which General Johnston Was Wounded," 187–88.

14. WTS, *Memoirs*, 1: 243–44; Sword, *Shiloh*, 424–25; Daniel, *Shiloh*, 296–97.

15. Daniel, *Shiloh*, 304–09; WTS, *Memoirs*, 1: 244; WTS, *Home Letters of General Sherman*, 224–25.

16. WTS, *Memoirs*, 1: 246.

17. Marszalek, *Sherman's Other War*, 79; WTS to EES, Apr. 11, 14, 1862; both, SFMSS, UNDL.

18. Marszalek, *Sherman's Other War*, 77–79; Reid, *Radical View*, 1: 136.

19. WTS to EES, Apr. 14, 1862; John Sherman to WTS, May 19, 1862, WTS MSS, LC.

20. OR, I, 10, pt. 1: 98; Grant, *Papers of Ulysses S. Grant*, 5: 32–36; Heitman, *Historical Register and Dictionary*, 1: 882.

21. WTS, *Memoirs*, 1: 249.

22. OR, I, 10, pt. 2: 99; Marszalek, *Commander of All Lincoln's Armies*, 122–23.

23. Grant, *Memoirs*, 193; Grant, *Papers of Ulysses S. Grant*, 5: 114–15; OR, I, 10, pt. 2: 182–83.

24. OR, I, 10, pt. 1: 676, 683; pt. 2: 286, 288; Marszalek, *Commander of All Lincoln's Armies*, 123–25.

25. OR, I, 10, pt. 2: 288; WTS, *Memoirs*, 1: 254.

26. WTS to Thomas Ewing, May 3, 1862, WTS MSS, GLC; WTS, *Memoirs*, 1: 254–55.

27. WTS, *Memoirs*, 1: 255.

28. Ibid.

29. T. Harry Williams, *McClellan, Sherman, and Grant* (New Brunswick, N.J., 1962), 46.

30. JEJ, *Narrative of Military Operations*, 139; Cooper, *Jefferson Davis, American*, 381.

31. Richard M. Lee, *General Lee's City: An Illustrated Guide to the Historic Sites of Confederate Richmond* (McLean, Va., 1987), 89–91.

32. Hughes, *General Johnston*, 153–54; Maury, *Recollections of a Virginian*, 151.

33. Sears, *To the Gates of Richmond*, 146–307.

34. Mrs. D. Giraud Wright, *A Southern Girl in '61: The War-time Memories of a Confederate Senator's Daughter* (New York, 1905), 80; Alvy T. King, *Louis T. Wigfall, Southern Fire-eater* (Baton Rouge, La., 1970), 133–34; Govan and Livingood, *Different Valor*, 161–62; Thomas Lawrence Connelly and Archer Jones, *The Politics of Command: Factions and Ideas in Confederate Strategy* (Baton Rouge, La., 1973), 120–21.

35. Symonds, *Joseph E. Johnston*, 175–77.

36. Ibid., 178–79.

37. OR, I, 17, pt. 2: 90; Marszalek, *Commander of All Lincoln's Armies*, 128.

38. Grant, *Memoirs*, 200–02; OR, I, 17, pt. 2: 99, 110–11; WTS, *Memoirs*, 1: 259.

39. WTS, *Memoirs*, 1: 265–66; Smalley, "General Sherman," 460–61.

40. WTS, *Memoirs*, 1: 265–78; WTS, *Sherman's Civil War: Selected Correspondence of William T. Sherman, 1860–1865*, ed. by Brooks D. Simpson and Jean V. Berlin (Chapel Hill, N.C., 1999), 258–59; Fellman, *Citizen Sherman*, 135–38; Mark A. Smith, "Sherman's Unexpected Companions: Marching through Georgia with Jomini and Clausewitz," *Georgia Historical Quarterly* 81 (1997): 1–2.

41. Noel C. Fisher, "'Prepare Them for My Coming': General William T. Sherman, Total War, and Pacification in West Tennessee," *Tennessee Historical Quarterly* 51 (1992): 75–79; OR, I, 17, pt. 2: 236.

42. OR, I, 17, pt. 1: 144–45; pt. 2: 235–36, 261–62; Mark Grimsley, *The Hard Hand of War: Union Military Policy Toward Southern Civilians, 1861–1865* (New York, 1995), 114–19.

43. Grimsley, *Hard Hand of War*, 117.

44. Fisher, "'Prepare Them for My Coming'," 79–85; OR, I, 17, pt. 2: 259–62; III, 2: 349; WTS, *Sherman's Civil War*, 253–64.

45. Fellman, *Citizen Sherman*, 142–47; Grimsley, *Hard Hand of War*, 170–74.

Twelve:

1. OR, I, 17, pt. 2: 260–61; WTS to John Sherman, Aug. 26, 1862, WTS MSS, LC.

2. OR, I, 17, pt. 2: 260–61.

3. Bruce Catton, *Grant Moves South* (Boston, 1960), 324–26.

4. WTS, *Memoirs*, 1: 260–62; Grant, *Memoirs*, 210–14; OR, I, 17, pt. 1: 64–75, 117–24; Cresap, *Appomattox Commander*, 83–87.

5. WTS, *Memoirs*, 1: 262–64; Grant, *Memoirs*, 215–19; OR, I, 17, pt. 1: 154–76, 375–89.

6. Grant, *Memoirs*, 219–22.

7. Ibid., 222; OR, I, 17, pt. 1: 469; pt. 2: 282; Richard L. Kiper, *Major General John Alexander McClernand, Politician in Uniform* (Kent, Ohio, 1999), 129–31; Catton, *Grant Moves South*, 324–26, 522n.

8. OR, I, 17, pt. 2: 347–48; WTS, *Memoirs*, 1: 278–80.

9. WTS, *Memoirs*, 1: 280–81; WTS to John Sherman, Nov. 24, 1862, WTS MSS, LC.

10. WTS, *Memoirs*, 1: 281; WTS to John Sherman, Dec. 6, 1862, WTS MSS, LC; Michael B. Ballard, *Vicksburg: The Campaign That Opened the Mississippi* (Chapel Hill, N.C., 2004), 105–06.

11. WTS, *Memoirs*, 1: 281–89; Grant, *Memoirs*, 222–25; WTS to EES, Dec. 14, 1862, SFMSS, UNDL.

12. WTS, *Memoirs*, 1; 282.

13. Ibid., 286–89; WTS to John Sherman, Dec. 15, 1862, WTS MSS, LC.

14. Brian Steel Wills, *A Battle from the Start: The Life of Nathan Bedford Forrest* (New York, 1992), 87–96.

15. Ballard, *Vicksburg*, 121–28; Edward G. Longacre, *Mounted Raids of the Civil War* (South Brunswick, N.J., 1975), 46–65.

16. Wright, *Southern Girl in '61*, 90–91; JEJ, "Jefferson Davis and the Mississippi Campaign," *B&L* 3: 473; Robert E. Lee, *Lee's Dispatches: Unpublished Letters of General Robert E. Lee, C.S.A., to Jefferson Davis and the War Department of the Confederate States of America, 1861–65*, ed. by Douglas Southall Freeman and Grady McWhiney (New York, 1957), 48; Thomas Lawrence Connelly, *Army of the Heartland: The Army of Tennessee, 1861–1862* (Baton Rouge, La., 1967), 203–80.

17. Herman Hattaway and Archer Jones, *How the North Won: A Military History of the Civil War* (Urbana, Ill., 1983), 220–30.

18. Ibid., 232–34, 240–44.

19. JEJ, *Narrative of Military Operations*, 147–48; E. J. Harvie, "Gen. Joseph E. Johnston," *CV* 18 (1910): 521; Richard Taylor, *Destruction and Reconstruction: Personal Experiences of the Late War*, ed. by Charles P. Roland (Waltham, Mass., 1968), 206.

20. JEJ, *Narrative of Military Operations*, 148–50, 231–32; Symonds, *Joseph E. Johnston*, 187–91; Archer Jones, *Confederate Strategy from Shiloh to Vicksburg* (Baton Rouge, La., 1961), 82–83, 104–10; Connelly and Jones, *Politics of Command*, 112–13, 187; Glatthaar, *Partners in Command*, 119–22.

21. JEJ, *Narrative of Military Operations*, 148–49; McMurry, "Enemy at Richmond," 9.

22. T. C. DeLeon, *Belles, Beaux and Brains of the 60's* (New York, 1907), 401–02.

23. JEJ, *Narrative of Military Operations*, 150–51; Jones, *Confederate Strategy from Shiloh to Vicksburg*, 114.

24. JEJ, *Narrative of Military Operations*, 151–52; Wright, *Southern Girl in '61*, 106; Jones, *Confederate Strategy from Shiloh to Vicksburg*, 125–26; JEJ, Telegram Book of Atlanta Campaign Dispatches and Postwar Comments on Sherman's *Memoirs*, JEJ MSS, W&ML.

25. WTS, *Memoirs*, 1: 289–90; OR, I, 17, pt. 1: 605–07, 616, 620–22.

26. WTS, *Memoirs*, 1: 290–91; OR, I, 17, pt. 1: 607; Edwin C. Bearss, *The Vicksburg Campaign* (3 vols. Dayton, Ohio, 1985–86), 1: 175–91; D. Alexander Brown, "Battle at Chickasaw Bluffs," *CWTI* 9 (July 1970): 4–9; Ballard, *Vicksburg*, 133–40.

27. WTS, *Memoirs*, 1: 291.

28. George W. Morgan, "The Assault on Chickasaw Bluffs," *B&L* 3: 467–68; OR, I, 17, pt. 1: 608, 638–39; Ballard, *Vicksburg*, 141.

29. WTS, *Memoirs*, 1: 291–92, 295; OR, I, 17, pt. 1: 608, 655–56; Bearss, *Vicksburg Campaign*, 1: 194–202; Ballard, *Vicksburg*, 141–44; William Ernest Smith, *The Francis Preston Blair Family in Politics* (2 vols. New York, 1933), 2: 148–50.

30. Bearss, *Vicksburg Campaign*, 1: 201–03; Brown, "Battle at Chickasaw Bluffs," 46.

31. WTS, *Memoirs*, 1: 292–93; OR, I, 17, pt. 1: 609–10; Bearss, *Vicksburg Campaign*, 1: 213–21; Ballard, *Vicksburg*, 145–47; Glatthaar, *Partners in Command*, 169.

32. WTS, *Memoirs*, 1: 293, 295; WTS to John Sherman, Jan. 6, 1863, WTS MSS, LC.

33. WTS, *Memoirs*, 1: 293–94, 296; OR, I, 17, pt. 1: 612; pt. 2: 534–35.

34. WTS, *Memoirs*, 1: 296; Bearss, *Vicksburg Campaign*, 1: 349–55; Edwin C. Bearss, "The Battle of the Post of Arkansas," *Arkansas Historical Quarterly* 18 (1959): 237–39.

35. WIS, *Memoirs*, 1: 296–97; Kiper, *John Alexander McClernand*, 158–59; Robert S. Huffstot, "Post of Arkansas," *CWTI* 7 (Jan. 1969): 11–13; Glatthaar, *Partners in Command*, 170.

36. WTS, *Memoirs*, 1: 297–301; OR, I, 17, pt. 1: 702–08, 754–57, 780–82; pt. 2: 570–71; Bearss, *Vicksburg Campaign*, 1: 355–405; Bearss, "Battle of Post of Arkansas," 239–74; Huffstot, "Post of Arkansas," 13–18; Ballard, *Vicksburg*, 149–53; WTS to EES, Jan. 12, 16, 1863; both, SFMSS, UNDL; WTS to Thomas Ewing, Jan. 16, 1863, WTS MSS, USAMHI; WTS to John Sherman, Jan. 17, 1863, WTS MSS, LC.

37. WTS, *Memoirs*, 1: 301; WTS to Thomas Ewing, Jan. 16, 1863, WTS MSS, USAMHI.

38. Grant, *Memoirs*, 271–76; OR, I, 17, pt. 2: 553–54, 559–62, 564, 566–68, 570–71.

39. Grant, *Memoirs*, 276–77; Kiper, *John Alexander McClernand*, 181–82.

40. Thomas Lawrence Connelly, *Autumn of Glory: The Army of Tennessee, 1862–1865* (Baton Rouge, La., 1971), 44–68; Stanley F. Horn, *The Army of Tennessee* (Norman, Okla., 1953), 190–210; Grady McWhiney, *Braxton Bragg and Confederate Defeat: Volume I, Field Command* (New York, 1969), 346–73.

41. Connelly, *Autumn of Glory*, 69–76; Horn, *Army of Tennessee*, 222–26; McWhiney, *Braxton Bragg*, 374–79.

42. JEJ, *Narrative of Military Operations*, 161–62, 499–500; Connelly, *Autumn of Glory*, 77–78.

43. JEJ, *Narrative of Military Operations*, 151–53; JEJ, "Jefferson Davis and the Mississippi Campaign," 474.

44. JEJ, *Narrative of Military Operations*, 153–54.

45. Ibid., 154–55.

46. Ibid., 161–62; McWhiney, *Braxton Bragg*, 379.

47. JEJ to Jefferson Davis, Feb. 3, 1863, JEJ MSS, DUL.

48. JEJ, *Narrative of Military Operations*, 162; Symonds, *Joseph E. Johnston*, 196–97; Connelly, *Autumn of Glory*, 77–80; Cooper, *Jefferson Davis, American*, 423; McWhiney, *Braxton Bragg*, 379–80.

Thirteen:

1. Marszalek, *Sherman's Other War*, 119–23; Royster, *Destructive War*, 112–13.

2. Marszalek, *Sherman's Other War*, 123–31; WTS to John Sherman, Jan. 31, Feb. 4, 12, 18, 1863; all, WTS MSS, LC; WTS to David D. Porter, Feb. 3, 1863, WTS MSS, LC; WTS to Thomas Ewing, Feb. 6, 17, 1863, both, WTS MSS, USAMHI; WTS to EES, Feb. 6, 26, 1863; both, SFMSS, UNDL; WTS to Stephen A. Hurlbut, Mar. 13, 1863, WTS MSS, GLC; OR, I, 17, pt. 1: 892–93; pt. 2: 587–90; WTS, *Sherman's Civil War*, 386; WTS, *Sherman at War*, 390–92.

3. Marszalek, *Sherman's Other War*, 132–49.

4. WTS, *Memoirs*, 1: 314–17; Grant, *Memoirs*, 231; Marszalek, "'A Full Share of All the Credit'," 17–18.

5. WTS, *Memoirs*, 1: 305.

6. Grant, *Memoirs*, 231–35; Bearss, *Vicksburg Campaign*, 1: 431–591; Ballard, *Vicksburg*, 157–59, 171–90.

7. WTS, *Memoirs*, 1: 306–09; OR, I, 24, pt. 1: 432–33; ORN, I, 24: 474–80; Richard S. West, Jr., "Gunboats in the Swamps: The Yazoo Pass Expedition," *CWH* 9 (1963): 157–66.

8. WTS, *Memoirs*, 1: 309.

9. Ibid., 309–10.

10. Ibid., 310; OR, I, 24, pt. 1: 433–35; Glatthaar, *Partners in Command*, 172.

11. JEJ, *Narrative of Military Operations*, 162; Wright, *Southern Girl in '61*, 123–35.

12. R. G. H. Kean, *Inside the Confederate Government: The Diary of Robert Garlick Hill Kean, Head of the Bureau of War*, ed. by Edward Younger (New York, 1957), 46, 50.

13. JEJ, *Narrative of Military Operations*, 163–64; Symonds, *Joseph E. Johnston*, 200–01; McWhiney, *Braxton Bragg*, 384–88.

14. Symonds, *Joseph E. Johnston*, 199; Glatthaar, *Partners in Command*, 122.

15. JEJ, *Narrative of Military Operations*, 164.

16. Ibid., 165–68; Longacre, *Mounted Raids of the Civil War*, 66–122.

17. JEJ, *Narrative of Military Operations*, 168–69.

18. Ibid., 170–71.

19. Ibid., 171–72; Ballard, *Vicksburg*, 222–50.

20. JEJ, *Narrative of Military Operations*, 172–76; Ballard, *Vicksburg*, 251–71; OR, I, 24, pt. 1: 239; pt. 3: 859; Davis, *Rise and Fall of the Confederate Government*, 2: 404–05.

21. JEJ, *Narrative of Military Operations*, 176–78, 506; OR, I, 24, pt. 1: 239–40.

22. WTS, *Memoirs*, 1: 315–17; OR, I, 24, pt. 3: 179–80.

23. WTS, *Memoirs*, 1: 319; OR, I, 24, pt. 1: 752; ORN, I, 24: 552–55; WTS to EES, May 2, 1863, SFMSS, UNDL; Edwin C. Bearss, "Sherman's Demonstration Against Snyder's Bluff," *Journal of Mississippi History* 27 (1965): 168–86.

24. WTS, *Memoirs*, 1: 319–21; OR, I, 24, pt. 1: 752–53; WTS to EES, May 9, 1863, SFMSS, UNDL.

25. WTS, *Memoirs*, 1: 321; OR, I, 24, pt. 1: 753–54; Force, *General Sherman*, 123–24.

26. WTS, *Memoirs*, 1: 321–22; OR, I, 24, pt. 1: 754.

27. JEJ, *Narrative of Military Operations*, 178; OR, I, 24, pt. 1: 240.

28. JEJ, *Narrative of Military Operations*, 178–80; OR, I, 24, pt. 1: 240–41; pt. 3: 876–77; Larry J. Daniel, "Bruinsburg: Missed Opportunity or Postwar Rhetoric?" *CWH* 32 (1986): 265.

29. JEJ, *Narrative of Military Operations*, 181; Ballard, *Vicksburg*, 282–85.

30. OR, I, 24, pt. 1: 263–66; Ballard, *Vicksburg*, 285–308.

31. JEJ, *Narrative of Military Operations*, 184–85; OR, I, 24, pt. 1: 266–69; pt. 3: 887; Ballard, *Vicksburg*, 309–18.

32. JEJ, *Narrative of Military Operations*, 185–87; OR, I, 24, pt. 1: 241.

33. JEJ, *Narrative of Military Operations*, 187–88; OR, I, 24, pt. 1: 241–42; pt. 3: 888–90; JEJ, "Jefferson Davis and the Mississippi Campaign," 480.

34. WTS, *Memoirs*, 1: 323–24.

35. Grant, *Memoirs*, 275–77.

36. WTS, *Memoirs*, 1: 323–25; OR, I, 24, pt. 1: 54; Warner, *Generals in Blue*, 145–47; Grant, *Memoirs*, 277; WTS to EES, May 19, 1863, SFMSS, UNDL.

37. OR, I, 24, pt. 2: 257–59; Smith, *Francis Preston Blair Family*, 2: 159.

38. WTS, *Memoirs*, 1: 325–26; OR, I, 24, pt. 1: 55.

39. WTS, *Memoirs*, 1: 327–28; OR, I, 24, pt. 1: 55–56.

40. Hattaway and Jones, *How the North Won*, 378–84; OR, I, 24, pt. 1: 157–86; James Harrison Wilson, *Under the Old Flag: Recollections of Military Operations in the War for the Union, the Spanish War, the Boxer Rebellion, etc.* (2 vols. New York, 1912), 1: 182–86; Kiper, *John Alexander McClernand*, 267–75, 282, 301, 305; WTS to John Sherman, May 29, 1863, WTS MSS, LC.

Fourteen:

1. JEJ, *Narrative of Military Operations*, 189–91, 196–97, 507; OR, I, 24, pt. 1: 242–43; pt. 3: 896, 903, 916, 929; JEJ, "Jefferson Davis and the Mississippi Campaign," 480; William Whann Mackall, *A Son's Recollections of His Father* (New York, 1930), 187–88.

2. JEJ, *Narrative of Military Operations*, 194; OR, I, 24, pt. 1: 244; pt. 3: 963.

3. JEJ, *Narrative of Military Operations*, 195, 197, 199; OR, I, 24, pt. 1: 243–44.

4. JEJ, *Narrative of Military Operations*, 197–98.

5. Ibid., 198–200, 508–12; OR, I, 24, pt. 1: 243.

6. JEJ, *Narrative of Military Operations*, 200–01, 514; John C. Pemberton, *Pemberton, Defender of Vicksburg* (Chapel Hill, N.C., 1942), 295–303.

7. Kean, *Inside the Confederate Government*, 76; Josiah Gorgas, *The Journals of Josiah Gorgas, 1857–1878*, ed. by Sarah Woolfolk Wiggins (Tuscaloosa, Ala., 1995), 69.

8. JEJ, *Narrative of Military Operations*, 196, 201–11; OR, I, 24, pt. 1: 244–46; Ballard, *Vicksburg*, 407–10; Lowell H. Harrison, "Jackson . . . Is a Ruined Town," *CWTI* 15 (Feb. 1977): 4–7, 45–47.

9. WTS, *Memoirs*, 1: 328, 331–33; WTS, General Orders No. —, July 5, 1863, WTS MSS, GLC; Ballard, *Vicksburg*, 406–07.

10. Ballard, *Vicksburg*, 405–07; WTS, *Memoirs*, 1: 335–42.

11. Ballard, *Vicksburg*, 410; OR, I, 24, pt. 3: 531–32.

12. Hattaway and Jones, *How the North Won*, 397–409.

13. Heitman, *Historical Register and Dictionary*, 1: 681, 882; WTS, *Memoirs*, 1: 344–45.

14. WTS, *Memoirs*, 1: 346–47; Hattaway and Jones, *How the North Won*, 446–54.

15. Hattaway and Jones, *How the North Won*, 454–58.

16. WTS, *Memoirs*, 1: 348; Marszalek, *Sherman*, 237–38; McAllister, *Ellen Ewing*, 266–69.

17. WTS, *Memoirs*, 1: 349; WTS to C. C. Smith, Oct. 4, 1863, SFMSS, UNDL.

18. WTS, *Memoirs*, 1: 349; WTS to EES, Oct. 6, 1863, SFMSS, UNDL.

19. WTS, *Memoirs*, 1: 350–53; Marszalek, *Sherman*, 238–39.

20. WTS, *Memoirs*, 1: 357; Marszalek, *Sherman*, 239–40; OR, I, 31, pt. 1: 16–32; WTS to EES, Nov. 17, 1863, SFMSS, UNDL.

21. Grant, *Memoirs*, 308–13; WTS, *Memoirs*, 1: 354.

22. WTS, *Memoirs*, 1: 361; Howard, *Autobiography*, 1: 473–74.

23. WTS, "The Grand Strategy of the Last Year of the War," *B&L* 4: 250; Howard, *Autobiography*, 1: 474.

24. Howard, *Autobiography*, 1: 474; Longacre, *Mounted Raids of the Civil War*, 202–24.

25. Connelly, *Autumn of Glory*, 245–46; Horn, *Army of Tennessee*, 283.

26. Connelly, *Autumn of Glory*, 261–65; Horn, *Army of Tennessee*, 294–95; Longstreet, *From Manassas to Appomattox*, 481–82; Wert, *General James Longstreet*, 338–41.

27. JEJ, *Narrative of Military Operations*, 211; Ballard, *Vicksburg*, 409–10; Gorgas, *Journals of Josiah Gorgas*, 74.

28. Kean, *Inside the Confederate Government*, 83.

29. JEJ, *Narrative of Military Operations*, 229; OR, I, 24, pt. 1: 202–07; McMurry, "Enemy at Richmond," 13; Mackall, *Son's Recollections of His Father*, 191; King, *Louis T. Wigfall*, 179.

30. Symonds, *Joseph E. Johnston*, 220; Chesnut, *Mary Chesnut's Civil War*, 482–83.

31. JEJ, *Narrative of Military Operations*, 230–52; OR, I, 24, pt. 1: 209–13; Symonds, *Joseph E. Johnston*, 221.

32. JEJ, *Narrative of Military Operations*, 214–29; OR, I, 24, pt. 1: 249–331; Symonds, *Joseph E. Johnston*, 221–22.

33. JEJ, *Narrative of Military Operations*, 253–54; Symonds, *Joseph E. Johnston*, 245; Connelly and Jones, *Politics of Command*, 135.

34. JEJ, *Narrative of Military Operations*, 255; Robert A. Toombs to JEJ, Aug. 21, 1863, JEJ MSS, W&ML; Symonds, *Joseph E. Johnston*, 224–25; Hughes, *General Johnston*, 208–09; King, *Louis T. Wigfall*, 180–81.

35. OR, I, 24, pt. 1: 248.

36. Grant, *Memoirs*, 313–18; OR, I, 31, pt. 1: 50–59, 77–78; pt. 2: 27–29.

37. OR, I, 31, pt. 2: 571–72; Peter Cozzens, *The Shipwreck of Their Hopes: The Battles for Chattanooga* (Urbana, Ill., 1994), 128–42; Larry J. Daniel, *Days of Glory: The Army of the Cumberland, 1861–1865* (Baton Rouge, La., 2004), 372–73; Steven E. Woodworth, *Nothing But Victory: The Army of the Tennessee, 1861–1865* (New York, 2005), 467; Cleaves, *Rock of Chickamauga*, 194–95.

38. OR, I, 31, pt. 2: 573–74; Cozzens, *Shipwreck of Their Hopes*, 149–58, 199–216, 241–43, 391–92; James Lee McDonough, *Chattanooga: A Death Grip on the Confederacy* (Knoxville, Tenn., 1984), 120–21; Woodworth, *Nothing But Victory*, 468–69.

39. OR, I, 31, pt. 2: 574–75; WTS, *Memoirs*, 1: 364; McDonough, *Chattanooga*, 143–60; Woodworth, *Nothing But Victory*, 470–77.

40. OR, I, 31, pt. 2: 575–76; Daniel, *Days of Glory*, 373–77; Woodworth, *Nothing But Victory*, 477–78; Cleaves, *Rock of Chickamauga*, 195–200.

Fifteen:

1. Connelly, *Autumn of Glory*, 277–78; Horn, *Army of Tennessee*, 305–06.

2. Nathaniel Cheairs Hughes Jr., *General William J. Hardee, Old Reliable* (Baton Rouge, La., 1965), 183–84; Connelly, *Autumn of Glory*, 281–82; King, *Louis T. Wigfall*, 183–84; Horn, *Army of Tennessee*, 306–07.

3. Wright, *Southern Girl in '61*, 155.

4. Mackall, *Son's Recollections of His Father*, 198.

5. JEJ, *Narrative of Military Operations*, 262–64.

6. Ibid., 265–69.

7. Connelly, *Autumn of Glory*, 289–93; Horn, *Army of Tennessee*, 308–12; JEJ to Beverly R. Johnston, Feb. 15, 1864, JEJ MSS, W&ML; Larry J. Daniel, *Soldiering in the Army of Tennessee: A Portrait of Life in a Confederate Army* (Chapel Hill, N.C., 1991), 56–61.

8. Daniel, *Soldiering in the Army of Tennessee*, 119–22; Mackall, *Son's Recollections of His Father*, 210.

9. Daniel, *Soldiering in the Army of Tennessee*, 132–33, 138–39; Christopher Losson, *Tennessee's Forgotten Warriors: Frank Cheatham and His Confederate Division* (Knoxville, Tenn., 1989), 133–35.

10. Daniel, *Soldiering in the Army of Tennessee*, 138–41; Horn, *Army of Tennessee*, 312–13; Mackall, *Son's Recollections of His Father*, 205; F. D. Stephenson, "Reminiscences of the Last Campaign of the Army of Tennessee, from May, 1864, to January, 1865: Paper No. 1," *SHSP* 12 (1884): 32–33; C. B. Denson, "William Henry Chase Whiting, Major-General C. S. Army: An Address . . .," *SHSP* 26 (1898): 158–59.

11. Connelly, *Autumn of Glory*, 318–21; Horn, *Army of Tennessee*, 313–14; Symonds, *Joseph E. Johnston*, 260–61.

12. Symonds, *Joseph E. Johnston*, 264; Richard M. McMurry, *John Bell Hood and the War for Southern Independence* (Lexington, Ky., 1982), 86–89; Richard M. McMurry, "The Mackall Journal and Its Antecedents," *CWH* 20 (1974): 323–24; Thomas Robson Hay, "The Davis-Hood-Johnston Controversy of 1864," *Mississippi Valley Historical Review* 11 (1924): 54–58, 81; Cooper, *Jefferson Davis, American*, 474; John P. Dyer, *The Gallant Hood* (Indianapolis, 1950), 231–32; Chesnut, *Mary Chesnut's Civil War*, 583.

13. Connelly, *Autumn of Glory*, 283–84.

14. Ibid., 295–97; Wert, *General James Longstreet*, 369–70.

15. OR, I, 38, pt. 3: 612–13; Connelly, *Autumn of Glory*, 298–304; McMurry, "Enemy at Richmond," 26–27; JEJ to John P. Nicholson, Dec. 7, 1875, JEJ MSS, GLC.

16. McMurry, "Enemy at Richmond," 27.

17. WTS, *Memoirs*, 1: 365–66; OR, I, 31, pt. 2: 577; Woodworth, *Nothing But Victory*, 478.

18. WTS, *Memoirs*, 366–68; OR, I, 31, pt. 2: 577–80; pt. 3: 459.

19. OR, I, 32, pt. 1: 173–75; Richard M. McMurry, "Sherman's Meridian Expedition," *CWTI* 14 (May 1975): 24, 26–27.

20. OR, I, 32, pt. 1: 175–76; WTS, *Memoirs*, 1: 390–95; McMurry, "Sherman's Meridian Expedition," 27–31; WTS to EES, Feb. 7, 1864, SFMSS, UNDL.

21. OR, I, 32, pt. 1: 176–77, 251–60; Wills, *Battle from the Start*, 158–68.

22. Grant, *Memoirs*, 358–59; WTS, *Memoirs*, 1: 399–400; Glatthaar, *Partners in Command*, 154.

23. OR, I, 32, pt. 3: 18, 49; Grant, *Memoirs*, 359.

24. Warner, *Generals in Blue*, 425–26; WTS, *Memoirs*, 2: 5–8; WTS to EES, Mar. 10, 12; both, SFMSS, UNDL; WTS to John Sherman, Apr. 5, 1864, WTS MSS, LC.

25. WTS, *Memoirs*, 2: 8–12, 398–400; Stephen Davis, *Atlanta Will Fall: Sherman, Joe Johnston, and the Yankee Heavy Battalions* (Wilmington, Del., 2001), 20–21; Jesse C. Burt, "Sherman, Railroad General," *CWH* 2 (1956): 45–54; Armin E. Mruck, "The Role of Railroads in the Atlanta Campaign," *CWH* 7 (1961): 264–71; Errol MacGregor Clauss, "Sherman's Rail Support in the Atlanta Campaign," *Georgia Historical Quarterly* 50 (1966): 413–20.

26. WTS, *Memoirs*, 1: 386; 2: 25–30; WTS, "Last Year of the War," 247–48; OR, I, 32, pt. 3: 245–46.

27. OR, I, 32, pt. 3: 221, 312–14; WTS, *Memoirs*, 2: 24–29.

28. WTS to EES, May 4, 1864, SFMSS, UNDL.

29. JEJ, *Narrative of Military Operations*, 304–05; Connelly, *Autumn of Glory*, 326–31.

30. JEJ, *Narrative of Military Operations*, 305; OR, I, 38 pt. 3: 614; Connelly, *Autumn of Glory*, 331–34; Albert Castel, *Decision in the West: The Atlanta Campaign of 1864* (Lawrence, Kan., 1992), 126–30.

31. JEJ, *Narrative of Military Operations*, 305–06; OR, I, 38, pt. 3: 614; Symonds, *Joseph E. Johnston*, 275–77; Castel, *Decision in the West*, 132–35; James Lee McDonough and James Pickett Jones, *War So Terrible: Sherman and Atlanta* (New York, 1987), 102–03; Richard M. McMurry, *Atlanta 1864: Last Chance for the Confederacy* (Lincoln, Neb., 2000), 63–64.

32. Davis, *Atlanta Will Fall*, 35, 42–44; Connelly, *Autumn of Glory*, 335–39.

33. OR, I, 38, pt. 3: 614; JEJ, *Narrative of Military Operations*, 306–07; WTS, *Memoirs*, 2: 32; WTS, "Last Year of the War," 252; OR, I, 38, pt. 4: 88–89, 99, 105, 110–12; Castel, *Decision in the West*, 136–41; Lewis, *Fighting Prophet*, 357.

34. OR, I, 38, pt. 1: 63–64; WTS, *Memoirs*, 2: 33; Castel, *Decision in the West*, 136–39; Albert Castel, "Prevaricating through Georgia: Sherman's *Memoirs* as a Source on the Atlanta Campaign," *CWH* 40 (1994): 54–55.

35. WTS, *Memoirs*, 2: 35; JEJ, *Narrative of Military Operations*, 308, 316–17; OR, I, 38, pt. 3: 614–15; Richard M. McMurry, "Resaca: 'A Heap of Hard Fiten'," *CWTI* 9 (Nov. 1970): 8–10.

36. OR, I, 38, pt. 1: 64; Castel, *Decision in the West*, 178–79; McDonough and Jones, *War So Terrible*, 109–10.

37. OR, I, 38, pt. 3: 615; JEJ, *Narrative of Military Operations*, 309–11; Castel, *Decision in the West*, 156–61; McDonough and Jones, *War So Terrible*, 110–12.

38. OR, I, 38, pt. 3: 615; JEJ, *Narrative of Military Operations*, 311; Castel, *Decision in the West*, 164–68; McDonough and Jones, *War So Terrible*, 113–14; McMurry, "Resaca," 12.

39. OR, I, 38, pt. 1: 64–65; WTS, *Memoirs*, 2: 35–36; Castel, *Decision in the West*, 169–80; McMurry, "Resaca," 44–46.

40. OR, I, 38, pt. 3: 615; JEJ, *Narrative of Military Operations*, 312–14.

41. JEJ, *Narrative of Military Operations*, 314–15; Symonds, *Joseph E. Johnston*, 281.

Sixteen:

1. JEJ, *Narrative of Military Operations*, 319–20; OR, I, 38, pt. 3: 615; McDonough and Jones, *War So Terrible*, 122–31.

2. JEJ, *Narrative of Military Operations*, 320; OR, I, 38, pt. 3: 615; Symonds, *Joseph E. Johnston*, 288.

3. JEJ, *Narrative of Military Operations*, 321; McDonough and Jones, *War So Terrible*, 132–34.

4. JEJ, *Narrative of Military Operations*, 321–22; Symonds, *Joseph E. Johnston*, 292–93; Thomas B. Mackall diary, May 19, 1864, W&ML; McMurry, *John Bell Hood*, 108–09, 198–99.

5. JEJ, *Narrative of Military Operations*, 322–24; OR, I, 38, pt. 3: 616.

6. OR, I, 38, pt. 4: 728; McDonough and Jones, *War So Terrible*, 133–34.

7. JEJ, *Narrative of Military Operations*, 324.

8. Chesnut, *Mary Chesnut's Civil War*, 607; Gorgas, *Journals of Josiah Gorgas*, 109.

9. WTS, *Memoirs*, 2: 38–41.

10. Ibid., 41–42.

11. Ibid., 42–43; Symonds, *Joseph E. Johnston*, 296; OR, I, 38, pt. 1: 66; pt. 3: 616.

12. OR, I, pt. 1: 66; pt. 3: 616; Castel, *Decision in the West*, 221–26; McDonough and Jones, *War So Terrible*, 147–54; Davis, *Atlanta Will Fall*, 61–67; McMurry, *Atlanta 1864*, 88–89; Richard M. McMurry, "The Hell Hole," *CWTI* 11 (Feb. 1973): 32–43; Posey Hamilton, "Battle of New Hope Church, Ga.," *CV* 30 (1922): 338–39.

13. WTS, *Memoirs*, 2: 44–45.

14. OR, I, 38, pt. 3: 616; JEJ, *Narrative of Military Operations*, 329–32; Castel, *Decision in the West*, 233–41; McDonough and Jones, *War So Terrible*, 155–66; Philip Secrist, "Scenes of Awful Carnage," *CWTI* 10 (June 1971): 5–9, 45–48; Castel, "Prevaricating through Georgia," 56.

15. JEJ, *Narrative of Military Operations*, 332–33; Castel, *Decision in the West*, 241–47; McDonough and Jones, *War So Terrible*, 166–69; Thomas B. Mackall diary, May 28, 1864, W&ML.

16. JEJ, *Narrative of Military Operations*, 333–341; OR, I, 38, pt. 3: 616.

17. WTS, *Memoirs*, 2: 46, 50, 55–56; Henry O. Dwight, "Each Man His Own Engineer," *CWTI* 4 (Oct. 1965): 30.

18. Hattaway and Jones, *How the North Won*, 519–24, 539–45, 552–58, 560–62, 572–76; Symonds, *Joseph E. Johnston*, 294–95.

19. Joseph Wheeler to Braxton Bragg, July —, 1864, Bragg MSS, DUL.

20. JEJ, *Narrative of Military Operations*, 359–62; Connelly, *Autumn of Glory*, 372–90; McMurry, *Atlanta 1864*, 97–99, 111, 131–36, 198–202; McDonough and Jones, *War So Terrible*, 124–26; John P. Dyer, *Fightin' Joe Wheeler* (Baton Rouge, La., 1941), 172–73; OR, I, 52, pt. 2: 704–07.

21. Wills, *Battle from the Start*, 200–46.

22. WTS, *Memoirs*, 2: 51–52.

23. Ibid., 53–54; OR, I, 38, pt. 3: 617; JEJ, *Narrative of Military Operations*, 337; JEJ, "General Polk's Death: General Joseph E. Johnston Describes How He Was Killed," *SHSP* 18 (1890–91): 380–81; Howard, *Autobiography*, 1: 563–64.

24. OR, I, 38, pt. 3: 617; WTS, *Memoirs*, 2: 54–55; Symonds, *Joseph E. Johnston*, 307; Castel, *Decision in the West*, 280–82.

25. Hattaway and Jones, *How the North Won*, 588–93; McPherson, *Ordeal by Fire*, 439–41.

26. OR, I, 38, pt. 1: 68; pt. 3: 617; WTS, *Memoirs*, 2: 57–59; Castel, *Decision in the West*, 288–99; McDonough and Jones, *War So Terrible*, 180–81; Richard M. McMurry, "The Affair at Kolb's Farm," *CWTI* 7 (Dec. 1968): 20–27.

27. WTS, *Memoirs*, 2: 59–60; Fellman, *Citizen Sherman*, 195.

28. Castel, *Decision in the West*, 303–05.

29. OR, I, 38, pt. 1: 69; pt. 3: 617; WTS, *Memoirs*, 2: 60–61; JEJ, *Narrative of Military Operations*, 341–44; Castel, *Decision in the West*, 309–20; McDonough and Jones, *War So Terrible*, 186–90; Davis, *Atlanta Will Fall*, 86–87; McMurry, *Atlanta 1864*, 108–10; Connelly, *Autumn of Glory*, 359–60; Horn, *Army of Tennessee*, 333–37; Richard M. McMurry, "Kennesaw Mountain," *CWTI* 8 (Jan. 1970): 25, 28–32.

30. OR, I, 38, pt. 5: 91–92; Castel, *Decision in the West*, 320–21; McDonough and Jones, *War So Terrible*, 181–83; WTS to EES, July 9, 13, 1864; both, SFMSS, UNDL; Castel, "Prevaricating through Georgia," 56–57; WTS to anon., June 21, 1885, WTS MSS, GLC.

31. OR, I, 38, pt. 1: 68; Hattaway and Jones, *How the North Won*, 577–83.

32. JEJ, *Narrative of Military Operations*, 345–46; Symonds, *Joseph E. Johnston*, 315; Francis A. Shoup, "Dalton Campaign—Works at Chattahoochee River—Interesting History," *CV* 3 (1895): 262–65.

33. JEJ, *Narrative of Military Operations*, 347; WTS, *Memoirs*, 2: 68–70; Castel, *Decision in the West*, 336–39; Thomas B. Mackall diary, July 9, 10, 1864, W&ML.

34. Symonds, *Joseph E. Johnston*, 310; Gorgas, *Journals of Josiah Gorgas*, 119, 121.

35. Mackall, *Son's Recollections of His Father*, 218; Richard M. McMurry, "Confederate Morale in the Atlanta Campaign of 1864," *Georgia Historical Quarterly* 54 (1970): 226–43.

36. Daniel, *Soldiering in the Army of Tennessee*, 141–42.

37. JEJ, *Narrative of Military Operations*, 348, 364; Symonds, *Joseph E. Johnston*, 321–23, 175–76; "In Memoriam: General Joseph Eggleston Johnston," *SHSP* 18 (1890–91): 175–76; Thomas B. Mackall diary, July 14, 1864, W&ML; McMurry, *John Bell Hood*, 117–18; Maury, *Recollections of a Virginian*, 147–48.

38. OR, I, 38, pt. 5: 881; McMurry, *John Bell Hood*, 118–20; Glatthaar, *Partners in Command*, 129–30; Hay, "Davis-Hood-Johnston Controversy," 63–65.

39. OR, I, 38, pt. 5: 885.

Seventeen:

1. WTS, *Memoirs*, 2: 72; WTS, "Last Year of the War," 253; Samuel Carter III, *The Siege of Atlanta, 1864* (New York, 1973), 193.

2. WTS, *Memoirs*, 2: 72; "Major Boyd's Sketch of General Sherman," *CV* 18 (1910): 453.

3. WTS, *Memoirs*, 2: 72–73; OR, I, 38, pt. 1: 71; WTS to George H. Thomas, July 19, 1864; WTS to James B. McPherson and John A. Logan, July 20, 1864; both, WTS MSS, GLC; John Bell Hood, *Advance and Retreat: Personal Experiences in the United States and Confederate States Armies* (New Orleans, 1880), 161–72; Castel, *Decision in the West*, 369–70, 372–73, 375–77, 380–82; McDonough and Jones, *War So Terrible*, 211–13; Connelly, *Autumn of Glory*, 440–43.

4. OR, I, 38, pt. 1: 71; Castel, *Decision in the West*, 369–73, 375–78, 380–83; McDonough and Jones, *War So Terrible*, 213–18; Davis, *Atlanta Will Fall*, 133–36; Castel, "Prevaricating through Georgia," 57.

5. WTS, *Memoirs*, 2: 73.

6. Ibid., 74; Castel, *Decision in the West*, 383–84.

7. Castel, *Decision in the West*, 385–87, 389, 393–94; WTS, *Memoirs*, 2: 75.

8. WTS, *Memoirs*, 2: 76.

9. Ibid., 76–84; OR, I, 38, pt. 1: 72–75; WTS to EES, July 26, 1864, SFMSS, UNDL; Hood, *Advance and Retreat*, 173–84; Castel, *Decision in the West*, 394–414; McDonough and Jones, *War So Terrible*, 228–37; Davis, *Atlanta Will Fall*, 145–48; McMurry, *Atlanta 1864*, 154–55, 187–88; Connelly, *Autumn of Glory*, 448–50; Horn, *Army of Tennessee*, 355–59; W. H. Chamberlin, "Hood's Second Sortie at Atlanta," *B&L* 4: 326–31.

10. Castel, *Decision in the West*, 405–12.

11. WTS, *Memoirs*, 2: 85–86; Howard, *Autobiography*, 2: 16–17; Force, *General Sherman*, 229; McDonough and Jones, *War So Terrible*, 241–46, 262; WTS to Thomas T. Gantt, June 8, 11, 12, 1886; all, WTS MSS, LC.

12. WTS, *Memoirs*, 2: 88–89; Castel, *Decision in the West*, 424–28.

13. WTS, *Memoirs*, 2: 88–89; OR, I, 38, pt. 1: 77; Hood, *Advance and Retreat*, 194–95; Castel, *Decision in the West*, 428–36; McDonough and Jones, *War So Terrible*, 256–62; Connelly, *Autumn of Glory*, 454–56; Horn, *Army of Tennessee*, 360–61.

14. WTS, *Memoirs*, 2: 91.

15. Ibid., 96–98, 436–43; David Evans, *Sherman's Horsemen: Union Cavalry Operations in the Atlanta Campaign* (Bloomington, Ind., 1996), 217–354.

16. Castel, *Decision in the West*, 454–61; McDonough and Jones, *War So Terrible*, 264–68; Albert Castel, "Union Fizzle at Atlanta: The Battle of Utoy Creek," *CWTI* 16 (Feb. 1978): 26–32.

17. Castel, *Decision in the West*, 448–50, 452, 466, 469–70, 484–86, 490–91; Connelly, *Autumn of Glory*, 434, 457–58, Evans, *Sherman's Horsemen*, 394–95; Dyer, *Fightin' Joe Wheeler*, 187–98.

18. WTS, *Memoirs*, 2: 103; Edward G. Longacre, "Judson Kilpatrick," *CWTI* 10 (Apr. 1971): 31–32; WTS to Edgar A. Hamilton, Dec. 11, 1881, WTS MSS, GLC.

19. WTS, *Memoirs*, 2: 104; OR, I, 38, pt. 1: 79–80; Evans, *Sherman's Horsemen*, 404–67.

20. WTS, *Memoirs*, 1: 104–05; OR, I, 38, pt. 1: 80.

21. Hood, *Advance and Retreat*, 203–04; Castel, *Decision in the West*, 538–39; Connelly, *Autumn of Glory*, 458.

22. OR, I, 38, pt. 1: 80; WTS, *Memoirs*, 2: 105.

23. OR, I, 38, pt. 1: 81–82; WTS, *Memoirs*, 2: 106–07; Hood, *Advance and Retreat*, 206.

24. OR, I, 38, pt. 1: 81; WTS, *Memoirs*, 2: 107; Castel, *Decision in the West*, 502–07; McDonough and Jones, *War So Terrible*, 301–04; Connelly, *Autumn of Glory*, 462–64; Horn, *Army of Tennessee*, 364–65; Davis, *Atlanta Will Fall*, 183–91; A. A. Hoehling, *Last Train from Atlanta* (New York, 1958), 387–95; Errol MacGregor Clauss, "The Battle of Jonesborough," *CWTI* 7 (Nov. 1968): 12–23.

25. OR, I, 38, pt. 1: 81–82; WTS, *Memoirs*, 2: 107–08; Hood, *Advance and Retreat*, 206–08; Castel, *Decision in the West*, 510–22; McDonough and Jones, *War So Terrible*, 304–07; Howard, *Autobiography*, 2: 39–40; Horn, *Army of Tennessee*, 365–66; Hoehling, *Last Train from Atlanta*, 400–07.

26. OR, I, 38, pt. 1: 82; WTS, *Memoirs*, 2: 108.

27. WTS, *Memoirs*, 2: 108–09.

28. Ibid., 109.

29. OR, I, 38, pt. 1: 87; pt. 5: 763, 777.

30. JEJ, *Narrative of Military Operations*, 349; Thomas B. Mackall diary, July 19, 1864, W&ML; Wright, *Southern Girl in '61*, 181–82.

31. Wright, *Southern Girl in '61*, 193–94; Symonds, *Joseph E. Johnston*, 331–35.

32. Symonds, *Joseph E. Johnston*, 331–32; "In Memoriam: General Joseph Eggleston Johnston," 174–75.

33. Symonds, *Joseph E. Johnston*, 332; *OR*, I, 38, pt. 5: 888.

34. Symonds, *Joseph E. Johnston*, 327–29; Davis, *Atlanta Will Fall*, 115–17.

35. Ellsworth Eliot, Jr., *West Point in the Confederacy* (New York, 1941), 110.

36. WTS, *Memoirs*, 2: 110–12, 118–29; Hood, *Advance and Retreat*, 229–42; Grimsley, *Hard Hand of War*, 185–90.

37. McDonough and Jones, *War So Terrible*, 2: 111; *OR*, I, 38, pt. 5: 839; 39, pt. 2: 503; EES to WTS, Sept. 17, 1864, SFMSS, UNDL.

38. WTS, *Memoirs*, 2: 129–30; Lee Kennett, *Marching through Georgia: The Story of Soldiers and Civilians during Sherman's Campaign* (New York, 1995), 238–42; Marszalek, *Sherman*, 299; McDonough and Jones, *War So Terrible*, 314–21; Castel, *Decision in the West*, 548–55.

39. WTS, *Memoirs*, 2: 112–13, 130, 140; Horace Porter, *Campaigning with Grant* (New York, 1897), 289–96; *OR*, I, 39, pt 2: 411.

40. WTS, *Memoirs*, 2: 144–50; Hood, *Advance and Retreat*, 243–57; Marszalek, *Sherman*, 291–92; Victor Hicken, "Hold the Fort," *CWTI* 7 (June 1968): 18–27.

41. WTS, *Memoirs*, 2: 150–56; Hood, *Advance and Retreat*, 257–69; Connelly, *Autumn of Glory*, 470–85; Roman, *Military Operations of Beauregard*, 2: 287–94.

42. WTS, "Last Year of the War," 255; WTS, *Memoirs*, 2: 152–56.

43. *OR*, I, 39, pt. 3: 162.

Eighteen:

1. Hattaway and Jones, *How the North Won*, 640–43.

2. Joseph T. Glatthaar, *The March to the Sea and Beyond: Sherman's Troops in the Savannah and Carolinas Campaigns* (New York, 1985), 119–21; S. M. Bowman and R. B. Irwin, *Sherman and His Campaigns: A Military Biography* (New York, 1865), 271–72.

3. Burke Davis, *Sherman's March* (New York, 1980), 39–40; Kennett, *Marching through Georgia*, 262–73; Edward G. Longacre, ed., "'We Left a Black Track in South Carolina': Letters of Corporal Eli S. Ricker, 1865," *South Carolina Historical Magazine* 82 (1981): 224.

4. WTS to EES, Oct. 21, 1864, SFMSS, UNDL; Glatthaar, *March to the Sea and Beyond*, 120–21.

5. Glatthaar, *March to the Sea and Beyond*, 130, 137; "Sherman's Hairpins," in Patricia L. Faust, ed., *Historical Times Illustrated Encyclopedia of the Civil War* (New York, 1986), 683.

6. Dyer, *Fightin' Joe Wheeler*, 207–08; Longacre, "Judson Kilpatrick," 33.

7. WTS, *Memoirs*, 2: 187–88.

8. Kennett, *Marching through Georgia*, 274–76, 283, 285; Davis, *Sherman's March*, 58–67; James C. Bonner, "Sherman at Milledgeville in 1864," *Journal of Southern History* 22 (1956): 273–91.

9. Davis, *Sherman's March*, 53–56.

10. Nathaniel Cheairs Hughes, Jr., and Gordon D. Whitney, *Jefferson Davis in Blue: The Life of Sherman's Relentless Warrior* (Baton Rouge, La., 2002), 307–14; John J. Hight, *History of the Fifty-eighth Regiment of Indiana Volunteer Infantry* (Princeton, Ind., 1895), 431, 490.

11. Marszalek, *Sherman*, 312–15; WTS to EES, Jan. 15, 1865, SFMSS, UNDL.

12. WTS, *Memoirs*, 2: 250–52.

13. Marszalek, *Sherman*, 314–15; Fellman, *Citizen Sherman*, 165–67; Willie Lee Rose, *Rehearsal for Reconstruction: The Port Royal Experiment* (Indianapolis, 1964), 327–30, 354–57, 377; Andrew Johnson, *The Papers of Andrew Johnson*, ed. by Paul H. Bergeron et al. (10 vols. Knoxville, Tenn., 1967–83), 10: 20–21, 21n.

14. *OR*, 44: 10–11, 701–02; WTS, *Memoirs*, 2: 193–201; WTS to EES, Dec. 16, 1864, SFMSS, UNDL; Kennett, *Marching through Georgia*, 308–09; Bowman and Irwin, *Sherman and His Campaigns*, 292–93.

15. WTS, *Memoirs*, 2: 202–03, 216–19; OR, I, 44: 6–7, 783; Charles C. Jones, Jr., "The Siege and Evacuation of Savannah, Georgia, in December, 1864," *SHSP* 17 (1889): 60–85.

16. WTS, *Memoirs*, 2: 213–16, 219.

17. OR, I, 44: 809; WTS to EES, Jan. 5, 1865, SFMSS, UNDL; John F. Marszalek, *Sherman's March to the Sea* (Abilene, Tex., 2005), 122–24; Kean, *Inside the Confederate Government*, 179.

18. OR, I, 44: 797–98, 841.

19. WTS, *Memoirs*, 2: 797; 47, pt. 1: 17; Davis, *Sherman's March*, 141–42.

20. Longacre, ed., "'We Left a Black Track in South Carolina'," 221: Glatthaar, *March to the Sea and Beyond*, 141; Bowman and Irwin, *Sherman and His Campaigns*, 353.

21. Glatthaar, *March to the Sea and Beyond*, 142; John G. Barrett, *Sherman's March through the Carolinas* (Chapel Hill, N.C., 1956), 66–93; Royster, *Destructive War*, 5–33; Marion Brunson Lucas, *Sherman and the Burning of Columbia* (College Station, Tex., 1976), 163–67; Emma LeConte, *When the World Ended: The Diary of Emma LeConte*, ed. by Earl Schenck Miers (New York, 1957), 42–50; Thomas Ward Osborn, *The Fiery Trail: A Union Officer's Account of Sherman's Last Campaign*, ed. by Richard Harwell and Philip N. Racine (Knoxville, Tenn., 1986), 127–38; James Ford Rhodes, "Who Burned Columbia?" *American Historical Review* 7 (1902): 485–93.

22. Glatthaar, *March to the Sea and Beyond*, 146; Davis, *Sherman's March*, 206; Barrett, *Sherman's March through the Carolinas*, 127–30; Sharyn Kane and Richard Keeton, *Fiery Dawn: The Civil War Battle at Monroe's Crossroads, North Carolina* (Tallahassee, Fla., 1999), 40–79.

23. Glatthaar, *March to the Sea and Beyond*, 15–16.

24. Symonds, *Joseph E. Johnston*, 339–40; Mackall, *Son's Recollections of His Father*, 224–25.

25. JEJ, *Narrative of Military Operations*, 464–65; Symonds, *Joseph E. Johnston*, 340–41; OR, I, 38, pt. 3: 621.

26. Symonds, *Joseph E. Johnston*, 341–42.

27. Ibid.; Kean, *Inside the Confederate Government*, 181; Chesnut, *Mary Chesnut's Civil War*, 698; Cooper, *Jefferson Davis, American*, 521.

28. Hughes, *General Johnston*, 260 and n; Mackall, *Son's Recollections of His Father*, 226–27.

29. OR, I, 47, pt. 2: 1303–11; Symonds, *Joseph E. Johnston*, 342–43; Hudson Strode, *Jefferson Davis* (3 vols. New York,1955–64), 3: 149–50.

30. JEJ, *Narrative of Military Operations*, 430–40; Symonds, *Joseph E. Johnston*, 352; OR, I, 38, pt. 3: 628–36.

31. JEJ, *Narrative of Military Operations*, 371–72; Symonds, *Joseph E. Johnston*, 344.

32. Symonds, *Joseph E. Johnston*, 344, 346; OR, I, 47, pt. 2: 1328.

33. Mark L. Bradley, *This Astounding Close: The Road to Bennett Place* (Chapel Hill, N.C., 2000), 8.

34. JEJ to Robert E. Lee, Feb. 25, 1865, Confederate Military Leaders Collection, MoC; OR, I, 47, pt. 2: 1247, 1256–57, 1271; JEJ, *Narrative of Military Operations*, 371–72.

35. John G. Barrett, *The Civil War in North Carolina* (Chapel Hill, N.C., 1963), 318–19; WTS, *Memoirs*, 2: 299–300.

36. JEJ, *Narrative of Military Operations*, 383–87; Wade Hampton, "The Battle of Bentonville," *B&L* 4: 701–02; Hughes, *General William J. Hardee*, 281–86; Barrett, *Sherman's March through the Carolinas*, 148–63; Symonds, *Joseph E. Johnston*, 348–50; WTS, *Memoirs*, 2: 303; Osborn, *Fiery Trail*, 192–94.

37. JEJ, *Narrative of Military Operations*, 388–89; OR, I, 47, pt. 1: 1056–60, 1131; pt. 2: 1437–39, 1447, 1451–52, 1457–59; Hampton, "Battle of Bentonville," 703–05; Howard, *Autobiography*, 2: 145–47; Barrett, *Sherman's March through the Carolinas*, 163–84; Bradley, *This Astounding Close*, 20–26; Jay Luvaas, "Bentonville—Last Chance to Stop Sherman," *CWTI* 2 (Oct. 1963): 8–9, 38–39.

38. WTS, *Memoirs*, 2: 304.

39. Ibid., 304–06; Hampton, "Bentonville," 704–05; Barrett, *Sherman's March through the Carolinas*, 180–81; Luvaas, "Last Chance to Stop Sherman," 40–42.

40. WTS, *Memoirs*, 2: 304.

41. Ibid., 306, 322–27; Bowman and Irwin, *Sherman and His Campaigns*, 375.

42. WTS, "Unpublished Letters of General Sherman," *North American Review* 152 (1891): 372–75; WTS to David D. Porter, Oct. 19, 1868, WTS MSS, GLC; Raoul S. Naroll, "Lincoln and the Sherman Peace Fiasco—Another Fable?" *Journal of Southern History* 20 (1954): 459–83.

43. WTS, *Memoirs*, 2: 334–44; Bradley, *This Astounding Close*, 103–05.

44. WTS, *Memoirs*, 2: 345–48; Bradley, *This Astounding Close*, 148–49.

45. JEJ, *Narrative of Military Operations*, 396–400; Symonds, *Joseph E. Johnston*, 353–54; Roman, *Military Operations of Beauregard*, 2: 394–95; Williams, *P. G. T. Beauregard*, 254–55; Cooper, *Jefferson Davis, American*, 525–26; Bradley, *This Astounding Close*, 140–41.

46. WTS, *Memoirs*, 2: 348–49; JEJ, *Narrative of Military Operations*, 402–04; Bradley, *This Astounding Close*, 157–62; David P. Conyngham, *Sherman's March through the South: Sketches and Incidents of the Campaign* (New York, 1865), 365; JEJ, "My Negotiations with General Sherman," *North American Review* 143 (1886): 183–97.

47. WTS, *Memoirs*, 2: 349.

48. Ibid., 349–50.

49. Ibid., 351–52.

50. Ibid., 352–57; JEJ, *Narrative of Military Operations*, 404–07; "Memorandum of Agreement between Generals Johnston and Sherman for the Surrender of the Confederate Troops, with Associated Letters and Notes by [Col.] B. S. Ewell," Apr. 18, 1865, JEJ MSS, W&ML; Symonds, *Joseph E. Johnston*, 356–57; Bradley, *This Astounding Close*, 169–77; John S. Wise, *The End of an Era* (Boston, 1899), 450–62.

51. WTS, *Memoirs*, 2: 357–59; JEJ, *Narrative of Military Operations*, 410–11; Bradley, *This Astounding Close*, 207–11; McPherson, *Ordeal by Fire*, 484–85.

52. WTS, *Memoirs*, 2: 362–77; JEJ to John C. Breckinridge, Apr. 23, 24, 25 [three letters], 1865; all, Confederate Military Leaders Collection, MoC; Fellman, *Citizen Sherman*, 245–47; Marszalek, *Sherman*, 341–59; John F. Marszalek, "The Stanton-Sherman Controversy," *CWTI* 9 (Oct. 1970): 4–12.

53. JEJ, *Narrative of Military Operations*, 412–19; JEJ to John C. Breckinridge, Apr. 26, 1865, Confederate Military Leaders Collection, MoC; JEJ, General Orders No. 18, Apr. 27, 1865, JEJ MSS, GLC; WTS, Special Orders No. 15, Apr. 27, 1865; WTS to JEJ, Apr. 27, 1865; WTS to H. Copper, May 21, 1865; all, WTS MSS, GLC; Bradley, *This Astounding Close*, 215–17, 227–32, 255.

Epilogue:

1. JEJ, *Narrative of Military Operations*, 418–19.

2. Ibid., 419–20; Symonds, *Joseph E. Johnston*, 359–60; "In Memoriam: General Joseph Eggleston Johnston," 196; JEJ to Robert W. Hughes, Oct. 1, 1865, Floyd-Johnston-Preston MSS, W&ML.

3. Symonds, *Joseph E. Johnston*, 360; Johnson, *Memoir of Joseph E. Johnston*, 245; Gorgas, *Journals of Josiah Gorgas*, 210; JEJ to "My Dear Little Lizzie," Nov. 22, 1866, Floyd-Johnston-Preston MSS, W&ML.

4. Symonds, *Joseph E. Johnston*, 361–65.

5. Ibid., 366–70; Johnson, *Memoir of Joseph E. Johnston*, 242; Burke Davis, *The Long Surrender* (New York, 1985), 253–54.

6. Hughes, *General Johnston*, 282–83, 287; James L. Kemper to JEJ, Sept. 27, Oct. 9, 1875; both, JEJ MSS, W&ML; Cooper, *Jefferson Davis, American*, 624; Symonds, *Joseph E. Johnston*, 4, 380; "The Monument to General Robert E. Lee," *SHSP* 17 (1889): 303–04; Davis, *Long Surrender*, 268–69; "Joseph E. Johnston Monument at Dalton," *CV* 21 (1913): 286–88; Robert M. Hughes, "Joseph Eggleston Johnston, Soldier and Man: Address . . . at Unveiling of Bust of General Johnston in the Old Hall of the House of Delegates of Virginia, February 3, 1933," *William and Mary College Historical Magazine* ser. 2, 13 (1933): 63–84.

7. JEJ to John W. Johnston, May 24, 1876, Oct. 8, 1877; both, JEJ MSS, W&ML; Merrill, *William*

Tecumseh Sherman, 364; Symonds, *Joseph E. Johnston*, 374.

8. "In Memoriam: General Joseph Eggleston Johnston," 179; Symonds, *Joseph E. Johnston*, 374–78; JEJ to Thomas T. Gantt, Mar. 16, May 14, 1880, May 25, 1887, May 29, 1888; JEJ to Ann Mason Lee, Sept. 26, 1888; all, JEJ MSS, W&ML; Hughes, *General Johnston*, 284; Johnson, *Memoir of Joseph E. Johnston*, 246–50.

9. Hughes, *General Johnston*, 285–89; Symonds, *Joseph E. Johnston*, 379–81; Johnson, *Memoir of Joseph E. Johnston*, 268–76; JEJ to Sally Johnston Lee, Mar. 31, 1887, JEJ MSS, W&ML; JEJ to "Judge Hughes," Feb. 11, 1879; JEJ to "My Dear Lizzie," Jan. 27, 1886; both, Floyd-Johnston-Preston MSS, W&ML; Maury, *Recollections of a Virginian*, 154–55; Robert G. Athearn, *William Tecumseh Sherman and the Settlement of the West* (Norman, Okla., 1956), 10–11.

10. George C. Rable, "William T. Sherman and the Conservative Critique of Radical Reconstruction," *Ohio History* 93 (1984): 147–51; Marszalek, *Sherman*, 364–66; Merrill, *William Tecumseh Sherman*, 306; WTS and John Sherman, *Sherman Letters*, 254.

11. Ralph K. Andrist, *The Long Death: The Last Days of the Plains Indians* (New York, 1964), 97, 154–55; Fellman, *Citizen Sherman*, 259–76; Royster, *Destructive War*, 393–98.

12. Fellman, *Citizen Sherman*, 264–65; Andrist, *Long Death*, 97–100; Merrill, *William Tecumseh Sherman*, 307; WTS to George A. Custer, June 17, 1867; WTS to David D. Colton, Sept. 26, 1878; both, WTS MSS, GLC; Athearn, *Sherman and the Settlement of the West*, 98–99.

13. WTS and John Sherman, *Sherman Letters*, 279–80; WTS, *Home Letters of General Sherman*, 358–75; Rable, "Sherman and the Conservative Critique of Radical Reconstruction," 152–53; Benjamin P. Thomas and Harold M. Hyman, *Stanton: The Life and Times of Lincoln's Secretary of War* (New York, 1962), 558–75; Merrill, *William Tecumseh Sherman*, 313–27.

14. WTS and John Sherman, *Sherman Letters*, 331–32, 346; Fellman, *Citizen Sherman*, 277–98; Merrill, *William Tecumseh Sherman*, 332–60; Force, *General Sherman*, 324–27.

15. Mark R. Grandstaff, "Preserving the 'Habits and Usages of War': William Tecumseh Sherman, Professional Reform, and the U.S. Army Officer Corps, 1865–1881, Revisited," *Journal of Military History* 62 (1998): 537–45; WTS, "The Grand Strategy of the War of the Rebellion," *Century Magazine* 13 (1888): 597–98; Merrill, *William Tecumseh Sherman*, 343–48; J. C. Audenreid, "General Sherman in Europe and the East," *Harper's New Monthly Magazine* 47 (1873): 225–42, 481–95, 652–71; WTS and John Sherman, *Sherman Letters*, 340–43.

16. WTS to "Messrs D. Appleton & Co.," May 14, 1886; WTS to Thomas T. Gantt, June 14, 1886; both, WTS MSS, LC; John F. Marszalek, "Sherman Called It the Way He Saw It," *CWH* 40 (1994): 72–78; Henry V. Boynton, *Sherman's Historical Raid: The Memoirs in the Light of the Record . . .* (Cincinnati, 1875); C. W. Moulton, *The Review of General Sherman's Memoirs Examined, Chiefly in the Light of Its Own Evidence* (Cincinnati, 1875); Royster, *Destructive War*, 392–93; Force, *General Sherman*, 328–30; Merrill, *William Tecumseh Sherman*, 360–61; WTS to J. C. Audenreid, Apr. 27, 1876; WTS to John E. Tourtelotte, May 4, 1884; WTS to "Alfred," May 24, 1884; all, WTS MSS, GLC.

17. Fellman, *Citizen Sherman*, 341–415; WTS to Mary Audenreid, Feb. 19, Oct. 1, 1883; both, WTS MSS, GLC; Marszalek, "General and Mrs. William T. Sherman," 153–56; Merrill, *William Tecumseh Sherman*, 369–72; McAllister, *Ellen Ewing*, 349–50, 366–68; Joseph T. Durkin, *General Sherman's Son* (New York, 1959), 47–68; WTS to Thomas T. Gantt, May 23, 1886, WTS MSS, LC; WTS, *Sherman at War*, 168–73; Sherman, *John Sherman's Recollections*, 2: 1101–05.

18. WTS, *Memoirs*, 2: 39–41, 53.

19. WTS and John Sherman, *Sherman Letters*, 330; *Joint Committee on the Conduct of the War* (3 vols. in 8. Washington, D.C., 1863–68), 6: 3–23.

20. Symonds, *Joseph E. Johnston*, 370; Marszalek, *Sherman*, 405; Howard, *Autobiography*, 2: 554; WTS, *Sherman at War*, 166.

21. Symonds, *Joseph E. Johnston*, 380; WTS, *Sherman at War*, 170; WTS, *Home Letters of General*

Sherman, 393; WTS to Robert M. McLean, Mar. 9, 1889; WTS to John W. Noble, July 31, 1889; JEJ to WTS, May 17, 1889; all, WTS MSS, LC.

22. WTS to JEJ, Jan. 5, 1891, WTS MSS, LC.

23. Howard, *Autobiography,* 2: 553–54; "In Memoriam: General Joseph Eggleston Johnston," 196; Symonds, *Joseph E. Johnston,* 380; Marszalek, *Sherman,* 496; Charles Bracelen Flood, *Grant and Sherman: The Friendship That Won the Civil War* (New York, 2005), 397–98.

BIBLIOGRAPHY

Unpublished Materials

Bragg, Braxton. Papers. William R. Perkins Library, Duke University, Durham, N.C.

Davis, Jefferson. Papers. Virginia Historical Society, Richmond.

Downs, Alan Craig. "Gone Past All Redemption? The Early War Years of General Joseph Eggleston Johnston." Ph.D. dissertation, University of North Carolina at Chapel Hill, 1991.

Ewell, Benjamin S. Papers. Earl Gregg Swem Library, College of William and Mary, Williamsburg, Va.

Hughes, Robert Morton. "Some Reminiscences of Joseph E. Johnston." Robert Morton Hughes Papers. Patricia W. and J. Douglas Perry Library, Old Dominion University, Norfolk, Va.

Johnson, Bradley T. Papers. William R. Perkins Library, Duke University.

Johnston, George B. Letter of April 17, 1907. Beverly Bland Munford Papers, Virginia Historical Society.

Johnston, Joseph E. Cadet Papers. United States Military Academy Library, West Point. N.Y.

_____. Correspondence. Beverly Randolph Wellford Papers, Virginia Historical Society.

_____. Correspondence. Century-Civil War Collection. New York Public Library, New York. N.Y.

_____. Correspondence. Confederate Military Leaders Collection. Eleanor Brockenbrough Library, Museum of the Confederacy, Richmond, Va.

_____. Correspondence. Floyd-Johnston-Preston Papers. Earl Gregg Swem Library, College of William and Mary.

_____. Correspondence. Gilman Lehrman Collection, New York, N.Y.

_____. Correspondence. James Ewell Brown Stuart Papers, Virginia Historical Society.

_____. Correspondence. Robert Morton Hughes Papers. Earl Gregg Swem Library, College of William and Mary.

_____. Correspondence. Robert Morton Hughes Papers. Patricia W. and J. Douglas Perry Library, Old Dominion University.

_____. Correspondence. Robert William Hughes Papers. Earl Gregg Swem Library, College of William and Mary.

_____. Correspondence. William Whann Mackall Papers, Southern Historical Collection. Wilson Library, University of North Carolina at Chapel Hill.

_____. Papers. Alderman Library, University of Virginia, Charlottesville.

_____. Papers. Earl Gregg Swem Library, College of William and Mary.

_____. Papers. Henry E. Huntington Library, San Marino, Calif.

_____. Papers. William R. Perkins Library, Duke University.

Lee, Robert E. Correspondence. Eleanor Brockenbrough Library, Museum of the Confederacy.

_____. Correspondence. Lee Family Papers. Virginia Historical Society.

_____. Correspondence. Lee Headquarters Papers. Virginia Historical Society.

_____. Letter of July 24, 1861. Letters of Confederate Generals Robert E. Lee, Stonewall Jackson, Jeb Stuart, and Joseph E. Johnston, 1861–64. Albert and Shirley Small Special Collections Library, University of Virginia.

Mackall, Thomas B. Diary, 1864. Swem Library, College of William and Mary.

McNeill, William James. "The Stress of War: The Confederacy and William Tecumseh Sherman during the Last Year of the Civil War." Ph.D. dissertation, Rice University, 1973.

Menius, Arthur C. "A Beginning to Reconstruction: The Surrender of J. E. Johnston to W. T. Sherman." M.A. thesis, University of North Carolina at Chapel Hill, 1982.

Sherman, John. Papers. Library of Congress, Washington, D.C.

Sherman, William T. Cadet Papers. United States Military Academy Archives.

_____. Correspondence. Century-Civil War Collection. New York Public Library.

_____. Correspondence. Ellen Ewing Sherman Papers. Ohio Historical Society, Columbus.

_____. Correspondence. Gilder Lehrman Collection.

_____. Correspondence. Hugh Boyle Ewing Papers. Ohio Historical Society.

_____. Correspondence. Philemon Beecher Ewing Papers. Ohio Historical Society.

_____. Correspondence. Robert Anderson Papers. Library of Congress.

_____. Correspondence. Sherman Family Papers. University of Notre Dame Library, South Bend, Ind.

_____. Correspondence. Thomas Ewing and Family Papers. Library of Congress.

_____. Correspondence. U.S. Army Military History Institute, Carlisle Barracks, Pa.

_____. Papers. Bentley Historical Library, University of Michigan, Ann Arbor.

_____. Papers. Henry E. Huntington Library.

_____. Papers. Library of Congress.

_____. Papers. Ohio Historical Society.

Wigfall, Louis T. Papers. Library of Congress.

Newspapers

Daily Richmond Examiner

New York Herald

New York Times

New York Tribune

Richmond Enquirer

Richmond Sentinel

Richmond Whig

Articles and Essays

Alexander, E. Porter. "The Battle of Bull Run." *Scribner's Magazine* 41 (1907): 80–94.

Ambrose, Stephen E. "Sherman: A Reappraisal." *American History Illustrated* 1 (January 1967): 5–11, 54–57.

_____, and Edwin C. Bearss. "Struggle for Vicksburg: The Battle & Siege That Decided the Civil War." *Civil War Times Illustrated* 6 (July 1967): 4–66.

Armistead, Drury L. "The Battle in Which General Johnston Was Wounded." *Southern Historical Society Papers* 18 (1890–91): 185–88.

Ashe, S. A. "The Confederate Loss at Vicksburg." *Confederate Veteran* 37 (1929): 12–14.

Audenreid, J. C. "General Sherman in Europe and the East." *Harper's New Monthly Magazine* 47 (1873): 225–42, 481–95, 652–71.

Barrett, John G. "Sherman and Total War in the Carolinas." *North Carolina Historical Review* 37 (1960): 367–81.

Bearss, Edwin C. "The Battle of the Post of Arkansas." *Arkansas Historical Quarterly* 18 (1959): 237–79.

———. "The Day at Shiloh." *Register of the Kentucky Historical Society* 63 (1965): 39–69.

———. "Sherman's Demonstration Against Snyder's Bluff." *Journal of Mississippi History* 27 (1965): 168–86.

Beauregard, G. T. "The First Battle of Bull Run." In Robert Underwood Johnson and Clarence Clough Buel, eds., *Battles and Leaders of the Civil War*. 4 vols. New York: Century Co., 1887–88. 1: 196–227.

———. "The Shiloh Campaign." *North American Review* 142 (1886): 1–24, 159–94.

Billings, Elden E., ed. "Letters and Diaries: The St. Louis Riots." *Civil War Times Illustrated* 2 (June 1963): 39–40.

Black, Robert C., III. "The Railroads of Georgia in the Confederate War Effort." *Journal of Southern History* 13 (1947): 511–34.

Bonner, James C. "Sherman at Milledgeville in 1864." *Journal of Southern History* 22 (1956): 273–91.

Bowman, S. M. "Major-General William T. Sherman." *United States Service Magazine* 2 (1864): 113–24, 240–55.

———. "Sherman's Atlanta Campaign." *United States Service Magazine* 3 (1865): 304–23.

———. "Sherman's Georgia Campaign—from Atlanta to the Sea." *United States Service Magazine* 3 (1865): 426–46.

Boyd, David French. "General William T. Sherman as a College President." *American College* 2 (1909–10): 6–7.

Bradford, Gamaliel. "Union Portraits III: William T. Sherman." *Atlantic Monthly* 114 (1914): 318–29.

Brockett, L. P. "Major-General William Tecumseh Sherman." In *Our Great Captains: Grant, Sherman, Thomas, Sheridan, and Farragut. (*New York: Charles B. Richardson, 1866), 87–162.

———. "William Tecumseh Sherman, General of the Army of the U.S." In *Men of Our Day; or, Biographical Sketches of Patriots, Orators, Statesmen, Generals, Reformers, Financiers and Merchants* . . . (Philadelphia: Zeigler, McCurdy, 1868), 69–97.

Brockman, Charles J., Jr., ed. "The John Van Duser [Van Duzer] Diary of Sherman's March from Atlanta to Hilton Head." *Georgia Historical Quarterly* 53 (1969): 220–40.

Brown, D. Alexander. "Battle at Chickasaw Bluffs." *Civil War Times Illustrated* 9 (July 1970): 4–9, 44–48.

Bryan, Charles F., Jr. "Stalemate at Seven Pines." *Civil War Times Illustrated* 12 (August 1973): 5–6, 8, 10–11, 3947.

Buell, Don Carlos. "Major-General W. T. Sherman and the Spring Campaign of 1862 in the West." *Historical Magazine* 18 (1870): 74–82.

———. "Shiloh Reviewed." In Robert Underwood Johnson and Clarence Clough Buel, eds., *Battles and Leaders of the Civil War*. (4 vols. New York: Century Co., 1887–88), 1: 487–536.

Buford, M. M. "Surrender of Johnston's Army." *Confederate Veteran* 28 (1920): 170–72.

Burt, Jesse C. "Sherman, Railroad General." *Civil War History* 2 (1956): 45–54.

Byers, S. H. M. "The March to the Sea." *North American Review* 145 (1887): 235–45.

———. "Sherman's Attack at the Tunnel." In Robert Underwood Johnson and Clarence Clough Buel, eds., *Battles and Leaders of the Civil War*. (4 vols. New York: Century Co., 1887–88), 3: 712–13.

———. "Some Personal Recollections of General Sherman." *McClure's Magazine* 3 (1894): 212–24.

Bynum, Hartwell T. "Sherman's Expulsion of the Roswell Women in 1864." *Georgia Historical Quarterly* 54 (1970): 169–82.

Castel, Albert. "Prevaricating through Georgia: Sherman's *Memoirs* as a Source on the Atlanta Campaign." *Civil War History* 40 (1994): 48–71.

_____. "Union Fizzle at Atlanta: The Battle of Utoy Creek." *Civil War Times Illustrated* 16 (February 1978): 26–32.

_____. "W. T. Sherman: The Life of a Rising Son." *Civil War Times Illustrated* 18 (July 1979): 4–7, 42–46; 18 (August 1979): 12–22; 18 (October 1979): 10–21.

Chamberlin, W. H. "Hood's Second Sortie at Atlanta." In Robert Underwood Johnson and Clarence Clough Buel, eds., *Battles and Leaders of the Civil War*. (4 vols. New York: Century Co., 1887–88), 4: 326–31.

Chesney, Charles C. "Sherman and Johnston and the Atlanta Campaign." *Fortnightly Review* 24 (1875): 611–24.

_____. "Sherman's Campaign in Georgia." *Journal of the Royal United Service Institution* 9 (1865): 204–20.

Clauss, Errol MacGregor. "The Battle of Jonesborough." *Civil War Times Illustrated* 7 (November 1968): 12–23.

_____. "Sherman's Failure at Atlanta." *Georgia Historical Quarterly* 53 (1969): 321–29.

_____. "Sherman's Rail Support in the Atlanta Campaign." *Georgia Historical Quarterly* 50 (1966): 413–20.

Coleman, William T. "San Francisco Vigilance Committees, by the Chairman of the Committees of 1851, 1856, and 1877." *Century Magazine* 20 (1891): 133–50.

Cooper, William J., Jr. "A Reassessment of Jefferson Davis as War Leader: The Case from Atlanta to Nashville." *Journal of Southern History* 36 (1970): 189–204.

Coulter, E. Merton. "Sherman and the South." *North Carolina Historical Review* 8 (1931): 41–54.

Cox, Jacob D. "General Sherman." *Nation* 53 (1891): 153–55.

_____. "The Sherman-Johnston Convention." *Scribner's Magazine* 28 (1900): 489–505.

Dabney, F. Y. "Anecdotes of the Peninsular Campaign. I.—General Johnston to the Rescue." In Robert Underwood Johnson and Clarence Clough Buel, eds., *Battles and Leaders of the Civil War*. (4 vols. New York: Century Co., 1887–88), 2: 275–76.

Daniel, Larry J. "Bruinsburg: Missed Opportunity or Postwar Rhetoric?" *Civil War History* 32 (1986): 256–67.

Davis, Jefferson. "President Davis in Reply to General Sherman." *Southern Historical Society Papers* 14 (1886): 257–75.

Davis, Theodore R. "With Sherman in His Army Home." *Cosmopolitan* 12 (1891): 165–205.

De Laubenfels, David J. "Where Sherman Passed By." *Geographical Review* 47 (1957): 381–95.

_____, ed. "With Sherman through Georgia: A Journal." *Georgia Historical Quarterly* 41 (1957): 288–300.

Denson, C. B. "William Henry Chase Whiting, Major-General C. S. Army: An Address . . ." *Southern Historical Society Papers* 26 (1898): 129–81.

Downs, Alan C. "'The Responsibility Is Great': Joseph E. Johnston and the War in Virginia." In Steven E. Woodworth, ed., *Civil War Generals in Defeat*. (Lawrence: University Press of Kansas, 1999), 29–70.

Doyle, J. E. P. "Sherman's Sixty Days in the Carolinas." *United States Service Magazine* 3 (1865): 511–14.

Dwight, Henry O. "Each Man His Own Engineer." *Civil War Times Illustrated* 4 (October 1965): 4–7, 30–31.

Eaton, Clement, ed. "Diary of an Officer in Sherman's Army Marching through the Carolinas." *Journal of Southern History* 9 (1943): 238–54.

Ellis, Edward S. "Reminiscences of General Sherman." *Chatauquan* 27 (1898): 474–75.

Fisher, Noel C. "'Prepare Them for My Coming': General William T. Sherman, Total War, and Pacification in West Tennessee." *Tennessee Historical Quarterly* 51 (1992): 75–86.

Fitzgerald, David. "Annotations by General Sherman." *Journal of the Military Service Institution of the United States* 14 (1893): 978–79.

Forbes, J. M. "Recollections of Sherman and Porter." *Nation* 52 (1891): 192–03.

Fry, James B. "McDowell's Advance to Bull Run." In Robert Underwood Johnson and Clarence Clough Buel, eds., *Battles and Leaders of the Civil War*. (4 vols. New York: Century Co., 1887–88), 1: 167–93.

Gannon, Anthony. "A Consistent Deist: Sherman and Religion." *Civil War History* 42 (1996): 307–21.

Gow, June I. "Military Administration in the Confederate Army of Tennessee." *Journal of Southern History* 40 (1974): 183–98.

Graham, Stephen. "Marching through Georgia: Following Sherman's Footsteps To-Day." *Harper's Magazine* 140 (1920): 612–20, 813–23.

Grandstaff, Mark R. "Preserving the 'Habits and Usages of War': William Tecumseh Sherman, Professional Reform, and the U.S. Army Officer Corps, 1865–1881, Revisited." *Journal of Military History* 62 (1998): 521–45.

Grant, Ulysses S. "The Battle of Shiloh." In Robert Underwood Johnson and Clarence Clough Buel, eds., *Battles and Leaders of the Civil War*. (4 vols. New York: Century Co., 1887–88), 1: 465–86.

_____. "Chattanooga." In Robert Underwood Johnson and Clarence Clough Buel, eds., *Battles and Leaders of the Civil War*. (4 vols. New York: Century Co., 1887–88), 3: 679–711.

_____. "Preparing for the Campaigns of 1864." In Robert Underwood Johnson and Clarence Clough Buel, eds., *Battles and Leaders of the Civil War*. (4 vols. New York: Century Co., 1887–88), 4: 97–117.

_____. "The Vicksburg Campaign." In Robert Underwood Johnson and Clarence Clough Buel, eds., *Battles and Leaders of the Civil War*. (4 vols. New York: Century Co., 1887–88), 3: 493–539.

Guernsey, A. H. "Sherman's Great March." *Harper's New Monthly Magazine* 31 (1865): 571–89.

Halstead, Murat. "Recollections and Letters of General Sherman." *Independent* 51 (1899): 1610–13, 1682–85.

Hamilton, Posey. "Battle of New Hope Church, Ga." *Confederate Veteran* 30 (1922): 338–39.

Hampton, Wade. "The Battle of Bentonville." In Robert Underwood Johnson and Clarence Clough Buel, eds., *Battles and Leaders of the Civil War*. (4 vols. New York: Century Co., 1887–88), 4: 700–05.

Harrison, Lowell H. "Jackson . . . Is a Ruined Town." *Civil War Times Illustrated* 15 (February 1977): 4–7, 45–47.

Hartje, Robert. "Van Dorn Conducts a Raid on Holly Springs and Enters Tennessee." *Tennessee Historical Quarterly* 18 (1959): 120–33.

Harvie, E. J. "Gen. Joseph E. Johnston." *Confederate Veteran* 18 (1910): 521–23.

Hay, Thomas Robson. "The Atlanta Campaign." *Georgia Historical Quarterly* 7 (1923): 99–118.

_____. "The Battle of Chattanooga." *Georgia Historical Quarterly* 8 (1924): 121–41.

_____. "Confederate Leadership at Vicksburg." *Mississippi Valley Historical Review* 11 (1925): 543–60.

_____. "Davis, Bragg, and Johnston in the Atlanta Campaign." *Georgia Historical Quarterly* 8 (1924): 38–48.

_____. "The Davis-Hood-Johnston Controversy of 1864." *Mississippi Valley Historical Review* 11 (1924): 54–84.

Henry, Robert Selph. "Chattanooga and the War." *Tennessee Historical Quarterly* 19 (1960): 222–30.

Hicken, Victor. "Hold the Fort." *Civil War Times Illustrated* 7 (June 1968): 18–27.

Holman, J. A. "Concerning the Battle of Bentonville." *Confederate Veteran* 6 (1898): 153–54.

Holmes, James G. "The Artillery at Bentonville." *Confederate Veteran* 3 (1895): 103.

Hood, John B. "The Defense of Atlanta." In Robert Underwood Johnson and Clarence Clough Buel, eds., *Battles and Leaders of the Civil War*. (4 vols. New York: Century Co., 1887–88), 4: 336–44.

Howard, Oliver Otis. "The Battles about Atlanta." *Atlantic Monthly* 38 (1976): 385–99, 559–67.

_____. "Chattanooga." *Atlantic Monthly* 38 (1876): 203–19.

_____. "Sherman's Advance from Atlanta." In Robert Underwood Johnson and Clarence Clough Buel, eds., *Battles and Leaders of the Civil War*. (4 vols. New York: Century Co., 1887–88). 4: 663–66.

_____. "Sherman's Campaign of 1864." *United Service* 13 (1885): 660–73; 14 (1886): 142–47.

_____. "The Struggle for Atlanta." In Robert Underwood Johnson and Clarence Clough Buel, eds., *Battles and Leaders of the Civil War*. (4 vols. New York: Century Co., 1887–88), 4: 293–325.

Huffstot, Robert S. "Post of Arkansas." *Civil War Times Illustrated* 7 (January 1969): 11–19.

Hughes, Robert M. "Joseph Eggleston Johnston, Soldier and Man: Address . . . at Unveiling of Bust of General Johnston in the Old Hall of the House of Delegates of Virginia, February 3, 1933." *William and Mary College Quarterly Historical Magazine* ser. 2, 13 (1933): 63–84.

_____, ed. "Some Letters from the Papers of General Joseph E. Johnston." *William & Mary College Quarterly Historical Magazine* 11 (1931): 319–24.

_____, ed. "Some War Letters of General Joseph E. Johnston." *Journal of the Military Service Institution of the United States* 50 (1913): 319–28.

Hurst, T. M. "The Battle of Shiloh." *Tennessee Historical Magazine* 5 (1919): 81–96.

Huston, James A. "Logistical Support of Federal Armies in the Field." *Civil War History* 7 (1961): 36–47.

Imboden, John D. "Incidents of the First [Battle of] Bull Run." In Robert Underwood Johnson and Clarence Clough Buel, eds., *Battles and Leaders of the Civil War*. (4 vols. New York: Century Co., 1887–88), 1: 229–39.

_____. "Jackson at Harper's Ferry in 1861." In Robert Underwood Johnson and Clarence Clough Buel, eds., *Battles and Leaders of the Civil War*. (4 vols. New York: Century Co., 1887–88), 1: 111–25.

"In Memoriam: General Joseph Eggleston Johnston." *Southern Historical Society Papers* 18 (1890–91): 158–209.

James, Alfred P. "General Joseph Eggleston Johnston, Storm Center of the Confederate Army." *Mississippi Valley Historical Review* 14 (1927): 342–59.

Johnston, Joseph E. "The Battle of Bull Run: An Important Letter from Joseph E. Johnston." *Historical Magazine* ser. II, 2 (1867): 232–37.

_____. "General Joseph E. Johnston's Campaign in Georgia: Some Letters Written by Him That Have Never Before Been Published." *Southern Historical Society Papers* 21 (1893): 314–21.

_____. "General Polk's Death: General Joseph E. Johnston Describes How He Was Killed." *Southern Historical Society Papers* 18 (1890–91): 380–81.

_____. "Gen. Johnston's Report of the Battle of Manassas." *The Land We Love* 2 (1886–87): 155–63.

_____. "Jefferson Davis and the Mississippi Campaign." In Robert Underwood Johnson and Clarence Clough Buel, eds., *Battles and Leaders of the Civil War*. (4 vols. New York: Century Co., 1887–88), 3: 472–82.

_____. "Manassas to Seven Pines." In Robert Underwood Johnson and Clarence Clough Buel, eds., *Battles and Leaders of the Civil War*. (4 vols. New York: Century Co., 1887–88), 2: 202–18.

_____. "My Negotiations with General Sherman." *North American Review* 143 (1886): 183–97.

_____. "Opposing Sherman's Advance to Atlanta." In Robert Underwood Johnson and Clarence Clough Buel, eds., *Battles and Leaders of the Civil War*. (4 vols. New York: Century Co., 1887–88), 4: 260–77.

_____. "Responsibilities of the First [Battle of] Bull Run." In Robert Underwood Johnson and Clarence Clough Buel, eds., *Battles and Leaders of the Civil War*. (4 vols. New York: Century Co., 1887–88), 1: 229–39.

Jones, Archer. "The Vicksburg Campaign." *Journal of Mississippi History* 29 (1962): 12–27.

Jones, Charles C., Jr. "The Siege and Evacuation of Savannah, Georgia, in December, 1864." *Southern Historical Society Papers* 17 (1889): 60–85.

Jones, J. William. "General Sherman's Method of Making War." *Southern Historical Society Papers* 13 (1885): 139–53.

"Joseph E. Johnston Monument at Dalton." *Confederate Veteran* 21 (1913): 286–88.

Jordan, Thomas. "The Campaign and Battle of Shiloh." *United Service* 12 (1885): 262–80, 393–410.

_____. "The Vicksburg Campaign of 1862–1863." *United Service* 12 (1885): 632–49; 13 (1885): 22–33.

Keim, DeB. Randolph. "Sherman: A Memorial Sketch." In Thomas W. Symons, comp., *Sherman: A Memorial in Art, Oratory, and Literature by the Society of the Army of the Tennessee with the Aid of the Congress of the United States of America* (Washington, D.C.: Government Printing Office, 1904), 125–383.

Keller, Allan. "On the Road to Atlanta: Johnston vs. Sherman." *Civil War Times Illustrated* 1 (December 1962): 18–22, 32–35.

Kelly, R. M. "Holding Kentucky for the Union." In Robert Underwood Johnson and Clarence Clough Buel, eds., *Battles and Leaders of the Civil War*. (4 vols. New York: Century Co., 1887–88), 1: 373–92.

Kiper, Richard L. "John Alexander McClernand and the Arkansas Post Campaign." *Arkansas Historical Review* 56 (1979): 56–79.

Lancaster, Jane F. "William Tecumseh Sherman's Introduction to War, 1840–1842: Lesson for Action." *Florida Historical Quarterly* 72 (1993): 56–72.

Lash, Jeffrey N. "Joseph E. Johnston and the Virginia Railways, 1861–62." *Civil War History* 35 (1989): 5–27.

Lee, Stephen D. "The Campaign of Vicksburg, Mississippi, in 1863, from April 15 to and Including the Battle of Champion Hills, Baker's Creek, May 16, 1863. *Publications of the Mississippi Historical Society* 3 (1900): 21–53.

_____. "Sherman's Meridian Expedition and Sooy Smith's Raid to West Point: A Review." *Southern Historical Society Papers* 8 (1880): 49–61.

Little, Robert D. "General Hardee and the Atlanta Campaign." *Georgia Historical Quarterly* 29 (1945): 1–22.

Little, W. C. "The Sherman of Early Days." *Overland Monthly* n. s., 17 (1891): 358–61.

Longacre, Edward G. "Judson Kilpatrick." *Civil War Times Illustrated* 10 (April 1971): 25–33.

_____, ed. "'We Left a Black Track in South Carolina': Letters of Corporal Eli S. Ricker, 1865." *South Carolina Historical Magazine* 82 (1981): 210–24.

Luvaas, Jay. "An Appraisal of Joseph E. Johnston." *Civil War Times Illustrated* 4 (January 1966): 5–7, 28–32.

_____. "Bentonville—Last Chance to Stop Sherman." *Civil War Times Illustrated* 2 (October 1963): 7–9, 38–42.

_____. "Johnston's Last Stand—Bentonville." *North Carolina Historical Review* 33 (1956): 332–58.

Maddox, Robert. "The Grog Mutiny: One Merry Christmas at West Point." *American History Illustrated* 16 (December 1981): 32–37.

"Major Boyd's Sketch of General Sherman." *Confederate Veteran* 18 (1910): 453–54.

Marszalek, John F. "'A Full Share of All the Credit': Sherman and Grant to the Fall of Vicksburg." In Steven E. Woodworth, ed., *Grant's Lieutenants: From Cairo to Vicksburg*. (Lawrence: University Press of Kansas, 2001), 5–20.

_____. "General and Mrs. William T. Sherman, A Contentious Union." In Carol K. Bleser and Leslie J. Gordon, eds., *Intimate Strategies of the Civil War: Military Commanders and Their Wives*. (New York: Oxford University Press, 2001), 138–56.

_____. "Sherman Called It the Way He Saw It." *Civil War History* 40 (1994): 72–78.

_____. "The Stanton-Sherman Controversy." *Civil War Times Illustrated* 9 (October 1970): 4–12.

Maury, Dabney H. "Interesting Reminiscences of General Johnston." *Southern Historical Society Papers* 18 (1890–91): 171–81.

McClellan, George B. "The Peninsular Campaign." In Robert Underwood Johnson and Clarence Clough Buel, eds., *Battles and Leaders of the Civil War*. (4 vols. New York: Century Co., 1887–88), 2: 160–87.

McClurg, Alexander C. "The Last Chance of the Confederacy." *Atlantic Monthly* 50 (1882): 389–400.

McMurry, Richard M. "The Affair at Kolb's Farm." *Civil War Times Illustrated* 7 (December 1968): 20–27.

———. "The Atlanta Campaign of 1864: A New Look." *Civil War History* 22 (1976): 5–15.

———. "Cassville." *Civil War Times Illustrated* 10 (December 1971): 4–9, 45–48.

———. "Confederate Morale in the Atlanta Campaign of 1864." *Georgia Historical Quarterly* 54 (1970): 226–43.

———. "'The *Enemy* at Richmond': Joseph E. Johnston and the Confederate Government." *Civil War History* 27 (1981): 5–31.

———. "The Hell Hole." *Civil War Times Illustrated* 11 (February 1973): 32–43.

———. "Kennesaw Mountain." *Civil War Times Illustrated* 8 (January 1970): 20–33.

———. "The Mackall Journal and Its Antecedents." *Civil War History* 20 (1974): 311–28.

———. "A Policy So Disastrous: Joseph E. Johnston's Atlanta Campaign." In Theodore P. Savas and David A. Woodbury, eds., *The Campaign for Atlanta and Sherman's March to the Sea* (2 vols. Campbell, Calif.: Savas-Woodbury, 1994), 2: 223–48.

———. "Resaca: 'A Heap of Hard Fiten'." *Civil War Times Illustrated* 9 (November 1970): 4–12, 44–48.

———. "Sherman's Meridian Campaign." *Civil War Times Illustrated* 14 (May 1975): 24–32.

Meade, Robert Douthat. "The Relations Between Judah P. Benjamin and Jefferson Davis: Some New Light on the Working of the Confederate Machine." *Journal of Southern History* 6 (1939): 468–78.

Medkirk, Robert W. "The Skirmishing in Sherman's Front [at Shiloh]." In Robert Underwood Johnson and Clarence Clough Buel, eds., *Battles and Leaders of the Civil War.* (4 vols. New York: Century Co., 1887–88), 1: 537.

"Memorial Services [for Joseph E. Johnston] in Memphis, Tenn., March 31, 1891." *Southern Historical Society Papers* 18 (1890–91): 189–99.

Miller, Nyle H., ed. "Surveying the Southern Boundary of Kansas: From the Private Journal of Col. Joseph E. Johnston." *Kansas Historical Quarterly* 1 (1932): 104–39.

Monnett, Howard Norman, ed. "'The Awfulest Time I Ever Seen': A Letter from Sherman's Army." *Civil War History* 8 (1962): 283–89.

"The Monument to General Robert E. Lee." *Southern Historical Society Papers* 17 (1889): 187–335.

Moore, John Hammond. "Sherman's 'Fifth Column': A Guide to Unionist Activity in Georgia." *Georgia Historical Quarterly* 68 (1984): 382–300.

Morgan, George W. "The Assault on Chickasaw Bluffs." In Robert Underwood Johnson and Clarence Clough Buel, eds., *Battles and Leaders of the Civil War.* (4 vols. New York: Century Co., 1887–88), 3: 462–70.

Mruck, Armin E. "The Role of Railroads in the Atlanta Campaign." *Civil War History* 7 (1961): 264–71.

Mullen, James M. "Last Days of Johnston's Army." *Southern Historical Society Papers* 18 (1890–91): 97–113.

Murray, Robert K. "General Sherman, the Negro, and Slavery: The Story of an Unrecognized Rebel." *Negro History Bulletin* 22 (March 1959): 125–30.

Naisawald, L. Van Loan. "The Battle of Dranesville." *Civil War Times Illustrated* 4 (May 1965): 5–10.

Naroll, Raoul S. "Lincoln and the Sherman Peace Fiasco—Another Fable?" *Journal of Southern History* 20 (1954): 459–83.

Neely, Mark E., Jr. "The Generalship of Grant and Sherman: Was the Civil War a Modern 'Total' War? A Dissenting View." In John Whiteclay Chambers, II, and G. Kurt Piehler, eds., *Major Problems in American Military History: Documents and Essays.* (Boston: Houghton Mifflin Co., 1999), 178–86.

Nichols, Roy F., ed. "William Tecumseh Sherman in 1850." *Pennsylvania Magazine of History and Biography* 75 (1951): 424–35.

Oakey, Daniel. "Marching Through Georgia and the Carolinas." In Robert Underwood Johnson and Clarence Clough Buel, eds., *Battles and Leaders of the Civil War.* (4 vols. New York: Century Co., 1887–88), 4: 671–80.

Osborn, George C., ed. "Sherman's March through Georgia: Letters from Charles Ewing to His Father." *Georgia Historical Quarterly* 42 (1958): 323–27.

"Papers of Convention between Sherman and Johnston: From the Papers of Col. B. S. Ewell." *Southern Historical Society Papers* 39 (1914): 45–53.

Perry, Leslie J. "Davis and Johnston: Light Thrown on a Quarrel Among Confederate Leaders . . ." *Southern Historical Society Papers* 20 (1892): 95–108.

Proceedings of the Senate and Assembly of the State of New York, on the Life and Services of Gen. William T. Sherman . . . Albany: James B. Lyon, 1892.

Rable, George C. "William T. Sherman and the Conservative Critique of Radical Reconstruction." *Ohio History* 93 (1984): 147–63.

"Recollections of Sherman." *Harper's New Monthly Magazine* 30 (1865): 640–46.

Reid, Whitelaw. "Lieutenant-General Wm. Tecumseh Sherman." In *Ohio in the War.* (2 vols. Columbus: Moore, Wilstach & Baldwin, 1868), 1: 417–93.

Rhodes, Charles D. "The Vicksburg Campaign." *Journal of the Military Service Institution of the United States* 42 (1909): 193–209.

Rhodes, James Ford. "Sherman's March to the Sea." *American Historical Review* 6 (1901): 466–74.

_____. "Who Burned Columbia?" *American Historical Review* 7 (1902): 485–93.

Rice, Allen Thorndike. "Sherman on Grant." *North American Review* 142 (1886): 111–13.

Robinson, Leigh. "General Joseph E. Johnston." *Southern Historical Society Papers* 19 (1891): 337–70.

Ropes, John Codman. "General Sherman." *Atlantic Monthly* 68 (1891): 191–204.

Rosecrans, William Starke. "The Campaign for Chattanooga." *Century Magazine* 34 (1887): 129–35.

_____. "The Mistakes of Grant." *North American Review* 141 (1885): 580–99.

Secrist, Philip. "Scenes of Awful Carnage." *Civil War Times Illustrated* 10 (June 1971): 5–9, 45–48.

Shanks, W. F. G. "Chattanooga and How We Held It." *Harper's New Monthly Magazine* 30 (1868): 137–49.

_____. "Recollections of Sherman." *Harper's New Monthly Magazine* 30 (1865): 640–46.

Sherman, Janan. "The Jesuit and the General: Sherman's Private War." *Psychohistory Review* 21 (1998): 255–94.

Sherman, Minnie Ewing. "My Father's Letters." *Cosmopolitan* 12 (1891): 64–69, 187–94.

"Sherman's Winter Campaign through Georgia." *United States Service Magazine* 3 (1865): 164–69.

Sherman, William T. "The Battle of Pittsburg Landing: A Letter from General Sherman." *United States Service Magazine* 3 (1865): 1–4.

_____. "General Sherman in Russia: Extracts from the Diary of General W. T. Sherman." *Century Magazine* 35 (1899): 868–75.

_____. "General Sherman's Last Speech: The Old Army." *Century Magazine* 20 (1891): 189–92.

_____. "General Sherman's Opinion of General Grant." *Century Magazine* 51 (1897): 821.

_____. "General Sherman's Tour of Europe." *Century Magazine* 35 (1899): 729–40.

_____. "The Grand Strategy of the Last Year of the War." In Robert Underwood Johnson and Clarence Clough Buel, eds., *Battles and Leaders of the Civil War.* (4 vols. New York: Century Co., 1887–88), 4: 247–59.

_____. "The Grand Strategy of the War of the Rebellion." *Century Magazine* 13 (1888): 582–98.

_____. "Grant, Thomas, Lee." *North American Review* 144 (1887): 437–50.

_____. "A Sheaf of Sherman Letters, 1863–81, with Comments by James Grant Wilson." *Independent* 54 (1902): 213–15.

_____. "Sherman and the San Francisco Vigilantes: Unpublished Letters of General W. T. Sherman." *Century Illustrated Monthly Magazine* n. s. 21 (1891): 296–309.

_____. "Sherman's Estimate of Grant." *Century Magazine* 70 (1905): 316–18.

_____. "Unpublished Letters of General Sherman." *North American Review* 152 (1891): 371–75.

_____. "Why General Sherman Declined the Nomination in 1884: Being a Letter Hitherto Unpublished, from General W. T. Sherman to U.S. Senator J. B. Doolittle, of Wisconsin, June 10, 1884." *North American Review* 171 (1900): 243–45.

Sherman, William T., and John Sherman. "Letters of Two Brothers: Passages from the Correspondence of General and Senator Sherman." *Century Magazine* 45 (1892–93): 88–101, 425–40, 689–99, 892–903.

Shoup, Francis A. "Dalton Campaign—Works at Chattahoochee River—Interesting History." *Confederate Veteran* 3 (1895): 262–65.

Slocum, Henry W. "Final Operations of Sherman's Army." In Robert Underwood Johnson and Clarence Clough Buel, eds., *Battles and Leaders of the Civil War*. (4 vols. New York: Century Co., 1887–88), 4: 754–58.

_____. "Sherman's March from Savannah to Bentonville." In Robert Underwood Johnson and Clarence Clough Buel, eds., *Battles and Leaders of the Civil War*. (4 vols. New York: Century Co., 1887–88), 4: 681–95.

Smalley, E. V. "General Sherman." *Century Illustrated Monthly Magazine* n. s. 5 (1884): 450–62.

Smith, Gustavus W. "Two Days of Battle at Seven Pines." In Robert Underwood Johnson and Clarence Clough Buel, eds., *Battles and Leaders of the Civil War*. (4 vols. New York: Century Co., 1887–88), 2: 220–63.

Smith, Helen Ainslie. "William Tecumseh Sherman." In *One Hundred Famous Americans*. (London: George Routledge & Sons, 1902), 186–89.

Smith, Mark A. "Sherman's Unexpected Companions: Marching through Georgia with Jomini and Clausewitz." *Georgia Historical Quarterly* 81 (1997): 1–24.

Smith, William Farrar. "Chattanooga: Was It Fought as Planned?" *Century Magazine* 31 (1886): 146–47.

_____. "Shiloh." *Magazine of American History* 15 (1885): 292–304, 382–90, 470–82.

Smith, William Wrenshall. "Holocaust Holiday: Vacationing at Chattanooga, 1863." *Civil War Times Illustrated* 18 (October 1979): 28–40.

Stephenson, F. D. "Reminiscences of the Last Campaign of the Army of Tennessee, from May, 1864, to January, 1865: Paper No. 1." *Southern Historical Society Papers* 12 (1884): 32–39.

Stewart, Alexander P. "The Army of Tennessee: A Sketch." In John Berrien Lindsley, ed., *The Military Annals of Tennessee, Confederate . . .* (Nashville: J. M. Lindsley & Co., 1886), 55–111.

Stinson, Byron. "Night Blindness in CW Soldiers." *Civil War Times Illustrated* 4 (January 1966): 33.

Stone, Henry. "Repelling Hood's Invasion of Tennessee." In Robert Underwood Johnson and Clarence Clough Buel, eds., *Battles and Leaders of the Civil War*. (4 vols. New York: Century Co., 1887–88), 4: 440–64.

Stowe, Harriet Beecher. "William T. Sherman." In *Men of Our Times; or, Leading Patriots of the Day . . .* (Hartford, Conn.: Hartford Publishing Co., 1868), 423–44.

Sword, Wiley, "The Battle of Shiloh." *Civil War Times Illustrated* 17 (May 1978): 4–50.

Thompson, Joseph D. "The Battle of Shiloh." *Tennessee Historical Quarterly* 17 (1958): 345–67.

Thompson, J. P. "Major-General William T. Sherman." *Hours at Home* 2 (1865): 11–22.

Trefousse, Hans L. "Civil Warriors in Memory and Memoir: Grant and Sherman Remember." *Georgia Historical Quarterly* 75 (1991): 542–56.

Walters, John Bennett. "General William T. Sherman and Total War." *Journal of Southern History* 14 (1948): 447–80.

Weller, Ella Fraser. "Stranger Than Fiction: A True Short Story, Told Mainly in a Series of Unpublished Letters by General Sherman." *McClure's Magazine* 8 (1897): 546–50.

West, Richard S., Jr. "Gunboats in the Swamps: The Yazoo Pass Expedition." *Civil War History* 9 (1963): 157–66.

Widney, Lyman S. "Campaigning with Uncle Billy." *Neale's Monthly* 2 (1913): 131–43.

Williams, T. Harry. "Beauregard at Shiloh." *Civil War History* 1 (1955): 17–34.

Wilson, James Grant. "General Sherman." In *Sketches of Illustrious Soldiers*. (New York: G. P. Putnam's Sons, 1874), 447–66.

Wilson, James Harrison. "A Staff-Officer's Journal of the Vicksburg Campaign, April 30 to July 4, 1863." *Journal of the Military Service Institution of the United States* 43 (1908): 93–109.

Wolseley, Viscount. "General Sherman." *United Service* 178 (1891): 97–116, 193–216, 289–309.

Woods, Robert Mann. "Gen J. E. Johnston—by a Federal." *Confederate Veteran* 15 (1907): 214–16.

Young, Jared W., ed. "General Sherman on His Own Record: Some Unpublished Comments." *Atlantic Monthly* 108 (1911): 289–300.

Books and Pamphlets

Alexander, E. P. *Fighting for the Confederacy: The Personal Recollections of General Edward Porter Alexander*. Edited by Gary Gallagher. Chapel Hill: University of North Carolina Press, 1989.

_____. *Military Memoirs of a Confederate: A Critical Narrative*. New York: Charles Scribner's Sons, 1908.

Alfriend, Frank H. *The Life of Jefferson Davis*. Cincinnati: Caxton Publishing House, 1868.

Allen, Felicity. *Jefferson Davis, Unconquerable Heart*. Columbia: University of Missouri Press, 1999.

Ambrose, Stephen E. *Duty, Honor, Country: A History of West Point*. Baltimore: Johns Hopkins University Press, 1966.

_____. *Halleck, Lincoln's Chief of Staff*. Baton Rouge: Louisiana State University Press, 1962.

Anders, Curt. *Fighting Confederates*. New York: G. P. Putnam's Sons, 1968.

Andrist, Ralph K. *The Long Death: The Last Days of the Plains Indians*. New York: Collier Books, 1964.

Angley, Wilson, et al. *Sherman's March through North Carolina: A Chronology*. Raleigh: North Carolina Division of Archives and History, 1995.

Arnett, Ethel Stephens. *Confederate Guns Were Stacked: Greensboro, North Carolina*. Greensboro: Piedmont Press, 1965.

Athearn, Robert G. *William Tecumseh Sherman and the Settlement of the West*. Norman: University of Oklahoma Press, 1956.

The Atlanta Campaign: Organization of the Union (Field) Forces (Commanded by Major-General William T. Sherman), May 5–31, 1864. Washington, D.C.: Government Printing Office, 1888.

Badeau, Adam. *Military History of U.S. Grant, from April, 1861 to April, 1865*. 3 vols. New York: D. Appleton & Co., 1868–81.

Bailey, Anne J. *The Chessboard of War: Sherman and Hood in the Autumn Campaigns of 1864*. Lincoln: University of Nebraska Press, 2000.

_____. *War and Ruin: William T. Sherman and the Savannah Campaign*. Wilmington, Del.: SR Books, 2002.

Ballard, Michael B. *A Long Shadow: Jefferson Davis and the Final Days of the Confederacy*. Jackson: University Press of Mississippi, 1986.

_____. *Pemberton: A Biography*. Jackson: University Press of Mississippi, 1991.

_____. *Vicksburg: The Campaign That Opened the Mississippi*. Chapel Hill: University of North Carolina Press, 2004.

Barnwell, Robert Woodward. *Sherman and Grant Considered (for Historians)*. n. p.: privately issued, 19—.

Barrett, John G. *The Civil War in North Carolina*. Chapel Hill: University of North Carolina Press, 1963.

_____. *Sherman's March through the Carolinas*. Chapel Hill: University of North Carolina Press, 1956.

Bass, Cynthia. *Sherman's March*. New York: Villard Books, 1994.

Bauer, K. Jack. *The Mexican War, 1846–1848*. New York: Macmillan Publishing Co., Inc., 1974.

Bearss, Edwin C. *Decision in Mississippi: Mississippi's Important Role in the War Between the States*. Jackson: Mississippi Commission on the War Between the States, 1962.

_____. *The Vicksburg Campaign*. 3 vols. Dayton, Ohio: Morningside, 1985–86.

_____, and Warren Grabau. *The Battle of Jackson, May 14, 1863 . . . The Siege of Jackson, July 10–17, 1863 . . . Three Other Post-Vicksburg Actions*. Baltimore: Gateway Press, 1981.

Bearss, Margie Riddle. *Sherman's Forgotten Campaign: The Meridian Expedition*. Baltimore: Gateway Press, 1987.

Beauregard, Pierre G. T. *A Commentary on the Campaign and Battle of Manassas of July, 1861, Together with a Summary of the Art of War*. New York: G. P. Putnam's Sons, 1891.

_____. *With Beauregard in Mexico: The Mexican War Reminiscences of P. G. T. Beauregard*. Edited by T. Harry Williams. Baton Rouge: Louisiana State University Press, 1956.

Bender, Averam B. *The March of Empire: Frontier Defense in the Southwest, 1848–1860*. New York: Greenwood Press, 1968.

Black, Robert C. III. *The Railroads of the Confederacy*. Chapel Hill: University of North Carolina Press, 1952.

Bowers, John. *Chickamauga and Chattanooga: The Battles That Doomed the Confederacy*. New York: HarperCollins, 1994.

Bowman, S. M., and R. B. Irwin. *Sherman and His Campaigns: A Military Biography*. New York: Charles B. Richardson, 1865.

Boyd, James P. *The Life of General William T. Sherman*. Philadelphia: Publishers' Union, 1891.

Boynton, Henry V. *Battles About Chattanooga, Tenn., November 23–25, 1863: Orchard Knob, Lookout Mountain, Missionary Ridge . . .* Washington, D.C.: Government Printing Office, 1893.

_____. *Sherman's Historical Raid: The Memoirs in the Light of the Record . . .* Cincinnati: Wilstach, Baldwin & Co., 1875.

Bradley, Mark L. *Last Stand in the Carolinas: The Battle of Bentonville*. Mason City, Ia.: Savas Publishing Co., 1996.

_____. *This Astounding Close: The Road to Bennett Place*. Chapel Hill: University of North Carolina Press, 2000.

Broadwater, Robert P. *Battle of Despair: Bentonville and the North Carolina Campaign*. Macon, Ga.: Mercer University Press, 2004.

Brown, Joseph M. *The Great Retreat: Could Johnston Have Defended Atlanta Successfully? The Policy of the Great Southern General Defended . . .* Atlanta: Railroad Record Printing Co., n. d.

Brown, Kent Masterson, ed. *The Civil War in Kentucky: Battle for the Bluegrass State*. Mason City, Ia.: Savas Publishing Co., 2000.

Buker, George E. *Swamp Sailors in the Second Seminole War*. Gainesville: University Press of Florida, 1997.

Burne, Alfred H. *Lee, Grant and Sherman: A Study of Leadership in the 1864–65 Campaign*. New York: Gale & Polden Ltd., 1938.

Burton, Katherine. *Three Generations: Maria Boyle Ewing (1801–1864), Ellen Ewing Sherman (1824–1888), Minnie Sherman Fitch (1851–1913)*. New York: Longmans, Green & Co., 1947.

Byers, S. H. M. *Twenty Years in Europe: A Consul-General's Memories of Noted People, with Letters from General W. T. Sherman*. Chicago: Rand, McNally, 1900.

Campbell, Jacqueline Glass. *When Sherman Marched North from the Sea*. Chapel Hill: University of North Carolina Press, 2003.

Carter, Samuel III. *The Final Fortress: The Campaign for Vicksburg, 1862–1863*. New York: St. Martin's Press, 1980.

_____. *The Siege of Atlanta, 1864*. New York: Bonanza Books, 1973.

Castel, Albert. *Decision in the West: The Atlanta Campaign of 1864*. Lawrence: University Press of Kansas, 1992.

Catton, Bruce. *Grant Moves South*. Boston: Little, Brown & Co., 1960.

_____. *Grant Takes Command*. Boston: Little, Brown & Co., 1968.

Ceremonies, Unveiling of the Bust of Joseph Eggleston Johnston, Old Hall of the House of Delegates, State Capitol, Richmond, Virginia, Friday, February 3, 1933, 3:30 o'clock P.M. Richmond, Va.: n. p., 1933.

Chase, Edward. *The Memorial Life of General William Tecumseh Sherman*. Chicago: R. S. Peale & Co., 1891.

Chesnut, Mary Boykin. *Mary Chesnut's Civil War*. Edited by C. Vann Woodward. New Haven: Yale University Press, 1981.

Clarke, Dwight L. *William Tecumseh Sherman, Gold Rush Banker*. San Francisco: California Historical Society, 1969.

Cleaves, Freeman. *Rock of Chickamauga: The Life of General George H Thomas*. Norman: University of Oklahoma Press, 1948.

Coburn, Mark. *Terrible Innocence: General Sherman at War*. New York: Hippocrene Books, 1993.

Coffman, Edward M. *The Old Army: A Portrait of the American Army in Peacetime, 1784–1898*. New York: Oxford University Press, 1986.

Connelly, Thomas Lawrence. *Army of the Heartland: The Army of Tennessee, 1861–1862*. Baton Rouge: Louisiana State University Press, 1967.

_____. *Autumn of Glory. The Army of Tennessee, 1862–1865*. Baton Rouge: Louisiana State University Press, 1971.

_____, and Archer Jones. *The Politics of Command: Factions and Ideas in Confederate Strategy*. Baton Rouge: Louisiana State University Press, 1973.

Conyngham, David P. *Sherman's March through the South: Sketches and Incidents of the Campaign*. New York: Sheldon & Co., 1865.

Cooper, William J., Jr. *Jefferson Davis, American*. New York: Alfred A. Knopf, 2000.

Correspondence Between the President and General Joseph E. Johnston, Together with That of the Secretary of War and the Adjutant and Inspector General, during the Months of May, June and July, 1863: Published by Order of Congress. Richmond, Va.: R. M. Smith, 1864.

Coulter, E. Merton. *The Confederate States of America, 1861–1865*. Baton Rouge: Louisiana State University Press, 1950.

Cox, Jacob D. *Atlanta*. New York: Charles Scribner's Sons, 1882.

_____. *The March to the Sea, Franklin and Nashville*. New York: Charles Scribner's Sons, 1886.

Cozzens, Peter. *The Shipwreck of Their Hopes: The Battles for Chattanooga*. Urbana: University of Illinois Press, 1994.

Cresap, Bernarr. *Appomattox Commander: The Story of General E. O. C. Ord*. San Diego, Calif.: A. S. Barnes & Co., Inc., 1981.

Cullen, Joseph P. *The Peninsula Campaign, 1862: McClellan & Lee Struggle for Richmond*. Harrisburg, Pa.: Stackpole Books, 1973.

Cullum, George W., comp. *Biographical Register of the Officers and Graduates of the U.S. Military Academy*. 3 vols. Boston: Houghton Mifflin & Co., 1891.

Cunliffe, Marcus. *Soldiers & Civilians: The Martial Spirit in America, 1775–1865*. Boston: Little, Brown & Co., 1968.

Daniel, Larry J. *Cannoneers in Gray: The Field Artillery of the Army of Tennessee—Revised Edition*. Tuscaloosa: University of Alabama Press, 2005.

_____. *Days of Glory: The Army of the Cumberland, 1861–1865*. Baton Rouge: Louisiana State University Press, 2004.

_____. *Shiloh, The Battle That Changed the Civil War*. New York: Simon & Schuster, 1997.

_____. *Soldiering in the Army of Tennessee: A Portrait of Life in a Confederate Army*. Chapel Hill: University of North Carolina Press, 1991.

Davis, Burke, *The Long Surrender*. New York: Random House, 1985.

_____. *Sherman's March.* New York: Random House, 1980.

Davis, Jefferson. *Message of the President Jan. 4, 1865 [Transmitting a Communication from the Secretary of War, Covering a Copy of the Official Report of General Joseph E. Johnston, Relative to Operations of the Army of Tennessee, Submitted Oct. 20, 1864].* Richmond, 1865.

_____. *The Papers of Jefferson Davis.* Edited by Linda L. Crist and M. S. Dix. 11 vols. to date. Baton Rouge: Louisiana State University Press, 1971– .

_____. *The Rise and Fall of the Confederate Government.* 2 vols. New York: D. Appleton & Co., 1881.

Davis, Stephen. *Atlanta Will Fall: Sherman, Joe Johnston, and the Yankee Heavy Battalions.* Wilmington, Del.: SR Books, 2001.

Davis, William C. *Battle at Bull Run: A History of the First Major Campaign of the Civil War.* Garden City, N.Y.: Doubleday & Co., Inc., 1977.

_____. *The Cause Lost: Myths and Realities of the Confederacy.* Lawrence: University Press of Kansas, 1996.

_____. *An Honorable Defeat: The Last Days of the Confederate Government.* New York: Harcourt, Inc., 2001.

_____. *Jefferson Davis: The Man and His Hour.* New York: HarperCollins, 1991.

_____. *Look Away! A History of the Confederate States of America.* New York: Free Press, 2002.

Dawley, T. R. *The Life of Wm. T. Sherman.* New York: privately issued, 1864.

Deaderick, John Barron. *Battles of Shiloh and Memphis.* Memphis, Tenn.: S. C. Toof & Co., 1961.

_____. *The Truth about Shiloh.* Memphis, Tenn.: C. S. Toof & Co., 1942.

DeLeon, T. C. *Belles, Beaux and Brains of the 60's.* New York: G. W. Dillingham Co., 1907.

Denkewicz, Robert M. *Vigilantes in Gold Rush California.* Palo Alto: Stanford University Press, 1985.

Detzer, David. *Donnybrook: The Battle of Bull Run, 1861.* New York: Harcourt, Inc., 2004.

Dodd, William E. *Jefferson Davis.* Philadelphia: G. W. Jacobs, 1907.

Dodge, Grenville M. *The Battle of Atlanta and Other Campaigns . . .* Council Bluffs, Ia.: Monarch Printing Co., 1910.

_____. *Personal Recollections of General William T. Sherman.* Des Moines, Ia.: privately issued, ca. 1902.

_____. *Personal Recollections of President Abraham Lincoln, General Ulysses S. Grant and General William T. Sherman.* Council Bluffs, Ia.: Monarch Printing Co., 1914.

Downey, Fairfax. *Storming of the Gateway: Chattanooga, 1863.* New York: David McKay Co., Inc., 1960.

Durkin, Joseph T. *General Sherman's Son.* New York: Farrar, Strauss & Cudahy, 1959.

Dyer, John P. *Fightin' Joe Wheeler.* Baton Rouge: Louisiana State University Press, 1941.

_____. *The Gallant Hood.* Indianapolis: Bobbs-Merrill Co., Inc., 1950.

Eaton, Clement. *Jefferson Davis.* New York: Free Press, 1977.

Eckenrode, H. J. *Jefferson Davis, President of the South.* New York: Macmillan Co., 1923.

Eisenschiml, Otto. *The Story of Shiloh.* Chicago: Norman Press, 1946.

Eliot, Ellsworth, Jr. *West Point in the Confederacy.* New York: G. A. Baker & Co., 1941.

Elliott, Charles Winslow. *Winfield Scott, the Soldier and the Man.* New York: Macmillan Co., 1937.

Evans, Clement A., ed. *Confederate Military History: A Library of Confederate States History . . .* 12 vols. Atlanta: Confederate Publishing Co., 1899.

Evans, David. *Sherman's Horsemen: Union Cavalry Operations in the Atlanta Campaign.* Bloomington: Indiana University Press, 1996.

Ewing, Presley Kittredge, and Mary Ellen (Williams) Ewing. *The Ewing Genealogy, with Cognate Branches: A Survey of the Ewings and Their Kin in America.* n. p.: privately issued, 1919.

Faust, Patricia L., ed. *Historical Times Illustrated Encyclopedia of the Civil War.* New York: Harper & Row, 1986.

Fellman, Michael. *Citizen Sherman: A Life of William Tecumseh Sherman*. New York: Random House, 1995.

Ferguson, John H. *On to Atlanta: The Civil War Diaries of John Hill Ferguson, Illinois Tenth Regiment of Volunteers*. Edited by Janet Correll Ellison and Mark A. Weitz. Lincoln: University of Nebraska Press, 2001.

Fleming, Thomas J. *West Point: The Men and Times of the United States Military Academy*. New York: William Morrow & Co., 1969.

Fleming, Walter L. *General W. T. Sherman as College President: A Collection of Letters, Documents, and Other Material, Chiefly from Private Sources, Relating to the Life and Activities of General William Tecumseh Sherman, to the Early Years of Louisiana State University, and to the Stirring Conditions Existing in the South on the Eve of the Civil War, 1859–1861*. Cleveland: Arthur H. Clark Co., 1912.

Flood, Charles Bracelen. *Grant and Sherman: The Friendship That Won the Civil War*. New York: Farrar, Straus & Giroux, 2005.

Forbes, Ida B. *Gen'l Wm. T. Sherman: His Life and Battles; or, From Boyhood to His "March to the Sea."* New York: McLoughlin Brothers, 1886.

Force, Manning F. *General Sherman*. New York: D. Appleton & Co., 1899.

Freeman, Douglas Southall. *Lee's Lieutenants: A Study in Command*. 3 vols. New York: Charles Scribner's Sons, 1942–44.

_____. *R. E. Lee: A Biography*. 4 vols. New York: Charles Scribner's Sons, 1934–35.

Frye, Dennis. *2nd Virginia Infantry*. Lynchburg, Va.: H. E. Howard, Inc., 1984.

General and Field Orders: Campaign of the Armies of the Tennessee, Ohio and Cumberland, Maj. Gen. W. T. Sherman, Commanding, 1864–5. St. Louis: R. P. Studley & Co., 1865.

Gen. J. E. Johnston Correspondence to Jefferson Davis: The Fall of Vicksburg. Richmond, Va.: R. M. Smith, 1864.

Gibson, John M. *Those 163 Days: A Southern Account of Sherman's March from Atlanta to Raleigh*. New York: Coward-McCann, 1961.

Glatthaar, Joseph T. *The March to the Sea and Beyond: Sherman's Troops in the Savannah and Carolinas Campaigns*. New York: New York University Press, 1985.

_____. *Partners in Command: The Relationships between Leaders in the Civil War*. New York: Free Press, 1994.

Goetzmann, William H. *Army Exploration in the American West, 1803–1863*. New Haven, Conn.: Yale University Press, 1959.

_____. *Exploration and Empire: The Explorer and the Scientist in the Winning of the American West*. New York: Alfred A. Knopf, 1966.

Gorgas, Josiah. *The Journals of Josiah Gorgas, 1857–1878*. Edited by Sarah Woolfolk Wiggins. Tuscaloosa: University of Alabama Press, 1995.

Govan, Gilbert E., and James W. Livingood. *A Different Valor: The Story of General Joseph E. Johnston, C.S.A.* Indianapolis: Bobbs-Merrill Co., Inc., 1956.

Grant, Ulysses S. *The Papers of Ulysses S. Grant*. Edited by John Y. Simon et al. (28 vols. to date. Carbondale: Southern Illinois University Press, 1967– .

_____. *Personal Memoirs of U.S. Grant*. Edited by E. B. Long. New York: Da Capo Press, 2001.

Grimsley, Mark. *The Hard Hand of War: Union Military Policy Toward Southern Civilians, 1861–1865*. New York: Cambridge University Press, 1995.

Hallock, Judith Lee. *Braxton Bragg and Confederate Defeat: Volume II*. Tuscaloosa: University of Alabama Press, 1991.

Harrison, Lowell H. *The Civil War in Kentucky*. Lexington: University Press of Kentucky, 1975.

Harrison, Mrs. Burton. *Recollections Grave and Gay*. New York: Charles Scribner's Sons, 1912.

Haskell, John Cheves. *The Haskell Memoirs*. Edited by Gilbert E. Govan and James W. Livingood. New York: G. P. Putnam's Sons, 1960.

Hattaway, Herman. *General Stephen D. Lee*. Jackson: University Press of Mississippi, 1976.

_____, and Archer Jones. *How the North Won: A Military History of the Civil War*. Urbana: University of Illinois Press, 1983.

_____, and Richard E. Beringer. *Jefferson Davis, Confederate President*. Lawrence: University Pres of Kansas, 2002.

Haughton, Andrew. *Training, Tactics and Leadership in the Confederate Army of Tennessee: Seeds of Failure*. Portland, Ore.: Frank Cass, 2000.

Hazen, William B. *A Narrative of Military Service*. Boston: Ticknor & Co., 1885.

Headley, Joel Tyler. *Grant and Sherman: Their Campaigns and Generals*. New York: E. B. Treat & Co., 1865.

Headley, P. C. *Life and Military Career of Major-General William Tecumseh Sherman*. New York: William H. Appleton, 1865.

Hedley, Fenwick V. *Marching Through Georgia: Pen-Pictures of Every-day Life in General Sherman's Army from the Beginning of the Atlanta Campaign Until the Close of the War*. Chicago: Donohue, Henneberry & Co., 1890.

Heitman, Francis B., comp. *Historical Register and Dictionary of the United States Army*. 2 vols. Washington, D.C.: Government Printing Office, 1903.

Hennessy, John. *The First Battle of Manassas: An End to Innocence, July 18–21, 1861*. Lynchburg, Va.: H. E. Howard, Inc., 1989.

Hewett, Janet et al., eds. *Supplement to the Official Records of the Union and Confederate Armies*. 3 pts., 99 vols. Wilmington, N.C.: Broadfoot Publishing Co., 1994–2001.

Hight, John J. *History of the Fifty-eighth Regiment of Indiana Volunteer Infantry*. Princeton, Ind.: privately issued, 1895.

Hirshon, Stanley P. *The White Tecumseh: A Biography of William T. Sherman*. New York: John Wiley & Sons, Inc., 1997.

Hitchcock, Henry. *Marching with Sherman: Passages from the Letters and Campaign Diaries of Henry Hitchcock, Major and Assistant Adjutant General of Volunteers, November 1864–May 1865*. Edited by M. A. DeWolfe Howe. New Haven, Conn.: Yale University Press, 1927.

Hoehling, A. A. *Last Train from Atlanta*. New York: A. S. Barnes & Co., Inc., 1958.

_____. *Vicksburg: 47 Days of Siege*. Englewood Cliffs, N.J.: Prentice-Hall, 1969.

Hood, John Bell. *Advance and Retreat: Personal Experiences in the United States and Confederate States Armies*. New Orleans: Hood Orphan Memorial Fund, 1880.

Hoole, William Stanley, and Hugh L. McArthur. *The Battle of Resaca, Georgia, May 14–15, 1864*. University, Ala.: Confederate Publishing Co., 1983.

Horn, Stanley F. *The Army of Tennessee*. Norman: University of Oklahoma Press, 1953.

Hough, Alfred L. *Soldier of the West: The Civil War Letters of Alfred Lacy Hough*. Edited by Robert G. Athearn. Philadelphia: University of Pennsylvania Press, 1957.

Howard, O. O. *Autobiography of Oliver Otis Howard, Major General, United States Army*. 2 vols. New York: Baker & Taylor Co., 1907.

Hughes, Nathaniel Cheairs, Jr. *Bentonville: The Final Battle of Sherman and Johnston*. Chapel Hill: University of North Carolina Press, 1996.

_____. *General William J. Hardee, Old Reliable*. Baton Rouge: Louisiana State University Press, 1965.

_____, and Gordon D. Whitney. *Jefferson Davis in Blue: The Life of Sherman's Relentless Warrior*. Baton Rouge: Louisiana State University Press, 2002.

Hughes, Robert M. *General Johnston*. New York: D. Appleton & Co., 1893.

Johnson, Andrew. *The Papers of Andrew Johnson*. Edited by Paul H. Bergeron et al. 10 vols. Knoxville: University of Tennessee Press, 1967–83.

Johnson, Angus James II. *Virginia Railroads in the Civil War*. Chapel Hill: University of North Carolina Press, 1961.

Johnson, Bradley T. *A Memoir of the Life and Public Service of Joseph E. Johnston* . . . Baltimore: R. H. Woodward & Co., 1891.

Johnson, W. Fletcher. *Life of Wm. Tecumseh Sherman, Late Retired General, U.S.A.* Philadelphia: Edwood Publishing Co., 1891.

Johnston, Joseph E. *Narrative of Military Operations Directed during the Late War Between the States.* New York: D. Appleton & Co., 1874.

_____. *Official Report of Gen. Joseph E. Johnston, Vineville, Ga., October 20, 1864.* Richmond, Va.: privately issued, 1865.

_____. *Report of General Joseph E. Johnston of Operations in the Department of Mississippi and East Louisiana, Together with Lieut. General Pemberton's Report of the Battles of Port Gibson, Baker's Creek, and the Siege of Vicksburg: Pub. by Order of Congress.* Richmond, Va.: R. M. Smith, 1864.

_____. *Southern Boundary Line of Kansas: Letter from the Secretary of War, Transmitting the Report of Colonel Johnston's Survey of the Southern Boundary Line of Kansas.* Washington, D.C.: U.S. War Department, 1858.

_____, et al. *Official Reports of Generals Johnston and Beauregard of the Battle of Manassas, July 21st, 1861* . . . Richmond, Va.: Enquirer Book & Job Press, 1862.

Joint Committee on the Conduct of the War. 3 vols. in 8. Washington, D.C.: Government Printing Office, 1863–68.

Jones, Archer. *Civil War Command and Strategy: The Process of Victory and Defeat.* New York: Free Press, 1992.

_____. *Confederate Strategy from Shiloh to Vicksburg.* Baton Rouge: Louisiana State University Press, 1961.

Jones, Charles Colcock. *General Sherman's March from Atlanta to the Coast: An Address Delivered before the Confederate Survivors' Association, in Augusta, Georgia* . . . Augusta: Chronicle Printing Establishment, 1884.

_____. *The Siege of Savannah in December 1864, and the Confederate Operations in Georgia* . . . *during General Sherman's March from Atlanta to the Sea.* Albany, N.Y.: Joel Munsell, 1874.

Jones, J. Pickett. *Black Jack: John A. Logan and Southern Illinois in the Civil War Era.* Tallahassee: Florida State University Press, 1967.

Jones, John B. *A Rebel War Clerk's Diary.* Edited by Earl Schenck Miers. New York: Sagamore Press, 1958.

Jones, Katharine M. *When Sherman Came: Southern Women and the "Great March."* Indianapolis: Bobbs-Merrill Co., 1964.

Jordan, A. L. *Gen. Jos. E. Johnston: A Review of His Military Career* . . . Pulaski, Va.: B. D. Smith and Bros., n. d.

Kane, Sharyn, and Richard Keeton. *Fiery Dawn: The Civil War Battle at Monroe's Crossroads, North Carolina.* Tallahassee, Fla.: Southeast Archeological Center, National Park Service, 1999.

Kean, R. G. H. *Inside the Confederate Government: The Diary of Robert Garlick Hill Kean, Head of the Bureau of War.* Edited by Edward Younger. New York: Oxford University Press, 1957.

Kellogg, Sanford C. *The Shenandoah Valley and Virginia, 1861 to 1865: A War Study.* New York: Neale Publishing Co., 1903.

Kennett, Lee. *Marching through Georgia: The Story of Soldiers and Civilians during Sherman's Campaign.* New York: HarperCollins, 1995.

_____. *Sherman: A Soldier's Life.* New York: HarperCollins, 2001.

Kerksis, Sydney C., comp. *The Atlanta Papers.* Dayton, Ohio: Press of Morningside Bookshop, 1980.

Kerr, Laura E. *William Tecumseh Sherman: A Family Chronicle.* Lancaster, Ohio: Fairfield Heritage Association, 1984.

Key, William. *The Battle of Atlanta and the Georgia Campaign.* New York: Twayne Publishers, 1958.

Keyes, E. D. *Fifty Years' Observation of Men and Events, Civil and Military.* New York: Charles Scribner's Sons, 1884.

King, Alvy T. *Louis T. Wigfall, Southern Fire-eater*. Baton Rouge: Louisiana State University Press, 1970.

Kinney, William L. *Sherman's March: A Review*. Bennettsville, S.C.: privately issued, 1961.

Kiper, Richard L. *Major General John Alexander McClernand, Politician in Uniform*. Kent, Ohio: Kent State University Press, 1999.

Lash, Jeffrey N. *Destroyer of the Iron Horse: General Joseph E. Johnston and Confederate Rail Transport, 1861–1865*. Kent, Ohio: Kent State University Press, 1991.

LeConte, Emma. *When the World Ended: The Diary of Emma LeConte*. Edited by Earl Schenck Miers. New York: Oxford University Press, 1957.

Lee, Richard M. *General Lee's City: An Illustrated Guide to the Historic Sites of Confederate Richmond*. McLean, Va.: EPM Publications, Inc., 1987.

Lee, Robert E. *Lee's Dispatches: Unpublished Letters of General Robert E. Lee, C.S.A., to Jefferson Davis and the War Department of the Confederate States of America, 1861–65*. Edited by Douglas Southall Freeman and Grady McWhiney. New York: G. P. Putnam's Sons, 1957.

_____. *The Wartime Papers of R. E. Lee*. Edited by Clifford Dowdey and Louis H. Manarin. Boston: Little, Brown & Co., 1961.

Lewis, Lloyd. *Captain Sam Grant*. Boston: Little, Brown & Co., 1950.

_____. *Sherman, Fighting Prophet*. New York: Harcourt, Brace & Co., 1932.

Liddell Hart, B. H. *Sherman, Soldier, Realist, American*. New York: Da Capo Press, 1993.

Life and Reminiscences of General Wm. T. Sherman, by Distinguished Men of His Time. Baltimore: R. H. Woodward Co., 1891.

Logan, John A. *The Volunteer Soldier of America . . . with Memoirs of the Author and Military Reminiscences from General Logan's Private Journal*. Chicago: R. S. Peale & Co., 1887.

Long, A. L. *Memoirs of Robert E. Lee: His Military and Personal History . . .* Philadelphia: J. M. Stoddart & Co., 1886.

Longacre, Edward G. *Mounted Raids of the Civil War*. South Brunswick, N.J.: A. S. Barnes & Co., Inc., 1975.

Longstreet, James. *From Manassas to Appomattox: Memoirs of the Civil War in America*. Philadelphia: J. B. Lippincott & Co., 1896.

Losson, Christopher. *Tennessee's Forgotten Warriors: Frank Cheatham and His Confederate Division*. Knoxville: University of Tennessee Press, 1989.

Lucas, Marion Brunson. *Sherman and the Burning of Columbia*. College Station: Texas A&M University Press, 1976.

Macartney, Clarence E. *Grant and His Generals*. New York: McBride Co., 1953.

_____. *Lincoln and His Generals*. Freeport, N.Y.: Books for Libraries Press, 1970.

Mackall, William Whann. *A Son's Recollections of His Father*. New York: E. P. Dutton & Co., Inc., 1930.

Mahon, John K. *History of the Second Seminole War, 1835–1842*. Gainesville: University of Florida Press, 1967.

Major, Duncan K., and Roger S. Fitch. *Supply of Sherman's Army during the Atlanta Campaign*. Fort Leavenworth, Kans.: Army Service School Press, 1911.

Marszalek, John F. *Commander of All Lincoln's Armies: A Life of General Henry W. Halleck*. Cambridge, Mass.: Harvard University Press, 2004.

_____. *Sherman: A Soldier's Passion for Order*. New York: Free Press, 1993.

_____. *Sherman's March to the Sea*. Abilene, Tex.: McWhiney Foundation Press, 2005.

_____. *Sherman's Other War: The General and the Civil War Press*. Memphis, Tenn.: Memphis State University Press, 1981.

Martin, Samuel J. *"Kill-Cavalry," Sherman's Merchant of Terror: The Life of Union General Hugh Judson Kilpatrick*. Madison, N.J.: Fairleigh Dickinson University Press, 1996.

Mathews, Byron H., Jr. *The McCook-Stoneman Raid*. Philadelphia: Dorrance & Co., 1976.

Maury, Dabney H. *Recollections of a Virginian in the Mexican, Indian and Civil Wars.* New York: Charles Scribner's Sons, 1894.

McAllister, Anna. *Ellen Ewing, Wife of General Sherman.* New York: Benziger Brothers, 1936.

McDonough, James Lee. *Chattanooga: A Death Grip on the Confederacy.* Knoxville: University of Tennessee Press, 1984.

_____. *Schofield: Union General in the Civil War and Reconstruction.* Tallahassee: Florida State University Press, 1972.

_____. *Shiloh—In Hell before Night.* Knoxville: University of Tennessee Press, 1977.

_____, and James Pickett Jones. *War So Terrible: Sherman and Atlanta.* New York: W. W. Norton & Co., 1987.

McElroy, Robert. *Jefferson Davis, the Unreal and the Real.* 2 vols. New York: Harper & Brothers, 1937.

McKinney, Francis F. *Education in Violence: The Life of George H. Thomas and the History of the Army of the Cumberland.* Detroit: Wayne State University Press, 1961.

McMurry, Richard M. *Atlanta 1864: Last Chance for the Confederacy.* Lincoln: University of Nebraska Press, 2000.

_____. *John Bell Hood and the War for Southern Independence.* Lexington: University Press of Kentucky, 1982.

_____. *The Road Past Kennesaw: The Atlanta Campaign of 1864.* Washington, D.C.: National Park Service, 1972.

_____. *Two Great Rebel Armies: An Essay in Confederate Military History.* Chapel Hill: University of North Carolina Press, 1989.

McWhiney, Grady. *Braxton Bragg and Confederate Defeat: Volume I, Field Command.* New York: Columbia University Press, 1969.

Meade, Robert Douthat. *Judah P. Benjamin, Confederate Statesman.* New York: Oxford University Press, 1943.

Merrill, James M. *William Tecumseh Sherman.* Chicago: Rand McNally & Co., 1971.

Miers, Earl Schenck. *The General Who Marched to Hell: William Tecumseh Sherman and His March to Fame and Infamy.* New York: Alfred A. Knopf, 1951.

_____. *The Web of Victory: Grant at Vicksburg.* New York: Alfred A. Knopf, 1955.

Mindil, George W. *The Battle of Fair Oaks: A Reply to General Joseph E. Johnston.* Philadelphia: privately issued, 1874.

Morrison, James L., Jr. *"The Best School in the World": West Point, the Pre-Civil War Years, 1833–1866.* Kent, Ohio: Kent State University Press, 1986.

Moulton, C. W. *The Review of General Sherman's Memoirs Examined, Chiefly in the Light of Its Own Evidence.* Cincinnati: Robert Clarke & Co., 1875.

Munroe, John A. *Louis McLane, Federalist and Jacksonian.* New Brunswick, N.J.: Rutgers University Press, 1973.

Nenninger, Timothy K. *The Leavenworth Schools and the Old Army: Education, Professionalism, and the Officer Corps of the United States Army, 1881–1918.* Westport, Conn.: Greenwood Press, 1978.

Newton, Steven H. *Joseph E. Johnston and the Defense of Richmond.* Lawrence: University Press of Kansas, 1998.

Niccolls, S. J. *A Tribute to General William Tecumseh Sherman . . . Delivered at the Public Memorial Service of Ransom Post No. 131, Department of Missouri, G. A. R., May 30th, 1891.* St. Louis: privately issued, 1891.

Nichols, George Ward. *The Story of the Great March, from the Diary of a Staff Officer.* New York: Harper & Brothers, 1865.

Nichols, Samuel J. *A Tribute to General William Tecumseh Sherman . . .* Ransom, Mo.: privately issued, 1891.

Northrop, Henry Davenport. *Life and Deeds of General Sherman, Including the Story of His Great March to the Sea.* Philadelphia: Globe Publishing Co., 1891.

Official Records of the Union and Confederate Navies in the War of the Rebellion. 2 series, 30 vols. Washington, D.C.: Government Printing Office, 1894–1922.

Official Register of the Officers and Cadets of the U.S. Military Academy, West Point, New York. West Point, N.Y.: privately issued, 1826–29, 1837–40.

Osborn, Thomas Ward. *The Fiery Trail: A Union Officer's Account of Sherman's Last Campaign.* Edited by Richard Harwell and Philip N. Racine. Knoxville: University of Tennessee Press, 1986.

Papp, Stefan. *General Joseph E. Johnston: Militarische Biographie.* Wuy auf Foehr, West Germany: Verlag fur Amerikanistik, 1989.

Parks, Joseph Howard. *General Edmund Kirby Smith, C.S.A.* Baton Rouge: Louisiana State University Press, 1954.

_____. *General Leonidas Polk, C.S.A., The Fighting Bishop.* Baton Rouge: Louisiana State University Press, 1962.

Patrick, Rembert W. *Jefferson Davis and His Cabinet.* Baton Rouge: Louisiana State University Press, 1961.

Pemberton, John C. *Pemberton, Defender of Vicksburg.* Chapel Hill: University of North Carolina Press, 1942.

Pepper, George W. *Personal Recollections of Sherman's Campaigns in Georgia and the Carolinas.* Zanesville, Ohio: Hugh Dunne Co., 1866.

Porter, Anthony T. *In Memoriam: Gen. Joseph E. Johnston . . . at the Church of the Holy Communion, Sunday Evening, April 26th, 1891 . . .* Charleston: Walker, Evans & Cogswell Co., 1891.

Porter, Horace. *Campaigning with Grant.* New York: Century Co., 1897.

Rafuse, Ethan S. *McClellan's War: The Failure of Moderation in the Struggle for the Union.* Bloomington: Indiana University Press, 2005.

_____. *A Single Grand Victory: The First Campaign and Battle of Manassas.* Wilmington, Del.: SR Books, 2002.

Reid, Whitelaw. *A Radical View: The "Agate" Dispatches of Whitelaw Reid, 1861–1865.* Edited by James G. Smart. 2 vols. Memphis, Tenn.: Memphis State University Press, 1976.

Report of the Joint Committee on the Conduct of the War. 3 vols. in 8. Washington, D.C.: Government Printing Office, 1863–68.

Reports of Secretary of War, with Reconnaissances of Routes from San Antonio to El Paso by Brevet Lt. Col. J. E. Johnston . . . Washington, D.C.: Union Office, 1850.

Reston, James, Jr. *Sherman's March and Vietnam.* New York: Macmillan Publishing Co., 1984.

Rice, DeLong. *The Story of Shiloh.* Jackson, Tenn.: McCowat-Mercer Press, 1924.

Robertson, James I., Jr. *Stonewall Jackson, the Man, the Soldier, the Legend.* New York: Macmillan Publishing USA, 1997.

Robins, Edward. *William T. Sherman.* Philadelphia: George W. Jacobs & Co., 1905.

Robinson, Leigh. *Joseph E. Johnston: An Address Delivered before the Association of Ex-Confederate Soldiers and Sailors of Washington, D.C. . . . .* Washington, D.C.: R. O. Polinhorn, 1891.

Roll of the Cadets [of the United States Military Academy] Arranged According to Merit in Conduct, for the Year Ending 30th June, 1826. West Point: privately issued, 1826.

Roman, Alfred. *The Military Operations of General Beauregard in the War between the States, 1861 to 1865 . . .* 2 vols. New York: Harper & Brothers, 1884.

Rose, Willie Lee. *Rehearsal for Reconstruction: The Port Royal Experiment.* Indianapolis: Bobbs-Merrill Co., Inc., 1964.

Royster, Charles. *The Destructive War: William Tecumseh Sherman, Stonewall Jackson, and the Americans.* New York: Alfred A. Knopf, 1991.

The Savannah Campaign: Organization of the Union Forces (Commanded by Major-General William T. Sherman), November 15–December 21, 1864. Washington, D.C.: Government Printing Office, 1888.

Schofield, John M. *Forty-six Years in the Army*. New York: Century Co., 1897.

Sears, Stephen W. *To the Gates of Richmond: The Peninsula Campaign*. New York: Ticknor & Fields, 1992.

Senour, F. P. *Major General William T. Sherman and His Campaigns*. Chicago: H. M. Sherwood, 1865.

Sharland, George. *Knapsack Notes of General Sherman's Grand Campaign through the Empire State of the South*. Springfield, Ill.: Jackson & Bradford, 1865.

Sherman, Ellen Ewing. *Memorial of Thomas Ewing of Ohio*. New York: Catholic Publication Society, 1873.

Sherman, John. *John Sherman's Recollections of Forty Years in the House, Senate and Cabinet: An Autobiography*. 2 vols. Chicago: Werner Co., 1895.

Sherman, Thomas Townsend. *Sherman Genealogy, Including Families of Essex, Suffolk, and Norfolk, England* . . . New York: Tobias A. Wright, 1920.

Sherman, William T. *Address of General W. T. Sherman to the Officers and Soldiers Composing the School of Application at Fort Leavenworth, Kansas, October 25, 1882*. Fort Leavenworth: privately issued, 1882.

_____. *The California Gold Fields in 1848: Two Letters*. n. p.: privately issued, 1964.

_____. *General Sherman's Official Account of His Great March through Georgia and the Carolinas, from His Departure from Chattanooga to the Surrender of General Joseph E. Johnston* . . . New York: Bruce & Huntington, 1865.

_____. *Home Letters of General Sherman*. Edited by M. A. DeWolfe Howe. New York: Charles Scribner's Sons, 1909.

_____. *A Letter of Lieut. W. T. Sherman Reporting on Conditions in California in 1848: From the Original in the Collection of Thos. W. Norris*. Carmel, Calif.: privately issued, 1947.

_____. *Major-General Sherman's Reports: I. Campaign against Atlanta; II. Campaign against Savannah; III. Campaign through the Carolinas; IV. Johnston's Truce and Surrender; V. Story of the March through Georgia* . . . New York: Beadle & Co., 1865.

_____. *Memoirs of General William T. Sherman, by Himself*. 2 vols. New York: D. Appleton & Co., 1875.

_____. *Memoirs of General William T. Sherman: Second Edition, Revised and Corrected*. 2 vols. New York: D. Appleton & Co., 1886.

_____. *Military Orders of General William T. Sherman, 1861–65*. Washington, D.C.: privately issued, ca. 1869.

_____. *Reply of Maj. Gen. Sherman to the Mayor of Atlanta* . . . Washington, D.C.: Union Congressional Committee, 1864.

_____. *Sherman's Civil War: Selected Correspondence of William T. Sherman, 1860–1865*. Edited by Brooks D. Simpson and Jean V. Berlin. Chapel Hill: University of North Carolina Press, 1999.

_____. *Two Letters from General William Tecumseh Sherman to General Ulysses S. Grant & William T. McPherson: In the Collection of W. K. Bixby of Saint Louis*. Boston: privately issued, 1919.

_____. *"War Is Hell": William T. Sherman's Personal Narrative of His March through Georgia*. Edited by Mills Lane. Savannah, Ga.: Beehive Press, 1974.

_____, and John Sherman. *The Sherman Letters: Correspondence between General Sherman and Senator Sherman from 1837 to 1891*. Edited by Rachel Sherman Thorndike. New York: Da Capo Press, 1969.

A Short History of Gen. J. E. Johnston. New York: Knapp & Co., 1888.

Smith, Gustavus W. *Generals J. E. Johnston and P. G. T. Beauregard at the Battle of Manassas, July, 1861*. New York: C. G. Crawford, 1892.

Smith, Justin H. *The War with Mexico*. 2 vols. New York: Macmillan Co., 1919.

Smith, William Ernest. *The Francis Preston Blair Family in Politics*. 2 vols. New York: Macmillan Co., 1933.

Stohlman, Robert F., Jr. *The Powerless Position: The Commanding General of the Army of the United States, 1864–1903.* Manhattan, Kans.: Military Affairs Press, 1975

Strode, Hudson. *Jefferson Davis.* 3 vols. New York: Harcourt, Brace & World, 1955–64.

Sword, Wiley. *Mountains Touched with Fire: Chattanooga Besieged, 1863.* New York: St. Martin's Press, 1995.

_____. *Shiloh: Bloody April.* New York: William Morrow & Co., Inc., 1974.

Symonds, Craig L. *Joseph E. Johnston: A Civil War Biography.* New York: W. W. Norton & Co., 1992.

Taylor, Richard. *Destruction and Reconstruction: Personal Experiences of the Late War.* Edited by Charles P. Roland. Waltham, Mass.: Blaidsdell Publishing Co., 1968.

Texas & New Mexico on the Eve of the Civil War: The Mansfield & Johnston Inspections, 1858–1861. Edited by Jerry Thompson. Albuquerque: University of New Mexico Press, 2001.

Thomas, Benjamin P., and Harold M. Hyman. *Stanton: The Life and Times of Lincoln's Secretary of War.* New York: Alfred A. Knopf, 1962.

Van Horne, Thomas B. *History of the Army of the Cumberland: Its Organization, Campaigns, and Battles. . .* 2 vols. Cincinnati: Robert Clarke Co., 1875.

Van Orden, William H. *Gen. W. T. Sherman: A Story of His life and Military Services.* New York: Novelist Publishing Co., 1885.

Vetter, Charles Edmund. *Sherman, Merchant of Terror, Advocate of Peace.* Gretna, La.: Pelican Publishing Co., 1992.

Wainwright, Charles Shiels. *A Diary of Battle: The Personal Journals of Colonel Charles S. Wainwright, 1861–1865.* Edited by Allan Nevins. New York: Harcourt, Brace & World, 1962.

Walters, John Bennett. *Merchant of Terror: General Sherman and Total War.* Indianapolis: Bobbs-Merrill Co., Inc., 1973.

Warner, Ezra J. *Generals in Blue: Lives of the Union Commanders.* Baton Rouge: Louisiana State University Press, 1964.

_____. *Generals in Gray: Lives of the Confederate Commanders.* Baton Rouge: Louisiana State University Press, 1959.

The War of the Rebellion: A Compilation of the Official Records of the Union and Confederate Armies. 4 series, 70 vols. in 128. Washington, D.C.: Government Printing Office, 1880–1901.

Weigley, Russell F. *History of the United States Army.* New York: Macmillan Publishing Co., Inc., 1967.

Wert, Jeffry D. *General James Longstreet, the Confederacy's Most Controversial Soldier: A Biography.* New York: Simon & Schuster, 1993.

Whaley, Elizabeth J. *Forgotten Hero, General James B. McPherson: The Biography of a Civil War General.* New York: Exposition Press, 1955.

Wheeler, Richard. *Sherman's March.* New York: Thomas Y. Crowell Co., 1978.

_____. *We Knew William Tecumseh Sherman.* New York: Thomas Y. Crowell Co., 1977.

Who Burnt Columbia? Part 1st. Official Depositions of Wm. Tecumseh Sherman and Gen. O. O. Howard . . . Charleston: Walker, Evans & Cogswell Co., 1873.

Williams, T. Harry. *Lincoln and His Generals.* New York: Alfred A. Knopf, 1952.

_____. *McClellan, Sherman, and Grant.* New Brunswick, N.J.: Rutgers University Press, 1962.

_____. *P. G. T. Beauregard, Napoleon in Gray.* Baton Rouge: Louisiana State University Press, 1954.

Wills, Brian Steel. *A Battle from the Start: The Life of Nathan Bedford Forrest.* New York: HarperCollins, 1992.

Wilson, David L., and John Y. Simon, eds. *Ulysses S. Grant: Essays and Documents.* Carbondale: Southern Illinois University Press, 1981.

Wilson, James Grant. *General Grant.* New York: D. Appleton & Co., 1897.

Wilson, James Harrison. *Under the Old Flag: Recollections of Military Operations in the War for the Union, the Spanish War, the Boxer Rebellion, etc.* 2 vols. New York: D. Appleton & Co., 1912.

Winter, William C. *The Civil War in St. Louis: A Guided Tour*. St. Louis: Missouri Historical Society Press, 1994.

Wise, John S. *The End of an Era*. Boston: Houghton, Mifflin Co., 1899.

Wiseman, C. M. L. *Centennial History of Lancaster, Ohio* . . . Lancaster: privately issued, 1898.

Woodworth, Steven E. *Davis and Lee at War*. Lawrence: University Press of Kansas, 1995.

_____. *Jefferson Davis and His Generals: The Failure of Confederate Command in the West*. Lawrence: University Press of Kansas, 1990.

_____. *No Band of Brothers: Problems in the Rebel High Command*. Columbia: University of Missouri Press, 1999.

_____. *Nothing But Victory: The Army of the Tennessee, 1861–1865*. New York: Alfred A. Knopf, 2005.

_____. *Six Armies in Tennessee: The Chickamauga and Chattanooga Campaigns*. Lincoln: University of Nebraska Press, 1998.

_____. *This Grand Spectacle: The Battle of Chattanooga*. Abilene, Tex.: McWhiney Foundation Press, 1999.

_____, ed. *Leadership and Command in the American Civil War*. Campbell, Calif.: Savas-Woodbury, 1995.

Wright, Benjamin C. *Banking in California, 1849–1910*. San Francisco: H. S. Crocker Co., 1910.

Wright, Mrs. D. Giraud. *A Southern Girl in '61: The War-time Memories of a Confederate Senator's Daughter*. New York: Doubleday, Page & Co., 1905.

PHOTO CREDITS

Archives of the University of Notre Dame: pp. 15, 129, 221, and 316.

F. T. Miller, ed., *Photographic History of the Civil War* (New York, 1911): pp. 240 and 301.

Fairfield Historical Association: p. 209.

Frank Leslie's Illustrated Newspaper: pp. 187 and 305.

Harper's Weekly: p. 204.

Library of Congress: pp. 1, 13, 21, 40, 45, 47, 53, 61, 70, 78, 83, 84, 107, 113, 125, 137 (bottom), 142, 157, 176, 190, 230, 239, 277, 278, 282, 283, and 313.

Mrs. D. G. Wright, *A Southern Girl in '61* (New York, 1905): pp. 32 and 168.

National Archives: pp. 37, 66, 72, 90, 98, and 126 (top and bottom).

R. U. Johnson and C. C. Buel, eds., *Battles and Leaders of the Civil War* (New York, 1887–88): pp. 134, 137 (top), 147, 252, 258, and 264.

S. M. Bowman and R. B. Irwin, *Sherman and His Campaigns* (New York, 1865): pp. 185, 224, 245, and 293.

Smithsonian Institution: p. 28.

U. S. Army Military History Institute: pp. 12 and 123.

U. S. Navy: p. 44.

INDEX

Numbers in *italics* indicate pages with illustrations and maps. Abbreviations used in the index are JEJ for Joseph E. Johnston and WTS for William T. Sherman.